THE DARKNESS IS LIGHT ENOUGH

To all the people who helped and still help me protect the badgers here I dedicate this book.

But most especially to: the three farmers of my area, the local police officers and their Inspector, and the RSPCA inspector who gave so much of his time and encouragement and said, 'Why don't you write a book?'

Chris Ferris

The Darkness is Light Enough

THE FIELD JOURNAL OF A
NIGHT NATURALIST

Foreword by Ernest Neal

THE ECCO PRESS

New York

The Ecco Press
26 West 17th Street
New York, NY 10011

Published by arrangement with Michael Joseph Ltd.

Printed in the United States of America
First published by The Ecco Press in 1988

Library of Congress Cataloging-in-Publication Data

Ferris, Chris.
The darkness is light enough.

Reprint. Originally published:
London : M. Joseph, 1986.
1. Nocturnal animals—Behavior.   I. Title.
QL755.5.F47   1988   87-24600

ISBN 0-88001-168-8

FOREWORD

It is a very great privilege to write a foreword to this remarkable book. Seldom has a relatively small area of countryside been studied in such detail; and never by such a perceptive naturalist concentrating largely on what goes on when most of us are at home and sleeping.

Chris Ferris has brilliantly depicted the nocturnal behaviour of foxes, badgers and tawny owls in particular, but also that of a great variety of other wildlife which she has come to know intimately over fifteen years of concentrated observations.

Most people who watch nocturnal animals start around dusk and return before midnight. Chris, by contrast, has her few hours of sleep first and watches from around midnight until dawn or later. This she has done in all weathers, week after week, for about five nights each week. This is a magnificent accomplishment which I venture to say has never before been achieved by any naturalist.

Chris has the artist's remarkable ability to observe detail and her diary is full of vivid behavioural observations and experiences. These are of great scientific value, as she writes them up immediately wherever she happens to be, capturing those details and the significant circumstances surrounding their occurrence which otherwise would so quickly fade.

Most badger- and fox-watching has been done around the sett or earth. This is comparatively easy: the difficult part is following the animals when they have left their homes. In recent years infra-red binoculars and telemetry have enabled researchers to make much progress in this respect, but even these techniques have their limitations as human scent and sound can be a problem when you are following wild animals. Chris Ferris's outstanding achievement has been to habituate badgers and foxes to her presence. In her early months of watching, night after night, she was just there. At first the badgers and foxes avoided her, later they became curious but kept their distance, but finally they accepted her presence completely as part of their world. Badgers claimed her as part of their social group by musking her and when they found her scent trail, would follow and find her. This trust made it possible for her to give first aid to injured animals and bring them back to health with antibiotics. This greatly strengthened the bond between them, so much so that they would play, groom and even forage together. Thus she could observe at close quarters their feeding techniques, their social behaviour and even their matings. In addition, through the years, she developed exceptional nightvision which added another dimension to her observations.

Night wanderings had other repercussions. It was not long before she realised how vulnerable the wildlife was to human predation. Shooting was usual, badger-digging was rife, and lampers trespassed on the farms which formed part of her study area using lights, nets, guns and lurchers. With outstanding courage she tried to prevent her wildlife being harmed. Encounters with lampers left her with concussion and other injuries and she was forced to spend a period in hospital. She had her arm broken with the butt of a gun and was fired at several times, presumably to scare her. But these events did not deter her. The police and the R.S.P.C.A have co-operated and in places her diary reads like crime detection. Badgers and foxes have been lost in the battle, but many have been saved . . . that is her reward.

This book will open the eyes of the public to what wildlife is up against in so many parts of the country. It will arouse anger and frustration, but hopefully also deep concern and positive action. Chris Ferris is a realist, not a sentimentalist; she is content to describe events as they happen and leave the judgement to others. Meanwhile she keeps up the fight to preserve what she loves and so vividly describes in this book . . . the beauty and charm of the countryside and its wildlife.

Ernest Neal

INTRODUCTION

This was never meant for others to read, but was written as a record of the place that I had come to regard as 'my' area. The first person outside my immediate friends to whom I explained myself was Ernest Neal. He had for some considerable time, patiently (and promptly!), answered my letters on badger behaviour. Part of a letter to him read as follows:

9 February 1984

Dear Ernest,

I think perhaps the time has come for me to explain how I came to go out at night. I never have to you before, as people that don't really know me (past police patrols included), have tended to regard me, to quote Steve Hammond of the R.S.P.C.A, as a 'nutter'. This in fact was what he thought when first told of me. It will, however, help you to understand some of the information (especially of the badger matings) that I've passed to you; so here goes.

Twenty years ago I damaged my back. I found that I couldn't sleep without pain for more than two or three hours at a time and, in consequence, used to roam about indoors doing odd jobs that could be done without disturbing my family. Eventually I found that walking eased the pain, and, although sometimes stopped and questioned by the police, I have been going out at night ever since. This over the years has eased, and for much of the time I'm not aware of pain, but you will understand that I never started out to watch badgers – or anything else – the whole business gradually evolved.

When Karen was five or six years old and Ross eight, we gave the children a pup, and when the dog was old enough to walk the distance to Ashcroft Woods and be reasonably well behaved, she came with me. It's difficult to explain Wendy or the devoted friend she became; she's been dead some years now. In our watches together, I can only describe her behaviour as that of a guide dog on duty. Have you ever known a blind person and their dog? On duty it is the eyes of its owner – watchful, quiet, incredibly patient; off duty it is as silly and playful as any of its kind. I think she may be the only dog that badger-watched with its owner. She had a great liking for badgers and there was an affinity between us that then I took for granted. She taught me much about animals, by observing her – but that is a story in itself. Then one Easter morning, well after dawn, I confronted a group of shooters in the woods and took an injured tawny owl from them. They surrounded me and one raised his rifle threateningly. Whether he would have struck me I never found out, for Wendy sprung between us and took the blow across her head. After that I never took her out at night – she meant too much to me.

I have rarely watched in the evening for badgers to emerge. Most of my evening work was spent doing a tawny census and plotting their territories (Dr Southern was a great help here). Wendy and I used to wait for the badgers to return in the early morning, but I quickly found this only answered a few of my questions. To note during the day what the farmer had done to his fields was to find at night where the badgers foraged – a logical study, really. And I've always held the view that if you're going to watch animal behaviour, you don't stay at home when the weather is adverse. I've deliberately gone out in thunder storms and gales to see what animals were around then too. In the end the badgers accepted me, till, like Old Joe and his daughter Lesley, they picked up my scent-trail and found *me* – it's as simple as that.

My foxes were rather different. Foxes fascinated me (watching badgers you inevitably see them too), they seemed to me so elusive, incredibly beautiful – I was determined to trail them and set about improving my nightvision and getting to know my area at night almost as well as the fox. It seemed to me that radio-tracking and infra-red binoculars (even if you could afford the equipment) were limited in scope. I wanted to get to *know* the animal. In the event, I suppose the inevitable happened; my foxes became as curious about me as I of them. My big advantage, besides good nightvision, is my size, or lack of it. I'm barely seven stone in weight and a little over five feet in height. I go through this wood via its animal trails, creep into small places out of sight, and take the ancient boundary ditches out on to the fields. I shelter under the ground-hanging foliage of the hollies from deep frost and driving rain like my foxes, and found that crouching down or sitting arms round knees I was smaller than my badger Old Joe. And smallness is invaluable with animals.

C.F.

At first, my night walks took me to a wood, but as time passed I included a place of rough land and derelict orchard and, finally, the greater part of three farms; in all, 800 acres. This gave me wonderful scope for studying wildlife and as I never relied on artifical light by which to see, my nightvision became good. (Later I improved on this for fox-trailing.) Farmers are much criticised these days, but I can only speak from experience, having known help, interest, enthusiasm and concern from those who farm my area. The badgers there – and myself – owe these farmers much.

Another badger to set its scent on me (or musk me) was a cub I called Jessie. Her parents mysteriously disappeared when she was still quite young and it was probably this which strengthened the bond already between us. At the time, I wondered whether it was good for an animal in the wild to come to know me in this way, but have since realised that we all have a different scent or smell. Just as a domestic dog knows its owner's scent from that of a stranger, so do the badgers and foxes here know mine. Jessie eventually developed an abscess that affected her severely. If I hadn't known her so well, I could never have lanced it, nor fed her antibiotic capsules night after night till she was well.

Long before my fox-trailing nights, I came to know a young vixen cub. She and her brothers were on friendly terms with an old mother cat and her half-grown kittens, and I'd see them all sitting in the middle of the lane of an early morning. As Vicky grew, so she would come to meet me, and our relationship gave me a lasting fascination with her kind.

All the people, animals and events of this book are true and, therefore, all names have had to be changed. For reasons of space (and readability!) much has been omitted and some events have been condensed. This of course creates gaps on the one hand and an impression of 'everything happening' on the other. But this is the way of editing.

I wanted this book published for two reasons. First, to show that badgers with their individual differences and temperaments are great fun and well worth protecting. Second, to demonstrate that with all the help I have, as the law stands at present it is well-nigh impossible *to* protect them. If I have succeeded in either of these, then this book has not been in vain.

Finally I would like to thank Dr Ernest Neal for all his patience with my letters on badgers and his immense help and advice with this book. Also Dr H. N. Southern, for the loan of his paper and for answering my queries on tawny owl behaviour.

Chris Ferris, 1986

WINTER 1980–81

Saturday 1 November 1980
Everything is descending earthwards this morning – leaves, twigs, berries, acorns and nuts. The American name for autumn, 'fall', is very apt. Just now, was standing watching an industrious bank vole when a large, prickly chestnut case landed on the back of my neck; felt I was being beheaded with a blunt axe! The weather has turned very cold and bright with heavy frosts at night. After sitting completely still early this morning in the moonlight for two hours watching the Briarmead Lane tawny owls, I found my anorak was white with hoar. Could run my finger through it – especially thick in the creases of the sleeves.

Now at 10 a.m. the scene has changed; the ground is still rock hard, but the frost all gone. This wood is alive with creatures collecting *their* harvest before the bitter winter weather. Standing quietly here, all around me is a-scurrying and a-hurrying; a multitude is gathering for the hard times ahead.

1

Monday 3 November
Since 1.20 a.m. have been at the Chantry which is just around the corner from, and above, the Bank Sett. The two badger cubs have decided to go independent and have re-dug out the old, small sett here. They appear very pleased with themselves − typical adolescents! − and, though keeping in touch with the original sett on the Bank, become quite aggressive if the parents approach theirs. (Feel like calling the twins' den the Jet Sett.) The two youngsters have been bustling about very importantly; taking turns to dig, bickering, sucking up 'spaghetti' worm snacks and indulging in games of Chase Me Charlie over the heaps of straw lying on Great Chantry Field. In the last half-hour, there has been more play and eat than work, as yesterday the tractor ploughed a firebreak round the Chantry and the twins are now finding plenty to eat in the soft earth.

I'm standing at first light on the headland of the Chantry, looking far out over the countryside. The sun touches the horizon, its radiance slipping through the night sky in wave after wave of deepest pink − the morning star fades as I watch. Light floods the valley as far below appears a vista of trees, fields and lush pasture through which the Bourne flows its serpentine course. This point may once have been a look-out post; indeed, the human history of the place on which I stand stretches far back beyond recorded time.

Friday 14 November
11 a.m. Dull, overcast morning. Have spent the past two hours checking setts. In the deepest part of the Chantry now. The trees have grown very tall and straight in their efforts to reach the light. It's impossible to see their crowns from the floor and great hanging creeper stems of traveller's joy, as thick as my arm, descend jungle-like from above. It's a physical battle to attain the heart of the Chantry, but well worth it. The badger twins have extended their sett into this dark tangle of undergrowth, and should be well protected from man and weather for the winter. Much dead timber is here and, in consequence, fungi of all descriptions; giant ferns, too. A twilight world of great beauty. I hope no one ever tries to 'clear up' here. There should be a Chantry in every wood and forest, a little wilderness left to itself and quite free of man's influence.

Wednesday 19 November
The autumn leaves are wonderful. The sun shines on their wet surfaces making the ground seem clothed in burnished copper. Many of the bramble leaves, and of course the holly, are still a deep green. The bracken is all shades from yellow to russet and the birches' lovely silver trunks show to perfection. Just found a solitary herb robert in flower − the delicate pink petals a welcome sight.

Been thinking about the lack of interest in the welfare of this wood − lack of official interest, that is. No one wants to be bothered about the shooting, the vandalism and animal harassment. Apparently Warby Parish Council's influence is nil (like mine – at least we have that in common!). Trouble is, trees do not necessarily make a wood, neither do they make wildlife habitat. Since I have known it, this woodland has been imperceptibly altering, changing, diminishing. Soon it will be a wood in name only – a mention on the map, wedged between main roads, en route to nowhere.

Thursday 20 November
Wendy died this morning.

Friday 28 November
High, gusty wind making the snow drift; very cold night with good visibility. Been at the Chantry since 2 a.m., first badger-, then fox-watching. All members of the dog family (Canidae) have the same teeth arrangement. Thus a fox, like Wendy, will swallow whole any food it can. But to tear off pieces, both must turn their heads sideways to use their carnassial or shearing teeth. Been watching a fox kill and then eat a rabbit so close to me that the gnawing, shearing noise was distinct – as was the smell of warm rabbit guts steaming in the cold air! Last spring, I observed young fox cubs chewing twigs like this, reminiscent of Wendy's pups years ago.

It's in such small events that I'm missing Wendy most. She made me observant. Watching her, I saw creatures I never dreamed were there. It's only recently that I've come to realise she *could* be the only dog that's ever badger-watched with its owner. As a very young animal, she came with me at night as well as day. I trained her to freeze at a touch and lie for hours whilst we waited and watched, she teaching me where to look for voles, snakes and slow-worms – by observing her. I owe her much. Add to this affection, protectiveness and companionship, and you have the essence of my black mongrel.

Wednesday 3 December
Where the bank of Great Chantry Field meets Briarmead Lane there's a terrific badger slide – can't call it a path. The animals slide down on to the little lane here, cross over the tarmac to the opposite bank, and pass through the roots of a yew tree and so into Barry Hains's meadow behind Newby Farm. Their passing has made a large passageway, wearing the roots shiny as their bodies brush through.

I'm on the Top Field, Prosser's Wood; it's 3.30 p.m. and will soon be dark. The sky is a mixture of different cloud formations against a pink and blue backcloth. There are areas of a mackerel sky (that I prefer to call flocks of sheep), heavy fluffs of grey-black rain clouds scurrying across in the wind and strips of very fine white vapour tinged with flame through which the azure creeps. Wish I had brought the camera!

3

Sunday 7 December

3.15 a.m. The stars are pinpoints of light showing brightly through the bare branches. Have been fox-watching on the frozen High Ridge; everywhere white with hoar, the grass crackles underfoot – good visibility. Followed my fox out to the farmland. The Hayfield has been turned under. I walked the fox way – in the deep furrow made by the plough 'twixt Wheat- and Hayfields. They are intelligent animals (if the ability to learn from new experiences is an attribute of intelligence). Not only is this furrow a quick route from wood to copse, but you are hidden from view and sheltered from the bitter wind too – if you're fox-size.

My creature is a dog fox and, typically for this time of year, he's less concerned with food than scent and scat-marking the boundaries of his territory against male newcomers. For the second time in the last hour, he has given voice on the move – a deep, hoarse, rasping bark, repeated again and again. His scent is very strong; it seems to hang, suspended in the freezing atmosphere. As he barks, his ears turn forward, mask raised, breath vaporising in the starlight. His route encompasses the ploughed Hayfield till the Damson Bank is reached. From here, still barking, he moves behind the Old Barn to the woodland fringe and suddenly there's an answering bark from beneath the trees – another fox is there.

They meet in the space before the trees and circle each other, their brushes curved upward. This is clearly a serious fight, not a war of nerves. Surprisingly little noise is made (far less than a dogfight); I can hear their laboured breathing as well as see it. They appear well matched size for size and sometimes use their tails to brush across the opponent's face. This seems done to momentarily confuse in order to close in and get a tooth-grip. No holds barred here, no breath wasted in noise, each bite telling. One slips backwards off the unploughed edging into the deep furrow and immediately the other is on top, securing a mouth-hold on the fox beneath him. Under the clear sky they appear larger than life, the near-silent combat eerie – somehow un-foxlike. Fur is coming away, though doubtless their winter coats offer good protection, at least on their backs and shoulders. Their movements are slower now; one, crouching down panting, belly to the ground, ears flattened back, silently snarls up at his rival. The latter darts forward, bites deep into his shoulder and hangs on. Both foxes are tiring fast now, and when the underdog finally breaks away and runs off, the other makes a move as if to follow, but instead stands panting.

5.30 a.m. Homeward bound, I'm wondering for the umpteenth time why a fox's coat is so brightly coloured. Birds are often brightly plumaged for courtship display and recognition, but then they have colour vision. Foxes, along with most other mammals excepting the primates, are colour-blind (so the experts say), so courtship display isn't the answer here. I've never found their winter coats blend into any surroundings except bracken; in fact, the reverse applies – they stand out most conspicuously. So why?

4

Tuesday 9 December

Been round to the Chantry watching the badger twins. Much too frozen for worming on the woodland edge – another bright, frosty night. Everywhere beautiful in the moon's rays; each seedhead, twig and blade glitteringly white. Haven't seen the parent badgers from the Bank Sett either last night or this, but since December is the adults' most dormant month unless the weather is mild and damp, this isn't perhaps surprising.

The twins have been searching for acorns and mast – also chestnuts, I think. It's amazing how much is still on the ground from the autumn. This time of year, badgers are very dependent on a wood. In the deep undergrowth under the trees, the ground often isn't frozen, so worms, slugs, etc. can still be found there, unlike the open farmland.

By the dead tree at the Bank Sett, I came upon a fox curled up and asleep in the long grass. I stayed quite still, watching and listening. It wasn't in a deep sleep, but rather cat-napping and breathing lightly. Every little while it roused, ears alert, and looked carefully round – its head facing into the wind to catch the scent of anything approaching. Seven times it alerted in this way, then finally, rousing and sniffing the air, it yawned, stretched and trotted along the path leading to the View – I followed.

My association with Vicky has left me with a lasting fascination with her kind, over all other creatures. The more I observe and learn, the more I am aware of my ignorance of their foxy ways. They rarely walk – unless not going anywhere! Their normal gait is a trot – our brisk walking pace. But when they run or lope, the fox for me is the epitome of grace and beauty. There's an aesthetic sensual pleasure in seeing a fox loping in the full glory of its winter coat – the effortless, dreamlike movement, the glorious brush floating after, lighter than thistledown. And galloping, a fox is unbeatable – except for the hare. On the Ridge I've seen one pursued by a fox. As the hare zigzagged diagonally down the Big Slip (their method of progressing fast down a steep slope with those long hind legs), the fox followed suit, its brush moving the opposite side to that of the body, to counterbalance its weight. The hare escaped!

Tuesday 16 December

Have been out fox-watching the past four nights – done a great deal of 'following after' unobserved, and learnt more than I thought possible! Tawny owl situation so far this month unsatisfactory, either through disturbance or poor weather conditions.

1.20 p.m. After a night of heavy frost, it's a lovely sunny day. Watching the end of another apple orchard. These trees were well cut back in October. Now a yellow tractor-like machine with a pair of metal jaws on a long arm is slowly crossing the area. The jaws fasten over the top of each tree, grip, and with a rending sound the trunk tears from the ground, its roots bleeding earth as the machine moves backwards. And so on, the length and breadth of the field, till it is strewn with prone trees like so many grotesque matchsticks – giant's play. (Wonder if I'm foreseeing the end of this wood?)

Came down the Warby Hill Road side of this wood above the Oak Dell to see how the Council workmen had left things. Last week they had erected a portable shelter off the path, as they had been coppicing here. Intrigues me that each night they left four lights round the shelter – can't think why. Am less likely to walk into it than into a tree (wonder they don't put red lights round them!). Take it they have finished collecting their Christmas logs and holly, etc. All that remains now is their rubbish littered about and the ashes of a fire.

Just seen a plastic carrier bag moving, and on opening it discovered a hedgehog so caught around with more plastic bags and greaseproof paper as to be unable to untangle himself, let alone curl up. There are remains of sandwiches and cheese inside, and obviously the 'urchin' was attracted by the smell. Took quite a time to free him, and when I did, he started to curl. Tried stroking him with my gloved hand down his spiny coat from his neck over his back – and lo and behold, he straightened out again! Quaint little chap; hope he's learnt a lesson about garbage. Ross once found a hedgehog with its head trapped deep in a yoghurt carton and nearly pulled its head off with the container, so hard was it forced in.

6.00 p.m. This evening, in excellent weather conditions, have checked for tawny owls. The Briarmead and Old Barn pairs are in residence, but had no luck with those in the Oak Dell area. Either they are not territorially hooting tonight (which is unlikely) or have been disturbed/shot (much more likely).

Monday 22 December

2.20 a.m. Met Jessie and her mate on the Enclosed Path – wasn't expecting to – our first encounter since October. They both 'fluffed up' and one (I think the boar) snorted. Then, sniffing the air, they scented me. The male stood still as Jessie came up in greeting. I squatted down and she pushed her face into mine, making that funny, bubbly, purring noise in her throat. Scratched her forehead above the eyes and then behind her teddybear ears – she loves that – and the noise grew louder. Don't know who was more pleased to see who! Tried to imitate her noise, but I never get it right. This made her really excited and she jumped up and knocked me over. Serves me right. I always seem to end up on my back when Jess is around!

Now at 10.30 a.m. I'm on High Ridge, and it's a sunny, damp morning, very mild. Just found some fly agaric under the birches – their fairytale caps have pushed up through the bramble leaves. The sky is a vivid blue. Under the fallen leaves, the mud and water have thawed, making the going treacherous. This woodland echoes to the sounds of the birds – it's like spring. Impossible to distinguish any one single voice amidst the general clamour. Sheltered amongst the bracken, I

6

discovered a long trail of untouched black bryony berries. Many fresh molehills here and on the Ridge. Like the fox and the badger worming, the mole, too, takes advantage of the soft earth after a thaw. From the top of the Ridge, I've watched a kestrel for the past half-hour, hunting in the sunshine over the Motorway. Wonder if the drivers glance up and spot her; she's clearly silhouetted against the blue.

Tuesday 23 December
7 p.m. and the night sky is clear, the moon at the full, and visibility excellent. Have been out checking tawnies, with special interest in the Oak Dell pair, but again have drawn a blank there. Am now at Briarmead Lane, above the Wildflower Path, and watching the pair here. The male flew quite near to me and commenced hunting from the dead trunk on the bank. He soon pounced on a small rodent, and returned – passing me – the short distance to their roost. Alighting on the home branch, he turned his head this way and that, the prey dangling from his beak. I heard the soft call as did he, 'oo-wip, oo-wip' – her courtship call to him – and watched as he silently flew off with his offering. Since then he has been hooting and is now quite close again, but he's being disturbed somewhat by a fox also hunting.

Intend going home via the Ashtree Path, so avoiding the Wheatfield badgers' territory. Lovely seeing young Jessie yesterday, but don't want to make a habit of it, for her sake. Two cars have been trying to pass one another just here on Briarmead – not much room. Amazing how many people walk their dogs after dark round the fields. The tawnies have quit the area for now. The fox clearly is the dominant predator – he's scent-marking too.

Christmas Day
4.20 a.m. Been out since 1 a.m. Raining steadily, brisk breeze, overcast sky. Strangely, I have *very* good visibility; must be growing nocturnal myself! Fox-trailing around the lower Briarmead and Great Chantry Field area. Rather interesting that though a fox's eyesight is superior to a dog's, nevertheless a fox will often overlook a human figure in the landscape if that figure is completely still – a dog generally recognises the human form, stationary or not. I've noticed foxes seem to sleep a lot above ground. Wonder if this impression is accurate or not? Understandable to find them lightly sleeping at night, as they are probably sleeping off a full stomach and will wake and continue hunting later on. But during daylight, have come upon them too, and usually then in a far deeper sleep – curious. I'll have to try and find out.*

*'If adequate surface cover is available, foxes do not seek holes or rocks except in breeding season ... mainly surface dwelling where cover is abundant; in such areas, may seek refuge underground after heavy, prolonged rainfall and in early part of cubbing season' – H. G. Lloyd in *The Handbook of British Mammals*, G. B. Corbet and H. N. Southern (eds.), Blackwell Scientific Publications, 1964, second edition 1977.

Another point regarding *Vulpes vulpes* behaviour intrigues me. If a domestic dog sees something unexpected in a familiar landscape, he will check, stiffening, hackles slightly raised, circle it cautiously and approach upwind to examine it. Then, if satisfied it is harmless, he continues on his rounds. A fox, on seeing something alien but unmoving, will check and stiffen ... and wait ... a long time. If emerging from a den entrance, it may go back in and re-emerge later – then the whole procedure is repeated. If, however, it can't get the object's scent and the object itself hasn't moved, it will continue its interrupted pursuit. But it *doesn't* approach close to, as a dog would. This has happened to me several times in cases of vixens with cubs above ground. In an instance last year, I was virtually left with the cubs whilst the mother went off to hunt. Then I was incredibly near and only half a metre off the ground, but she never approached me at all. Obviously the fox's behaviour pattern is quite different from its relation in this respect. That is not to say that it is less intelligent, or a bad mother. Oh, to get inside the mind of a fox!

The rain has ceased. The moon is a hazy blur, striving to break through the cloud veil – no stars showing. 5.50 a.m. Sitting at the View – the windy side of this wood, very gusty here. Ah, the moon has made it! The Motorway and Main Road are very quiet this Christmas morn. The village lights of Warby below me are beginning to twinkle; a bird makes a tentative twitter in the branches above my head. Just a solitary car's headlights showing on the Motorway. No other traffic at all.

Friday 26 December

1.30 a.m. The moon is in her glory this morning – no words can express the beauty of the treescape around me. It is past the full, but each lunar phase seems to shed a different quality of radiance impossible to explain. The shadows of the trees by the Oak Dell are thick, black fingers snaking across the ground as if to bar my way. All is amazingly quiet and still. Nothing seems to move or breathe. It is eternity, clothed in silence, suspended in space. By this light, the wood is ageless, perpetual; a distant fox barks and the spell is broken. I move on once more.

4.10 a.m. I'm sitting on an old stump in the shadow of a giant holly tree, just watching. A badger has been chittering, chattering (I imagine to another, though that is outside my range), and now a rabbit is grooming itself, not a yard from where I sit. Carefully he licks the pads of his front paws, then simultaneously rubs them down each side of his face. Licks his paws again and pulls first one ear and then the other down between his wettened pads. Licks his chest and sides, with each side washed to his spine. A pause, quite still, to listen and look, then the grooming finishes with his feet. All at once he dashes off noisily over the fallen leaves. He's chased after another rabbit that came into view.

Followed a vixen to the beech that crowns the Ravine, but she became uneasy, so I stopped here. This old tree's roots make a fine seat! 6.10 a.m. Watched Jess and boar mating in the Gully end of Briarmead. She squealed when he grasped the back of her neck to steady himself. Approx. 17 minutes' duration.

Saturday 27 December

Ross [my son] and I went for a walk together today. We stood looking down at the countryside from the View and mutually felt drawn to Warby. The village was very mellow and peaceful under the morning sun. The old bridge over the Bourne seemed eternal. We took the Crosshampton footpath that keeps this meandering river company – all is beautiful, even in winter. The sunlight dappling the water's surface, the blue vault above us, lush meadowgrass beneath. My companion found the most superb jew's ear fungus on a rotting elder trunk that I've ever seen, very fresh and translucent brown, the 'ear' lobes clear-cut and distinct. (Judas is reputed to have hanged himself from an elder, hence the name.)

After Crosshampton, we continued until we re-crossed the river. Discussing rivers, both decided we prefer miniatures such as ours to large navigable kinds. The last time I came here was with Wendy – haven't had the heart to since. Yet now I can recall her with pleasure. The regret is still with us standing together today looking at the flowing stream, but the pain is less acute. She was the dog of his childhood – now he is a man.

Sunday 28 December

Left home at first light to walk to the Water Meadows at Newby Farm.

Very severe frost, ground stone hard, grass stiff underfoot; colourful dawn sky. Everything very quiet – nothing stirring – till retracing my way along the river, I spied a fox amongst the herd in the meadow there. It carefully avoided the bovines, but one cow of a sudden broke into a lumbering run and, at its approach, Reynard turned and, flattening his ears down and outwards, snarled open-mouthed. The cow changed its mind and veered off back to the herd where, from the safety of her companions, she gave voice. The fox promptly barked in answer, its body pushing forward. (The sharp, staccato bark – wonder if it was scenting its territory before the cow charged?) The cow lowed again; the fox barked. The situation had all the qualities of a farce. Then the herd joined in. The noise was deafening and the fox, probably losing its nerve, turned and quickly slipped away under the wire fence.

Wednesday 31 December
2.10 a.m. Crescent moon leaning on its side, very gusty wind, but mild and good visibility. Observed the Chantry twins and their parents from the Bank Sett. Worms the main item on the menu this morning. Talk about noisy spaghetti-eaters! When they locate a worm in the soft, damp earth of the field with the aid of their big, flexible snouts, it is vacuum-sucked up and swallowed. If it's a very long one, it will be crunched some way along before it enters the throat. One animal very close to me has eaten twenty-three consecutively, before moving on a few paces and starting again.

The wind is violent now in the bare treetops, masking most sounds, so I easily followed the Bank Sett pair till they split up, one going over Briarmead Lane via the Slide and into the meadow, the other keeping the Wildflower side and gradually moving along the lane's bank – I followed the latter. It seemed to find plenty to eat there in the herbage and is eating grass too (as opposed to accidentally taking it with other items). It startled a long-tailed field mouse that leaped to safety. Much too quick for a badger to catch, though they will dig up the nestlings and eat them, as they will young rabbits in their nursery stops.

7 p.m. New Year's Eve. The floodlit church spire stands guard above the village. From the stile at the View, bright little Warby bespangled with lights eclipses the stars above. Sitting at the highest point of the Chantry. No reason for coming out tonight – unless the sheer love of the place and the tranquillity of being alone in a wood at night can be termed 'a reason'. Looking down and across, the illuminated villages stretch along the valley. There's an urge, a need to come here, which has nothing to do with the wildlife – but everything to do with the place. The sky above me is very clear as the last cloud remnant is drawn back gently over the horizon and is nearly gone.

I can hear a car going up Briarmead – dogwalkers? Then silence. Listening to tawnies hooting and replying, very melodious. 9.30 p.m. The night grows chill and I'm becoming numbed, so I move on with regret. I'll go and watch those tawnies, then home via the Ashtree Path.

Well, another car, three dogs barking furiously inside! Know who they are. Wendy was always afraid of the youngest, an alsatian cross – it seemed to bring out the worst in the other two.

[The following entry for this date not completed until Saturday 3 January.] At the Ashtree Path, I heard a great commotion from near the Old Barn; shouting, dogs snarling and barking. I thought possibly one dog had caught a rabbit and the others were fighting over it. Then turning to walk into the woods, I distinguished different sounds – those of a badger.

Seemed to take an age covering the distance, and now I knew by the absence of badger noise that I was too late. The man was standing with his back to me, urging on his alsatian which was worrying and tearing at something on the bank. The other dogs, obviously tired, were licking at a patch of ground a yard or so away. The alsatian turned at me as I knelt down and wedged my shoulder between it and Jess lying on her back in the grass – her eyes open, nose and muzzle blood-spattered. Foolishly, I stared at her belly, puzzled at the glistening coils steaming in the clear night air. Then realisation dawned – the dog had ripped out her entrails. Helplessly I looked and saw recognition in her eyes. I stroked her forehead and she made a sound in her throat, but only blood came flowing from her mouth as she died. Don't know how long I knelt there under the stars, but when I finally looked round me, man and dogs were gone and the only sound was the wind sighing in the long grass.

I couldn't bear to leave here there (which seems silly), but was undecided what to do with her body. Finally, I wrapped her in my sweater, trying the arms tightly around her, and put the bundle under the pile of wood waiting to be burnt in what had been the apple orchard. The effort of dragging the roots and boughs away and then replacing them as nearly as possible to resemble the original heap gave an outlet for the anger that threatened to engulf me, for never have I felt so near to physical violence.

Saturday 3 January 1981
Left home at nine this evening to try and trace Jessie's mate. I gave no thought to him last Wednesday. He *could* have been underground, foraging a distance away, or even injured himself, though a mature boar such as him would have given a good account of himself with any dogs. They are normally very protective and possessive towards their sows and since he nearly attacked me when I lanced Jessie's abscess, I can't imagine he fled when she was set on by the dogs. However, that's something I'll never know, but I want to make sure he's not hurt.

Covered the territory in search of him, starting with the Wheatfield Copse. Past the Enclosed Path area, the back of the Ridge, and then walked round to Briarmead at the Main Pond. 11 p.m. Held up here by human activity, but finally able to leave 11.45 p.m. and passed through

11

this wood on to the open lane. The Old Barn and then the ploughed Hayfield. Thank heavens – one large badger by the Damson Bank. I checked, making sure it really was him, by kneeling and trying to copy her purring bubble. Yes, it's Jessie's mate, apparently unharmed. Since he was so much older than her, I think he had probably lost a previous mate too. He looked very vulnerable standing there on the bank.

Till now, whenever things have occurred here (senseless acts or calculated cruelty over which I have felt anger or bitterness), I have in my frustration shut the door, as it were, on this piece of countryside and stayed away for a time, only to be drawn back by my affection for the place. Jessie's death – no, her manner of dying – has altered that. The door now is not so much wedged open as taken right off its hinges. In a sense, I no longer have a choice – I am committed.

We are a strange nation. On the one hand, we have an incredibly sentimental attitude towards the animals for which we care (a vet once remarked to me, 'There are few problem pets, but many problem owners!'), yet on the other, we can deliberately inflict pain for our own pleasure. Years ago, I found a wooden box taken from the surrounding fields and placed in the middle of the path leading to the View. A pigeon had been nailed to it alive (the claws gripped the slats so tightly that, in death, they were forced into the wood). Then it had been used as target practice, the head all shot away. I walked up unknowingly, and two men made off. They weren't teenagers, but *men in their forties*. Indeed, much of the vandalism, burning and shooting that occurs here is, in my experience, carried out by that age group. But to report them you must have another witness to substantiate what you say and, as in the case of the pelt hunters of May 1979, a carcase found in their possession. With the young badger Tossy and his siblings, I knew the men had shot the other cubs as the family returned home that morning, but when I confronted the apparent leader, he laughed and challenged me to prove it. As he pointed out, by the time I reported him and his Land-rover's number to the police, they would have hidden the bodies to collect later. Incidentally, the strange mentality that will pay high prices for a stuffed badger will pay even more for a 'sweet' little cub.

Like the law 'protecting' owls, the Badger Act is in name only. There are so many ways round it that it has become just a mockery. The only difference it has made is, in my experience, to make people careful of how they go about killing. It has driven them underground with the badger, so to speak.

Tuesday 6 January
10 a.m. Mild, overcast day. Gorse in bloom by the Main Pond and the tiny new leaves of the honeysuckle make a brave show along each twine of stalk. The Yewtree Grove stands aloof and mysterious and from the dark shelter of one veteran, I'm surrounded unseen by a host of small birds. There's a coal tit in my yew, inches from my face, and several great

12

tits. What an odd 'song' the latter make – like two pieces of metal rubbed together. They seem to descend to the woodland floor more readily than other tits. There's a handsome bullfinch and two squirrels on the Scots pine near by. The squirrels aren't upsetting the birdlife as they tend to do in suburban gardens, but then there's plenty of scope and food here, so no real competition. I'm thrilled to see a tree-creeper (can't remember when last I watched one) spiralling upwards like a mouse. These yews have an aura of antiquity and indirectly offer much to the life of the wildwood.

In the early hours of this morning, I followed a vixen to this grove. She cached food in three places close by – a rabbit she had caught and partly eaten, she buried here under my yew; a dead pigeon hidden by the pine; and something left by the Council men yesterday (couldn't make out what it was), under the holly. I think movement to a great extent triggers off the urge to kill in the fox; sound does also, like the squeaking of voles. Certain creatures, e.g. weasels, shrews and moles, are regularly killed but rarely eaten, I have noticed, but then all these small mammals have a musky odour. Foxes bury food by excavating a shallow hole with the front feet. The cache is dropped in (just one item per hole in my observation) and the loose earth *nosed* over it, dog-like.

N.B. Walking past the Wheatfield Copse, I see the pile of wood is burnt. So nothing now remains of Jess and orchard – but a memory.

Wednesday 7 January
Left home at 2.20 a.m. Snowing steadily, but too damp to lie – wind in a sulky mood, reasonable visibility. Met Jessie's mate in the dead bracken by the Enclosed Path. We stood regarding one another. The soft snow settling on his face hides the black stripes; he blinks as a snowflake touches his eye. But for us, the world seems deserted.

7.30 a.m. By daylight, the varying coloured soils of the ploughed Hayfield contrast with the dark brown furrows near by, but now the white blanket is trying to conceal all. Followed a fox from the Old Barn, then watched it through the monocular (8.40–9.0 a.m.) scenting and rolling on what it had scented, on the top hayfield of Briarmead. It quartered the field doing this, to human eyes aimlessly, but probably with good purpose to the fox. By the stretch of trees that divides this hayfield with the next lower down the lane, it backed into the bank and scent-marked, then rubbed its shoulders against the place – then its rump. Think it may have been a vixen but can't be sure. By now I'm too benumbed with cold to walk silently, so am returning home.

Sunday 11 January
Since 2.10 a.m. have been following a fox on John Shaw's land. Everywhere glittering under the stars – the huge puddles frozen sheets of reflecting glass. At the farm buildings by the Poplar Row, it met up with a vixen – they obviously knew one another. She crouched down, tail

13

waving at the male's approach, then they both ran towards each other. One or both whined and made little guttural noises and a sound like panting (this latter by the vixen only), as they circled round, often on hind legs. The vixen's brush curved up and over her back in a bushy question mark. Under the night sky their dancing movements had an airy grace. Once the partners stood facing one another on hind legs, licking each other's muzzles. By now their gyrations had brought them but a short distance from me as I stood in the black shadow of a poplar trunk. The vixen seemed to be shivering; both were open-mouthed with tongues lolling and breath vaporising in the freezing air. Now the only sounds were the shivering, breathing, and the soft crunching of the frozen grass stems under their paws – they might have been the last moving creatures in a petrified landscape.

Then the dog fox mounted the female, she moving slightly at first under his weight. They remained in position perhaps fifteen to twenty minutes, finally facing dog-like in opposite directions. The male seemed almost to be asleep, head held low, till distant barking alerted him and they moved apart. They stood for a moment side by side, heads turned towards the sound, then as if in mutual agreement, first dog then vixen passed between the poplars, crossing the farmland beyond and so out of my sight.

[Finished my tawny census for January last Sunday and Tuesday evenings – ideal weather conditions. The Oak Dell pair definitely not in residence now. Great deal of shooting in this wood and the surrounding farmland. Some at dawn: a car is regularly parked near the top of Briarmead around 5 a.m., three men with guns (*see* entry for 24 January). Also other cars at dusk, especially Friday/Saturday/Sunday of any week.]

Thursday 15 January
Midnight. After *very* wet day, there's a clear, starry sky with moon two-thirds full and wind very gusty. Fox-watching – plenty of activity. Saw a pair of foxes out together, running side by side. Very playful – making little runs at one another – a quick lick round the mouth – gently bumping one another – both skittish and affectionate. Feel they have probably mated and will now remain together till the birth of the cubs.

The wind is trying to freeze the waterlogged soil, making the going very treacherous. Surface is not hard enough to walk on yet and below is soft, yielding mud. Moon hanging very low in the sky behind Newby Farm. It's a curious orange colour tonight, though it still sheds a white radiance, glinting on the diamond shapes of the leaded windows. Wonder if this orange hue is caused by climatic conditions, or the amber reflection of the distant Main Road.

I'm very used now to judging distances at night, viz. jumping down from a wall or bank. Night light makes heights appear greater. I'm out five nights of the week on average, and when I do walk my area by day,

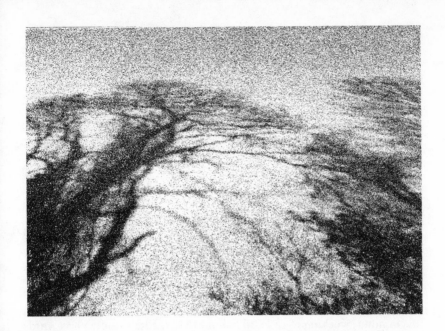

the result is rather a let-down, for everywhere seems small and rather insignificant by comparison.

Friday 16 January
Have been observing the three herons on the Bourne – and find them rather comic. Their feathers are mainly grey, and they have white heads and long necks with black plumes resembling untied bootlaces hanging behind their heads; two rows of broken stripes down their white fronts, long yellow bills and bamboo stilts for legs. Each heron is standing on one stilt in the stream (it's looking rather crowded!), all hunched up so that their long necks disappear into their shoulders; they each look bored to death. 'Three after-dinner speakers in search of a topic.' Occasionally, one will open its bill in a yawn, shut it with a rattle-like snap and raise its head. The long neck will appear, the straggling laces dangling behind and a second leg will be lowered down briefly into the water (yes, they *do* have two legs – I was beginning to wonder!). Then back they hunch in their dinner suits for another spell of inertia, the snowy covering all around adding a tablecloth touch. Well, at least they've kept me amused, which is more than I can say for most speakers!

Saturday 17 January
9.50 a.m. Rounding a corner of a quiet little lane, fields of sheep on my right, ploughed land and a copse to my left, I saw two birds busy tearing

at something on the grass verge. Was so near that I easily made out it was a squirrel from which a pair of kestrels was feeding. Never have I viewed them so close. Those keen eyes alerting between mouthfuls; the curved talons and hooked beaks; the sunlight accentuating their black-spotted plumage – what a noble pair of falcons! Whether the squirrel was a road casualty, had been shot, or the birds had killed it, it's impossible to say. They eventually left the carcase and rose up high in the air in what was surely an aerial display – I really must find out more about kestrels.

Monday 19 January

2.30 a.m. The moon has finally given up the struggle and disappeared behind a blanket of cloud. No stars showing, but I can see well. *Very* mild, wet night, with gentle breeze. Sitting on Meg's Fallen Birch writing this – the old trunk is gradually diminishing as it settles into the ground.

Been observing a vixen (possibly the same one as on 6 January?) stalk and kill a rabbit on the hayfield facing me. She crouched belly-low to the ground, flattening her body. This is when you realise how slender they are; no larger than a good-sized house cat under that fur. She stalked it in this manner, working round and behind the grazing rabbit. Three yards away, she made a lightning dash – one high-pitched squeal, one meal!

At 4.45 a.m. a blackbird began his lovely territorial song on the woodland fringe. No artificial light shows here, so I don't know what stimulated him to start so early – not dawn till approx. 7 a.m. Tremulous, lilting melody, a pure joy to hear.

Stood a long, enjoyable while with the Old Barn tawnies. I say 'with' as they knew quite well I was there. Oddly enough, walking home I heard a tawny at the far end of Madden Lane, but can't stop to locate it; also heard the Holmoak Lane pair by the ponies' field. Was late getting home – 6.15 a.m!

Saturday 24 January

Been badger-watching since midnight at the Bank Sett. The pair of animals here are very entertaining – a solid, middle-aged couple and the parents of the Chantry twins. They have dug out further along the Bank this year, but since the ancient workings go the length of this long, narrow field, they have plenty of accommodation from which to choose. The Council men are still burning and sawing here. Hope the badgers don't feel threatened and move. (There's been shooting since dawn this morning and now at 8 a.m. a police car has caught up with one lot of our regulars who had crossed the Hayfield to park their car.)

The grey of the overcast sky is giving way to streaks of blue and palest vermilion over the bare tree shapes of the Bank Sett. Before me on the Wildflower Path is the ploughed earth of the Long Field, the length of leafless trees (from which Yaffle* is making more noise than all the other

*Green woodpecker.

16

birds put together), and clearly showing in the background is the beautiful undulating curve of Great Chantry Field, greenly sown to the horizon. I can see the squirrel drey, far over the extreme side of the field, apparently suspended in air. Looks very odd from here, especially if you didn't know what it was. Under cover of the slight rustle caused by the breeze playing in the dead leaves, I've crept close up to Master Yaffle – one of nature's bigheads; every species has one!

9 a.m. Amongst the trees behind the View Sett now. No badgers here since Joe and Josephine were disturbed last summer and moved away. The birds love the mixture of Scots pine, birch and sweet chestnut; the woodpeckers like the dead wood for its insect life, whilst the brambles give cover to the small mammals. When badgers lived here, one could guarantee to see a fair selection of woodland wildlife in a couple of hours' quiet sitting – it was here that I saw Joe and his hedgehog that evening. Unfortunately, though, many shooters have also found this area profitable, so the mortality rate is high.

Tuesday 27 January
Sitting on the View stile 3.30 a.m., listening to a cock blackbird singing near the Main Road – confused by the lights perhaps – and watching a mist creep up over Warby; very peaceful here.

Had just written the last, when I heard a noise in the wood some way behind me, and though not thinking much about it, nevertheless moved out of sight under the tree cover. A few minutes and it became clear that something(s) much larger than a badger was on the move. A little longer, and two men appeared at the stile. One seemed very nervous and wanted to be off. (Couldn't decide whether he was fearful of being in a wood at night – strangely, some people are – or whether he sensed the presence of a third party?) The second man was calmer, looking slowly and carefully around as they emerged into the light, and, at one time, straight in my direction. (Rather glad I had covered my face with gloved hands as when animal-watching, that being the only light part of me showing.) After a moment, he seemed satisfied and, speaking curtly to his companion, hurriedly led the way down towards the cul-de-sac and the main road. Was tempted to track them and see if they too had a car parked there, but since they had been uneasy, thought better of it.

Saturday 31 January
Left home well before midnight. Sky clear, turning very cold, though the footpaths are still muddy. Crescent moon, but thick fog from ground level to twelve feet in the air, so limited visibility. Followed a pair of foxes (possibly those of 11 January) past the Glebe Farm land till we came to the main road at Crosshampton, where I left them. Went down to the river and here the mist has gone, the night bitter. Frost lies thick on each twig and grassblade. The river sparkles under the stars, endlessly murmuring as it tumbles on its way. Walked upriver, past Newby Farm

17

and under the Motorway towards Warby. Seemingly, nothing stirs here this frozen night except the river and me, each forever passing the other.

At Warby, stayed a long while observing a pair of barn owls hunting low over the fields – such an age since last I saw this species – what a joy to behold! Think they may roost in an old outhouse in the main street. Eventually moved on to the Chantry and spent the remaining hours of darkness there, since this is the best vantage point from which to view the sunrise over the valley.

The Bank Sett badgers, with their cubs, have quit this area – too much disturbed by the Council men sawing and burning along their bank the past week. Their old claw-scratching log that had been used by a decade of badgers was burnt, along with a great tangle of cuttings, barely a metre from the main entrance – and left burning all night. The two spindle trees and that of the guelder rose have been sawn down to eight-inch stumps. These cannot be coppiced like chestnut, though the guelder may survive by producing sucker shoots. Both guelder and spindle are small trees or shrubs, the greatest recorded height for the guelder being sixteen feet.* The spindle is an attractive, dainty little tree in any season: their destruction seems futile and, like Gerard Manley Hopkins mourning his aspens, I feel

> O if we but knew what we do
> When we delve or hew –
> Hack and rack the growing green!
> Since country is so tender ...
> After-comers cannot guess the beauty been.

6.15 a.m. The hoar has transformed the young corn to curly whisker tufts on the granite-ground. The heavy sky glows orange in the east and the birds twitter over the sleeping field. The machine-sown rows, each marching to infinity, disappear in ranks over the brow of Great Chantry. Now the night is dissolving and only the finely etched crescent of the old moon remains in the morning sky.

Have been very lucky this morning. The fox whose territory includes this area (who on several occasions I have discovered asleep) has mated quite recently and I have successfully tracked them by their clawmarks – too frozen for pawprints. I find they are at present denning together up here. Later, as her parturition approaches, the vixen only will den here and the dog fox will lie up away from the nursery. A short while ago, I found evidence of foxy grooming – a wad of fur with tooth marks clearly visible (the animal runs its teeth through the coat, collecting up the loose hairs).

The sun's great disc is well above the horizon now at 8.40 a.m. My lengthening shadow diminishes me as it stretches far long the fieldside. The morning rays have caught the top of my pine tree in a blaze of light –

*H. L. Edlin in *Wayside and Woodland Trees*, Warne & Co., 1964.

the dark green needles are tawny, its upper trunk afire. Below me the Bourne Valley is a swirling mist; just the tree and house tops visible. Near my Scots pine, a dying beech with giant boughs outstretched stands 'gaunt against the wintry sky, forever crucified'*, and at the lowest point of each twig, a frozen droplet hangs suspended.

There are a myriad rabbits playing and eating over by the Bank Sett. I am sitting here at the headland, monocular-gazing. Squirrels are amongst them too, all quite amicable. Sometimes, one of the latter will run up a tree in a rough-and tumble but with apparently no animosity, as a few moments later all will be feeding again. A great spotted woodpecker has flown down quite close to me on to a rotting log lying at the field's edge. His bright crimson patches behind the head and beneath the tail beautifully combine with his black and white plumage. This trunk is riddled with holes and he's improving on them in his quest for food. He's finding plenty; one, a long centipede-type he had to pull quite hard at. Now a pine cone has taken his fancy and he's gouging out the seeds. He has sounded a harsh churring note as a pair of jays alight near him.

Walking home, I see the Old Barn is being demolished, the rafters carefully removed and placed in neat piles. Here, too, I found the dead heads of hedge-parsley all whitely draped in lacy spider-tatters, though where the light is touching the grass verges, they steam in the sunshine.

Wednesday 4 February
The dead elms of the Wheatfield Copse moan and creak fearfully in the gusty wind. Several would be lying on the ground long since, but are still uncertainly held aloft by their companions. Mild, cloudy night – can see well.

Near the ruin of the Old Barn, I met Jessie's mate – the only resident badger left in the whole area, now that the Chantry is being cleared of its undergrowth and dead timber. Easier for human walking, I suppose, but vulnerable for badger activity. How ironic I should have said of the twins' new home at the Chantry (on 14 November 1980), that here they should be, 'well protected from man and weather for the winter'. Nine months ago, there were more badgers than I had ever known in the vicinity. And there is nothing that I can do about it – there's the rub – no one is interested. How do you overcome apathy and ignorance? All I *can* do is what I've done for so many years – keep a record of this area. Think now I should call it *The Decline and Fall of Practically Everything – of Value!*

Tuesday 10 February
Ross and I walked together round these woods today. Horrified to find that the Council men who have been working here, have sawn down the

*From 'Spring', *The Land*, by V. Sackville-West.

few wild service trees. Spoke to them and, to prove my point, searched for and found a few of the speckled brown service fruits, then pointed out the stumps to the man in charge.

Went up to the Chantry – for both of us a mysterious place. The elders have their bright green leaflets; lesser celandine is in bud; dog's mercury flowers in the undergrowth of the wood; and from many of the birches hang their tassel-like catkins. Superficially, the bare-branched trees denote winter, but look closely, and the promise of another year is already a reality, the new growth stealthily pushing through the dead.

Saturday 14 February
Left just after midnight. Already a severe frost, ground iron-hard, no wind. Moon two-thirds full, orange and low in the sky. Stood long on the Ridge, at first fox-watching, then just enjoying the view. Glorious panorama – the night sky with its bright stars and great orange moon; the bark of a group of birches close by, shimmering whitely; the dark line of the distant wood behind, and below to my right, an echo of the moon in the amber-lit mouth of the Motorway tunnel.

Have completed my tawny census for February; position static. Twice have met Jessie's mate this week. Find the Chantry rather forlorn at night without its badgers. See the stumps of the wild service trees have been dug out. Tried to find a few more speckly fruits – most seem to have gone. Have just eight in all.

Monday 16 February
Left home 1.20 a.m. Heavy frost, no wind, moon nearly full, mist pockets over the fields and clear sky. The Sleet Path tawnies are calling and answering one another – been watching and listening some while. Seems to be a 'conversation' of soft calls by the female and disconnected hooting on the male's part – he gently touching her beak and face. Think she may have chosen her nest site just here; will have to watch throughout February/March to see.

On the Ridge the cold is intense. A fox began screaming near by – continued some minutes, then momentarily broke off as the animal came crashing (noisily for a fox) through the bracken. Now a few feet from me, it begins to scream again. (Can hear the rasp in its throat as it takes in a great gulp of air, ready to sound once more.) No other fox appears or barks – just silence.

Walking slowly and as quietly as possible over the long hummocky field (frosted grass makes a soft 'crunch' underfoot), I've surprised a hare. For ages, it crouched low to the ground, waiting for a movement on my part. Was so close I saw the black-tipped ears now flattened in apprehension against its head, and large prominent eyes. I stayed completely still a long time under the moon, trying to ignore the biting cold by concentrating on the rodent. Time passed; then, moving one step at a time, it began feeding on the herbage, the sound of nibbling clear in the still air. It kept a wary eye my way, but taking its time, continued feeding.

Wednesday 18 February
Dull, overcast night with snow flurries and slight wind. Visibility excellent – possibly because the moon is full behind the cloud blanket? Been with Jessie's mate – seems to tolerate my presence and gets down to foraging for himself. Digging around in the undergrowth just inside the wood, he unearthed a hibernating hedgehog. Batted it around for a while, but clearly hadn't Joe's knack of uncurling it. He discovered some withered chestnuts that he crunched – also beechmast, I think. When he moved on, I re-covered the hedgehog.

Large flurries of snow descending, but none settling. Heard a great deal of shooting on entering the wood at the Oak Dell. Seemed to be coming from my left and, since the shots sounded off almost simultaneously, I would say from several guns. The shooting probably put an end to the tawny owl pair, for this was their territory.

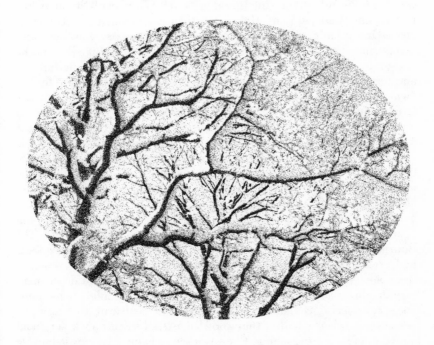

Friday 20 February
Met Jessie's mate almost immediately at the top of Briarmead Lane – wasn't expecting him just here. He stood regarding me – as I spoke to him – through the gently drifting snow that was doing its best to settle on the fields. Then, crossing the lane, the badger ambled along the bank till at the soakaway fence, he turned looking back at me. Our

21

relationship is good. Since Jessie's death, it is one of mutual tolerance. All of a sudden, I had an overwhelming desire to follow him – if he would allow it.

Thus with the big boar a short distance ahead, we passed down Briarmead, our pace steady yet unhurried. He was not foraging but clearly going somewhere, and occasionally looked back. Where this woodland meets Briarmead above the Wildflower Path, he re-crossed the tarmac and went under the wire and, unlike a fox, *across* the empty meadow – me following. Now we were at the Main Road, the few flakes that lay on the surface glinting as they caught the light; but at 3 a.m. quite deserted. Then he crossed and, flattening himself under the fence where it doesn't quite meet the uneven earth, he went into Newby Manor.

Here I couldn't follow, for though the main gate is near by, these are private grounds. In my experience, it is not wise to be seen so early in the morning around human habitation, so I walked down Newby Lane and into the meadows opposite the old house. (Strange how I seem to find my way here; I'll end up knowing this area as well as my own!) Stood awhile just looking and enjoying the scene, then a movement by the river alerted me. A badger had just crossed the Bourne, very shallow here, and was purposefully moving towards a cluster of molehills. Like Wendy, he passed by some, deliberated at others, then, scenting something in another, dug swiftly down. But whereas my dog would have dug for the owner-occupier, Jessie's mate – for it was he – was seeking the owner's larder, and he found it first time! He began eating the store of worms* in a most un-badgerlike fashion. Normally the ones they find are caught individually and alive, so the single prey writhes and twists briefly as it is sucked up – or breaks off, the predator 'snuffling' down hastily to locate the remainder. This morning, the boar was hungry, and biting into the inanimate mass, they dangled from his mouth making him look more like a spaghetti-eater than ever!

Walking back, I marvelled that until today I hadn't realised the big boar I watch in Newby's Water Meadows was one known to me. The Bourne is barely a mile from the Wheatfield Copse – no distance for a badger. Wonder if he originates from the river area? Although much of their behaviour is instinctive (captive cubs will 'musk' and do elementary digging), certain aspects are probably taught by adult behaviour. Joe's cubs have seen him uncurl hedgehogs, so learnt by example. Jessie's mate clearly hadn't that knowledge (*see* 18 February), yet, in all my years of badger-watching, I've never seen a badger so knowledgeable

---

*Checked up on moles: 'Larger, more permanent mounds or fortresses incorporating a nesting chamber are sometimes made – they can be recognised by the associated smaller molehills . . . Food is commonly stored in or near the nest chamber in autumn and winter. Stores consist mainly of earthworms with the anterior segments mutilated, and up to 470 worms have been found' – *The Handbook of British Mammals.*

about mole fortresses; wonder if later in the year he will dig for mole nestlings?

Reaching the top of Briarmead Lane, there are two cars parked here (5.30 a.m.), both with gun-carrying cases on the back seats. Jessie's mate will go to earth in the Newby area – I hope. There must be a sett in the grounds there somewhere. Is there any part of England now where the wildlife doesn't run the risk of being shot – or its habitat destroyed? Rather doubt it. Even on the hills, shooting goes on and snares are set for foxes (especially in the lambing season), which invariably catch other animals too. Come to that, is there anywhere that one can observe, unbothered by other human activity? Again, I rather doubt it. Only last September I was shot at as I walked up Briarmead Lane after midnight one Saturday morning (by the occupants of a passing car I had startled – they had left another car burning by the pond). Still, perhaps that keeps me alert – provided they miss, of course!

Homeward bound and a lovely, mild morning. It's turned noticeably warmer the past hour and one would never think it had snowed in the night. Dawn sky streaked with layer upon layer of brown, red and orange. I never see a beautiful sky without recalling Gerard Manley Hopkins: this sunrise now is 'brown brink eastward'. And how many 'brinded' 'couple-colour' skies have I seen; clouds that are 'silk-sack' or 'meal-drift moulding and melting'; and sunsets in the 'dappled-with-damson west'?

Tuesday 24 February
Have been walking in the woods today and looking at trees – this is an experience in itself. A vivid blue sky and a vision of trees. To see them, without foliage is to see to the 'bare bones', though many aren't bare of course. Some oaks have the dead year's brown leaves; the Scots pine and holly remain green.

But most of all, the birches take my attention this lovely morning. The airy grace of their besom branches and the intricate patterning of the bark. The two varieties are so different, yet have many good looks in common.

Observed a stoat on the Ashtree Path eating a squirrel. When it had completed the meal, it carefully groomed its fur. Have noticed they show great curiosity. If ever I surprise one, I keep quite still. Very often a stoat will return after a while to have a better look – its bright-eyed, bewhiskered face with its upright ears, more softly rounded than its weasel cousin, and the longer tail always black-tufted.

Walked along the Wildflower Path looking at the felling and burning there. The undergrowth has gone or, more accurately, the undercover and foliage of the plants that would soon have flowered, before the undergrowth becomes thick. Disturbed to find the area where the asarabacca (*Asarum europaeum*) grew has apparently been used as a

23

fire-site – hope I'm wrong and the plant grew farther over. Will have to check later in the year.*

Thursday 26 February
Mid-day; dull, overcast. Met two groups of shooters. One man of the second group came towards me with something bright dangling from his hand. Seeing my glance go to it, he proudly showed me his trophy, saying, 'Takes expertise to hit such a small target.' It probably does, since it was a male bullfinch he was swinging by a leg – its pink breast and underparts had caught my eye.

A few orange berries still clung to the stinking iris growing off the Wildflower Path. Found a perfect, unblemished crab apple amongst the flowering dog's mercury near by; the foxes must have missed it. Left it sitting on top of an old stump for them to find.

Think I had better move. Another car of shooters has arrived – don't want to be a bullfinch!

Saturday 28 February
The last morning of February – and a most enjoyable one. Left home before 2 a.m. – the hours of darkness in the silent grip of a deep frost. No wind, each star bright in the cloud-clear sky. My breath as the footpath crosses the fields a continuously white ebb and flow about my face. Such a night must be the last of any creature weak or sick.

Trailed a fox from the Old Barn area to that of the Bank Sett, then deserted it to enjoy the hunting and parleying of the tawny pair. Tawnies are the greatest – no, perhaps barn owls are – my loyalties are somewhat divided! The cold finally won, and leaving the exposed fields, my anorak glistening like everything else, I retreated to the depths of the wood and the cover of a friendly holly tree. The evergreen boughs of this giant pass down to sweep the ground, and once inside its protecting shelter the cold soon became bearable again.

6 a.m. and no desire to return home, so walked up the gentle main street of Warby. This small village has for me a great attraction and its people contain the quality of the place.

Found a letter from Ernest Neal waiting for me on my return. He suggests Jessie's mate could have dug down and found the stored worms after hearing/smelling the mole – good point that; I feel he's probably right. Also interesting that he writes, 'I once analysed the stomach contents of a badger run over by a car – after a cold night – and this contained many earthworms and two moles.' The significant words here are 'after a cold night'. A badger can't worm for himself in hard ground (as the worms go deep below the surface), and moles store against

*Checked 6 May: this *was* the area.

24

difficult digging conditions. The two moles must have been a welcome addition to the worm menu! His letter demonstrates how helpful it is to be able to *discuss* an observation like this and get another's viewpoint.

SPRING 1981

Sunday 1 March 1981

8 a.m. and dull, mild morning. Successfully avoided becoming a target as I followed the footpath up through Prosser's Wood to the Top Field. Met David on the way over. He told me that a while ago, walking along Burr Lane, a very large badger crossed the road in front of him by the farm and proceeded with haste towards Newby and the river. I told him about Jessie's mate – wonder if it was him?

At the Wheatfield Copse now. A perfect badger print in the soft earth under the dead elms – the five claws, toes and the big, broad pad – the ideal clue you rarely find! Have to be careful here as some uprooted trees are very precariously balanced by another's dead branches. The badger has been digging for roots, bulbs, and wild arum corms. (Jessie's family living here last year did this so often that it comes as a surprise there *was* anything to come up.) Some old bedding is freshly pushed out containing straw, grass, fronds of bracken, two heads of last year's wheat minus the grain and – a piece of very chewed blue plastic fertiliser bag! Bet that was one of Jessie's trophies! Only Jessie could have been such a clot as to have included that in the bedding! Bluebell greenery is bitten off close to the ground, though that may have been done by rabbits – think a vixen is denning here too. The earth of this copse is very sandy and easily worked.

At the Fallen Log and View Setts (still empty as yet), the green of brambles, bluebells and nettles is well advanced. Observed a rabbit here on the dead logs, 'chinning' and nibbling moss, then sampling bramble leaves. A jay's sudden cry made him dash for cover with a white flash of scut. There's a bright-breasted robin under the Scots pine here as I eat my apple. He's watching me with great curiosity – his neat little head to one side and his eyes alert. Strange, now that I don't have to share my apple with my dog, it doesn't seem to have the same flavour.

Tuesday 3 March
2.40 a.m. After thirty-six hours of rain, the fields are somewhat water-logged. Still raining, but not so heavy; visibility fair. For the past twenty minutes have been fox-following. Strangely, it hasn't looked back once! (It has looked around as it hunted, but never back.) Usually, they trot a little; swerve sideways or pounce; look around and behind; trot a little; look around and behind; scent-mark; look around, etc. At first, the pattern seems haphazard, but over the weeks of fox-following and keeping my eyes on the animal all the time (this is where knowing *my* territory intimately is essential), I seem to sense when it will turn, just before it does. Because there *is* a certain pattern in all this. Barring the odd scent/sound disturbance (the fox hunts into the wind so the prey's scent is borne downwind to him; equally his scent is borne downwind to me, not mine to him), they tend to look about them at certain times and in certain places – not necessarily the obvious ones to us.

In theory, the openness of farmland should be more difficult to trail through than woodland but in fact this isn't so. First, the fox loves the fieldsides, hedges, banks, the last furrow, overgrown grassy paths be-tween fields, the Poplar Row. And the ploughman's deep furrow to help drainage, or division between two crops, is a fox's dream. Secondly, field-workers tend to be untidy, e.g. odd boxes thrown here and there, too many straw bales brought on to the field to hide the birdscarers and the surplus left lying around. Scarecrows, too, are erected at irregular inter-vals. Not your Worzel Gummidges (romantic image of yesteryear), but plastic fertiliser bags hanging from tall sticks; modern Gummidge would have to search the 'nearly new' or jumble sales' Therefore, the fox on open farmland is well used to a man-made change in his landscape. At seven stone in weight and five foot two in height, I'm not overlarge by human standards, and if I squat down just before he turns (this only travelling *across* fields generally, and rare), my shape protrudes little on my surroundings. I've found also that if a fox does turn and

27

look hard at me, provided I keep *still*, it will move on – to suddenly look back again after a short trot. If I've stayed in the same position at the second examination, I'm accepted as part of the scene. Foxes *do* cross open fields at times, e.g. the fox scent-marking the hayfield (*see* 7 January), but not as a general rule. Also, many foxy patterns of behaviour occur during the rut, which are exceptions to the remainder of the year.

The rain has ceased. Today's fox has made a high pounce and now is eating something small. Realised quite recently that, although I started animal-watching years ago, by waiting at a given point – den, sett, pond or trail – I am very mobile these days. Suppose that is the natural progression, really. A lot due to training myself to see under most conditions, knowing the terrain very well at night, and an incredible amount of luck – and, not least of all, the goodwill of Barry Hains. I'll doubtless do more stationary watching when the respective cubs are above ground (doubt if badgers will have returned to the area though, unless they are harassed at their present sett) and that late in the year the dawn will break before I need to return home.

Wednesday 4 March
Dry, mild day though overcast. Walked round the woods this afternoon. Checking the Wheatfield Sett, was puzzled to find several deep little holes around each entrance. Only when I discovered a two-inch mesh net (still pegged in and forgotten by its owner) over one secluded entrance did light dawn. Very concerned as I haven't seen Jessie's mate all this week. [Re-checked carefully again – I'm wrong. The big main entrance above the bedding-chamber has *not* been netted; no marks here.] What was the net owner out to catch/kill – rabbits, fox or badger? I know of two methods of catching rabbits with nets – gassing*, and putting a ferret down – but I'm sure smaller mesh netting is used to prevent the ferret escaping; must check this. However, what must be abundantly obvious to any rabbit-catcher is the size of the these holes. There *is* a vixen denning here, and Jessie's mate is living here and at Newby Manor. He had a massive dig-out last Sunday morning from several entrances and, of course, turned out the old bedding too – all clear evidence of a badger.

Ministry officials dig in the entrances leaving one free, through which cyanide powder is pumped into the sett. As soon as the powder mingles with the air, it turns into gas. Moreover, *they* aren't after badger pelts (which is just as well or then they would have to start digging). Anyone

*Five years ago I wrote: 'Watched a man this morning shooting rabbits by the Old Cherry Tree in the woods. He stopped up most of the entrances just leaving the three nearest to him. He inserted a hose connected to a gas canister into a burrow, blocked in round it, and turned the tap on; then stood with his gun by the old tree. In moments the rabbits emerged, about a dozen in all. I only saw him miss one. I just hope he doesn't try this with Joe and Josephine; the View Sett is only round the corner and two prime badger pelts would make him far more easy money than any amount of rabbits.'

could get hold of a gas cylinder, and shoot or net the badger as he emerged from the uncovered entrance – if Jessie's mate was here. Or have I just a suspicious mind?

[Spoke to Richard yesterday evening about the net. He said that net and mesh *are* right for rabbiting with ferrets – the latter *should* be able to pass through the mesh and tame enough not to attempt to escape. He queried how the net was placed over the entrance. There were four pegs in all (and four pegmarks at each entrance but one); the net stretched taut across the hole and securely pegged into the ground. Richard shook his head and remarked that the net owner wasn't after rabbits then, as for those it should be fixed by its one peg loosely over the entrance with the surplus net lying on the ground inside the hole. The rabbit sees the net but, with the ferret behind, springs into it, pushing itself, net and all, out into the open air; the drawstring tightens up and you have one net-bag with one rabbit inside. Slip the peg out of the ground and retrieve your ferret. He said rather thoughtfully that someone was after much larger game – I just nodded and left it at that. Remembered how hard the pegs had been forced into the ground, right up their hilts, and had to be dug out with my penknife before I could remove the net.]

Thursday 5 March

Searched from midnight to dawn, moving from the Ridge down to the Water Meadows and the Bourne, then along the Burr Lane area (just in case David's badger was also mine), and slowly back again. No sign of Jessie's mate. Not that that proves anything much – only time will tell.

1.30 p.m. Walked to Ashcroft Woods this afternoon via the side of the Motorway and Madden Lane. The wood is quiet – nothing stirs. At the Wheatfield Sett could find no evidence of fresh dung in the pits. The beauty of this countryside hurts – a 'Silent Spring'?

[I've just read a magazine article about a young sow badger who was saved from torture and certain death at the hands of badger-baiters. I've never seen badger-baiters at work, so don't know whether it is carried out with terriers still, as of old, or whether there are more modern methods. Those very qualities that make the badger so endearing to some humans – its sociability, family groups and cleanliness – make it vulnerable to mistreatment by others. Add to this the legalised gassing in some counties where bovine tuberculosis is known to be present in cattle (in south-west England an estimated *10,000* badgers have been killed 'officially' since the operation started in 1974 by the Ministry of Agriculture teams), and the picture is gloomy indeed.]

Tuesday 10 March

Persistent rain since Friday; very mild. Been out every night searching, but seen nothing of my badger, which is ominous. Waited till midnight on two evenings at the Wheatfield Sett for him to emerge; regretfully must conclude he is no longer in that vicinity. He is not in the Newby area either, which means that if he is still living he has moved right out of his territory. For this time of year that would be extraordinary behaviour for a solitary boar. The months of February/March are usually those in which the cubs are born and also the principal time of mating. The resident boar of each territory is very aggressive towards any strangers – so are the sows. A yearling boar *might* just be unwise enough to trespass, but not a mature one like Jessie's mate. I'll go on searching, but he's almost certainly dead; the last of the badgers in this area.

I've been wondering how the Bank Sett sows fared after they were disturbed and moved at the end of January. During the autumn, badgers generally dig out in different places within their territory, but since the Bank Sett is such a long and ancient one, they merely dug out further along. Then the felling and all-night burning forced them to move right away at the worst possible time. If the cubs were still unborn *and* the group could find a vacant sett with a reasonable foraging range, their chances of survival would be good. If the cubs were born, I doubt if they would survive the move. The sows would have had to leave the litters while they carried one cub at a time a considerable distance in freezing conditions (we had severe frosts on the nights of 28/29/30 January). The remaining cubs left a long time without their mother's body warmth would then be carried under the same conditions. If the first cub survived the carrying ordeal, it would then be left along in a new sett and already be suffering from exposure. By the time of the sow's return with the next of the litter, the first would probably be dead.

Thursday 12 March
A mild, gentle morning; the rain really seems to have left us for a time. The warm, damp conditions have encouraged all the young growth to surge upwards in an effort to reach the light. The clouds are well broken and moving quickly across a blue sky. There must be a strong wind high up in the atmosphere, but down below just a slight breeze. Every bird sings in the competition for territory; the bare branches are acquiring a greenish tinge and I've given up counting the different fungi – spring has returned once more.

Towards the wood's end of the Enclosed Path, I discovered woolly male aspen catkins blown down by the wind and the rain – their purple anthers in marked contrast to the yellow pollen, resembling so many plump, gaudy caterpillars. Past the Main Pond, a solitary bee was crawling across the detritus, occasionally opening its wings to the sun only to fold them again and continue its journey.

Many blue and great tits busy in the wood. The dark-blotched, spear-shaped leaves of wild arum are growing fast. On the stony scree of the Ridge, watched with great pleasure the ridiculous antics of the 'trotty-wagtails' as they searched for insects amongst the pebbles.

Friday 13 March
Twice last week I observed a fox drop food near the Chantry Den, sniff at the entrance and make a soft 'mmmmmmmmm' (the same sound I've heard vixens make when returning with food to their cubs, and the sound I made to Vicky whenever we used to meet); then he scent-marked in several places – including near the food – and left. I've definitely established it now (the third time witnessed) to be a dogfox 'bringing back' for its vixen in whelp, as this time before he'd disappeared, the vixen herself emerged. She looked at her retreating mate who hadn't seen her, went over to the catch – and then the dogfox turned, whined, and made to come across to her. Whereupon, the vixen growled, ears flattened – and he hastily retreated. She stood looking after him awhile, then began to eat – stopped with ears alert and eyes on the den entrance, then went to earth with her meal. This is the pair of Chantry foxes. The vixen has moved since the burning and felling disturbance to this den, but it's only a short distance away.

Yesterday afternoon after that lovely spring morning, we had heavy thunderstorms which are only now easing. One or two stars are trying to peep between the cloud spaces; time 2.20 a.m. Very, very mild with excellent visual conditions. Extremely happy up here though I miss my badgers – but humans willing, there'll be others one day perhaps.

I'm interested in what the Chantry dogfox has been leaving here for his mate – hindquarters of a rabbit the first night; a pigeon, three skylarks and several voles the next (fetched at intervals); and a rabbit now, apparently whole. The skylarks (ground-nesting birds) are quite easy to catch at night. This will sound far-fetched, but I caught one myself back in January, as I crossed Ingrims Fields one bitterly frosty night. They fly up as I pass by and they leave it so late that I'm often brushed by their wings. This particular night, I sensed seconds before it happened that it was about to and, putting out a hand, caught it easily. Stood bird in hand, looking at its tiny crest, its long 'larkspurs' and terrified eyes, feeling ashamed that I was the cause of its fear yet marvelling that so tiny a creature could in daylight create such a torrent of bubbling music over the fields. Placed it gently back on the frozen ground, pitying its wretched resting place. Have a great respect for their ability to soar up high – no wonder they have such large and broad wings to their sparrow-like bodies. Continuing on my way, I reflected that much as I love the skylark's silver chain of song so effortlessly delivered on the wing, the skylark is, like most eminent songsters, intensely territorial. And as I had proved that night, very vulnerable to predators!

Still checking for Jessie's mate but know, if I'm honest with myself, that he's a pelt long since. Well, perhaps not a pelt when one remembers that magazine article about badger-baiting.

Tuesday 17 March
1.40 a.m. Snowing hard, though not at present settling – fields very wet

from recent rains. Been watching Old Barn tawnies parleying and hunting for some time until finally they moved out of my sight-range. As I made to move on, heard their trill for the first time this year. Couldn't myself say which bird made the high burst of song (it lasted some seconds, to be repeated, and repeated again), although Dr Southern states, 'The trill ... belongs mainly to the male and to the breeding season.'* Bad weather conditions have prevented my tawny evening census this month, but found through night-time observations that the position still the same.

9.30 a.m. Beautiful morning, though cold. Walked round the Wheatfield Copse. The women cutting cabbages were warming their hands at a fire made of broken boxes. I like these people very much – always friendly and smiling in spite of their cold, wet job. At the abandoned sett, all has a neglected air – found a giant puffball by an entrance. The footpath, undermined by the sett running beneath, is beginning to subside owing to the wet conditions – very wary of my footing here at night.

Met Barry Hains exercising his horse. Our conversation covered several topics, all I think of mutual interest. He was concerned over the badgers' disappearance (and Jessie's death). He told me that his father contacted the police about a car that came up Briarmead Lane late one evening recently, and stopped by the pond. The police intercepted it on its return down the lane, but not before his father had chased up in hot pursuit, parked his car and followed them into the wood on foot! The car's occupants had been sharing out the takings (radios) of a Warby shop broken into earlier on. Told him of the illegal activity I try to avoid – not always successfully – and suggested his dad was very unwise to get *out* of his car and accost people as I've seen him do of an early morning. He's fairly safe *in* it, but at seventy-eight and frail, liable to get hurt challenging folks. He agreed, but remarked rather sadly that his father didn't see it in the same light. He then warned me that the Prowler was back again – didn't know we had one! Mind you, after the night-time activities up here, a prowler in the day would be a little light relief. It's evidently upset both him and his tractor-driver. Afraid that I laughed so much, I startled his horse. Little Ashcroft Woods sound more like Hyde Park!

Wednesday 18 March

Have had every kind of weather condition tonight. Started out at 12.45 a.m. with a near-full moon and deep frost. Later had snow showers, but by 4.30 a.m. it had turned beautifully mild and later I walked home carrying my anorak! Spent much of my time at the Chantry, fox- and stoat-watching and just enjoying myself – such a glorious place to be,

*The Natural Control of a Population of Tawny Owls (Strix aluco) by H. N. Southern, from J. Zool. Lond. (1970).

feel I belong there. For a good while, listened to a fox barking at intervals on the move. The sounds indicated its owner crossed Briarmead lower down and passed above Newby Farm, then away across the fields. Not the wow-wow bark, but more open sounding, with a slight rise to the end of each phrase. The type of bark alters with the situation and the time of year. Wish there was some accurate means of studying the 'language' of the fox – it would answer a lot of my questions on the life of this elusive creature.

Friday 20 March
Beautiful, well-lit night with a gusty wind blowing thin, trailing 'scarves' of cloud across the face of the full moon. Everything clear-cut and distinct, though rather too bright for my vision. (Found during these past weeks of cloudy, raining nights, I can see unaided farther and farther into the distance as well as close to. It's definitely practice, though I've got that kind of sight that operates best in dusk-type conditions.)

On the Ridge watched the courtship ritual of two brown hares – not seen this before. One was grazing when another appeared from the gorse bush area. The grazing one looked up suddenly with a sound as if blowing violently through its nose. The other 'walked' slowly up in a curious way, hard to describe – almost lying along the ground, its extreme length of hind legs accentuated, its head pushing forward and ears back. They came nose to nose and stayed so awhile. Then the ground-lying hare gathered itself up, gently and smoothly in spite of its former ungainly position, until they both sat, four feet on the ground and still nose to nose. There they remained almost trance-like. Then with no apparent warning, both reared up on hind legs, their bodies long in the moonlight, and stood tall. One leapt away and next moment they were off, leaving the ground in great leaps and bounds over the open space – turning, twisting in mid-air as though trying to outstrip each other's performance, with the loose stones of the scree rolling and clattering under their feet. One or both urinated in mid-air (as rabbits do), but by now their movements were so fast, I found it impossible to tell them apart. Then one, the doe, crouched down quite still, with tail raised and hind feet pushing backwards. The buck still continued his leaps, seeming not to notice the other and moving further away. Then with a suddenness that came as a surprise, he leapt back – a long, low jump right across the space, and covered the crouching doe. Copulation was brief and similar to that of the rabbit, though whether this is usual with the hare, I don't know.

Dawn by the Main Pond very beautiful, the water full after the recent rains, and the birds busy in the early morning sun. No human sounds – just the woodland stirring in the day's first warmth. Looking out from the sheltering trees, over these fields and beyond, a great surge of joy rises from me to meet the skylark spiralling high and ever higher into the blue air – the liquid notes of his ecstasy spilling down to me far below. The same sun warming my upturned face glows on his feathers; the breeze that gently lifts my hair touches him also.

Jess and her mate are gone, not to return. I'll never walk this way again to see my badger come to greet me and hear her purr. But other badgers will live here one day – as long as this place remains, undefiled. For each small wood and every bank holds a promise for the future – our future and theirs – if we honour that promise.

Saturday 21 March

A curious thing happened this morning. Didn't leave home until quite late – for me – 4 a.m. Walked via the Motorway for quickness, into Madden Lane and up to the Chantry from the Oak Dell side of the wood. Watched first light approximately 5.15 a.m. and then the dawn from Great Chantry Field. Very mild; clear sky and full moon. At this time of year, the moon is still quite high in the sky at daybreak, so to the east across the valley I had the sunrise, whilst behind me through the leafless branches, the full disc of the moon seemed reluctant to quit the sky.

Having no deadline to return home today, I walked about the woodland listening and watching the birds, and came to the giant holly tree set into a bank – one of several such trees here and a particular favourite of mine. If unhampered in its growth a holly tree attains a considerable size, and unless the branches are lopped or pruned, the evergreen foliage will hang to the ground all around, entirely concealing the trunk. Such trees give me protection from wind, rain – and frost on bitter nights. This particular holly was split in three in its youth. Though it has rejoined and grown so massy, this has caused the trunk to have a wall-like appearance which, set into the bank, makes its sheltering boughs most cavernous. Generally if very cold or wet, I sit back against this trunk looking towards the 'curtain' entrance. Today I was neither, and ducking down under the trailing curtain of greenery, sat down – not against the trunk as usual, but a little to the right of the entrance. And there I stayed, head down, still listening to the birdsong all around.

Gradually became aware I was not alone. Very, very slowly lifting my head, found I was being stared at by a fox curled up in my usual seat – poor creature, he was surely more startled than me! Of course, I was all but covering his retreat, but was unsure quite what to do. It would have been kinder to have obeyed my first impulse to quit the hideout and leave the fox in charge, but curiosity to see what he – a dogfox certainly – would do made me stay, completely still and just watching.

There was a very long pause; a blackbird high up in the holly began its morning song, telling the rest of Ashcroft Woods that this was *his* territory. The recital opened with a lovely, lilting theme, and continued with variations *ad infinitum* – and still fox and I sat within three feet of each other! Then slowly, smoothly, sinuously, it uncurled, its long brush that had been curved around its body nearly touching me as its owner found his feet. Then, still regarding me carefully, but I think with less alarm, it walked stealthily around the green wall until it came up to the entrance near my left side. I fully expected it then to make a bolt for freedom – but it didn't. And that was the strangest thing of all. With freedom inches away, it just stood looking – if I had moved sideways we would both have been head on! It made as if to pass through the curtain, its gaze leaving mine; then changed its mind and looked at me again. Another long pause – by now it was gazing *back* at me as its steps had moved it slightly forward. Then, slowly and silently, it passed through and I was alone. A pause – I had the feeling it was still near by. Turning, I parted the foliage very gently to find myself again staring into foxy eyes. I had a desire to laugh – which would have wrecked the mutual interest! Still the blackbird proclaimed his territory above and still we gazed below. Then a movement ahead took Reynard's attention and with a last glance my way, he trotted out of sight.

Though I have many times smelt fox scent here, it has never occurred to me that the animal might use this shelter as I do. He must know my scent far better than I know his!

Had a very interesting discussion this evening with Brian Carpenter, who did research on night vision during the war, which has given me food for thought. He told me that pilots during the Second World War, though aided by radar, needed to see the enemy near to before they themselves were sighted. So tests were made on the individual's ability to see unaided in the dark and on adjusting and improving sensitivity. I mentioned how useful my thirty-minute walk across farmland to the

Ridge is in acclimatising myself, and how a car's headlights, even at a considerable distance (and the Main Road's lighting), can temporarily hamper my nightvision. Brian is the first person I've met who knows from his own experience that a human being can, with practice, see well at night even under cloudy conditions.

We went on to discuss the article 'Through an Owl's Eye' by Dr Graham Martin (*New Scientist*, 12 January 1978) which investigated the tawny owl's vision and visual system and came up with some surprising results 'concerning not only the vision of a nocturnal creature but also of man'. We have a 'view of man as a diurnal creature whose behaviour at night is chiefly limited by his poor visual sensitivity. It is simply not appreciated just how very sensitive the vision of man is ... The high similarity of owl and human visual sensitivity thresholds does not mean of course that we should regard man as a nocturnal creature, but it does suggest that our diurnal habits are not because we are any blinder in the dark than nocturnal animals.'

Discussed infra-red binoculars and infra-red photography – both infinitely beyond my pocket! Was told I should practise seeing with the monocular more at night – I've got lazy lately, so will take that to heart. I said that though I now have the flash attachment for my camera, I don't care to use it on animals. It frightens them and so defeats my objective as I want to continue observing the same animal regularly. Have no wish to startle any creature if I can possibly avoid it; it's not in their interests, or mine. Also, professionals with their experience and more sophisticated equipment take far better photographs than I could ever obtain. My only regret is that I never had the flash in time to take Jessie – she wouldn't have turned a guard hair! In the case of Vicky, even if I had obtained the flash in time, I don't think I would have attempted to photograph her, as our relationship was so tenuous. I valued the knowledge I gained from her far above a mere photo of a fox – she was my very first breakthrough with *Vulpes vulpes*.

Saturday 28 March
Came out at 12.50 a.m. after a week away. Very mild, warm night with clear, starry skies, half-moon and slight breeze. Fields wet after three days/nights of rain earlier this week – ponds and soakaways full to overflowing. Hate being absent for long; miss this place too much and get restless to be out at night.

Everything has grown in the interval; combination of warmth and moisture. Long before I reached Raven Lane, let alone turned the corner, I noticed the 'fragrant incense' smell, so knew without looking that Roger Johnson's balsam (poplar) trees had uncurled their new young leaves. This row of quick-growing poplars, like the Lombardy poplars, form a fine windbreak. Everywhere the fresh scents of spring are a pleasure – earth, grass, gorse – all things living and sweet.

My moon goes before me past the Wheatfield Copse – I've become a moon-worshipper, I think! Can understand the ancients believing in a lunar goddess (it *is* feminine), and creating a legend to explain its disappearance from the night sky at certain times. Briarmead Lane wet with running water; the light reflects on its gleaming surface. I'm walking down this lane – a rather risky thing to do at 2 a.m. on a Saturday – but enjoying myself too much to mind chancing a car coming up. Have reached the Bank Sett. The brow of Great Chantry looms ahead, its treeline profiled against the glittering sky. With an oak tree as a back rest I'm writing here, the shining moon ahead, a tawny owl calling from the Wildflower Path behind – what greater joy than this! The moonlight reveals the pattern of my oak's bark in greatest detail. On every side, scents are borne along on the breeze; no wonder a fox's world is one enveloped by smell – man's must once have been, too.

3.30 a.m. Been watching a pair of foxes, but too lazy and contented to attempt to trail. To my extreme far right, the bright amber of the Main Road – except for this, all is beautiful. Walking home through the moonlight wood, I hear the tawnies parleying. Stood awhile listening to the soft 'contact' call of the hen repeated several times and watched as a tawny flew back and forth across the track. Seems to be considerable pre-dawn activity with these owls. This female appears to have laid her clutch now, so her mate will need to provide all the food for them both and for the fledgling chicks for quite a time – provided the pair aren't disturbed and desert the clutch, of course.

Tuesday 31 March
Have been observing the Chantry foxes for the past three nights. The behaviour pattern here seems similar to that witnessed with other pairs in past years, so I imagine it to be the norm. For the first two to three weeks after the cubs' birth, the vixen hardly leaves them at all – unless her mate is not fetching food for her (there's no way of telling whether he's dead, or deserted her, of course), and she will not let him approach her or the cubs. After these few weeks, she will hunt near by the den and accept the dogfox back into the family circle, though she will growl at him if he approaches too near the entrance. He continues to hunt for himself and her, but does so farther afield – I trailed him tonight to the railway fencing, which I believe to be the limit of his territory in that direction as he never attempts to go on the embankment. In fact, dog and vixen don't meet up that often, since when he's away she's above ground, and when he fetches a kill back (he's brought back three times tonight) she's often below ground. However, when the visits *do* synchronise, there's much tail-wagging, whining and face-licking – their close relationship to the domestic dog is never so apparent as then.

Find this dog/fox similarity interesting. Wendy's listening attitude and high pounce on small rodents was very reminiscent of the fox, and hunting in the overgrown Old Orchard at Weldon, her bounds to see above the long grass were akin to *Vulpes vulpes* in the hay and cornfields

37

here. Both dog and fox enjoy a good roll, grunting as they twist and squirm about on their backs – especially in the moult. It seems to me that an incredible amount of nonsense has been written about the fox. Only a few days ago, I read an article which said that foxes seldom growl or snarl – whatever the stuffed foxes seem to be doing in their display cases. Rather like saying the same of dogs, or that man rarely shouts and never loses his temper. Given the right set of circumstances, of course foxes growl – and they *do* occasionally snarl, as at the cow on 28 December last.

Thursday 2 April
After days and nights of rain, this morning dawned misty but dry. Now at 2 p.m. the sun is trying without much success to break through the greyness. Ashcroft and Prosser's Woods are carpeted with wood sorrel, wood anemones and lesser celandine – splashes of white and yellow amongst the green-brown undergrowth. Luxuriant mosses below, tiny leaves unfurling above – and birds on every side.

The Damson Bank is clothed in whitest blossom. Everywhere the water level is seriously high. The Bourne, in common with other rivers hereabouts, has overflowed its banks at different points and the Water Meadows are living up to their name. At the View Sett, two of the entrances have been dug out recently but not, I think, by a badger. The primroses and violets along the Primrose Path are breathtaking. An elder just here has some fresh jew's ear fungus growing from it. Beginning to rain again ... very misty now, 4 p.m.

In a damp part of this woodland opposite the Oak Dell grows a great bank of spurge laurel, the finest in the area. This is a curious shrub (reminds me of miniature palm trees), as the long upright stem is brown and leafless except for its crown of leaves at the top. Amongst this bright evergreen foliage, the tiny, sweet-scented flowers are clustered with their yellow centres which will eventually turn into poisonous, blue-black berries. Going up to look at the spurge laurels just now, I saw a snake twined beneath one woody stem and partially obscured by dog's mercury and dead leaves. The reptile's markings appeared zigzag, though I've never seen an adder here. Nevertheless, I picked it up behind the head rather cautiously (with the practised grasp of the true animal lover – who has been bitten before!). It was a barred grass snake, however; the length of it alone – well over three feet – and the round pupil (not a vertical slit) proved that. Probably an old female as it lacked the orange or yellow 'collar' at the nape of the neck. But what an unusual one – the vertical black bars along each flank, nearly joined at the top of the body, giving it at a glance a zigzag effect. Stood admiring its coils now wound about my arm – even a small snake such as this has a surprising strength in its muscular body.

Saturday 4 April
Been watching the tawny owls at the Old Barn area for the past three hours. This particular pair are the easiest to observe without me being seen. The hen is incubating her clutch and I don't wish to alarm her. They are fascinating birds – there is a strong bond between the pair. They call frequently one to another; she from the nest, he answering from the field's bank where he is hunting for their food. Have to decide beforehand which to observe for the night and then stay put. If I'm by the female, I see her mate as he returns with the prey. If, however, I choose to watch him, I witness his hunting technique and his reaction to other predators, which is *very* interesting. The monocular is marvellous for detail which otherwise I would miss.

Tuesday 7 April
Very dull night with poorest visibility this year. Heard a skein of geese pass high overhead, calling as they flew northwards. They were many minutes passing, so imagine there was a considerable number. Tawnies very vocal – watched the Chantry foxes and stayed in the Great Chantry Field area most of the night. At 4 a.m., a mist is beginning to creep over

the countryside. Have a weasel for company as I write up my notes on the Ridge – can't sit down five minutes without being taken for part of the landscape!

Walked homeward at 5 a.m. reflecting that it's interesting how many habitations I pass at night that have dogs which, during daylight, will bark incessantly as I go by, yet in darkness make no sound at all. Just as well for me they don't bark, I suppose, or it could be awkward!

Thursday 9 April
6.40 a.m. Mild, overcast morning. Great spotted woodpecker very busy near by, his staccato drumming echoes through the trees. The green woodpeckers are in full 'yaffle' now; squirrels, birds, rabbits fill the living woodland with song and sound. Watched a weasel again, this time feeding on a rat where a great heap of grain was dumped last autumn – both bird and beast feed from it. Everything fulfils itself and nothing is wasted. One's death is another's life; one's life, another's death. Green is an extraordinary colour; so many shades and tints.

Friday 10 April
6.35 a.m. Been in the Chantry area since 11.30 p.m. yesterday – tawny- stoat- and most of all fox-watching, especially the Chantry vixen – very profitable night. The past half-hour, sat with my back against a beech, very comfortable, with my camera on my lap. Had hoped to photograph a dawn sky, but the mist isn't going to lift in time. A man with a gun has just come around the field edge and into the Chantry – stopped, startled, when he saw me. We both stayed very still just looking; then he raised his gun slowly and took aim. I've sometimes wondered what I would do in this situation and have just hoped it would never occur, but it's odd what you do without really thinking. I slipped the lens cover off the camera, got him perfectly in focus – and waited. Gun versus camera – which is the more deadly? The seconds passed; then, muttering something, he made off back the way he had come – but it's made me think.

Have walked round to the View and Felled Logs Setts to stretch my legs and write this. Been a cold, damp night with this ground mist, but now the sun is penetrating. Some bluebells in bloom. No badger evidence anywhere – the 'dig out' at the View was an exploratory fox. Perhaps this is just as well since the school Easter holiday began yesterday so there's bound to be disturbance.

8.45 a.m. Stalked a rabbit with my camera as it sat washing in the sunshine on the Wildflower Path under the gean blossom. It wasn't until I came close that I saw its face was disfigured with myxomatosis. It neither heard nor saw me even when I spoke close to. But as I went to pass by, my shadow fell across it and, turning, it stumbled up the bank under the trees. About one-third of all the rabbits Wendy caught had myxy in varying stages. This is not to say, of course, that a third of the rabbit population here are affected, as clearly the disease renders them vulnerable to predators.

Sunday 12 April
Found a tawny owl shot near the Old Barn at 7.45 this morning. Body *very* warm, so only recently killed. This is the male of the pair I regularly observe (last entry for them on 4 April). The hen will have to leave her clutch to hunt or she will starve.

We have passed three complete months of the year and I have been checking back in this field book at the entries for 1981 – makes rather depressing reading. Much has been expressed through the media recently on farmer versus wildlife. The Wildlife and Countryside Bill now before Parliament is of national concern. But wonder just how much real effect the bill will have? Perhaps I have been lucky in the farmers I know personally – it's the general public that are versus wildlife here. Only yesterday, a politician stated that 'people must have more access to the countryside' – a remark that intrigued me since much of the countryside is *private* farmland. The inference is that the countryside with its flora and fauna is there for 'people' to enjoy (an interesting theory, that) and the farmers are restricting that enjoyment. If the public have as little respect for the woods and parks open to them as they have for farmland in this area, it's a poor look out for wildlife!

The farmers who have given me permission to go on their land take an active interest in the wildlife of their part of this countryside and farm intelligently and with foresight; they also suffer considerable damage and harassment from the public. I myself have seen that badgers and owls especially (both so-called 'protected' species) benefit from open fields and hedgerows. In fact it is no exaggeration to say, if it wasn't for the enlightened attitude at Newby, there would have been no badgers here these past years. Certainly, the public in general and our Council in particular, have successfully, albeit unintentionally, killed off or driven badgers from the neighbourhood.

Ashcroft Woods, and what remains of Prosser's Wood, together with High Ridge and the surrounding farmland, all combine in their variety of habitat to make an area well worth conserving. But 'No man is an Island, intire of itselfe' and Ashcroft Woods cannot stand in isolation as wildlife habitat for it is directly linked to its environs. If Barry Hains moves right away as he wishes to do (and who wants to farm near increasing development?), the bell will toll not only for these fields, but for Ashcroft Woods also.

Saturday 18 April
The Chantry vixen's young cubs appear briefly at the den entrance when their mother emerges, but don't yet venture out. Can't tell at present how many she has – just eyes, movement and little woolly faces that linger until she leaves and then vanish. Another few days and they'll

41

start exploring the big world outside – I imagine they are approximately four weeks old. Very cold night with frost; beautiful pre-dawn sky. Not worth staying as the shooters are out in force.

Wednesday 22 April
Have decided, with regret, to alter my watching from night to evening and daytime. Various reasons for this. The shooting and disturbance reached such a pitch over Easter that:

1) the remaining tawnies are scattered and impossible to observe;
2) the Chantry vixen and her cubs have been dug out some time during the daylight hours of last Saturday – this isn't illegal, of course. The adult's pelt would have been of doubtful value as the moult has commenced – the pups, however, are another story;
3) there are wildflowers and young foliage that I want to photograph.

Therefore I am abandoning my night-watching until things improve.

An animal has been digging out along the Bank Sett; a near-perfect fox skull excavated with the earth (the lower mandible missing). Notice the beech leaves are some of the last to unfurl – the buds are still small and tight.

Checking this area on Easter Monday evening until after midnight, I found the shooters were causing the most disturbing activity I've ever encountered; thankfully I've good nightvision and am used to merging into my surroundings! (A friend remarked yesterday that animal-watching must be a lovely, peaceful hobby in the quiet of our countryside – I was too stunned to reply.)

A curious wind eddy has just blown violently over me as I sit at the Chantry headland. Have experienced this before and conclude it must be something to do with the rush of air being trapped in this field's strange undulations. A breeze passed across Chantry from my left, lifting dirt and twigs several feet in the air below me. When it met the rising hill to my right, it became stationary – a miniature whirlwind with a vortex which rises high into the air. Continues like this until the sun's warmth reaches it. Then up it drives over the brow of Chantry and hits the trees and me with great force, covering everything with sticks and stinging debris. If the sun doesn't shine, the whirling funnel shape will continue indefinitely.

[One very hot, dry summer, Ingrims Fields had been ploughed and rolled. Dust began to move below the hump-shaped mound, though where I stood on the footpath there appeared to be no wind. The dirt twirled faster and faster at this point, then rose up in a column, perhaps five feet in the air. Became aware of two more whirlwinds near by. Suddenly, all began to move to the right, one following another, rushing on at a great speed until they met the hedge. The atmosphere at this time was hot and airless, which made the scene appear the more bizarre.]

42

Thursday 23 April

Each evening this week I have attempted to watch in and around these woods and fields, but it's completely hopeless. Lost count of the numbers of men, youths (and one woman) I've seen shooting here since last Thursday. There was an uproar just now when one group came firing too near another; the situation is ridiculous – and disquieting. Everything and anything that moves is a target. Beware any child or dog that wanders under the trees.

Coming here this evening, I noticed a kestrel hunting between the bridge in Holmoak Lane and Rendcombe. The Prosser's Wood kestrels have vanished some time ago – they could have been shot or perhaps moved here? If they now nest near the village, they are more likely to gain protection from the residents who take a pride in their hamlet and its surroundings.

I hope badgers *don't* return to Ashcroft Woods. Even if they are harassed at their present site, it can't be worse for them than this area. I feel they have more chance of undisturbed survival in, say, a large garden of some of these isolated houses where, on the whole, there's more of an interest in wildlife, than in the banks, hedgerows and woods where the public roam.

Sunday 3 May

The countryside of the Bourne Valley seen from the View and the Chantry is bright with rape fields in bloom; vivid patches of yellow, glowing from these green hills. The ground beneath the woodland trees is carpeted with spring flowers. Every time I come here, I seem to find yet another kind in bloom – yellow archangel, lady's smock and lesser periwinkle are flowering now. The white bells of lily-of-the-valley compete with the bluebells to scent the air.

A vixen has recently moved her four cubs to an earth in the Old Cherry Tree area. For the third time this evening, I am watching them at play (they emerged at approximately 7.40 p.m.). The vixen, who no longer dens with her pups, has begun to wean them – they're about two months old. However, they are determined to suckle – and their mother is equally determined that they shall not. If she stands, they promptly start nursing, so she has just lain down, and in frustration they are noisily swarming over her. She's a very placid mum – now she is being used as a King of the Castle mound and the 'dirty rascals' are clinging on to her ears and fur in their efforts to keep on top. No wonder she's so tatty – it's a miracle she has any coat left at all. Her brush is great for creeping up on and attacking, and since it's a good twelve inches long, there's plenty to hang on to!

She's just bounded to her feet, the cubs scattering. The dogfox is here. He hasn't brought anything, but both adults are pleased to see one another, the dog smelling his mate and much mutual tail waving. The cubs are scampering around their father. One is searching through his belly fur and, thwarted, mews cat-like – it won't find much milk there! The largest pup begins to lick the dog's mouth – this is a handsome little chap. He persists in his licking – Wonder if the father has eaten something his offspring can smell? All at once the male coughs – and he's thrown up a mouse/vole which the youngster grabs and rushes with into the den! I've never seen a male fox regurgitate before, only the vixens, so that's interesting.

The parents have left now, 8.20 p.m. One cub remains above ground, chewing at a tree root that protrudes near the earth. Now he is tiring and looking round, finds he is alone. A movement in the branches above sends him scurrying to safety underground – and all is still.

Monday 4 May
Watching again since 7 p.m. at the Old Cherry Tree earth. Sounds of distant shooting and barking, so not surprised the cubs aren't above ground yet. Twice heard a 'whip-crack' just now and would put it down to human activity, but also heard it on two evenings last week well after everyone had left.

The last bird is silent, the gloom deepens and the insects – moths and gnats included – are numerous. I'm a sitting target for the latter, and not to scratch is an agony, but I'm determined I won't move!

9.10 p.m. The little foxes are out at last. They emerged from an entrance some distance away and are playing chase amongst the bluebells. Something has flown between us, far too large for a bat – its flight isn't bat-like either. Its agile, silent movements are owl-like and the white marks on the long tail and wings are clearly visible. It's a nightjar – that explains the sharp noise earlier. I've read they make that whip-crack with their wings, which is hard to credit as the feathers must be as downy as an owl's, so silent is their flight. We are right on the edge of the wood and the trees grow very sparse here, giving plenty of room to twist and turn. Four little heads move as one as the cubs sit amongst the bluebells following the nightjar's flight as it wheels and glides. No need to watch the bird to see where it is. Back and forth, up and down go the heads, bobbing above the flowers as gracefully as the bird amongst the trees.

Shots sound near by – in an instant, bird and cubs are gone.

Tuesday 5 May
Bright, dry morning though rather chill. The waterholes of the beech trees' roots are very full. Watched a green woodpecker in the area between the Main Pond and Meg's Sett, which remains vacant – still no badgers anywhere in the neighbourhood. A great spotted woodpecker is drumming just above my head from an oak – this woodland is alive with birds.

I'm following an ancient boundary ditch, along one side of which the moss grows in glory – a smooth, shining, green-clad bank. These ditches are a visible reminder of our history. In early times, the simplest way of defining your land (and preventing swine from straying) was to dig a trench, throwing up the earth on one side. These ditches were originally man-high (higher with their earth banks) and quite wide. Only in woods and the commons have they survived to tell the tale. No one knows just how old they are – the Anglo-Saxons did this, but so did the medieval peasantry. To whichever period these boundary ditches belong, they certainly deserve their 'ancient' title.

Saturday 9 May
The broad green blades of corn stand a foot high now in Ingrims Fields. The sun's orange disc sullenly glows well above the horizon, and from a tremulous speck on high, the skylark's song comes drifting. Heard the cuckoo call from the Enclosed Path as I stood by the Wheatfield Copse. Shortly after, it flew across and displayed first on a dead elm above the beehives and then on a hive itself!

Checked all setts and dens in my area today, so was kept pretty busy. No sign of badgers whatsoever. What I've discovered in scrambling about near setts in very steep banks is that trees growing at the bank bottom have their crowns level with the field above. How often can one examine a tree's leaf and branch formation from top to base – rarely, I imagine.

Tuesday 12 May
Had a two-year-old beech tree to plant, so was in Ashcroft Wood quite early. A fine, warm, sunny evening with a slight breeze and clear skies. A badger had dug a rooted beech mast up when worming (beech nuts sprout the spring after they fall); its tap root hadn't reached down into the earth very far and its two broad, fleshy seed leaves on their pinkish stalk had broken through the case. The ground was too dry to replant it, so I brought it home, potted it, and now it's a fine little tree – only a few inches high but with a marvellous root system. Have noticed both beeches and oaks spend most of their first few years of growth putting down a deep root system in search of water, though there's not much to show above ground. These trees in their infancy are very shade-tolerant, but must have water. Sadly, few young trees are growing now in this lovely woodland except the colonising birch.

Have been regularly observing the fox family at the Old Cherry Tree den. Up to and including Sunday, the dog as well as the vixen was bringing in food. However, I didn't see him at all on Monday although I came here from early evening until 5.30 a.m. The cubs are very venturesome – and the bluebells are showing the strain! All flattened by their play; occupied fox dens at this time of year are very obvious. I've twice seen this particular vixen regurgitate. Tonight she has returned first with a collared dove, then with a rabbit already partly eaten (by her, I imagine). She suckled the cubs briefly at 7.20 p.m., then lay down

45

on her teats. She seems very restless. Now she's helping her offspring pull the remaining rabbit to bits; they can cope individually now with small prey (if two pups grab the same vole, it tends to disintegrate!). When a youngster gets hold of food that he can easily handle, he dives underground with it, unlike the adults.

The two-thirds-full moon is up, the stars bright and gnats bearable – glorious evening watch. 8.40 p.m.: vixen pacing up and down. The Old Cherry Tree den has several entrances on a steep slope. There's a path hidden a good way behind me and above, a path also hidden with foliage below me, and another rises beyond that path – all out of sight though quite near. The vixen stands on an entrance mound, body jerked forward and taut, and commences a single harsh bark 'wooo' at five- to seven-second intervals, turning her head first one way, then another. The sound echoes between the slopes and is thrown back; occasionally she coughs. The cubs are at first startled, then resume their activities with considerably less enthusiasm – uneasy, or merely full up? The mother suddenly breaks off barking, runs down out of sight, and begins to bark again from the other slope. Continuous single, grating bark for twenty-five minutes – the sound indicates she is turning her head as before. Without their mother, the little foxes go to earth, except one (in each litter, there's always an odd one out). He yawns, jumps over some felled wood, falls flat on his muzzle, picks himself up, whines and, turning back, starts chewing the wood he didn't jump over! Stops, listens – obviously to the vixen still barking. All of a sudden, he becomes uneasy and disappears underground. The barks don't seem to have altered in all this time.

Silence – a few seconds and the vixen is back. She stands awhile on the original entrance mound, then lies down on it. See her very clearly in the moonlight. We are extremely close: I, in my tree just above; she lying head on front paws, ears forward, very alert and still on her vantage point ... waiting? ... for what? Easy to jump to the conclusion that she was calling her mate (haven't seen him since last Sunday – could be shot, of course), but dislike jumping to conclusions. Eight and a half minutes pass, everything still and silent. She stands looking quietly behind her and then, trotting off in the direction of the little upper path leading out of the wood and on to the Hayfield above, quickly passes from my sight. Time: 10.15 p.m.

Thursday 14 May
Walked here via the Sleet House footpath and the Ridge. The latter is a blaze of yellow now the broom and gorse are flowering. Walking up the Big Slip when, to my surprise, saw a weasel in a bush – very conspicuous amongst the yellow as it darted about. Think it may have been after eggs or their owners – these bushes contain a rich variety of nesting birds.

Reached the Old Cherry Tree den at 9.30 a.m. The whole area is becoming very messy and fly-ridden – feathers, two well-gnawed rabbit

46

bones and odd bits of fur strewn about. (I find the flies rather useful. The entrance that has the most buzzing around generally is that from which the cubs will emerge!) If a den becomes too fouled, the vixen may lead her family to a fresh one. This will help to conceal their whereabouts as well as giving them a clean start. Can see where the adult has been grooming herself. As she moults, she runs her teeth through the fur with a curry-comb effect and spits out a little wad of fur with teeth-holes in it. She had a great grooming session this past night – her belly is near-bald from the pups' rough treatment. She has the body of a lean whippet: even at their greatest bodyweight, there is never much fat under that massive coat; they are all muscle, sinew, senses and speed – they need to be to survive.

Birdsong and bluebells (those still upright, that is!) are indescribable. Everywhere fresh green young leaves and the sun mottling the ground below: Ashcroft Woods is the loveliest place to be. I sat here five hours yesterday evening and night – listening and watching vixen, cubs, nightjars and tawny owls – what a combination!

Just inside the wood, a short distance from the Old Cherry, I found a shot robin yesterday, and then a hawfinch, also shot. On the upper path above this den, I discovered just now a shot wren. The robin, shot neatly through the head and passing out the other side, appeared by the wound to have been killed by the same type of pellet as the other two. Just hope this marksman doesn't try for nightjars – he's terribly accurate.

Two pups have just emerged, 9.50 a.m. They came out cautiously sniffing the air and each would obviously prefer the other to be first! Their two little heads are just below me as I sit arms hugging legs, chin on knees, looking down. Though they will play noisily and with apparent abandon when satisfied it is safe to do so, this emerging is always performed with great caution. A strange scent, a falling leaf or a screech from the nearby jays, can send them below for another twenty minutes. And even when they are out playing, a cracking twig, distant voices (or no apparent reason) can send them all scurrying for safety. This play is for life and an alert sense of smell and hearing is the difference of a short or long life. Their mistakes pay the highest price – no second chances. The vixen, though denning only a short space away, makes no attempt to emerge in the day or have any contact with them. Their daytime survival depends on themselves – at night, she is involved. It is probably not in their interests to know she is near, and with four cubs and herself to feed unaided, she needs all the respite possible.

All the youngsters are above ground now. One is scratching. Another has found a pigeon's flight feather and dashes off with it, hotly pursued by the others. The victor, standing on a woodpile, triumphantly holds aloft his, by now broken and tatty, feather which his growling, barking brethren jostle for below.

Two cubs are scrapping – a rolling bundle of fur with no holds barred. One is nipped too hard, gives a yelp of pain and 'submits' on his back, belly exposed. This is accepted and, fight over, the winner runs off to play tag with another. Like puppies, one will 'ask' another to play. With chest on ground, bottom skyward and tail wagging eagerly, the cub will whine at his companion and then bark to attract his attention. If the other *will* play, then a mad rough-and-tumble commences – often a free-for-all with the four litter-mates taking part.

Left the den at midday to walk up Briarmead in the sunshine. The cow parsley that borders this lane already towers above my head. All around me is a busyness of bees and butterflies. (Karen [my daughter], as a child, insisted on calling the latter 'flutterbies', and watching them now over the wildflowers, I still think that's more apt a description.) Halfway up the lane, found a weasel dead by the roadside – appeared quite unmarked. Interesting to examine close to – their darting movements in life can be hard to follow.

Friday 15 May
11.40 a.m. The first time I've ever seen a police motorbike patrol in this wood. Been watching from 2.30 a.m. at the Old Cherry Tree area (also wandered to the Chantry and round the woodland generally). Then back home for breakfast and returned by 9.10 a.m. Cubs came out briefly a few minutes ago but dived back when they heard the cop's engine – must ask him to wheel his bike! They've been playing and fighting a lot underground this morning, which makes very entertaining listening. A slow-worm has carefully arranged itself in a tiny patch of sunshine next to my left shoe and is sleepily basking. Above me and directly ahead, great spotted woodpeckers are busily feeding their young.

48

Wednesday 20 May
Been foxcub-watching at the Old Cherry Tree den in very wet conditions
since last weekend. At first, the pups took little notice of the torrential
rain but it has continued for so long that even they were looking muddy
and bedraggled at dawn this morning – no wonder their stay above
ground was brief. If their coats become saturated, it must be difficult for
them to keep warm.

This evening, the rain has ceased for a while, so I would have expected
them above ground quite early. However, the den has been interfered
with and at 10.30 p.m. no sign of them or sounds of them playing below.
When I arrived here this evening, I found three long, muddy pieces of
metal amongst the flattened bluebells by the main den entrance – they
weren't here when I left after dawn yesterday morning. They resemble
giant skewers and two are very bent (as if they were pushed hard in the
ground and struck something immovable); one is perfect – measured
this, $11\frac{1}{2}$ inches long. Children wouldn't have played here today because
of the rain, and half-term doesn't start until next week, in any case.
Wonder what the skewers were used for. Holding down nets – or am I
getting suspicious again?

11.30 p.m. With regret, I can't stay any longer this evening. No sign of
foxcubs, vixen – or the nightjars, come to that. Last saw the latter on
Monday evening. Walked home past the Wheatfield Copse. See a section
of the undermined path has collapsed (judging from the tyre-marks, as a
tractor passed over), and has been dug out. Everywhere here is
honeycombed with old badger/fox/rabbit workings.

Friday 22 May
4.20 a.m. Standing on the Wildflower Path surrounded by birdsong. The
heavy disc of the moon hangs low over the treetops. Everywhere sodden.
From the cornfield before me come odd popping, gurgling sounds as the
saturated earth struggles in a watery embrace.

Haven't seen or heard the Old Cherry family since Wednesday
morning; the entire area seems deserted. I didn't leave until 5.30 a.m. on
Wednesday, well after dawn, and the pups were below ground then.
Wouldn't have thought their mother would have moved them in
daylight hours. Was back for evening watching at 6 p.m. It would seem
highly probable, therefore, that they were taken sometime during
daylight hours of Wednesday last.

SUMMER 1981

Tuesday 2 June 1981

Since I've been away, charlock, yellow rocket, goat's-beard, wood burdock, comfrey, woody nightshade, hogweed, white campion and elderflower are all in bloom. Deep blue of the spurred columbine is lovely. The area has had heavy rains – everywhere the corn and hayfields stand tall and lush. Walking near the Poplar Row at 1 a.m., saw a lorry burnt out – looks like one belonging to the farm.

At the Wheatfield Copse came silently upon three foxcubs tearing at a rabbit hindquarters on the path. Simultaneously heard sounds of play from within the tree-shelter, so must be more. For a moment hoped these were the Old Cherry Tree cubs moved during daylight after all, then sadly I realised they were strangers to me. Imagine a parent left the rabbit; the cubs were quite aggressive to one another. One tried to carry it off, found it impossible, and stood guard *on* it, snarling and growling. One cub had a surprising amount of white fur, extending from the chest round the throat and some way on the left shoulder towards the back of the neck.

At Briarmead, a wind sprung up, violent and sudden. The mist was gone, the sky black and visibility startlingly good. At 4.40 a.m., the storm struck just as I reached the wood – wind, fire and water, all intent on forcing the earth apart. The trees were bending until it seemed they must break, only to be hurled in another direction. Thunder and lightning instantaneous; the sheer volume of water made vision near-impossible.

Out beyond Madden Lane, the fields were swamped. Because of my fox interest, I deliberately go out in thunderstorms, though up to now haven't cared overmuch for them. Stood awhile by the car-port and a parked tractor. The size of the latter and the cold, solid feel of the wet metal under my hand was somehow reassuring. I could shelter between the vehicles and protect my camera from the wet, but instinctively (like Wendy of old, caught in the open by a storm) I wanted to get down small in the undergrowth, not stay here. So, buffeted by rain and wind, I did so, closing my eyes against the lightning's continual flash. To my surprise, could still clearly see the scene ahead – water spilling over the tractor, the rows of orchard trees, the car-port and Sleet House – all through closed lids. The on–off, on–off quality of the lightning gave a near continuous picture.

There was an indescribable sound as if my ears were bursting and simultaneously the tractor became a great explosion of colour. Fire danced on its surface and, still with eyes closed, I felt stunned. Then the colour had gone and the tractor was enveloped in a cloud of vapour – the smell of hot metal overpowering, the steam choking in my throat. And still the storm continued unabated.

I waited awhile, working out the best course home. The footpath had long since disappeared, the fields were under water. So I went by Raven Lane, into Rendcombe and along Holmoak Lane. It took me some while to realise I was deaf; lightning, wind and rain, but with the sound 'switched off'. (It was to be well into the afternoon before my hearing became normal.) Reaching the bridge, I had a shock – the next stretch of Holmoak was under water. The soakaway, unable to cope with the sheer volume of rain, had disappeared – just the tawnies' willows to mark the spot. If I was soaked before, it was nothing to battling through that icy water to reach higher ground and Ingrims barley fields. And I felt for the tawny/mallard families of the soakaway, wondering how *they* were faring.

Friday 5 June
Been observing the Wheatfield fox family each morning, from 2 a.m. onwards. Seen dog and vixen here together – there are six cubs. Surprised that the dog is still fetching in so much food, though perhaps the number of cubs accounts for this – they take a lot of feeding. The adults bring in a considerable number of rabbits, but then this is great

51

rabbit country. Yesterday, the youngsters had three to themselves. The parents leave the food farther away from the earth now, to encourage their growing family to venture afield and so to begin the rudiments of hunting on their own account. I've seen the pups crouching amongst the nettles by the beehives, watching the rabbits nibbling the young corn – but the rabbits have, too! This morning, I checked the area in daylight (9.35 a.m.) and found the remains of two rabbits, both only a bit eaten, plus a lot of odd pieces scattered about (a cub was playing with a rabbit scut yesterday).

Meant to watch here from midnight, but came via Madden Lane and so up by the Oak Dell. In the space close by the Main Pond, nearly walked into four men with a van and car. I was held up a long time until they finished handing over and counting their packages, and didn't care to back away in case I was heard.

Saturday 6 June
Sitting at the headland looking out over Chantry, 8 a.m. The sun warms the young green of this countryside as a breeze waves through the corn below, and the airborne martins dart and wheel, just skimming the growing crop. Earlier was watching a spotted woodpecker feed its nestlings in a hole only six feet from the ground in an old beech – the lowest I've come across, and very obvious from the fouling below the entrance.

Walked by a young leveret crouching in its form in the lower hayfield of Briarmead Lane. I could have picked it up, as it made no move, but afraid if the mother found my scent on it she might reject her offspring. Young hares are fully furred at birth and have their eyes open – their fur seems rather darker in colour than the adults, the ear tips are black.

Walked the length of the Bank Sett. The recent digging out *could* be badger, but more like fox. Found a blackbird standing with eyes closed, glossy black plumage and orange bill and eye rim very attractive, but quite evident it was ill. Put it in the orchard under the trees – less likely to attract the attention of people and their dogs.

Tuesday 9 June
Have been in the Ashcroft Woods area since yesterday evening. Have made an all-out effort to locate the nightjar pair, but with no success. Watched tawny parents feeding their three fledglings near the Main Pond. After the chaos caused by the shooters at Easter, there appear to be only two pairs of these owls in Ashcroft Woods and its environs, and just one of these has successfully produced young. The calling of the tawny chicks dominates the other night sounds of this woodland; they are not as yet hunting for themselves, but are quite active. The feathers showing through the down give them an untidy appearance. It's interesting just how many creatures, apart from the mole, prey on

52

earthworms: badgers, foxes, hedgehogs and, in common with many other birds, the tawny owl.

2.45 a.m. The Wheatfield vixen has found herself a worm bonanza in the wet soil at the field edge and is letting a cub tackle one – if you think spaghetti is difficult with a knife and fork, try a worm no-handed! He's chewed and swallowed, only to find a lot more worm to be chewed and swallowed. He's finally got the knack of biting through a length before swallowing. How complicated life is!

Another cub (the white-patch one) has decided to torment its father – and the dogfox is growling a warning. He's tolerated a fair amount of pup-play this morning, but has had enough now, gets up abruptly and trots purposefully away.

First light has crept over the fields almost unnoticed, but under the trees it will still be dark. A bird (skylark?) rises up out of the growing corn just in front of a pup who lunges forward – next moment, he shakes his head and feathers flutter. He dashes with his prize to the copse with two more cubs chasing after. One bundles the bird-carrying youngster and a fight begins as the bird drops to the path. The second cub reaches his battling litter-mates, goes to wade in too, then sees the cause of all the discontent, lying there. In a flash, he's picked it up and runs unseen into the bushes.

A coughing bark sounds – then another. One of the parents, I think, but neither in my field of view. The remaining cubs go to earth just as the sun touches the horizon and softly streaks the sky – paint on a wet canvas spreading between the thin layers of cloud. This for me is the moment of re-creation; the promise of a new day eternally fulfilled. In a while, as the sun quickly rises, the quality of light will alter and the moment is gone.

Walking round towards Briarmead, I heard a shot. That then is why the fox barked a warning! A car parked at the top of the lane – three men with guns on the field by the wood – time, 3.45 a.m.

Saturday 13 June
Dull, damp morning with a breeze – time, 5 a.m. Found a long-tailed tit shot, lying under the yew tree on the path that leads to the View. Such a tiny bird, never very common, the long tail out of all proportion to the miniature body. Only shot a short time ago as the body was still warm.

The Bank Sett and the Wildflower Path, which are parallel sides of the Long Field at Briarmead, have between them a fine variety of trees, flowers, insects, fungi and birds. There has been more digging out (including old bedding) at the Bank Sett. Think it could be a badger.

Afternoon. It's turned out to be a hot, sunny day with a gentle breeze – the first real summer day this year. Karen and I walked via Weldon to the Old Orchard and back through Crawfords Farm. No words can adequately describe this orchard left to its own devices for eleven years and fast reverting to wilderness. Wildflowers, butterflies and birds all

53

living and glowing in the sunshine – what more could one wish for? The cuckoo very vocal. Found a species of wild rose I can't identify despite all my wildflower books; it has a fragrant smell and is pure white.

Sunday 14 June

Left home at 1 a.m. to keep watch at the Bank Sett. Mild night with near-full moon and starry skies. This portion of the freshly excavated sett is the widest part of the bank and that nearest the wood. In consequence, the slope is gradual and, sitting near the top, I'm surrounded by trees. If I look through the upper foliage of a sycamore growing below, I can see way over the Long Field to the Wildflower Path beyond. It's a wonderful spot to sit at night – I'm deep in the shade and viewing the moonlit scene from above. Whether I'll see the badger – if there is one – is debatable, as it could go to earth by any entrance in the length of the bank, not necessarily the excavated ones. I was settled here an hour ago and now it's 3 a.m. The moon has disappeared in a slight haze and the sky is lightening; we could be about to have another hot day. A wood-pigeon behind me in the Chantry is the first bird to find voice, and after a few minutes he falls silent again – perhaps it *was* a bit too early!

3.20 a.m. A blackbird just above me begins his serenade to the morning. Soon he is answered by another at the Wildflower Path as the skylarks rise sunwards over the fields. A lone fox saunters into sight, sits on its haunches to scratch, then rolls in the dust at the corn's edge.

4 a.m. The rising sun is spilling light drop by drop through the tree cover and dappling the undergrowth around me. A thick branch of the sycamore just ahead glows in the day's first warmth. Rabbits are appearing on the field below, their young frisking through the green stems. The fox I have been watching comes up the bank but, before reaching me, turns and jumps with ease on to the sycamore branch, and stretches out his length in the sunshine. My view is now impeded by fox, and since no badger has appeared, I think it's time to back quietly away – 4.38 a.m.

Wednesday 17 June

Left home 12.40 a.m. Near the Ridge, I remembered I'd seen movement (foxcubs?) last night near the bottom of the Big Slip by the gorse and broom bushes. So instead of crossing by the stile – in full view of anything on the slopes – I followed the tunnel brickwork and the bottom of the Motorway, into Prosser's Wood and so on to High Ridge. Spent nearly an hour of pure enjoyment, standing amongst the bushes watching six cubs, one with a white patch left-shoulder – now I've found where my fox family from the Wheatfield Copse has moved!

Walked through Ashcroft Woods to the Main Pond and the tawnies. Their roosting place is moved nearer the Briarmead oak, probably because, with the concealing foliage so lush now, the adults are hunting where woodland meets hayfield, making it easier for them to see their prey. I've observed these tawnies bringing young rabbits, birds, earthworms, small rodents to their fledglings these past nights – also pieces torn from a dead cat, recently run over at the top of Briarmead Lane. (Watched a stoat and later a fox feeding from it, too – that carcass didn't last long!) Have read tawnies don't eat carrion, so this observation interested me.

Thought I'd walk round to the Bank Sett – for the third time this week. I'm sure a badger *is* living there. Arrived at 2.50 a.m. Full moon battling unsuccessfully with the cloud layers, which suits me fine. In common with the animals, I find the moon restricts my movement, and to pass across the fields unseen I must follow the shadowed side of the hedge. Had only been at the Bank Sett ten minutes when a sow badger with one cub came along the field edge below me (until that moment, I hadn't realised just how much I had missed badger-watching). Watched and waited until 5.15 a.m., but no sign of a boar or other cubs.

Passing round the top hayfield on my way home, saw a hare emerge from the long grass. They are very un-rabbit-like in the way they *walk* and appear very highly strung, with their ever-twitching noses and mobile ears. Their eyes are placed well up on the head, rather than at the side like a rabbit, and the long, coarse whiskers growing from the muzzle are distinctive. A leveret came after the hare from the concealing grass and both settled to a spell of serious eating. Have never seen a hare with a young one before; imagine it will soon be independent.

Tuesday 23 June
Afraid I've deserted my foxes for *Meles meles* these past nights – can't put into words the sheer joy of watching this little badger family. The Briarmead hayfields were cut last weekend and left to dry. At two this morning, I sat concealed at the fringe of these woods watching the lone cub playing with its mother close by – the sweet smell of cut grass was everywhere and, over all, the waning moon to light the scene. The young badger seems very nervous and keeps near its parent. If it looks up and doesn't immediately see the sow, it whickers anxiously. Wonder what happened to the rest of this family – obviously something did. (Cub has fur missing from an area just above its right front paw.)

4.15 a.m. and there's someone shooting. This is my worry with the badgers. Anyone with a rifle fitted with telescopic sights could shoot a badger and no one would be the wiser. Just another proud protagonist boasting to his friends that he had shot something larger than birds that morning.

Friday 26 June
Left home just on midnight. Had a great deal of rain the last two days – still raining slightly now. Made my way through the Water Meadows to

Warby. Trying to locate the barn owls, but with no success. Last observed them mid-May

3.15 a.m. Walked up to the View – sun spreading through the rain clouds. Everywhere the smell of wet earth and vegetation. Passed round the field with the Chantry on my right and Ashcroft Woods crowning the skyline – an unforgettable sight. There is something ancient and enduring about this place: its welfare has become of great importance to me.

Saw the badgers briefly on their way home – from their dirty snouts, they surely had been worming. The cub is a little shadow stuck close to Mum. That's one sow that has no problem locating Junior. Ten minutes after they went to earth, I heard guns and saw a man coming from the Primrose Path – 4.05 a.m.

Cut through the undergrowth and so along the Ashtree Path. Something interesting here. Where this path meets the cut hayfield, many rabbits feed in the early morning. You can pick out the ones with myxomatosis from the rest of the grazing colony: their stance, attitude and way of eating is quite different. A fox came from the wood fringe and stealthily crept round to a rabbit, but another alerted its companions to the danger and they all gained the safety of the undergrowth. Except the sick one, still grazing in that curiously hunched-up position. The fox started over to it ... paused ... and turned away. I've seen this happen twice recently. Certainly Reynard couldn't have been very hungry, but even so – here was an easy meal. When the coast was clear, I walked right up to the rabbit as before, and looked at it long and carefully. Apart from the grotesque head (the nose becomes distorted too), the flanks were losing their fur and the flesh beneath had a suppurating appearance. As with all myxy rabbits I've seen (including those Wendy brought me), it was well nourished. Whatever suffering the disease causes, it doesn't impair browsing. It surprises me that I see so many around. Should have thought that predators would kill these off first. Or is it that with so much food about, a fox can afford to be choosy. Reynard and I can see it is diseased, but can the fox smell it is too?

Returning home, heard a noise of a large juvenile bird in Ingrims barley by the side of Holmoak Lane. Investigating, I found a well-grown young pheasant 'talking to itself' in a space in the growing corn. Can't describe the noise made, but one of my books does it beautifully: 'a curious double bullfinch-like pipe followed by a creaking third note' – I like that! It hadn't yet acquired its tail and had a speckled appearance (and remarkably large feet!). It eventually flew off, rather lopsidedly, just skimming the crop – made my morning!

Sunday 28 June
Left home 2.10 a.m. Very mild night, slight breeze, crescent moon, with a thin cloud layer fast clearing. Watched the badgers until they went underground. The sow has been digging out. She has evidently decided

to settle with her cub here. 4 a.m. Dawn chorus becomes more subdued as summer proceeds (birds moulting).

Have been watching a fox catch a rat on the heap of old potatoes dumped inside the wood fringe on the lower hayfield, Briarmead. It had quite a tussle with it – rats die hard. Once on High Ridge, Wendy and I came upon a group of rats eating the remains of discarded fish and chips. The dog killed one outright (her usual method of gripping the back of the neck and shaking it), then went for another that turned at bay and bit her above the left eye – and held on. In a frenzy, she dashed it repeatedly against the ground until, dying, it relaxed its hold. All this while the remaining rats continued eating as if nothing was happening. Only when she rushed the group did they scatter. It struck me at the time that had they all turned at bay (as an individual rat will in the last resort), they could have warded her off. Certainly a case of 'united we stand, divided we fall'.

Tuesday 30 June
Sitting on the hay-turner at the Top Field, Briarmead, writing up my notes – lovely summer morning, 4.10 a.m. The badgers have been busy tonight on the lower hayfield, taking in fresh bedding. At least, the mother has been taking in and her cub has been dropping and picking up (with emphasis on the dropping). Badgers move backwards when they bring in like this – following their own scent trail back to the sett. It's quite a distance. Notice the cub's paw injury doesn't now appear to affect it. The sow is *very* selective in her choice of hay, taking bits here and bits there; raking them up with her long front claws into a large bundle under her chin and against her chest. She comes out on to Briarmead itself, follows the lane down to the Wildflower Path, goes halfway along, then goes through the corn. The first two journeys took her approximately thirty minutes each and the third, nearly forty-five – she was certainly tired by then. She's really been very busy, with Junior tagging on behind with his few wisps.

He starts off full of enthusiasm, gets distracted by something along the way, then suddenly recalls he's bringing in bedding, retrieves it, and scurries after Mum. At one point along the Wildflower Path, the adult paused to rest and her offspring, catching up, pulled at its parent's hay. The sow's face looking down over the pile – the cub's gazing up – there's something about badgers. They have marvellous patience with their cubs and great affection in their family groups. Adults are playful one with another and will mate throughout the year. I have seen them mate when their cubs are about this one's age, though they only give birth (delayed implantation) at the beginning of the year, and not always then. I think their strong family ties and their extreme cleanliness (in personal grooming, bedding renewal and use of dung pits) are very deep-rooted traits in the badger.

This morning, the cub, whilst hay-playing, found a young rabbit killed possibly when the field was cut – it was *very* pleased with its find. I've just looked up to see I'm surrounded by rabbits myself. Sitting here on the machinery, they haven't registered me. This countryside is very pleasant and peaceful; the sky streaked gold, vermilion. Time: 4.55 a.m.

Thursday 2 July
The tawny owls over the Madden Lane, lower Ridge area, have been very vocal pre-dawn, 3.10 a.m. Stood under the trees of the Gully, Briarmead, watching them hunt. They don't appear to have any fledglings. In the woods, came upon a long-tailed field mouse (wood mouse), drinking from water collected in a 'cup' where a large teasel leaf meets the plant's stem. Birds do this quite often, but have never seen a mouse do so before.

Later, I walked to the Yewtree Grove, as yesterday evening we were discussing one of the wood's unexplained (to us!) mysteries. We can't recall the date when this occurred although I think it was sometime in 1969. One weekday morning, we went with Wendy into these woods and wandered about under the yew trees. Towards the edge of the Grove, where bramble begins to grow as the light penetrates, we came across a hole, freshly dug. The earth here is mainly gravel, hard and unyielding, the place isolated. But someone had dug a neat oblong, straight-sided, flat-bottomed, the spade marks clear. We measured its sides as best we could, and agreed it was over six feet long and four feet wide. I was inclined to jump down into it and measure it against my height, but thought better of it, which was just as well! For when my companion found a dead branch and stood it in the hole, we found it was six feet deep! We mulled the matter over while walking home and decided it couldn't be a shooters' hole, for only a giant could use one that deep. The effort entailed would be considerable and, anyway, yew tree groves aren't ideal for pigeons and crows – you do better on the wood edge.

The next day I couldn't go back to the spot, but the following day I did – and couldn't find the hole! I searched backwards and forwards, for it's a place easy to confuse with somewhere else, and finally I sat down puzzled where I thought it had been. Then, looking very carefully around, something struck me as odd. The brambles trailed along the ground and, over one part, the leaves seemed to be wilting. I went over and pulled at a trailing stem – and it came away, as did the others over the oblong. The hole had been filled in, carefully smoothed down and the brambles laid across once more; the cuts ends pressed into the earth.

A week, two weeks later, and nothing to tell this spot from another. A dog buried here? Something left, to retrieve later? Somehow, we think not. Whatever went into that hole wasn't meant to come out of it.

Sunday 5 July
7 a.m. A bright, warm summer's morning; met my magpie friend on the Ridge. His mate is more cautious, but if I sit on the top slat of the fence, he will alight on it three feet away and then come right up. He first did this on 25 July last year and now makes a habit of it if I'm not in a hurry. I talk to him softly when he's close, but I've never fed him.

I walked the drovers's road of Briarmead through these woods. It took a long time as I would keep stopping to look about me. I've never really thought about it before, but nothing ever grows here. True, beech overshadow here and there, but so do oak and chestnut and normally plenty grows under them. As the track goes deeper into the wood, rosebay willow-herb and grass attempt to find root. There's a 'tortured' beech, much hacked about in its youth, which I like to look at along here. It has survived everything, its roots becoming part of the Gully bank. It has a small lower branch recently torn from the trunk – the sap still moist, the green leaves unwithered. In its life, it has seen much human passing – it will endure to witness more. We are but dust on the hour-glass of eternity; trees are rooted in time.

Friday 10 July
We've had storms and heavy rain in the past forty-eight hours, though nothing as bad as that of 2 June. Though the rain has ceased, everywhere is humid, the atmosphere close. Left home at 1 a.m. and went direct to the freshly ploughed cabbage field at the side of High Ridge. I find it pays to take a close interest in what is happening on the surrounding farmland through the year if I want to locate any badgers in the area without much effort. A dry spell, storms, then a field ploughed – a farmer can be a badger's best friend. Sure enough, sow and cub from the Bank Sett 'spaghetti-eating' as if their lives depended on it. *Very* glad John Shaw isn't a spray fanatic. Not only do the wildflowers at the field edge (rosebay willow-herb, foxgloves, bladder campion, viper's bugloss, etc.) *look* beautiful tonight, but they smell so too.

A half-grown foxcub has glided out of the bracken near me, and is also worming – near the young badger. Both youngsters are well aware of one another, and the fox is nervous. After a while, the badger, replete, sits back on its haunches, washes itself half-heartedly, then, seeing it is close to the burnt-out lorry (still left and ploughed round since early June), goes and explores under it. The foxcub is still worming, and every so often looks up when there's a 'clunk' from the lorry area. The badger is scrambling over the pieces of fast-rusting metal lying on the ground – all that remains of the trailer. The young fox's curiosity is getting the better of him, so, very cautiously, he approaches the lorry just as the other comes round the side. The two animals face one another, the fox taut and ready to flee. Then the badger turns and ambles under the vehicle – a momentary hesitation, and Reynard, cat-like, follows. I can only hear now as they are out of my sight, but the noises indicate the animals are still together. I would like to creep closer, but the sow is between me and the lorry. She has taken no notice whatsoever of the two youngsters and has been worming all this time. Her cub is certainly more self-reliant than when first they appeared at the Bank Sett, three weeks ago. The fur growing on its right front paw is white, over the healed injury.

The last I see of the badgers is the mother moving along the field edge by the Poplar Row and her cub rushing to catch her up. The fox has moved away from the lorry and stands looking after them. The sky is growing lighter – every leaf and blade of grass shimmers with moisture. The fox mounts the overgrown bank and comes along the indistinct path, straight towards me. I've been kneeling all this while on top of the bank watching through the monocular and it's far too late to move out of the way now. A pair of upright ears appears below me as he springs up the slope – and we're face to face. A growl of fear and surprise, and he crashes through the flowers to the left of me, reaches the Enclosed Path and safety, and is gone.

When it was fully light, went across the Ridge and through Ashcroft Woods, looking at the fungi that have appeared after the rain. The algae growing on many of the living trees, especially the birches, pattern their wet bark and in the early morning sunshine seem too brilliantly green to be real. The ponds are full once more, as are the beech trees' twisting roots. There is an interesting beech growing a short distance from the Main Pond. It has the fluted trunk of a hornbeam and the buttressed bole of a beech. It is an old tree and, moreover, a very beautiful one. Over the years, I have seen squirrels, birds, badgers and a fox drink from the rainwater that runs down its fluted columns into the root 'pools', though the ponds are quite near. Wendy, too, found this a favourite watering place. This beech's roots make excellent bird baths if the number of birds I've seen bathe here is any criterion.

Tuesday 14 July
8.45 a.m. For the past hour and a half, have been observing life in the Main Pond. Find that early morning seems to be the most productive time to watch. Plenty of newts and tadpoles – and a grass snake. They are marvellous swimmers, twisting and turning so effortlessly. Ignore

the rubbish thrown in and the place looks healthy enough. Birds like the partially submerged branches on which to alight, and probably feel safer than drinking from the water's edge. The grass snake is trailing a newt. Its tail lashes the water, driving the snake forward, and the newt is grasped from behind, only the head and fore limbs protruding from the predator's jaws.

Friday 17 July
Fitful morning – hot sunshine interspersed with heavy showers and gusty wind. The thick clouds hurry over the sky as their shadows chase the light across the fields. Watched a male common blue on a patch of horseshoe vetch. Many rabbits feeding in large groups, some of their offspring very young. One of the latter stumbled on to my boot and I picked it up. A perfect little creature, damp from the long grass and not yet old enough to be quick. Put it gently back and it rejoined the others still browsing.

Met Sam Mercer putting up his mist nets at the Main Pond, 8.30 a.m. Earlier this month he sent me lists of birds ringed and sighted in these woods. Said he doesn't now belong to the Barksham group – disillusioned with their methods. I see a plastic home-made tent has been erected at the Chantry; not children's work – too professional.

At the Bank Sett now, writing this. Regularly watching the badgers here at night – they are doing well. Plenty to eat with the heavy rains, like fungi, and more worms, cherries (birds, squirrels, foxes *and* badgers seem to enjoy the sour gean fruit that litter the ground). Everywhere the vegetation is very lush; woodland paths fast disappearing. The undergrowth seems to be creeping up the trees and, at night, the twining canopies of the fragrant honeysuckle scent the air.

Sunday 19 July
1.30 a.m., and a full moon. The footpath leading through Ingrims barley is overshadowed by the tall ripening crop, rustling drily as the wind passes through. Already a heavy dew everywhere, sparkling in the moonlight. The white campion has a clove-like scent at night and moths as well as bees seem attracted to it. Heard a stationary fox on High Ridge giving the rasping bark repeated at five-second intervals. Crept up within six feet of it to watch and listen. It turned its head sometimes as it barked, like the vixen on 12 May. Continued like this for twenty

minutes, the $<\,>$ type of bark, with a rise in the middle; occasional

cough-bark too.

Walked through Prosser's Wood to the Top Field. Burnt-out lorry has gone and the newly rolled field looks great under the moon. Watched two young foxes fighting near the Old Barn ruins. The mock fights of their puppy days are for real now – soon they will be going their separate ways.

Following the woodland edge round to the second hayfield, I located a tawny hunting from the elder tree by the pile of fast-rotting potatoes. It caught two rats while I watched. (Which reminds me that Sam Mercer warned me to beware the owls' talons especially when they have young. I've never been attacked yet, but guess there's always a first time.)

Near the Chantry, observed badger sow and fast-growing cub (he's really near his parent in size), tearing and eating fungus from a felled trunk. Don't know for sure what type it was, but think probably a Trametes. As the moon follows me through the trees, first light is appearing in the sky, 3.50 a.m. Over the fields, a few birds are 'tuning up' but those in the woodland are still silent. On the Ridge, 4.05 a.m., the streaked dawn is very beautiful. The moon is still charged with light, but the stars fast fade. Have just seen a stoat bound from the bracken cover and kill a rabbit, 4.35 a.m.

Thursday 23 July
The weather since Monday has been stormy and wet. This morning, I photographed fungi. Met David at Briarmead; his old dog, after greeting me, still looks round, whining softly for Wendy. Frog-bit (*Hydrocharis morsus-ranae*) in bloom at the Main Pond – used to think this was a water-lily not a floating water weed. Broad-leaved pondweed grows here profusely.

The moles, as always, have been busy in the undergrowth after the rain. Found a decomposing mole which moved as I watched. Turning it over gently, I discovered two completely black burying, or sexton, beetles burrowing under the body. The corpse gradually collapsed upon itself and sank into the hole, as the earth was thrown out to the sides. Left them to it as I couldn't see more without disturbing them further. They will dig a mortuary chamber slightly larger than the mole and up to eight inches deep. Then, having stripped the fur off with their jaws, the beetles will work and knead the mole into a ball. The female will then drive her mate away, and this ball will eventually become food for her larvae.

Friday 24 July
2.20 a.m. At the Bank Sett, watching the two badgers. Been pouring steadily since early evening yesterday. The edge of the Long Field where it meets this steep bank has temporarily become a stream, as the saturated earth can't absorb any more water. The sow and her cub have been worming energetically here, lapping water and splashing about generally. A short time ago, the youngster slipped down the muddy bank and landed loudly in the water. This gave him a marvellous idea for a game as he gallops up to the slope and slides down with a splash!

(However, I think the game is about to finish, as he's twice cannoned into Mum and she's getting a bit irate!)

5.10 a.m. Found a dead tawny at the Potato Dump. It must have been shot yesterday as the body is very cold, hard and wet. Wonder a fox hasn't got here before me and picked it up. (The amount of shot birds discovered by people must be a small proportion of those actually shot.) That leaves, in the whole area, one and a half pairs of tawny owls out of the original five pairs.

Monday 27 July
8.30 a.m. Shooting near Old Barn ruins. Fine, sunny morning with slight haze. Recent heavy rains have done a lot of damage to the cereal crops here. Only good thing about it on the Long Field is that it's obliterated the badgers' path that was becoming very obvious.

The fox wasn't using his sycamore branch this morning over the Bank Sett, so I've been sitting at the far end of it writing this, 9.35 a.m. I've just felt a slight bump and he's landed halfway along and settled down to have a good look across the field. He has his back to me and is about eight feet away – I'm curled up, notebook on knees, where this branch meets the main trunk. Know how he feels. There's a singularly secure feeling halfway up an enormous tree, quite hidden by foliage. (And I don't even have to climb to get here.) He's stretched out along the limb, head on front paws, and I know if something moves far over on the Wildflower Path, as his ears turn forward, he stiffens (even his brush stiffens); then very gently he raises his head – their sight is far better than ours. A woman with two small children and a dog pass by and into the wood (the school summer holidays start today).

He relaxes back, but the flies round his face are disturbing him. The upright ears twitch in irritation. He turns to dislodge them – and begins to groom, sometimes biting at his fur. He's spent some minutes teasing and pulling, as he curry-combs through with his front teeth. A thistle-head of the wood burdock is his objective – the long hooks covered now in loose hairs. He finally pulls it free and it drops on to the branch. Grooming complete, he stretches out once more. The sun is warm on my arms, though it's only dappling through the upper leafage, and the fox farther out in the sunshine is bathed in light. As he turns his head and yawns my way, I see his elliptical pupils have, cat-like, become mere slits. He's lying on his side now, tail hanging down over the branch, but for all that he's still very alert. The fur on his shoulders and back is slightly darker, making a cross. Most foxes have this, I think, but it shows up very clearly in this light.

A pair of jays are in amongst the ripe barley, but what they are pecking up from the ground (insects or grain) I can't see, and daren't use the monocular for fear the movement will disturb Reynard. It's very pleasant and peaceful here, the sun over the field of amber grain, the rich green of the trees all around, and my handsome fox in front of me. Oh,

63

peace shattered! A squirrel is scolding angrily just above my head and the fox has turned to see what all the noise is about. He stares at me lengthily and then looks up at the squirrel still chattering. He's standing up now. To get off this branch the way he came, he will have to come closer to me and I don't think he's going to risk it. No. He trots away along the branch and jumps effortlessly to an ash tree branch near by – and from there to the bank. I'll give him a few minutes, then leave myself, as the squirrel is still protesting!

Wednesday 29 July
Been out since midnight trailing and watching the badger cub. He met up with the sow twice and eventually came home with her, but he forages around on his own quite often now. I'm careful to give the Chantry a wide berth at night as a lone man is using the tent to sleep in most nights. Not a shooter, and apparently unaware of the wildlife here – except when a fox disturbed him last night. Don't greatly care to have him at my back when I'm at the Bank Sett, but haven't a choice, so am very wary. And don't want him to know he has company up here either.

The Briarmead bank and Wildflower Path are vivid with the contrasting blues of chicory and nettle-leaved bellflowers. And everywhere in the shady parts of this wood, the dainty, pale blooms of enchanter's nightshade stand out in the semi-darkness. There is a solitary kestrel that regularly hunts over the top hayfield of Briarmead. Stood watching it hover-wheel-hover-plummet earthwards this morning.

Friday 31 July
Lovely dawn, 4.35 a.m. Been watching the young badger playing at the side of the Wildflower Path. His mother went to earth some time ago. He's found a take-away carton and, after licking it out, he's been chasing around with it in his mouth. Now he's rolled on his back with it held between his front paws and is chewing it – the noise this makes seems to please him. The sun is streaking the dawn sky pink and mauve, the light catching the dew on the ears of barley.

5.10 a.m. The badger cub was very nearly shot just now. He was between me and the edge of Briarmead when a man appeared from the lane below. I just saw his head, shoulders and raised gun come slowly above the bank, and for a moment couldn't make out what it was against the light. I ran along the path between cub and man, shouting, and the badger dashed through the barley to safety. (Thankfully, they can move fast over short distances.) Another man appeared on the bank with the first. Then they both turned, rushed down the bank and up Briarmead with me running after them. Can't think why – just instinct, I suppose! A bit farther up the lane, they ran into the wood and I didn't follow them further. Mad really, chasing two armed men – guess I was angry. Late getting home as I walked all round Ashcroft Woods and

64

High Ridge to see if there was a vehicle parked. Nothing. Either they were locals, or they parked a distance away among other cars outside houses: this is the latest dodge to prevent car numbers being taken.

Saturday I August
Cold, wet, overcast morning. Saw the badgers safely go to earth – no humans around. Think yesterday's shooters were probably after birds but saw the cub and thought it would make a good target – that's the trouble. Many badgers must get maimed and killed this way, and who's to know?

Watched a young fox drinking from the Main Pond. Then it had a grooming session on the little crag before going down the Beech Path. Agrimony's rain-scented yellow spikes very pretty – the moisture makes its tiny flowers stand out. This and weld were both once used to dye wool and cloth.

5.50 a.m. Shooting started Old Barn area and back of High Ridge – no cars.

Sunday 2 August
It was a fine dawn though everywhere very wet. Shooting has only just started at 6.10 a.m., so the badgers went to earth undisturbed this morning. Plenty of fungi – stinkhorns (*Phallus impudicus*) especially, also many bracket fungi. Been watching the birds feeding on the insects

swarming over the Potato Dump, and a wren on the elder tree there. The pale green flowers of the wood sage, with their long brown stamens, are in bloom.

Walking down the Oak Dell Path at 7.15 a.m. when someone way ahead made to come out of the undergrowth to my right. Whoever it was moved hastily back and, as I passed by, a shotgun was fired across the path just in front of me. At such close range, it could only have been meant to intimidate. Wonder if it was one of Friday's badger shooters, but maybe not. Suspect I'm a thorn in the side of a lot of people.

Tuesday 4 August
2.30 a.m. A heavy mist lies over the countryside and the trees drip with moisture. The undergrowth nearest me is alive with tiny sounds and I can't decide what animals (for it's more than one) are the cause of them. Now something has darted out into the open and back – small, slender shapes, lightning fast. A family of weasels – hunting? For what? See now they're not hunting, but pulling and scrambling over a rabbit's carcass.

Have discovered what badger is excavating near the beehives (where the path is undermined, 20 May). It's the sow and her cub from the Long Field, Bank Sett area. She's moved a great deal of earth, but fortunately the mound is well hidden by the dense growth of nettles all around. (It would seem from this that she is uneasy and anxious to move again.) Left her to it, helped by her cub! – and returned to the wood, gradually working my way round to the Chantry.

3.30 a.m. Visibility improving, but there are still dense pockets of mist here and there. Saw two men with guns come down from the Bank Sett. Would have remained undetected standing amongst the geans, but was discovered by their terriers. None of us spoke as they passed on the Wildflower Path, but I had the distinct impression my presence wasn't welcome! Rather early for bird shooting; not dawn for another hour, and clearly they have been here some while (terriers aren't gun dogs, either). To keep track of them without the dogs scenting me, I went up Briarmead Lane a little, then moved back into the undergrowth, expecting to locate them as I came round in a circle. Found no sign of them, however, until nearly back at the Wildflower Path. Just inside the tree cover, saw two things simultaneously. The men and their dogs sitting quietly in a car parked off the path, and a third man with a spade over his shoulder, coming down to his waiting companions. He got in the car which was immediately driven away, 5.55 a.m.

The badgers must have gone to earth at their new sett – at least, I hope they decide it's to be their new home. A spade at this time of the year wouldn't be for foxes (adults are moulting anyway and vixens only den when their cubs are young). Almost certainly after the badgers, therefore, and they knew what they were doing – no noise or fuss, and well organised.

Thursday 6 August
Out at 2 a.m. this morning to keep watch on the badgers' new sett. Very quiet – no sign of men and dogs of Tuesday, though I feel it's only a question of time before they discover the sow and cub's whereabouts. It's an unsatisfactory situation – can't expect the police to be tied up waiting around. Think evenings will be safe as there are always people here then – motorbikers, children, dog-walkers etc. – until quite late, so I don't think the badgers would be taken then. It is their pre-dawn return that is the danger time, when no one is here. Came out yesterday and must do so each morning now, as I did with Tossy in the summer of 1979.

Dawn has been late coming as it's very misty. Notice that three of the beehives here are occupied – they sound like distant traffic! The three fledged tawnies are doing very well over the undulating fields between here and the back of Ashcroft Woods. Now that the pairs of adult tawny owls are reduced by the shooters from five pairs to one and a half pairs, it means that these three young birds have unlimited territory (good comes out of bad – provided *they* don't get shot, of course).

Sunday 9 August
In the distance, along the Wheatfield Copse path, saw the Glebe Farm's part-white cat with a fox. The two figures wandered along, each individually searching the overgrown verges, but nevertheless keeping together, finally disappearing from my view round a corner of the path. Hope they don't meet trouble, as shooting started 4.50 a.m. this morning, in spite of the wet conditions.

Tuesday 11 August
7.50 a.m. Sunny, dew-drenched morning. Watching the many rabbits on the Ridge – have seen no evidence of myxomatosis here. Bees on the flowering heather (ling) are rivalling the pylon cables for noise. Since I've been sitting here, a crow on the second horizontal strut of the pylon is cawing continuously as he walks back and forth. He's looking directly below him under the metal tower and is very agitated. I'm on a rise of ground here by the heather and with the monocular can just see three darting shapes – I'll try and work my way nearer.

Some minutes later and I'm in the concealing bracken near by – the crow has been joined by its mate. Together, they have tried to dive-bomb the weasels who have caught a crow fledgling, but the weasels refuse to be intimidated; in fact, an adult crow nearly fell prey to them also. The predators hissed, spat and made squealing barks as they reared up on hind legs in an attempt to grasp the crows as, airborne, they closed in. I admired the parents' tenacity, but three weasels are a lot of enemy.

All is quiet now. The weasels and their meal are gone; the crows have returned to their nest in a sweet chestnut tree near by. It is a very pleasant spot with insects, bees and butterflies active in the sunshine.

9.05 a.m. At the far end of the Enclosed Path, just inside Ashcroft

Woods, met a green woodpecker as I was searching for fungi. He was wary (it *was* a male) but not particularly nervous, and after a bit continued his quest for insects. Never realised before the amount an adult woodpecker can consume. Under the rotting bark of a fallen ash, he did particularly well with his long, probing beak. The light filtering through the upper foliage is making a spiderweb shimmer, and the tiny brown spider, just completing his snare, is bathed in sun. My green woodpecker is high above me in a birch now, with the warmth on his feathers as he sits to sunward, preening.

Thursday 13 August
In the kitchen at 2.10 a.m., ready to go out, when I heard a high-pitched whistling coming from the garden. When I opened the door, the light shone out on to the path and lawn to reveal our resident hedgehog with four small urchins in tow, and the sound was coming from the youngsters. Liza, Karen's half-bred Siamese cat, who is quite used to the adult hedgehog (both animals tend to disregard one another), was clearly upset by the whistling and, rushing into the sitting-room, hid beneath an armchair where she crouched growling and lashing her tail as she does during a storm! Left the back door wide open so that the kitchen light showed the scene clearly, and sat on the bottom step for a long time, watching the family.

They continued their activities (a worm was tackled on the lawn and slugs from the path and flowerbed areas), quite oblivious of the light or myself. It was the first time I had seen this hedgehog's young, though they were well grown and quite capable of coping with the slugs that were leaving their trails over the wet path. Liza finally left the safety of her armchair to come in search of me on the step. She sat on my lap, uneasily regarding them and occasionally making a very subdued form of her 'no' sound. The first time she made this sound, three young hedgehogs stopped in their tracks, then continued moving about. (The fourth youngster had disappeared temporarily, but the parent disregarded the sound.) She repeated the noise twice more whilst the hedgehogs foraged, with no apparent effect upon them whatever. In all, I sat watching for twenty-five minutes. At the end of that time, the adult suddenly moved up to the base of a large flowerpot containing a miniature rose – I *thought* to search for slugs. Her nose seemed to touch the plastic surface, whereupon she turned and, raising her body up, rushed under the tree and hedge cover by the fence, her four youngsters following after. I didn't hear her make any sound of warning, but she could have done so.

In consequence, I was well late leaving home. The badgers seem settled at the Beehive Sett and though I've seen the three men and their terriers again (early morning, Monday 10 August) exploring the Bank Sett, they haven't as yet traced sow and cub to here. Both badgers forage independently now; the youngster is nearly his mother's size and, being young and playful, unfortunately stays above ground well after dawn some mornings.

Monday 17 August
Perfect full moon and clear skies throughout the night until dawn – most unusual for this summer when clouds or mist have nearly always obscured the stars. Coming here, I listened and watched tawny fledglings over Ingrims Fields, and also those over the farmland and lower slopes of High Ridge. Moonlight floods the land as, streaming from sky to fields, its rays explore the curving hedgerow, the bewhiskered barley, and glints mica-like on each pebble and flint. I cast a long shadow and have to be careful if I wish to move undetected – tawnies and foxes, especially, have very keen sight.

The three fledged owls from the Old Barn area discovered me at the beehives and, at one time, I had them flying and calling around me as I waited for the badgers' return. Curiosity perhaps – certainly not fear. I notice that one young bird takes considerable interest in the occupied hives, alighting on them, walking on the roofs and watching the sluggish movements of the few bees that seem always to be on the entrance platforms. He takes no notice of the empty hives, nor does he actually interfere with the crawling insects. I imagine the fanning noise from inside and the movement on the platforms outside, attracts his attention. (*See* entry for 27 August.)

Dr Southern writes that: 'The young (tawnies) fall completely silent during the first week (of August) and evidence has accumulated to show that they are now independent of the parents, and a limited dispersal, involving considerable mortality, takes place.'* When I write to let him know how I have progressed, I'll mention this silence amongst young tawnies, as tonight and other nights recently, this brood have called their 'hunger' cry quite a lot, though it is the first August I have noticed this.

Tuesday 18 August
Have discovered that the young tawny isn't the only creature interested in the farmer's hives. I came upon the sow badger up on her hind legs trying to topple one at two-thirty this morning. It seemed very heavy, however (probably near full now that the pollen-flow is slackening), and she only succeeded in rocking it, accompanied by a crescendo of sound from the occupants. Should the cub see her, he might be more successful – he appears to be bigger and stronger each time I watch him.

Coming here across Ingrims Fields, I saw one of the Holmoak Lane tawnies perched on the little rusty footpath sign. With the barley now cut, I was able to detour round it so as not to alarm him. He stopped preening and regarded me carefully – can understand the expression 'to

The Natural Control of a Population of Tawny Owls (Strix aluco), by H. N. Southern, from *J. Zool. Lond.* (1970).

69

look at one owlishly'. When I had gone some distance away along the path, his head suddenly did that 180° swivel for which owls are noted, as he looked at me over his back. After all this time owl-watching, I still find that action comic.

Thursday 20 August
Raining hard, steady wind. Heard people coming round the field edge at the View approx. 3.10 a.m. Kept well out of the way – the men and terriers of 4 August. For the next hour, they worked round the woodland setts (all, of course, empty). Decided it would be best to let them see I was around – it wasn't a very pleasant encounter, but at least now they know they are still being observed. Relieved, though surprised, that they haven't explored more on to Barry Hains's land (do they feel that on open fields they are more likely to be seen?). Their terriers would soon locate the badger pair by the beehives if they did. Perhaps now that they have found the woodland setts deserted – and me around – they'll call it a day (and who's being optimistic?).

Saturday 22 August
After seeing the badgers this morning, thought I would move down to Warby and on through the Water Meadows. Beautiful dawn sky, bright with chill wind. The Bourne was full of life: watched a water vole hunting. Farther along this river, saw a flash of blue and orange dart

70

arrow-like upstream, very close to the surface. A few moments later, it returned and perched on a rock projecting above the water. My first experience of a kingfisher in this area, though fifty years ago I believe they were common here.

Walking back past the Old Barn area, watched a magnificent Emperor dragonfly (*Anax imperator*) over the barley field. The blue-green thorax is very striking. It rested awhile on the damson foliage, long wings outspread.

Sunday 23 August
Have had a marvellous two hours observing the young badger tonight. The dew-drenched grass makes the fur cling to his chunky body, and his white-patched front paw on otherwise black legs is most distinctive. First saw him and the sow worming in the damp, rolled field behind the woods. Then the mother curled up on the Damson Bank to sleep off her meal. However, Junior's surplus energy has got the better of him, so he's moved round to the wheat growing next to the Top Field, Prosser's Wood. The grain rustles drily in the ripe ears as he passes through, and when he disappears from sight I can still mark his progress by the gently waving crop. He's playing really, moving in little bursts of speed and whickering every so often. He doesn't appear to eat the grain, but then this summer has been wet with plenty of opportunity to worm. Notice he seems to enjoy this area especially – and why not? It contains all the animal's requirements: the Prosser's Wood edging, apart from trees, has a farm dump (a fine source of larvae, slugs), hazelnuts now, chestnuts later; there's grass and thick hedgerow with blackberries, elderberries, wireworms and snails; and Barry Hains's fields that are always being turned in or ploughed as crop follows crop (worms and beetles). The sun was high in the sky when he finally went to earth – no shooting – all's peace in my world.

Tuesday 25 August
The thin-edged moon is in the last quarter and will be very near the sun when it rises. Noticed before (15 January) that its position in the sky can vary a great deal according to the time of year.

Walked to the Oak Dell Path where I found to my horror that the proposed new road is about to become reality. A wide brown scar has been gouged through the landscape, chopping through the lower Gully of Briarmead and diagonally up across High Ridge. This time yesterday, those trees and undergrowth were living – now all in its path is overturned. Walked its length, stunned, not really accepting the enormity of it; scrambling over piles of fencing, coils of wire. Past the machine that had swiftly wrought such havoc, and up on to the Ridge I have grown to love. If I had not taught myself nightvision, I would have stumbled many times; as it was, all was clear – bewilderingly clear.

Walked deep in thought, round to the Wheatfield Copse. A slight

71

ground mist, though the crescent moon and stars were distinct. Suddenly to my right, high in the air, saw something bright descending very close. Turned, startled, to look at it. It may have made some noise coming through the air, but with the Motorway's sound and other night noises, difficult to say. It glowed redly and possibly wasn't larger than a sizeable flint (but can't really judge for sure, so may be quite wrong). It landed in the middle of the rolled and sown field with a tremendous thud and sound of stones on impact. The glow lessened after a few minutes and then darkness again. I was inclined to go across to see what it was but, a) it would have been a cheek to cross a sown field like that, and b) not at all certain I would have located it anyway; fields are pretty vast when you start crossing them. Time approx. 2.10 a.m. Rather glad it didn't land on me. Wonder what it was – meteorite?

Moved on to Briarmead. Near the Old Barn ruins, watched and heard two of the tawny fledglings – I have become rather attached to them. At Briarmead, stood looking across the hayfield enjoying the place. A group of large birds flew over the woods and landed in the field. This must be the morning when everything happens! Some kind of geese – a lot of dark on them, but some have white breasts and most have some white patches on them – Brent geese? [Too early in the year for Brents; they don't arrive in England until October.] Not particularly bothered at my presence when I crossed the lane and went over the field to them. I finished up with them all around me; one seemed as much interested in me as I was in them, and decided to keep me company awhile. Thought at first they had alighted here to rest (they probably had), but they were also enjoying the grass.

The area was clear of human activity – apart from mine! Waited for the badgers' return, 5.05 and 5.20 a.m.; all's well.

Thursday 27 August
During the week, much work has been done on the new road. It crosses the Top Field above Prosser's Wood now and is stoutly fenced all along with five-barred metal gates where it intercepts footpaths and farm tracks; High Ridge isn't big enough to survive a road cutting through it. Thick mist everywhere; I enjoy mist and its curious conditions – moisture drip-drips continuously from the trees.

Came out of the undergrowth on to the aspen-lined path. Stood awhile there feeling very uneasy – sensed that, humanwise, I wasn't alone. Looked carefully around me in the mist, instinctively trying to locate the place that felt wrong. Decided it was somewhere near the old cottage site, so passed along the path and through to the little space just off Briarmead where the bistort grows. Four sleeping-bags, four motorbikes crammed in side by side. Relieved that was all it was, and left them still sleeping peacefully.

Mist is lifting now; beautifully thin crescent moon and bright stars,

4.35 a.m. Saw the young boar badger ahead of me, foraging on the Enclosed Path, and trailed him out on to the wheatfield next to the Top Field, Prosser's Wood. The fencing of the new road snaking through the wheat seems to have upset him. As it was only erected here yesterday, chances are this was the first time he'd encountered it on his territory. He followed it along, occasionally rearing up against the wire, and continued in this fashion until he reached the point where, at present, it ends. Here he began, snout down, to explore the machine-torn earth of the 'road' itself, working slowly back the way he had come but now, of course, between the two rows of fencing, not outside it. The damp, raw earth was ideal for worming and nearly an hour was spent very profitably here until, sated, he sought a way out. Then the badger ran back and forth along the wire, sometimes rearing up at a post, clawing it and growling, and then dropping down on all fours again and running on. It was as if in a panic, he felt himself trapped but, young as he was, his reaction was anger as well as fear. This is the third time he has known human interference:

1) when he and his mother arrived here so abruptly in June; his paw injured and obsessive 'shadowing' of her;
2) the shooter aiming at him and the men and terriers searching the Bank Sett;
3) and now this 'alien' road and fences dividing up his territory.

He has my sympathy, this is no place for badgers. Watched him finally reach the open end of the new road and move up at a near-gallop back towards his sett and safety.

Took the footpath down through Prosser's Wood and so to the stile at the foot of the Ridge. Spoke to a police patrol near the Motorway Tunnel, as from Saturday I'll be away for a fortnight and want to have the badgers protected if possible. Understandably, he didn't seem very enthusiastic about patrolling Briarmead Lane of an early morning, but I hope someone does. The men and their terriers may not come back, but there's no way of telling.

(Had a letter from Dr Southern this morning. He writes: 'The persistence of calling by your fledged [tawny] young may be due to inherent variability ... attention paid to beehives may well be due to the habit of wood mice raiding them.' He adds: 'The fact that somebody shoots your tawnies is most unfortunate – and quite illegal. Can you not mobilise some action against this?' Wish I could.)

Friday 28 August
Watched Glebe Farm's cat meet its fox friend this morning. The dogfox saw the cat first coming towards him, and stopped short. The cat, less vigilant, took longer to register the other. It was the cat that seemed to take the initiative, slowly approaching the fox; typical cat action,

apparently casual, but in reality a calculated approach. Both animals proceeded back the way the cat had come, in the direction of the Old Barn ruins and Briarmead Lane. Here at the wood/field edge, they separately hunted awhile amongst the clumps of toadflax and wild chicory. The fox caught something small which it ate.

I last saw them meandering down the little lane together, just as the sun rose above the skyline, touching this quiet countryside with light, 5.20 a.m.

AUTUMN 1981

Monday 14 September 1981
Gloriously full moon, clear skies and slight breeze. Hains's wheat and barley all harvested – straw baled and drying on the field. Everywhere the blackberries are ripe and dropping, their scent lingers heavy on the air. Came back to hear the news that the new road is not a road at all, but a gas pipeline.

    3.10 a.m. and a beautiful night. Trailed a young vixen from the Main Pond area, through these woods and on to the Ridge, where I left it hunting as I wanted to see my badgers home. (Odd thing about this fox: though it can move quickly if it wants to, in repose its hindquarters have a curious 'hunched' appearance – deformity?) Sow badger returned 4.20 a.m., cub at 5.10 a.m.

Monday 21 September
2.25 a.m. Dull overcast night after four days and nights of storms and high winds. My visibility excellent – can see every detail of the ploughed

75

earth, tree bark and leaves at the same distance as by daylight – only a different kind of vision. Have been badger-watching and am now at the Chantry writing this. Could smell paraffin and traced it to the plastic tent area of the Chantry. People have been using it since I've been away and have left a plastic mini-rucksack containing two new choppers and three household boxes of matches and a length of rope. Tucked away under creeper, I discovered a metal can two-thirds full of the liquid – everywhere reeks of the stuff. I imagine it's a couple of youths playing 'camps' but it's very dangerous. It stays dry here as rain rarely penetrates. Will return in daylight and tidy up a bit. Have seen no sign this past week of the men and terriers, but have seen a motorbike patrol twice on Briarmead, so the police are doing their bit.

All very peaceful over Great Chantry; this field was ploughed whilst I was away and now the wet earth smells fantastic.

4.30 a.m. For the past two hours have watched the badgers bringing in bedding from the hayfield at the top of the lane. The hay is lying cut on the ground, waiting to be baled. The young badger has become an accomplished hay-carrier these days and went on fetching long after the sow had given up. The Beehive Sett is quite a distance and a lot of hay wisps and badger hairs are left to tell the tale on the lowest barbed-wire strand at the side of Briarmead. I wonder if Barry Hains will read the signs and guess how popular his hay is!

Wednesday 23 September
First frosty night this autumn – clear skies, perfect constellations. Checked for tawnies in my area. So far, I can only trace one pair, plus the one fledged owl near the beehives. After the five pairs recorded and observed last autumn, this is rather disappointing. However, I will continue to check at dusk throughout the months until March. Successfully avoided human activity at the Main Pond – a car was set alight later at 11.20 p.m. Badgers digging out at the Wheatfield Sett – a great deal of hard work put into it! Notice the young boar is beginning to assert himself; although his mother dominates at present, I don't think she will much longer.

When near the Old Barn ruins, I heard a vehicle on the gritty surface of Briarmead Lane at approximately 2 a.m., and men's voices, so avoided the lane. (A nuisance, as it meant I had to go the long way round to the Chantry.) Worked at the Chantry for the remaining hours of darkness. Stoat activity very interesting – I must endeavour to learn more about these animals.

Yesterday afternoon, I did my tidying up at the tent site here; relieved to see the back of the paraffin. Wonder if it might be wisest to rip up the home-made tent – seems mean, but the strange, frightened man that made it isn't likely to return. (If he had had a choice, I don't think he would have lived here as he did; there was something rather sad and isolated about him.) The 'paraffin' people have chopped down small

76

trees, burnt others and stripped tree-bark. Probably teenagers, certainly *not* the lone man. His one aim in life seemed to be not to attract attention for fear of discovery.

Thursday 24 September
Beginning to rain, 4.10 a.m. Very quietly I walked up Briarmead Lane as there have been some birds gleaning on the stubble there that I wished to identify. Find they are mallard. The past weeks during daylight hours, flocks of linnets and greenfinches have been feeding, first from the weedy wastes and now from the stubble also. I love the linnet's erratic flight. To get from A to B you don't fly in a straight line, but do all sorts of crazy twists, bounces and turns to make life interesting!

Daylight now. The rainclouds are moving to reveal a delicate blue sky touched here and there with fine wisps of translucent vapour; each plant, each leaf fresh-hued, bejewelled with shimmering raindrops.

Saturday 26 September
2.10 a.m. Raining hard, gusty wind and cloudy sky. Marvellous visibility, though – can see in detail and for a good distance. Been watching the sow worming on the rolled field at the Wheatfield Copse. The noise she is making rivals the sound of the rain driving on to the foliage under which I stand. It's a very fine night badgerwise! Think her son isn't far away as I can hear a lot of movement in the copse behind me. Now he's appeared to my left and joined her on the field – two badger minds with but a single thought!

They seem to alternate now between this sett and that by the beehives further along.

Moving slowly along the path, but careful not to disturb the foraging animals. The smell of wet nettles is indescribable – I think nettles are very underrated. Walking these sodden woods for the sheer joy of it. The rain sounds torrential on the still-thick leafage and the fragrant Scots pines have surely the loveliest scent in the world. Have a childish pleasure in wading through deep puddles, so I'm indulging this morning. The rain has penetrated to the skin and water runs down my spine, but the tawnies above me are calling and I haven't a care in the world, 5.40 a.m.

Sunday 27 September
Fine warm morning after heavy rains. By the Long Field, Briarmead Lane is flooded to a depth of ten inches. At the Wildflower Path, the red admirals rest on the leaves of dogwood and bramble. Have been checking badger setts in my area for signs of digging out – nothing so far. Don't somehow think that the Wheatfield sow and cub will overwinter here. Can't quite say why but feel they are unsettled – perhaps as well, though I shall miss them.

Sporadic shooting began approximately 7.20 a.m. Squirrels are busy in the geans above my head. The cherries' leaves are turning deep red

77

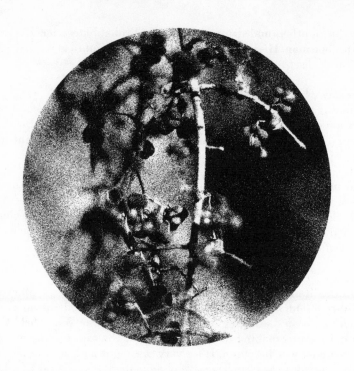

and falling already. Before daylight this morning, I saw from a distance one of the badgers blackberrying. Moved closer and had just identified it as the sow when a fox appeared from round the bush side and they came face to face. The badger dropped down on all fours, watching the fox who made a slight detour, avoiding *Meles meles*, and continued on its way – the badger resumed its feast.

Monday 28 September
7.15 p.m. Ideal weather conditions for commencement of tawny census. *One pair* of these birds checked at Briarmead/Wildflower Path area.

Wednesday 30 September
The trees are in turmoil tonight, bending and swaying helplessly as the wind's giant hand passes through. But for the dryness and the firm ground underfoot, I might be at sea. The surge and roar of the foliage, the occasional glimpses of sky, a momentary lull, then back with unseen ferocity, the storm rages once more. Leaves, berries, branches are hurled from above – dust and wreckage everywhere. Something soft and solid hits the path ahead, moves sickeningly and is still. Reaching it, I kneel and stroke a pigeon's warm body as chaos continues above. For all the danger from flying debris, I've never loved this woodland more. To encounter it in all its moods is to know and be one with it. Looking

upwards as I kneel by the dead bird, I try to imprint the sight, sound – and smell – of the gale on my mind for all time. It's an exhilarating experience; a never-ending seascape of sound.

Friday 2 October
1.10 a.m. Watched my sow badger eating shaggy parasol (*Lepiota rhacodes*) mushrooms growing in the grass under the damson trees at the side of Briarmead Lane. She started biting the side of one, uprooted it, and finished it stem, grass and all. Think there were five, including a 'drumstick' one, and two quite wide-capped. She polished them all off!

Very windy, wet, squally night with clouds racing across the sky. Sometimes I see the stars clearly, then a few moments later all is cloudy and raining again – very heavy at times and the wind makes it sting. Not that Mrs Badger is bothered – what with fungi, worms, blackberries and chestnuts since I've been trailing her, she must be fairly full by now.

Watched the 'hunched' vixen of 14 September foraging along the Damson Bank. Definitely something wrong with her; she's looking very very emaciated, coat poor.

Monday 5 October
There's a gentle breeze murmuring in the leaves of the Wheatfield Copse and blowing on my face. Everywhere is much less waterlogged and drying fast. One of the fledged tawnies has taken over this area; he calls, but so far appears to have no mate. The other two tawnies have disappeared – haven't seen them for a long time. I think my badgers have finally left the area altogether; haven't seen the cub since 26 September, and the sow since Friday. Autumn is a great time of movement with badgers. I only hope the place they choose to winter over is a safe one – certainly here is not.

Was standing inside the wire at the top of Briarmead when a light appeared at about the Ashtree Path entrance on the top field here. (Thought I saw a bobbing light earlier, approximately 1.10 a.m., at the side of this field when I was tawny-watching.) Three men came and stood on the tarmac close by me, talking quietly amongst themselves. It would seem that the torch-holding one had previously concealed something to be retrieved by the three under the cover of darkness. The undergrowth had since grown so much that he couldn't find the place. One suggested that 'they' might have been discovered and removed – but no, he just couldn't now make out the place. They would have to return in daylight and get 'them'. The others said this was too risky and finally it was amicably decided that the torch-bearing man should find the spot in daylight and they would then all return near the end of the week under cover of darkness and collect 'them'. They walked quietly down Briarmead and across the fields. Under the oak trees there they got into a parked car and drove away, 2.30 a.m. (Leaving the car there was intelligent of them, as in the open the glint of metalwork can be seen even on a dull night.) Think I'll give that part of Ashcroft Woods a wide berth at the end of the week!

Wednesday 7 October
2.25 a.m. Excellent visibility; a very cold night. My badgers have definitely quit this area; will miss them, but glad for their sake. Fox-trailed from the View to the Main Pond – foxes fond of fungi too! Many varieties everywhere.

The horse-chestnuts on the Sleet House footpath have a bumper crop of conkers this year. Collected some for the boys next door and returned by 5.45 a.m.

Thursday 8 October
2.20 a.m. Windy, wet night, but very mild. Walked down to Warby (no barn owls) and through Newby Water Meadows. The Bourne gurgles to itself as it slips away over the pebbles. Watched a water vole in the reeds and sedges. When eating, they tend to sit in a hunchback attitude, the grass stem etc. held in the front paws, generally end on. I like their chubby faces and neat round ears nearly hidden by fur. Think the term 'water-rat' is a bad one; they are neither related to nor look like rats – most vole-like. Very obvious where it has been feeding as a lot of bits and pieces are left around.

Past the Old Barn ruins when, silently as always, the young male tawny flew by. Waited, hoping and expecting him to return. A lovely bird with his mottled plumage effortlessly turning to glide back over this field. Again he came very close and I tried slowly and gently putting out my hand in his path. He veered very slightly to avoid it and went off, only to return again. (Tawnies have other vocal sounds besides their 'tu-wit' and 'kewik' but I can't describe them in words.) He and I have been curious about each other ever since I badger-watched at the Beehive Sett and *he* alighted on the occupied hives right by me. He never takes any notice of them now, so maybe his interest in them was the curiosity of a juvenile and not the wood mouse theory. Hope he never gets shot. Unfortunately, tawnies tend to roost in obvious places and a marksman walking round in daylight must soon become experienced in where to look. This must be the reason that their mortality rate here is so high. Have bought a torch and tried directing its beam over this field – it gives a red light. Never used one before, though Dr Southern writes that they are insensitive to red floodlight – and he's right. My owl flew into the beam, along it, past me, and then veered round again. Felt very elated. Have never plucked up courage to do this before – too afraid of scaring him off.

Friday 9 October
Raining hard, gusty wind, 3.10 a.m. Found a dead long-tailed field mouse yesterday, so decided I would try to get my tawny to perch on my

hand. Thought the weather conditions might have put him off, but near the Damson Bank I found him (or rather, he found me). Let him twice come past my outstretched hand, but the third time, I laid the field mouse on my upturned palm. (Should have held on to it, of course.) The next time round, his talons neatly caught the mouse – I never felt it go. One moment it was lying there; the next, I was empty-handed. 'The best laid schemes o' mice an' men, Gang aft a-gley!', i.e. I don't have much luck!

Tuesday 13 October
Another ideal evening for locating tawnies. Concentrating now on Corbett's land, but nothing at all owl-wise. At 7.15 p.m. I was leaning against a tree trunk near the wood edge when a fox came yawning and stretching to my side and then sneezed! In doing so, its nose touched my trouser leg. I know foxes can move fast but this one nearly flew!

Friday 16 October
Has been raining without pause for two days and nights – very windy. Passing the long grass of the Damson Bank at 5.20 a.m., discovered a vixen stretched out very near death. Believe it to be the 'hunched' one, but won't touch or disturb it. Breath very rasping, eyes wide, jaws open; its drenched, clinging coat accentuating its lack of flesh. The forelegs sometimes twitched, but hindlegs and brush quite still – alive, but only just. Walked home feeling very disturbed. If I was capable of cleanly killing it, I would. Twice have killed horribly maimed birds, though had to force myself to do so. But terrified I wouldn't kill a fox cleanly; it's such a large creature. Cursed my cowardice all the way back.

Returned at 9.10 a.m. Sky black, poor visibility as rain so torrential – earth is just no longer absorbing the water. Found the young vixen without difficulty, dead by now and the body beginning to stiffen. Knelt beside it in the sodden grass and, lifting it gently, tried to judge its weight. Doubt if it was any heavier than Karen's little cat – so emaciated was it. Realised the odd hindquarters weren't a deformity, as I'd first thought on 14 September, but a wire snare! At least, that's what it *must* be, but it was so embedded in the pelvic area that only a jagged end protruded halfway up the right side in front of the right hind leg, and that was all twisted and contorted. The agony it must have known these past weeks!

(Many years past, Wendy was caught in a wire snare set in the undergrowth near the View. She had the sense not to struggle after the first moment, and waited for me to come up and release her. Even so, the wire was tight around her leg. Some weeks later, the dog herself discovered a very young fox in a similar snare by the holly trees. It had mauled its front paw as it had chewed at the wire, and snapped and bit me in its fear. So I wrapped it in my anorak with just the foot exposed – [sounds easy, but it wasn't!] and so brought it close to where the wire was anchored, to relieve the tension. Even so, it took some time to free the paw – with a very sympathetic dog as onlooker. When I unwrapped my anorak and stood clear, the young fox got shakily to its feet, looking fearfully at us, hobbled a few paces and then made a bolt for the nearest cover on three legs. I've often wondered whether it had the use of the trapped paw in later life. And I can believe the stories of foxes severing a paw to escape a trap. The animal gnaws and worries at the trap and eventually starts on the paw.)

Thursday 22 October
Standing near the broken willow by Newby Water Meadows at 2.25 a.m. Very thin-edged moon leaning on its side and bright stars with clear skies. Watched a heron in the river, fishing by moonlight! For perhaps ten minutes, it stood in the shallow water, its neck poking forward and quite motionless. Then with a lightning stroke of his bill, he caught – not a fish, but a frog! A few stealthy steps forward and once more a patient vigil. (The pictures one so often sees of herons fishing with gracefully curved necks can't be accurate. In reality, they either stand with neck straight up, ready to strike or, more usually, the neck is poked forward at a forty-five degree angle.)

Now, whether the other heron fishing in the swamped meadow-grass near by moved too close, I don't know. But suddenly, the frog-eating

individual was out of the river (nearly colliding with the willow's trailing branch) then, sitting back on his tail, he stabbed at the other with his long beak! At first, the attacked bird successfully parried the other's stroke, taking it on the flat of his bill with a hollow, clashing sound. (I think he was half expecting an attack – I'm sure he was trespassing and knew it.) Then the aggressor came in again with great speed and the swordlike bill caught the other just below its left eye. The injured bird crouched low whilst the other towered above it, wings open and uttering a screeching, almost barking noise. Both remained like this for a moment. Then the vanquished heron ran a few paces still in that crouching low-to-the-ground position, and took heavily to the air.

Have never seen this before. I can't tell the difference between the sexes, but think possibly this was two males disputing over territory – may be wrong. Herons have a great vocal range – more, I think, than any other bird I've encountered. What formidable weapons those duelling bills are.

Saturday 24 October
Mild, dull morning. Black nightshade and viper's bugloss are still in bloom on the Prosser's Wood Top Field edge. Everywhere the leaves are falling fast – many chestnuts, but size and quality poor – very few acorns this autumn. Shooting started 7.40 a.m. (at the Chantry). Normally at this time of year, I have to be home well before dawn, so can't say when it starts in the week. Looking from the Bank Sett out over the Long Field, the brilliantly burnished foliage of the geans that line the Wildflower Path are afire in the early morning light.

Birds and squirrels are very busy and vocal here – the dry leaves rustle noisily underfoot. A slight movement from the side of the log on which I sit and a weasel appears from amongst the ivy. He moves silently away, his gaze ahead on the quarrelling squirrels. He disappears into a dense golden cluster of *Coprinus micaceus* only to re-emerge at the foot of an ash and very close to the unsuspecting disputers. With its back to the lurking weasel, the squirrel neither sees nor hears the darting movement. The acorn argument is suddenly terminated, the squirrels all gone bar one – the weasel's hunting is temporarily over. On several occasions now I've seen weasels catch squirrels – on the ground, and generally when the squirrel's attention is diverted. The method of killing is the same – a bite to the back of the neck.

Friday 6 November
This has been the Night of the Fox. Was out before 1 a.m.; new moon, clear skies and patches of ground mist (and strong smell of bonfires and fireworks until I reached the Ridge!). At Briarmead heard the regular, rasping bark-interval-bark of a fox and traced it easily to the Long Field. Mature dogfox (with *no* white tail tag – that should make for quick future identification). It was moving over the field scent-marking, a

83

large flint-chipping, for instance, a broken twig, a molehill. Then stood with body pushed forward and barked similarly again. I needed to keep at a distance or it would have crossed *my* scent path at some stage, so viewed it through the monocular. It kept up this scenting and barking in my sight for thirty-eight minutes (how long it had been doing this before I happened on the scene, I can't say). Its meanderings had brought it close to the Bank Sett where it froze, intently gazing upwards into the near-bare branches of a sycamore tree – moved a few paces – looked upwards again. Then I lost sight of it for a moment as it trotted diagonally up the steep bank – pause – and a noisy clapping of wings as the disturbed wood-pigeons flew out across the Long Field from where they had been roosting . . . and the dogfox reappeared near the bottom of the bank, in his jaws the one that didn't get away. Interesting to see a fox eating a sizeable bird. It neatly shears off the long primaries or flight feathers from the bone – such a find is the sure sign of a fox. They do this very quickly and, apart from a few scattered feathers and perhaps the feet, that's all you'll probably find.

Returning home along Holmoak Lane by the bullocks' field, 5.35 a.m. A fox is barking and scenting the far side of their field! The young bovines are lying down, cud-chewing – and don't seem very impressed.

(Doubt if I'll be embarking on a systematic trailing of foxes this winter in my area. Last winter proved to myself I can do it and learnt a great deal. But to get to know the foxes and every detail of their territories, I would need to build up information regularly as before and be out at least five nights in seven. For foxes aren't alike; they are as individual as dogs – or people. And trailing the same foxes regularly from October to March, I was able to build up in my mind a pattern of behaviour in *very* familiar countryside. Thus, when a strange fox entered another's range, its entire attitude stamped it as trespasser and even at a distance I could tell it didn't belong. Although the concentration for this sort of trailing is mentally exhausting, I don't think it would be nearly as successful shared with another person. So much of the information gained can't readily be verbally transmitted. Getting to know your foxes is a challenging, stimulating one-person job – and the rewards are infinite.)*

Thursday 12 November
Though for the past forty-eight hours a thick cloud-blanket has blotted out both sun and stars, the visibility tonight is fantastic. Somewhere behind the clouds is the full moon, which probably accounts for this. No wind. Very difficult to move silently in the woods; the dead dry leaves make the slightest movement noisy. Nevertheless, I managed to get fairly near two foxes sitting together, mutually grooming. They were amongst the thin undergrowth just off the path above the Oak

*Happened to re-read this entry on 22 February 1982. Seeing how much success I've had with foxes this winter, it's rather funny.

Dell, and partly hidden by the stump of a felled tree that had suckered. The foxes (alternately washing each other's face, ears and neck) became aware of me gradually – or rather, began to get uneasy. The grooming ceased, one slowly getting up and the other still lying down, but looking around. After a moment, the standing one trotted away deeper into the wood, whilst the other rose slowly to its feet, still looking round. It sprang lightly on to the stump, peering between the long shoots, and saw me standing there; and with a sharp bark of alarm, spun round and ran off after its companion.

Friday 13 November
9.30 a.m. Vivid blue skies and a light breeze. All around me, the falling leaves give colour and movement to this woodland. Discovered that the entrances at the back of the View Sett have very recently been dug out, almost certainly by a badger. This old sett is intriguing insomuch as quite accidentally I discovered (through Joe's cubs) that it connected with the Felled Logs Sett on the other side of this small hill. The main holes here are liable to subsidence in wet weather and are also very near the Primrose Path – these entrances are untouched, however; it is the back, hidden ones that are dug out. Besides chestnut and ash, this small slope has cherry and holly; in fact, the entire sett is in the shade of the last two named trees. The broken cherry branch from which I used to badger-watch has sunk nearer the ground. Creeper and several years' dead leaves cover it now like a shroud and with the drooping holly curtain near by, these back entrances to the sett are well camouflaged.

Just hope if it's Joe and his mate returned that they are not still crossing the Motorway. In his youth, he crossed there long before that section was built – and old habits die hard.

A fine clear afternoon, so went out about 4 p.m. to check again for tawnies. Still the total is one and a half pairs – perhaps the situation will improve later.

Tuesday 17 November
Fieldfares and redwings busy on the orchards' fallen fruit and the hawthorn and rowan berries. At times, the clamour of their cries is overpowering along the Sleet House footpath. A lovely sunny morning with a female kestrel hovering over the Ridge.

The men of the 'pipeline' are restoring the earth on the Ridge. In time, it should look little different from the surrounding slopes.

The vista of these woods from the bank top is glorious. Birds and tractor drivers very busy this morning. I'm going the rounds of the spindle trees today; the showers of coral-pink and orange berries are a lovely sight that no camera can do justice to. Spindle bark is attractive also, and I've photographed the largest tree here – which nevertheless is quite small!

The freshly green honeysuckle leaves are opening in the undergrowth.

85

It is always a small miracle to me – their appearance when most other leaves are withered on the twig.

Wednesday 18 November
1.10 a.m. Sitting in the shade on the steep slope near the 'grandfather' cherry – moonlight all around and a fox just ahead. Everywhere here is undermined with burrows of all descriptions, from rabbit to ancient badger. Near by was the foxcubs' den where I watched so often this spring. Moonlight slants through the restless branches and softly touches the leaf-strewn ground; it heightens the strange contortions of the old cherry bark just ahead. This tree leans at an angle, but still gives forth blossom and is very much alive.

The fox has pounced on a small rodent (wood mouse?) that jumps high in the air and is swallowed. (Notice foxes often do this, almost playing with a small dead catch.) The fox has moved nearer me and is listening intently – he can hear something below the leaves. Up on hind legs he swivels, large ears taking in every sound. He looks like a dancer turning on his toes; then a pounce, and this time I can see what he has – plump body, soft little ears, a bank vole. That also is chewed a bit before swallowing. Then he moves out of my line of vision, snapping at a moth that blunders near him.

I've come down on to the shaded Wildflower Path. One of the tawny pair sounds as it flies low over Long Field in the moonlight – its mate

86

answers, a long fluting tremulous wave of sound. Briarmead by moonlight – how does one describe it? This silver ribbon of a lane, barred with tall tree shadows falling across.

Friday 20 November
2 a.m. A mad, wild night with gale force winds both at sea and inland. Wind in the branches is deafening; scarcely any rain. Visibility on the whole very good. Stars appear briefly and are gone. Five large shapes (swans or geese) are flying on the wind but are having a hard time of it. Sudden gusts are plucking and snatching at the figures struggling past. They are *very* low in the air (and soundless beneath the wind's roar). Whether their lack of height is due to their struggle up from the valley to the highpoint of Great Chantry, or whether they are trying to avoid the force of the gale, I don't know. It hardly looks from where I stand that they will clear the tree tops of the Bank Sett, but they do – and I'm left with an impression of size and strength and white face flashes, but can't be certain of the last. Surely they weren't Canada geese? Have never seen any in the neighbourhood.

Stayed a while longer, but no other bird or beast seems to be braving the elements tonight. Walked slowly back through the woods towards the Main Pond. Dry and protected in the leeward side under the trees. Stopped close by the 'swap-shop' area (my nickname for the open space just off this path which is a favourite sharing-out spot with night visitors). Had a curious feeling I wasn't alone, but not really apprehensive, just puzzled. Walked slowly – and silently, thanks to the wind outside – round to the opening. Took a deep breath and looked through. Had to smile – the geese had beaten me to it. Snug and sheltered in the space, five beautiful birds preening and cleaning, one rubbing its face along the ground, first one side, then the other. Occasionally making little noises amongst themselves. One rising up to shake its wings and stretch them for a moment above its body before folding them to rest once more. And they *are* Canada geese – large with black head and long black neck and distinctive white face flash.

Left them to enjoy their well-earned rest. If this weather continues, no one is likely to come to these woods in daylight, so they should be safe enough.

Monday 23 November
10.15 a.m. Wind still very strong, so am spending a few hours in the Yewtree Grove where it's quiet and peaceful. Amongst all the other birds busy in this sheltered spot is a hawfinch feeding on the scarlet berries. Notice they seem to like the cherry *stones* from the geans in this wood, cracking them easily in their powerful beaks. I like the shy hawfinch greatly and only wish we had more of them in Ashcroft Woods. Sam

87

Mercer has ringed eleven here between 1975 and 1980. He erects his nets round the Main Pond and also at the spring. (See from his list that his most-ringed bird in this woodland is the redpoll, with a total of 1,218!)

Sunday 29 November
Foxes have dug out at many places in preparation for the spring. The interesting tree-root den at the Potato Dump is one. It's noticeable that mice, voles, foxes – and badgers – make no attempt to move, hide or disguise their excavated earth. Coming here I saw the debris from six tiny holes in the bank of Madden Lane; all fresh and plain to see by any predator. The badgers haven't settled so far at the View Sett though they have dug out more and used dung pits. On the whole, it would be better if they don't settle here, though, of course, I've no way of judging whether where they come from is safer than Ashcroft Woods or not.

As always in damp conditions, the moles have also been digging out or, rather, digging up in the undergrowth of this woodland! Watched a molehill being formed this morning – amazing what you can see by just staying still awhile.

WINTER 1981–82

Monday 7 December 1981
1.10 a.m. Mild, windless night with cloud blanketing the stars. Watched and listened to the Holmoak tawnies hunting over Ingrims Fields. Water lying on the fields. Each furrow is a miniature canal, a neatly straight band of light, identical to those on either side. Have seen three foxes. Trailed one from the Enclosed Path down into Prosser's Wood. Very *quiet* fox-wise. They seem to make most noise on cold, frosty, clear nights: then it is possible to differentiate between individuals' barking.

The day began with vivid blue skies and high wind. But from mid-morning onwards, a curious orange light covered the earth due to *brown* scurrying clouds blotting out the sun. Very eerie.

Wednesday 9 December
Wonderful night. At 1.20 a.m., a fantasy world of white with a near-full moon that's covered with a slight haze. The snow has frozen in the breeze

and crunches softly underfoot. Since the trees have shed their leaves, the tawnies (still only one pair, plus the young bird) are hunting in the woods once more, and not over the open fields. Near the Main Pond, watched a pair of foxes I had trailed from the Ridge. They were turning over the moss balls there to find the beetles, larvae and insects sheltered underneath. Every so often, the dogfox would stop his search and come behind the vixen to smell her – upon which she would spin round and growl. When his attentions became too pressing, she snapped. She clearly is not yet on heat, though they keep together. Noticed in previous winters that the vixens are receptive about mid-January, although a dogfox will try to mate from early December onwards.

These two foxes are glorious in their winter coats. A wonderful experience to stand unseen – the cold forgotten – and watch them hunting amidst the bracken. The perfect animals beautifully adapted – large ears turning to catch the slightest sound, their every aspect vital and alert to culminate in a high pounce, ears forward, on to their unsuspecting prey.

Now, in the distance, another fox barks and my two stand quietly listening. Then the dog barks back, a longer sound. Each bark rises and falls, rises and falls, and ends on a higher rise, thus ⌒⌒⧸ . A pause of a few seconds, and a similar bark. The vixen stays silent and still in the bracken. All is noiseless as they watch and wait in the moonlight. Then the barking stranger sounds again and this time nearer. Whereupon my dogfox (and it *is* the male) screams. A long-drawn eerie cry ending in a rasp (though I probably wouldn't have heard the rasp if I wasn't so near). He screams again and again, each sound a penetrating wail. He's taken a stand on the wall of the ancient boundary ditch and from that vantage point is giving voice. Body pushing forward, ears flattened against his head, and *tail curling upwards*, the whole animal stiff and inflexible. Now he has stopped screaming and his mate runs up the slope to stand next to him, both listening intently for any sound. But none comes. In the silence, I notice for the first time that a wind has got up – the branches above our heads are creaking and rubbing together. Apparently satisfied that the challenge or threat has not been taken up, my pair of animals, led by the dog, pass close by the holly under which I stand, and out of sight. (As she passed, I noticed that the vixen has a good deal of white to her tail – not a tip, but several inches.)

Walking home across the Ridge, and the snow gives an ideal light by which to see. Standing gazing down from the highest point of the scree slope, the scene below is magical; the wind blowing in my face bites deep, stinging eyes and lips: time, 4.50 a.m.

Came out in daylight to photograph trees etc. Though sky leaden, snow gives excellent light. Found myself at the boundary ditch where the dogfox screamed and thought I'd follow the double trail to see a) if they are denning together, and b) just where. Clear track evidence shows

90

they both continued hunting after they left the Main Pond area. Near the View Path, I found a dead weasel with fox prints, suggesting that one animal had killed and discarded it and the other had come up and inspected the prey, only to reject it also. Weasels have a musky odour and, like shrews, tend to be killed and left.

The trails curved back and forth and, with one fox following the other, a steady pace round the frozen field to – their den at the Potato Dump! Two trails leading in and none out. Now I know who lives there. Frozen yellow urine stains both here and at intervals along the route – also scats deposited on prominent objects or places. Their territory is well marked against intruders.

Sunday 13 December

Following Friday's snow, we now have eight inches – quite a record here for early December. Have never known it so cold. Took Ross's little thermometer with me and on High Ridge at 2.30 a.m. it registered –12°C. Snow very deep and frozen hard – walking is an odd sensation – and my boots make no impression on its gleaming, flawless surface. Everything is white – sky, ground, trees, bushes; nothing stirs in this petrified landscape. My hot breath as it cools makes my face ache with pain. Involuntarily, the eyes narrow to slits; the snow visibility gives a clarity that hurts. Nothing moves – no wind, no bird, no beast, no sound. The end of the world.

Tuesday 15 December

The great thaw – very dangerous conditions, as at night it freezes again. Water, water everywhere. The Bourne has broken from its narrow confines and surged over the land. Elsewhere, especially in the south-west, the situation far worse – livestock drowned; people isolated for days without electricity and heating; some found after the snow dead in their marooned cars. Still very cold, but more bearable.

Came across many dead birds, especially in the undergrowth where they had crept for shelter, but had frozen. On Ingrims Fields, I discovered seven dead skylarks (must have been many more), once frozen to the earth but now limp, wet and bedraggled. A dead male pheasant near the Chantry, blackbird, brambling, a goldcrest in the Yewtree Grove, two long-tailed tits – the list seems endless. Doubtless, they will soon be eaten by the surviving animals of the region.

Birds very noisy and *bold*; now they can feed again, they are busy finding grass seeds etc.; birches very popular. Near the 'grandfather' cherry, I stopped to admire the butcher's broom berries, bright splashes of colour. Tucked in at the stalk bases, amongst a tuft of grass, discovered three dead wrens huddled together for warmth – such tiny birds must quickly lose their body-heat.

Walking homeward at 3.30 p.m. saw a fox in the orchard by Sleet House. Moved closer and watched it searching and finding apples in the

91

long grass. Its foraging brought it close to the horse-chestnut trees, and by the hedge there, it turned up and ate three conkers. Not seen foxes eat these before, though sweet chestnuts are a firm favourite with both badgers and foxes.

Tuesday 22 December
It has been snowing for forty-eight hours, though not nearly so cold as 12/13 December. Have been fox-trailing at night and tracking during daylight hours. I find the snow conditions irresistible and the difficulties involved in closely following the animal at night in a snow-bright landscape (when I'm wearing clothes that are meant for the dark) a great challenge that requires foresight and ingenuity. Very many small birds dead, also fieldfares and redwings. I've never seen so many crows searching the countryside, and seagulls – the latter even in the woods. Saw two attack and kill a pied wagtail that offered little resistance (weak or sick). The gulls then fought noisily and viciously over the corpse.

Found a dead dogfox that had huddled for warmth in the ancient boundary ditch that runs between the Main and Aspen Paths.

Friday 25 December
Snow upon snow. Climbing the Ridge is quite a tricky business nowadays, especially since these slopes are used for tobogganing. Have to keep going or you slip backwards on the polished surface. If you can't stop slipping, it's best to twist round and come down on your rear – a lot less painful than your face ... then start climbing up once more!

On the open fields, only the top two inches of snow are frozen, so silent walking, and therefore fox-trailing, is impossible; have to admit myself beaten. Nevertheless, was able to watch a vixen eating dead birds. Two she dug out well under the snow, and what appeared to be a blackbird she found dead under the hedge by the beehives. Never known the birds so hard hit, but then conditions are extreme. For every one I see dead, there must be many more in this area that are eaten or hidden by further snow – rather a disquieting thought. Went up to my armpits in a drift at the bottom of Great Chantry Field. My own fault – had great difficulty getting out.

I was at the side of the field above the Oak Dell writing this at 7.35 a.m. when close by me appeared some dark, crumbly earth thrown up above the snow! What marvels these moles are; they never cease to delight me. I stayed crouching in the snow, notebook on knee, whilst two molehills were formed. When all was still once more, I ran my fingers through the nearest. What an experience to see and feel soft earth again amidst so much snow!

Saturday 26 December
The fog, which had been dense since about 2.10 a.m. lifted quite unexpectedly, to reveal stars twinkling amidst the trees' bare branches.

Heard the tawnies calling so persistently that I was able to trace and observe them. Since the numbers of these owls are so reduced in this woodland, this pair seem to have extended their territory. Very happy to see they have survived the bitter weather. Don't think my young tawny (Old Barn area) has – haven't heard or seen any sign of him since 9 December.

Shooting began 7.05 a.m. Coming out of these woods just after dawn, saw hare tracks in the snow leading on to the field. Idly followed them since they seemed so fresh. Here the brussels sprout tops just showed above the snow, and clearly the hare had stopped to nibble and sometimes to dig down a little, and sample the greenstuff. Came suddenly upon two animals. Nearest me, a stoat crouched behind a white hummock (how conspicuous they are in snow), and a few feet further from us, the owner of the tracks. Both were aware of me simultaneously, and both moved at speed. The hare with beautiful kangaroo-like grace, the stoat bounding off into the tree fringe. Here I lost his tracks (stoat prints tend to be in threes, or sometimes two superimposed on two) as well as the animal, as the trees often drip moisture during daylight hours and mar the snow's smooth surface.

Wednesday 30 December
Most of the snow has vanished now in this milder, damp atmosphere. Many trees in this woodland have been broken or felled by their recent snow covering. The Chantry is the most affected with giant beeches strewn about the ground. Jew's ear fungus much in evidence here. (Found a very thin, dead dogfox – no external injury – probably due to weather.)

At the View Sett, clear signs of badger occupation. It has only been used as temporary (overnight, as it were) living quarters until now, but today see freshly used dung pits, entrances cleared of leaves and debris, bulbs dug up and half-eaten, and fresh claw marks on two elder trunks. Perhaps surprisingly, the 'grandfather' cherry still stands. No noticeable deterioration due to the prolonged snow and sub-zero conditions – no recent branches snapped and it still leans at the same angle.

Crossed Briarmead and went on to John Shaw's land. The pear orchard has been a source of great interest to me throughout this month. Though the sound fruit was duly picked and carted away, there have been a lot of pears (windfalls, dropped or damaged) lying in the grass under the snow. Whether the foxes digging down for them have alerted the birds to what is below, I don't know, but certainly the redwings, fieldfares, blackbirds, starlings, and song and mistle thrushes have exploited the situation. The redwings with their black-tipped yellow beaks, yellow eye-stripes and red/brown wings, are colourful birds, although the fieldfare is the larger and, in this orchard at any rate, seems to be the most dominant thrush, routing the others – and even the starlings. These birds will leave an apple or pear looking near perfect, but

93

pick one up when the marauders have dispersed and your fingers will go straight through the hollowed fruit – only the skin has been left intact.

Today as it was growing dusk, I approached the orchard, and through the monocular watched at a little distance. Think the place was more alive with birds than ever – possibly the thaw had revealed pears previously overlooked. Their squabbling, twittering, squealing quarrels as first one kind of thrush, then another, secured possession of a favourite pear only to be outmanoeuvered by a more aggressive opportunist, were deafening. Strangely, I think cock blackbirds are perhaps the greatest aggressors – they seem to be fearless and will even chase a routed fieldfare. Had to smile. Whilst these activities had been in full swing, a greenfinch was quietly approaching a pear, almost disappearing inside the shell, peck-pecking, and just as unobtrusively, passing on to the next. Was almost certain he was taking the pear seeds – had to admire his audacity.

Don't know for how long I stood watching when there was an explosion (or rather, several nearly simultaneous). Next, some birds had taken to the air leaving many of their kind lying amongst the rotting fruit. The five shotgun owners who had been standing inside the hedge began to put the bodies into a sack. I approached and spoke to them but was threatened and surrounded. They weren't English – Cypriot? Difficult to understand, though their meaning was clear enough – I was in the way. Tried following them but they split up, so tailed the sack-carrying man down across the fields on to the road. On the farmland in the dark, he twice tried to give me the slip and once attempted to waylay me – but my nightvision was a great deal better than his, and I didn't step into puddles like he did, either! After following him some distance along the road, he eventually ran for a bus just leaving a stop some way ahead, so I lost him.

Saturday 2 January 1982
It has been raining steadily since New Year's Eve. Ponds in Ashcroft Woods very full and the ice on the Main Pond has only thawed around the bank edges.

At the ancient boundary ditch below the Main Path, I found spots of fresh blood shining on the leaves. The trail led me to a wood-pigeon peppered through the left wing and body, and bleeding freely. In its clumsy efforts to avoid me, it fell over a twig and lay beak down in the ground struggling feebly in a gush of blood. Put it out of its pain by breaking its neck. Not something I find easy to do, but to leave a creature in pain I find even harder. Had only gone a short distance farther when I discovered a lesser spotted woodpecker similarly maimed. Was able to get close, but not so near as to catch it, and it disappeared trailing a wing into a bramble thicket. Sometimes I thoroughly dislike my own kind.

Thursday 7 January
I have been collating my fox observations collected over the past fifteen months, based mainly on systematic trailing, though casual sightings have also been included. The following may appear to be inconsequential traits, I suppose, to many observers but are facets of their behaviour I find most interesting:

1) In 242 separate observations from September 1980 until now, involving eighteen different animals, only *one* fox preferred to use its left front paw as opposed to its right to turn over something it was unsure of; to scrape under a log etc. That is to say, only one was left-handed and seventeen were right-handed. (N.B. And of those eighteen foxes – eleven dogs and seven vixens – eight are now dead: four vixens and two dogs shot, and two dogfoxes frozen/starved to death.)

2) During the past snowy weather, I didn't see any food cached by foxes. Anything edible obtained by hunting, foraging or carrion was either eaten where found or, in cases where the animal was uneasy in its surroundings, taken to a more sheltered position and eaten. However, during plentiful months of last year, observed food hidden (often ineptly – e.g. part of rabbit cached with hind leg sticking up through leaf litter!). Once my foxes were known to me, it became increasingly obvious that two out of three owners of the cached surplus were not the fox that retrieved them. Noticed, also, that the fox burying its food, once it had pushed the earth/debris over it doglike with its nose, often though not always urinated on the spot. If this was intended to say 'Keep off', it wasn't particularly effective. Three times during this period, observed an animal retrieve its *own* cache, only to re-bury it a little further off.

3) Have found *on the whole* that however much a fox may wander within – or without – its territory, it seems to return to the same part to sleep although its actual 'bed' (made doglike by turning round several times in long grass, bracken etc.) varies from morning to morning. Thus I can generally trace it in the same area though not the same spot (which is very useful for observing it asleep) – which brings me to . . .

4) Foxes when not denning (denning occurs mainly with vixens in whelp and with cubs growing to independence) favour a slight elevation (e.g. behind a tree trunk, halfway up a bank) and sleep facing into the wind so that scent may be borne *to* them, and not *from* them. They do not like a biting wind any more than horses – or humans! And unless suffering from extreme cold (like the one I discovered dead in the boundary ditch during the snowy, bitter weather), tend to avoid sleeping in ditches or any place where they haven't the advantage of slight elevation for scent and sight.

5) If a fox finds dense, safe cover, e.g. bracken, it will sleep fairly soundly, though never so completely as the domestic dog. In uncertain, poorly protected countryside, however, it will cat-nap or sleep in snatches, starting up with ears alert to look carefully around every half minute to two minutes or so.

95

6) Foxes tend to sleep curled round in a ball with bushy brush over forepaws, nose and muzzle. This apparent covering over of the nose, however, certainly doesn't mean its sense of smell is impaired in any way. (N.B. Looking at and handling the tails of dead foxes, what is immediately apparent is how lightweight this long, cylindrical appendage is – no wonder it appears to 'float' horizontally after a galloping or loping animal. The vertebrae are slight, the length of individual hairs considerable, and a gentle puff of the breath easily blows these hairs apart.)

7) The only weather conditions that seem to deter foxes from going their rounds are storms and gales. This appears to be a definite fact as I've managed to go out in every available lightning/thunderstorm and gale at night this past year. Have found these are the only occasions that my area is remarkable for its non-foxy sighting, sounds and signs. Must conclude, therefore, that they lie up in such conditions. However, these chronic extremes apart, nothing else discourages them from their activities; not snow, wind, rain, fog, frost, cold – or bright moonlight. I add the last as some writers say moonlight puts off foxes and badgers, whereas I have found that neither is deterred. They *do* react with more caution certainly – but then so do I in bright visibility. We all keep to the dark side of the hedgerow and take advantage of the shadowy places. But the full moon stops none of our nocturnal activities!

Friday 8 January
Started snowing at 1 a.m. and has continued steadily. Now, at 3 p.m., there are six inches of snow on the ground and it is still snowing with strong gusts causing considerable drifting, temperature –3°C. Two hours after it began falling, I watched a fox successfully locate and kill a vole under the snow. Have noticed during December's snow, however, that with four or more inches lying on the ground, foxes are unable to find them, so the vole's high-pitched squeaking must be blanketed from the predator's acute hearing. The snow must also hamper the fox's sense of smell.

Watched Joe (the flank-marked badger that is now living at the View Sett) return home early at 3.10 a.m., powdered in white. His parents originated from the other side of the valley and were well aware of my presence. Indeed, my scent must have been everywhere then, as now. When he last was denning in this area (early autumn 1980, over a year ago), he had Josephine and the three 'buster' cubs with him also. This is the longest I've known him absent. It is good to see him back, though he is a loner now, so wonder what happened to his mate. Disregarding his snow-covering, he is getting an 'old' look and to describe his gait as stiff in the joints wouldn't be fanciful. I calculate he is now around ten years old.

Sunday 10 January
Missed the total eclipse of the moon last evening owing to the snow-laden sky. (Rather than be invisible, the full moon should have appeared as a dull red disc due to sunlight being bent by the earth's atmosphere, lighting up the shadow.) However, the moon has kept me company all night since the sky cleared and now at 5 a.m. it is a bright disc still high in the heavens.

Deep drifts over the fields, some with frozen crests that resemble waves about to crash down on a beach. Watched a Holmoak Lane tawny on top of the cattle's open-sided fodder barn. It has already killed and eaten a mouse and now is perched, feathers puffed out, in the moonlight. May appear to be asleep, but in reality is listening for the slightest sound below – not much misses a tawny. Wonder where its mate is?

Joe hasn't been abroad since yesterday's snowfall. No prints any-where; the snow around all entrances quite untouched except for a small bird's tracks under the holly tree and the delicate prints of – a bank vole? – by the cherry tree entrance. What a sensible chap Old Joe is – with his layer of fat accumulated in the plenty of autumn, a badger can go for days without venturing forth.

Tuesday 12 January
2.10 a.m. Determined to get down the hillside to the Water Meadows, though the wind on the Warby side has built up great drifts, some towering many feet above my head. Beautiful wind-made shapes –

minarets and castellations, then a sudden smooth area with its centre a thin twisting corkscrew three feet high and frozen rock-hard. A very desolate snowscape with the moaning wind and the eerie scream of a fox from above me in the Chantry.

At Newby the snow is lying thigh-deep and the cows have been moved. The Bourne is frozen here – without the murmur of water, it seems a different place, with only the line of old pollarded willows to mark its course. Caught sight of a fox tearing at something in the snow; large bird, feathers everywhere. Even *Vulpes vulpes* is having difficulty finding food. Though they hunt also by day in winter, the clear skies and wind are giving us intense cold and heavy frosts on snow.

Before this fox finished at the carcass, he scat-marked close by. Gave him time to move well away, then went over to find a partly eaten grey heron lying frozen in the snow. The fox must have had difficulty in tearing open the chest cavity and gut, unless another had been there before him. Head and neck quite untouched. Looking at the snow signs, the heron had been eaten where it died. No sign that it had been moved from the slight shelter of a beech. Whether it had died there from cold and starvation, or been killed, I can't say.

Wednesday 13 January
1.25 p.m. and bright sunshine after a night and early morning of freezing fog. Came across several fresh molehills in the undergrowth. Was intrigued to find a hole close by from which tracks led, winding back and forth amongst the trees. These prints were clear, recent and most distinctive, with a 'drag' mark between them; have not seen any quite like them in the snow before. The hind showed as normal five-toed prints, but the front were large clear impressions of five claws only – no pads. Decided they were probably mole tracks though wondered what it was doing roaming about in the snow. The obvious answer was to follow them. They twisted back and forth for a surprising distance, so much so, in fact, that I had quite convinced myself no mole would have gone so far above ground, when I saw him – and unfortunately he saw me or, more likely, heard or felt the ground vibrations I made.

It transpired later that a fox had been shot a short time earlier and it was *on* the dead animal that I first saw the mole who, at my approach, hastily (and with an almost breast-stroke motion) scrambled off and dug down into the nearest snow. In no time at all, the mole had disappeared, which, considering the state of the topsoil, was no mean feat. Stayed still a long while, hoping it might return, but apart from distant shots deeper in the wood and the twitterings of a flock of siskins and redpolls in their quest for seeds from a nearby clump of birches, all was still.

Later I had a careful look at the dead fox, which was still quite warm and limp – one of my 'regular' foxes. Of the original eighteen animals recorded, observed and trailed since September last, now only nine remain – six dogs and three vixens. The fox's body was lying hunched on

98

its right side in the snow. From its tracks, it had jumped over the stump near by – shot in mid leap – and fallen where it now lay. It had been shot at close quarters so that the charge had had little time to splay out; in consequence, most had gone straight into the skull. A quick death though a messy one. Thus, the left side of the head, left eye and neck were bloody and the mole had clearly gone to the source of blood. Its sense of smell rather than sight had guided it, as approaching from the tail end of the carcass it had climbed aboard, so to speak, and gone the fox's length until it reached the neck, and had chewed there. It would have been far less effort for so small a creature to have gone round, but this it had not done.

I have read that moles will eat carrion if hungry, but have never witnessed this before. Feel it must have been pure luck that this one found the shot animal as, apart from the distance, the erratic tracks weaving in and out don't suggest the mole was on a scent trail! Wonder if they normally move above ground much. Have seen moles apparently searching at the field edges in rain and have concluded this is due to the worms' habit of surfacing during a downpour. Today, the snow has shown me how far a mole *can* travel, and still have the energy to make a quick escape.

Walked on to Briarmead which is still blocked from just above the Wildflower Path to the wood entrance. The snow blown over the fields above has drifted into the little lane which is now on a level with its banks. It has been like this since last Friday which suits me fine – how selfish can I get! The great advantage to me, of course, is that I don't have to be alert for night visitors. This snow-bound wood is mine – and the animals'.

Monday 18 January
3.25 a.m. Damp, mild night. Watched the old badger Joe finishing the carcass of the fox shot last Wednesday. Don't know whether it was he who eviscerated the body but he probably has been here before. Most animals seem to go for the entrails first. This morning, he has literally turned the body skin inside out in his efforts to get at the last fresh remnants. It's been interesting to see him do this. He reached inside the now floppy skin, hung on to something inside and shook it hard. Then, holding down the reversed hide with his front paws, he stripped the remaining morsels off with his teeth, rolling up his flexible snout as he did so. Then, carefully and loudly, he snuffled over the bare skin – just in case anything was missed! The head of the fox has disappeared – may have been carried off by another scavenger. The brush, body fur/skin and part of the vertebrae are all that now remain.

Friday 22 January
12.45 a.m. Slight frost, clear skies, no moon. Everywhere saturated – only a few patches of snow still lingering. These past four nights, have

99

observed and trailed the Dump foxes – they mated on the twentieth, *very* noisy, in strong contrast to previous mating by Chantry pair, witnessed last year. Also trailed the Prosser's Wood pair. For some time past, I have been keeping a separate record of all the foxes of my area. Last year I chose one pair to concentrate on particularly – from mating, birth, rearing and dispersal of cubs, only to have them disappear at the crucial cub-exploring stage. Therefore, this year I will concentrate on two pairs of foxes, hoping to have better luck.

Saw Joe foraging round the View Sett, 2.20 a.m. To my surprise, he musked me – the first time since he has returned to this place. [When Joe and his parents came here to forage from the opposite side of this valley, they crossed a main road to do so. In time, I ceased to see his parents, but the young boar came to live in Ashcroft Woods, take a mate and have cubs of their own. Early on I found I could follow him, approach him or have him approach me. Eventually he musked me though I was careful not to become so familiar to his mate, since I was never sure of the wisdom of this.]

Now he was moving off at a steady pace across Corbett's fields. Have never seen exactly where he goes when he crosses the Motorway, so decided now was the time to find out. When it was in the process of being built, Joe still crossed back to visit his old haunts and still he crosses in the same place, although a floodlit gantry has been erected just here! He reached the bank, foraged about there nearly thirty minutes taking no notice of the traffic occasionally passing, then, without warning, he suddenly began to cross the 'lanes'. He didn't exactly hurry himself and gave me some anxious moments. Though the Motorway isn't busy at that time of night, a few heavy lorries come through, and with all the lights seen head-on, the speed of such vehicles is difficult to gauge at first, coming out of the night. Even which lane a lorry is in can be confusing till you get used to it. This first time I waited until he had crossed, then followed suit, picking up his trail again on the Warby side. His passing through the frosty grass gave it a bruised look, and soon I was following closely once more – up the bank, through a thicket and curved steadily round past grazing horses. Joe was out to get from A to B, no foraging now. (It's far easier to trail a badger than a fox, but I suppose once you've successfully fox-trailed, you can trail most things.)

We came out to the back of a big old house and an equally ancient dustbin – the latter was certainly where Joe's interest lay! I have never seen a badger overturn a dustbin before; the clatter was deafening in the quietness. He just reared up on his hind legs, flicked up the lid with his snout – it wasn't on properly in any case – and tried to reach down to the contents well below. He growled in frustration and then rocked the dustbin, bear-like, before pushing it away from him. He didn't wait for the noise to die away before he was nosing amongst the garbage. Clearly he wasn't expecting to be disturbed. I *was* intrigued to see how he went about scavenging. Tins he held down with his left front paw and scooped

100

in with a long-clawed right – he's right-handed. Notice he didn't put his snout in any – has he been cut before? Badgers generally have a mania for sticking their noses in things. He throughly enjoyed potato peelings, searching around for any stray bits like a vacuum cleaner! Things well wrapped he simply picked up and shook – then ran after the contents. Some very gone-off sausages were top of the menu, quickly and noisily gobbled up and the area snuffled over well. I couldn't tell what some of the things were that he ate and at one point he chewed on something that was later discarded. When he moved off with a prize bone to chew amongst the shrubs, I had a look at the discarded object – a man's old leather shoe with teethmarks and spittle clear. No accounting for taste!

Dustbin session over, Old Joe trotted steadily up the hillside to the tree-line. I followed at a little distance – his grey, swaying bulk very clear to see. Had a surprise at the trees. There's a steep bank here, obviously an old badger sett. There's been an earth fall, very recent, snow perhaps or flooding, and a great section has come down exposing the inner tunnelling and chambers. Joe nosed around, had a half-hearted dig but clearly found it too muddy and stood looking over towards Ashcroft Woods. This could be where he's been living until his recent return to the View Sett (see entries for 29 November and 30 December 1981). What a shame it's subsided; he's much safer from human interference here. The dustbin owners probably think it's a fox that explores their refuse!

It's not only the trunks of elders that badgers like for claw-cleaning; they'll use the corners of old garden sheds too! Standing upright to tear downwards on the rotten planking, he spent some minutes there as long slivers of wood dropped around him to the ground. The marks left showed clearly as lighter patches. Then he made tracks for home, coming out on the Main Road slightly lower down. He's *very* familiar with it here – quite evident he's on home ground. It's nearly 5 a.m. and the traffic is increasing. He's going to re-cross that Motorway but I haven't the nerve, so leave him to it and go down into Warby.

(Spoke to the owner of this place today and was given permission to go in the grounds. He told me the history of the house – very interesting.)

Tuesday 26 January
A very curious thing happened to me tonight. It has been raining hard the past eight hours, gusts of wind, but quite mild – ideal conditions for badger-/fox-trailing. I was crouching in the lee of the wood fringe, looking out over the Top Field and debating where I was most likely to find the Prosser foxes, when first the vixen, then the dog, appeared on the path. I had passed that way a short time earlier and they appeared to have my scent trail. The first animal cautiously looked around and at me, but didn't recognise what it saw (not unusual with foxes, if one stays perfectly still). It came on several paces. Then the dog reached its mate, caught my scent and froze. From their attitudes they were wary but not afraid; apprehensive, perhaps. We were almost of a height as they were

on the slightly elevated path, and I was crouched down, hands in pockets, head a little above knees. What happened then was unbelievable if you know foxes. Still with caution but not alarm, first one then the other skirted carefully round me, slowly and with backward glances – as foxes do a badger when they meet – and continued on their way through the rain. My presence was treated with respect – but not fear. Why – that is the question?

When I trail foxes throughout the night, they often travel in a circle and eventually re-cross their own scent trail – and mine. Often when worming in the rain along a field edge, they will retrace their steps and find my very recent scent, so they must be used to it. Shouldn't have thought, however, they would have reacted to me so calmly head on. Yet I feel very pleased. Surely that indicates I've reached a milestone in this fox-trailing? If anyone had said eighteen months ago this could happen, I'd have laughed!

(Should this ever occur again, will try making the soft 'mmmmmm' sound that I used as a contact with Vicky whenever we met. It's the sound the vixen makes at the mouth of the den to her young cubs, telling them of her return. There are great possibilities here.)

Wednesday 27 January

Fox call on Johnson's land, 2.22 a.m. ∧∧∧ < > 'Wow,

wow, wow' in quick succession; harsh, long-drawn bark dying away fast. Only at close range are the three 'wows' distinctly separable.

This is not an area I cover and therefore not a fox known to me, but the call is of interest, as after two winters' trailing and observing I know under what conditions it occurs. It's a dogfox with a vixen in tow and on the edge of its territory; it's warning off another dogfox.

Cold night, clouds moving fast in strong north wind. Alternate snow showers and clear periods. Visual clarity remarkable, can see to the horizon – no moon. The Dump foxes are hunting within sixteen feet of each other; occasionally one or other makes the soft contact bark. The territories of my two fox pairs – Dump and Prosser's Wood – run alongside at one point. There is no overlapping at this season, although this could be relaxed in the summer if rabbits are plentiful again, and the boundary is vocally, not physically defended.

These boundary clashes have included barking, screaming and the noise I call clattering, though there's probably a proper word for this jay-like sound. It's an obvious demarcation line to human eyes (often they're not), and even if I hadn't been present at so many challenge matches, the meeting of these territories would be clear from the abundance of ritual scat- and scent-marking. Both these dogs have their mates and ample territories thanks to the elimination of so many of their kind, so have no need to come to physical grips. This cannot be said of their other

boundaries where vixenless dogs (last year's cubs) have a lot to gain with displays of active aggression. This confrontation will soon be at an end now. The oestrus of both vixens (a three-week period of which a mere three to four days can prove fertile) is ended.

The mating observed last winter was almost entirely a silent one (11 January 1981) and I did not know the age of the vixen. In contrast, the mating seen this winter was, on the vixen's part, very noisy – one could say painfully so. This vixen was born last year and it is her first mating ... which might explain the apparent paradox.

Thursday 28 January
At the risk of sounding trite, there's a great deal of apparent affection between mated foxes. Though they may forage and hunt separately they will constantly come together throughout the night with much face and mouth licking and jumping around each other. They enjoy each other's company, resting together and mutually grooming. Even adult foxes will play.

Just now, after barking softly to her, the Prosser dogfox has brought a stick to his mate and puppy-like is asking for a game – bottom skyward, brush waving and head on one side. She, however, is more intent on food and, giving him a little nudge, returns to her search amongst the grass tussocks. He comes and sits on his haunches near her, then hears and pounces on a vole. Now occurs something I've never seen before in this situation. The vixen looks up eagerly and advances two paces. He inclines his head, small rodent in mouth, his tail upwards. He's almost inviting her to take it, but she hesitates. Then the dogfox deliberately drops it so that it falls between them. She finds it, chews and goes to swallow but changes her mind. Suddenly, *she's* in the stick-playing attitude, vole in mouth, rear in air, tail wagging. Then they're off, playing chase and bumping each other. They end up almost next to me by the trees. The vixen one paw on his shoulder, her mouth open and tongue lolling – he looking up in her face. Where the vole is I wouldn't know! Probably swallowed – she's forgotten all about food. Now they're off again, running together like carefree pups. There *is* affection here – and companionship.

Later, walking down Briarmead at 2.20 a.m., thoughts on foxes, hands thrust deep in pockets against the cold, when a car's headlights appeared above the top of the lane's little hump just ahead. Heard a shout, had a glimpse of three men inside as I jumped on to the bank. To my amazement, the car reversed at speed down the lane and out of sight – never seen a vehicle back so fast. Wonder what they were coming up here for?

Friday 29 January
Dull, overcast, cold morning with slight wind. The Dump vixen has moved home although I'll still call them the Dump foxes for easy reference. She and her mate have established themselves in an old entrance of the View Sett. They shared the digging, one working whilst the other rested and groomed. Like badgers – and Wendy – they are very fastidious where their paws are concerned, biting at the claws to loosen dirt and licking the pads meticulously. Moreover, the fox, unlike the badger, has hair growing between the pads which can become encrusted when the soil is wet.

Though they are round the far side of the holly tree from Joe, I'm rather wondering what his reaction is going to be. Badgers and foxes do exist amicably side by side, but the badger here is old, rather short-tempered and very clean in his habits (except regarding dustbins perhaps!). However, the vixen may change her mind again before she whelps. Quite often the dogfox stays underground with her, but somtimes I'll find him lying up in a clump of ferns a short distance away. However, he is always around and if I sight one, the other is soon spied.

The pile of grain that was dumped last year just inside the wood has, with snow, thaw, and general deterioration, slowly subsided and so now

104

covers a far greater area than before from which small trees like hazel and elder protrude. No wonder the tawny pair hunt here at night so profitably. Today, I watched the comings and goings of several short-tailed voles. Their stumpy forms and small rounded heads are very attractive and give them a chubby look. This whole area is a spongy mass that springs back, moss-like, at the touch, and these little voles have a series of runs just below the surface. Nothing like having your home in a larder, instead of a larder in your home! Some grain is rotting, some still whole, but much has sprouted and they seem to prefer these fresh green blades.

Walking home, I watched a dogfox foraging – very obvious in his winter coat. They have a highly developed sense of touch. Saw this animal put his right front paw down lightly, move it along gently, and hold down a large black beetle. Notice they often catch insects like this. In fact, beetles are amongst the first prey a cub learns to catch – only at that age, they might pounce rather than hold down. The high pounce seems to be inborn right from the beginning of play – whether in creeping up on a litter-mate, or catching a fluttering leaf. A cub may lack accuracy at first (or co-ordination), but age and practice soon gives it experience, for this 'play' is for life.

Saturday 30 January
3.40 a.m. Saw the Prosser dogfox sitting under the lights in the tunnel grooming himself, one hind leg up in the air. Thought he made off up the grass verge to the fence of High Ridge, but after standing where he had been for a few moments, I saw a movement (the Motorway tunnel lights temporarily impair my nightvision) and discerned him standing there watching me from the verge. Another movement higher up the bank and the vixen was there too. Knelt on the tarmac in the middle of the road and made the soft 'mmmmmm' sound. Seemed to wait ages – the muffled noise of a car overhead – and I repeated the sound. The vixen came down to join her mate – a long pause. Didn't wish to frighten them off, but decided to experiment with the situation, so moved slowly over to the far pavement and began to walk silently along Madden Lane with High Ridge stretching away to my left. Halfway along I turned and looked back. Two figures still there in the light of the tunnel, one sitting on its haunches, the other standing by its side, and both watching me. Had to chuckle – the watcher, watched – the laugh's on me!

Cold, wet, overcast night. Raining steadily; the shine of water lying on the fields. Very good visibility. Somewhere under that lowering cloud layer is a thin-edged crescent moon. Gusty wind. Probably the foxes were using the tunnel to groom themselves in the dry – they're not stupid.

5.10 a.m. Saw Joe coming up from the Motorway at the View. He stopped to drink halfway across the field where erosion has caused a deep cleft in the hillside and water collects. Made me reflect how Wendy made

105

herself ill by drinking from contaminated puddles on Ingrims land. The vet after doing tests decided that was what had poisoned her. Fertilisers, chemicals, etc. can collect in rainwater and not disperse. It would have killed her but for his prompt action. Wonder how many badgers, foxes, birds die in this way?

The tunnel unoccupied as I returned home. Just wisps of gingery fur blowing gently in the wind.

Monday 1 February
1.10 a.m. Very mild, warm, overcast night. No wind – fox scent hangs heavy on the air. Visibility excellent; can see for a considerable distance. No fox vocalisation anywhere. In complete contrast, medley of tawny hoots and flutings amazingly beautiful. First listened to the Holmoak pair harmonising, then the pair that frequent Johnson's land round the Sleet House area. Found to my delight that a male tawny has taken over the vacancy of lower High Ridge and the Motorway side of Madden Lane.

Discovered whilst out walking yesterday afternoon that the tawny owls who frequent the Long Field/Wildflower Path and lower woods (better call them the Long Field pair) are roosting together in an ivy- and clematis-clad tree at the side of Briarmead – many pellets have collected on the bank below. Have stood on the lane for an hour listening to them tonight – surely the loveliest night music of them all. If I could choose only one bird's song, it would be these fluting variations on a tawny theme – played tremolo!

Haven't bothered to trail foxes tonight, but found the Dump pair just the same at their new home – the View Sett. The female, in typical finicky fashion, was still doing some minor alterations to the den. The dog, seemingly bored with the whole procedure, was rolling on his back, squirming and twisting, arching his spine and rubbing his shoulders against the tree roots. All this accompanied by grunts and heavy breathing until, satisfied, he stood up and shook himself thoroughly.

A movement by the creeper 'curtain', and the old badger had returned home. Don't know what happened to the dogfox (perhaps he felt discretion was the better part of valour), but his mate promptly vanished into her renovated den. Joe ambled over and snuffled round the entrance – he didn't seem unduly perturbed, merely a bit inquisitive. As he turned away from the den, there sounded the most extraordinary noise I've ever heard. The vixen emerged, still making the noise, ears backward and turned slightly showing their black backs (the threat gesture of the fox), legs stiff and taut, exaggerating her height. Never seen a fox threaten a badger before – nor have I heard that awful noise. It was nothing like their bark, scream or growl; in fact, it didn't sound fox-like at all. If I hadn't seen as well as heard, would have concluded it to be made by a large duck or goose in distress. Seemed to have three or four stresses to each phrase, the phrases rising to a gobble of a cadence that

106

broke off on a high note. Having stated her case, the vixen turned tail and bolted back into her den – leaving Joe looking as I felt, physically shattered! He stood staring vaguely into space, came to with a start, and pottered into his home. Have a feeling he's going to find his new neighbours rather wearing ...

Tuesday 2 February
This morning out in the sunshine checking the kills – mainly pigeon – made by the Prosser foxes earlier. One dead pigeon had been roosting near the Motorway fencing by the old beech stump. Three more pigeon killed at the Wheatfield Copse. Remains are all similar – scat-marked, sheared off primaries and assorted large feathers. All these kills were *shared*. The hunt at the Wheatfield Copse of particular interest because it was *co-ordinated*; the vixen stood on the higher bank, whilst her mate moved about below and along the bank. Roosting birds disturbed. Some flew off well clear of the higher ground; others at a very low angle. Vixen jumped and snapped at one, dropped it, snapped and stood holding another still flapping around her face, just as the dog came up from below, holding another.

Walking home in bright sunshine, the sky a vivid blue, birdsong all around. Ashcroft Woods look wonderful. Thought to cross Cullen Rise and there amongst the broom and bracken found a dead, shot fox. Watched a woodlark ascending into the blue, his song bubbling down to me far below. Never tire of pinpointing the near-stationary speck in the sky, wings beating as the melody pours forth. Then the abrupt silence as it plummets earthwards. When almost at ground level, they usually fly horizontally a short distance before dropping into the concealing grass.

Idly watched an earthworm making a wriggling retreat from a waterlogged furrow when something darted forward and grasped its threshing body halfway along. It was a weasel. The first bite cleaved the prey in two and, leaving the twisting tail, the weasel quickly ate the other half, starting at the severed end it was holding down. It was a weird sight to watch, the 'serpent' writhing across the weasel's head and upper body as it was eaten. A miniature St George and the Dragon with the roles reversed and St George the villain. Meanwhile, the tail end had fallen by the water and was nearly submerged. The weasel soon found it, however, and made short work of that. Had no idea they eat earthworms; this large one made a good-sized meal.

Wednesday 3 February
Frosty, starry night. Two-thirds full moon low in the sky, time 12.45 a.m. The only tawnies sounding are the Long Field pair. A moving fox over Warby way giving the 'wow-wow-wow' bark. There's human activity at the top of Briarmead, so keeping clear. Happened upon Joe at the Chantry, worming in the moist earth at the bottom of Great Chantry Field. He moved off down past the mistletoe tree, across the

107

meadow and so to the Main Road. Followed him to the farmland by the river. Joe was turning over the flints lying on the field and crunching – beetles, snails? He drank at the Bourne and had a brief scratching session on the bank. Didn't seem his usual self – appeared taut, edgy.

Getting very quiet now – and cold. No foxes or owls sounding here, just the river gurgling along. Joe has suddenly moved off at speed and I've just realised why he is uneasy. He's on another boar's territory. He's being chased across the field, hotly pursued by a growling, squealing, snorting individual, and they disappear over the brow of the slope. As the sounds die away and I'm left by the quiet of the river, I'm hoping Joe made it to safety – got a soft spot for the old fella!

Sunday 7 February
Near-full moon, bright sky with white clouds moving fitfully across. Joe caught a partridge in the Chantry tonight. It was roosting in the undergrowth there. He pulled the head off and ate it, then ripped into the chest. Feathers everywhere. Afterwards, he searched a long time round about although the others had run off under cover long since.

Notice with my two pairs of foxes that it is the vixens who are scent-marking the most now. This tallies with last year's findings. After mating, the dog will still defend his territory and scent-mark, but the vixen, once she has made a choice of den, proclaims in this way her ownership of the surrounding land, though it is a much smaller area within his. She will continue to do this if she has cubs up to the time when the litter begins to disperse. Then as the family group breaks up so she loses her interest in scent/scat-marking and both adults become loners again. (Each time she moves her cubs to a fresh den – whether through disturbance or fouling of the old – she will scent-mark the environs of the new earth in like manner.)

Raining now – Long Field tawny pair hunting by the Old Cherry Tree. With no competition from other owls, these have an extended range to the top of Briarmead. The tawny on High Ridge now has a mate and has similarly extended *his* territory to the back of the Ridge and the surrounding woodland. Trailed the Prosser foxes back to the scrubland on the upper Ridge. Nearly witnessed the end of one of these owls, for as a tawny dropped on to something in the grass, the dogfox sprang at the owl which flew clear just in time. Can appreciate that foxes not infrequently catch tawnies. *Vulpes vulpes* doesn't have it all his own way though, especially when fledglings are in the nest. Tawnies go for the eyes, and their talons, like their beaks, are adept at tearing.

Wednesday 10 February
Mild, sunny morning with slight wind. Woods full of sound as the birds sing out their territories. I am finding my two pairs of foxes very interesting. Nowadays, I generally let the Prosser foxes know I'm around and shall compare their activities with the others to see, amongst

108

other things, if my presence inhibits their behaviour. As far as I can tell, the Dump foxes are unaware of my trailing and observation of them;* plus the added bonus that the latter are at Old Joe's sett and the badger/vixen situation has potential, to say the least. I've never had it so good!

The winter-sown corn of Long Field is growing fast. Watched a rabbit colony well out on the field feeding here by moonlight about 2.30 a.m. They sometimes do this, though grazing far out by moonlight doesn't seem to be a regular occupation and normally they keep close to the hedgerow. Seen in a group, rabbits exhibit a whole range of emotions, the dominant 'boss' ones standing out from the nervy, inferior ones. Though theirs is a matriarchal society, this wasn't evident today. A dominant male was depositing a few pellets on a molehill and chinning a dead twig. It will be his mate, however, who determines where the warren will be and the other does will be subordinate to her. It's odd that we humans tend to look upon wild animals as free, whereas in reality their social structure can be far more rigid than ours – their entire lives contained in a very small area.

It was whilst standing under the geans, monocular-gazing, that I saw the Dump dogfox appear halfway down the steep slope of the Bank Sett and almost opposite me across the width of the Long Field. No sign of his vixen, though I dared not move to check the area properly and she's not far away as a rule. You can see where the rabbits have been grazing – a big half-circle spreading out from the field edge with the shoots almost nibbled to soil level. One 'carefree' rabbit does a little run and a sidewards jump which is taken up by three others that become quite skittish. This causes a general move across the field to the Wildflower Path. Here the fresh shoots and varied herbage which are pushing through the soil make a tasty change. And the fox has moved down the Bank to disappear behind a fallen branch stretched out on the corn. Then I was aware of his mate as she slipped past me on the up-and-over path – her belly to ground, shoulder blades protruding skywards, head and ears strained forward, pupils large and round, intently watching one amongst the nearest group of rabbits.

It's almost too easy. The rabbit, sprung on from behind and bitten through the upper spine, hangs limp in the vixen's jaws. The others, amid a general thud, thudding of hind feet, scuts held upright clear in the moonlight, stream back across the field. A high-pitched scream – almost human in its pain or terror – echoes over the field and is abruptly cut off as the dogfox too made his kill. The vixen below me dropped her rabbit, and, nosing it over to expose the belly, tore into it. The warm smell of blood hung on the night air. Occasionally, one of the foxes would look up from its meal, across to the other, then, head lowered, would continue to feed. Perhaps half an hour passed in this way, then the dog walked over

*I was wrong!

109

to his mate on the Wildflower Path, carrying the remains of his much smaller prey. He finished off his, all but the tail – then they were both feeding from hers. A while longer and the vixen looked up, walked over to the tail, nosed and scat-marked it. Then she yawned hugely and, sitting back on her haunches, began to groom.

Much later, they disappeared into the entrance of the Primose Path, the vixen ahead and carrying the remains of her rabbit. She buried the remains of her kill near the Felled Logs Sett and, for a fox, made a good job of it. When she had finished pushing the earth back over it with her nose, the *dog* then scat-marked the cache whilst she looked on.

Sunday 14 February
The distant trees have a reddish tinge, with a touch of pale green. The morning sun is warm – everywhere peaceful. Have been watching a busy tree-creeper spiralling upwards and probing with his slightly down-curved beak for insects and grubs in the deeply fissured bark. His stiff, fan-shaped tail was held down, barkwards, rather like a woodpecker's. The limbs of this old oak drooped halfway along their length, so that when he reached the point of descent, he would fly off to the base of another great branch and creep mouse-like up again. Near by, a clump of birches are alive with redpolls and siskins – also bramblings and a solitary chaffinch; a very gregarious, noisy group!

Checked the View Sett this morning (Old Joe's and the Dump foxes'

110

home). The vixen and badger seem to have come to terms with the situation – the dogfox keeps well out of the picture. On Friday night, I waited for Joe to emerge. He came from the back Old Cherry Tree entrance and a short time later I followed him round to the Felled Logs area. He likes the bulbs here, also the slugs etc. in the damp leaf litter. These old logs harbour insects and beetles. He pushes over some of the smaller logs and finds worms and larvae beneath. He was interested in the cached area (do the fox's scats disguise the smell of the buried rabbit?), clearly felt the place worth examining, but appeared undecided. Came back to it five times in all to sniff over but not actually dig into. Finally, when I thought he was quitting the spot altogether, he suddenly made a bee-line for it, dug, and in a moment with those powerful claws, found the hidden rabbit – nearly two complete hind legs still attached to the pelvis and spine. Notice a badger prefers to tear the fur away where possible, unlike the fox. They both crack the bones.

Tuesday 15 February
2.45 a.m. Met the Prosser foxes at the Motorway tunnel and though I had really intended tawny-watching tonight, I rather fell for their easy acceptance of me and decided, if allowed, I'd keep with them. Damp, cold, miserable night with rather poor visibility. My foxes foraged in a desultory way over the Ridge to the Wheatfield Copse. They sat on a grassy bank and mutually groomed. Eventually the grooming became a kind of game amid much tail wagging and light-hearted nipping, until the vixen lay belly uppermost and panting on the grass and refused to play any more. Her mate ambled down the bank and had a good scratch.

Later he stood on the footpath looking out over the farmland – whether he had heard or seen something is impossible to say. I sometimes hear cats yowl or fight down near Glebe Farm and the collection of dwellings there. The vixen came and stood by him, shoulder to shoulder; she became bored at his stillness and tried to chew his ear. Flicking his ear away, he started at a trot towards the end of the Poplar Row, turned right there and moved steadily down to the farm. I thought at first the vixen wouldn't follow but after a short hesitation she did so, though at a distance and not too confidently. Wondered where his interest lay – is he a dustbin addict like Joe?

The little cluster of cottages was in darkness but, like the vixen, I preferred to stay well clear of human habitation, and crouched down near her by the outhouse. A short time passed and all was quiet but for an occasional click-click as of metal. The fox near me was crouched low on the ground, alert and uneasy. I moved my head slightly to pin-point the sound of the clicking and caught the reflective shine of her eyes – not unlike a cat's – as she turned her head towards me. She certainly knew what her mate was up to, though I didn't! My curiosity was by now thoroughly aroused (convinced it wasn't a dustbin lid being pushed up and down), so I followed the sound, and there inside a wire fence was the

111

dogfox at the door of a wooden shed. He came up to me as I knelt there with the wire between us and I spoke softly to him, anxious for his safety with the farm cottages so near. What on earth was his interest in the shed? He has been here before, that's for sure, and he seemed excited and eager. Then he turned his attention to the door again and I found the source of the click-clicking. A metal latch, usual design, dropping into a slot. He was standing upright, pushing it up out of the slot with his nose, only to see it click into place again – and again – and again. Then he sprang up once more, this time with all his strength, hard-pressed against the wood. The latch nosed up, the fox dropped to the ground just as the door opened a crack and the bar fell down on air! Then a sudden squawking and flapping, and enlightenment belatedly dawned on me – this was no shed, but a hen-house. The fox had disappeared inside and I had a desire to disappear too – back the way I had come, and fast!

I hesitated by the vixen, but she scarcely registered me and had crept a bit nearer, no longer so apprehensive, ears forward, intent on the chicken noises from ahead. Heard a shot as I reached the bank and sat down to await developments. Two or three windows showed lights and somewhere a dog barked. Then from the field just below me came a deep booming bang – not a gun. Just the bird-scarer starting; it must be after 4 a.m. Began to feel I had had enough excitement for one night, but worried about my foxes, so continued to sit and wait, eyes and ears strained for any indication of their whereabouts.

A movement along the field edge and there they were. A chicken – like a full-grown rabbit – is quite a weight to run with in your jaws. They stopped a few feet off and he dropped his burden on to the path. Panting, he stood looking back over the fields. As the vixen made a move towards the meal, he growled at her and looked over to me sitting, hands deep in pockets, on the bankside. The vixen whined softly and his gaze returned to her and then to his kill. Bending his head, he chewed through the neck using his side, carnassial teeth. Then with the chicken head dangling out of the corner of his mouth, he moved slightly away and the vixen began to feed. Foxes, like dogs, are gulpers; they chew very little. In fact, neither has teeth that are really meant for chewing. The carnassial teeth shear off chunks that are swallowed whole. Like Wendy, these foxes bolted their food and ate steadily until they were sated.

[At home, we discussed the dogfox lifting the latch. Doubt if it was intelligence – more like remembered accident. Ross reminded me how Wendy, impatient to be let into the dining-room where we all sat talking, reared up against the door, knocking down the end of the handle which released the spring and resulted in her almost falling into the room. Ever after, having learnt from that experience, she opened all the doors by bringing a paw smartly down on the end of the handles. She also learnt very quickly that once in with the door shut, she couldn't reverse the procedure. Henceforth, she let herself into a room and barked to be let out. If, as my dictionary says, intelligence is the capacity for understand-

112

ing, then this can't qualify as intelligence. Both dog and fox found through experience that a certain course of action had a certain result, but neither understood why.]

Saturday 20 February
A pheasant roosted in a rather unfortunate place tonight (rather unfortunate for the pheasant, that is) – in the elder Joe uses as his favourite claw-scratching tree situated directly outside the main entrance of the View Sett. Elders don't grow to a great height and this one is no exception, so the handsome bird was barely ten feet off the ground. It must have been there when the badger emerged last evening, but it was only when he returned about 4.25 a.m. and stretched upwards to use his claws that he registered the bulky shape in the leafless branches silhouetted against the sky. He stayed where he was, up on hind legs, his front legs stretched outwards along the tree's sloping trunk – sniffing the air. Could almost read his thoughts – breakfast! Looked at his chunky body and massive shoulders, then at the little tree, and wondered how he was going to come by his meal. He slowly began the ascent, pausing at about five feet. The roosting bird, perched in the angle where branch meets trunk, bobbed a little as if a sudden wind had sprung up, but slept on. The badger crept slowly upwards, the tree bent slowly downwards! By now, the pheasant was much nearer the ground than before. Something had to give, and it did.
I thought for the moment that the elder trunk had snapped, but no, there it was – *almost* as before, swaying violently and now relieved of its unaccustomed weight. Old Joe, his physique not built for climbing slender trees, had fallen – as had the unfortunate pheasant, which was sprung on by the badger before it had a chance to fly off.
He commenced eating this bird from the vent end. He's much fussier than a fox about eating feathers, too. Eating into the body from the vent and ripping wide open as he proceeded, guts, organs and flesh were swallowed, whilst most of the bird's skin and feathers were left intact. Badgers have a rather neat way of turning prey almost inside out. I think the neck and head were turned inside the skin, not eaten. Must check tomorrow. [Yes, they were.]

Sunday 21 February
Meant to do a tawny check and also investigate the bird call (little owl?) heard over the Poplar Row part of Shaw's land twice last week when I was in the company of the Prosser foxes, but went instead to the river and Newby meadows. Overcast sky, no moon or stars showing, strong breeze and excellent visibility. Coming back, I carefully avoided Glebe Farm (although I've John Shaw's permission to come and go, and the public footpath runs through the farm in any case – I've a slight conscience over a certain dead chicken!).
Walked through the pear orchard and so towards Top Field and

Prosser's Wood. Saw first one fox in the distance, then another. I was walking quickly and not thinking of foxes when first one then the other turned and moved swiftly away. They would never hear the soft vixen sound at that distance and it was pointless following them. Remembered the odd claw-and-drag marks I'd seen yesterday across the Primrose Path near Joe's sett, so sat down on an old sleeper and tried to draw them from memory in my notebook.

Had a feeling I wasn't alone and slowly looked up from writing to see the Prosser vixen watching me a few yards off. I made the soft vixen sound and she came right up to my knee – just as Vicky did. Just sat looking in her face – foxes are so beautiful. She's small and neat and, seen head on, has a narrow, high-domed little face, the black markings very clearly defined; the white 'cheeks' and white areas around nose and chin are immaculate. And all this topped by those big, pointed ears. Something moving diverted her attention from me as she looked, ears pricked, towards the far end of my sleeper. On impulse, I got up slightly and tucked my hands under it, gripping hard. Sleepers are very heavy – for me – but I thought that, if I jerked it, whatever was living beneath might run out. I twisted hard, the vixen moved back startled, then pounced . . . on a wood mouse. Noticed that, before swallowing it, she bit off its tail which dropped from the side of her mouth. Picking it up – it had nearly dropped *on* me – I saw it had been chopped off neatly at the base. Can understand her rejecting it; rather chewy and tasteless, I imagine! Had moved the sleeper slightly off its original place and the vixen picked up several slugs from the dead grass beneath which she ate with relish. (She obviously hasn't read *The Handbook of British Mammals*, which states that the fox 'shuns feeding on shrews, moles, toads and slugs'.)

At daylight, saw a woodcock in the dead leaves, very much where I used to see them. Their mottled plumage blends well in the undergrowth. They seem to like damp woodland places, probing about with that long bill. For a large, plump bird, its flight was very dextrous, swerving around the trees with skill.

SPRING 1982

Wednesday 3 March 1982
2.10 a.m. Gale force wind and driving rain, so not surprised to find no animals about. Joe did stick his snout out briefly, musked me but then promptly disappeared again. No foxy evidence at all.

Saturday 6 March
Sunny day after night of deep frost. Just off Briarmead, watched a lapwing tumbling in courtship display over these fields. It rose steadily on slowly beating wings; then tumbled in a rolling dive from on high, to end with an upwards twist and the sound of throbbing wings, its spring song accompanying the performance. (Was once told that the lapping sound of the wings was the origin of its name although, to my hearing, they seemed to throb rather than lap.)

Monday 8 March
Well met by moonlight! The Prosser foxes were there on the grass verge by the tunnel, 2.10 a.m. Thick frost, full moon, grass crunching softly underfoot. Went into Prosser's Wood via the Motorway ditch and came out at the beech stump. There's a Trametes growing from it that both animals disregarded, though under a larch farther in, they found and ate *Boletus elegans*. I generally avoid accidentally touching the foxes by keeping a yard or so away, but seeing they had overlooked one mushroom, I knelt and picked it to check the variety, whereupon the dogfox came up and stared at it lying on my palm. Held out my hand with it on, but he hadn't quite the assurance to take it; looking away, then at it, then away once more. I picked up the end of its stem between fingers and thumb and offered him the round cap. He took it up very gingerly in his teeth, moved slightly aside and ate it. Then he stood looking back at me kneeling there.

Left them and slowly made my way across Hains's land, hoping to hear again the unidentified call of what may be a little owl (heard on 10 and 19 February). Haven't heard it since and had no luck again tonight. It could have been passing through, of course. [Very many years ago, I recorded a long-eared owl for a brief time in Ashcroft Woods.] Probably the best time to do a proper check for a little owl in spring would be dusk.

Watched the Briarmead male tawny hunting under the geans by the Wildflower Path – wasn't calling and everything very quiet. Saw his silent shape disappear through the leafless branches. Suddenly I was startled by a scream followed by a shrill squawk above and to my left. Very high and penetrating – could only have been a bird – one of the tawny pair? Waited, but no further sounds and, by now, bitterly cold, 4.25 a.m.

[Checking through Dr Southern's paper for the origin of the tawny cry – 'Yet another very startling note – a high-pitched scream and cackle – is confined to a small period of the spring just when eggs are being laid. This is almost certainly connected with copulation. I could never discover whether it was characteristic of one sex only.']

Sunday 14 March
8.15 and a sunny, gusty morning with cloud shadows racing each other across the land. Shooting in Ashcroft Woods has just begun. Skylarks trilling over Briarmead; light sparkling on the water-covered earth.

Last Friday, the Prosser vixen moved her den to the Wheatfield Copse (Jessie's old home, but sadly altered now that many of the dead elms have fallen). She wouldn't allow the dog entry to the new den, so felt her time was near.

Tonight I met the dogfox without his vixen and went with him on to the Ridge in the moonlight. He was interested in the ground next to the gorse bushes, muzzle lowered, ears intently forward. Dug down and along, and presently upturned a nest of young rabbits. Ate three on the

116

spot, then, carrying the remaining couple, continued up the stony scree. He dropped one crossing the Enclosed Path, checked, and returned for it, and so continued to the Wheatfield Copse. Stood jaws full, listening at the mouth of the den. Then he left the baby rabbits on the freshly excavated earth and nosed them a little. The foxes have hunted together these past months so it is natural he should leave her share. If he doesn't yet sense what has happened, the whimpering cries will tell him in due time. Then he trotted the length of the coppice looking upwards every so often. His nose has discovered what my ears told me last dawn – there are pheasants roosting at the Wheatfield Copse, but he hasn't his mate to help him hunt now.

Old Joe is still at the View Sett. On Friday night, I saw his swaying figure going cross-country to the Motorway – dustbin destined?

Tuesday 16 March
Beautifully mild, gusty night. Half-moon sailing through dark, swirling clouds. Both Dump and Prosser vixens have cubs and are only venturing to their den entrances to retrieve kills left by their mates. Old Joe quickly took advantage of this easy meal and twice ate them (one was a rat, the other part of a rabbit) before the vixen appeared. However, she has learnt by experience and just now emerged as the dogfox arrived. He stood, pigeon in mouth, whining softly, brush lowered. He's a little unsure of his vixen now she has helpless pups to protect. She, in her turn, will tend to be aggressive towards him, warning him away from the den until the cubs' eyes are open and they are moving about.

Have been thinking about the relationship I have with the Prosser foxes and have decided at all costs that I *mustn't* familiarise their cubs with my scent and person once they are above ground. To learn to accept a human being would be their death-knell and fox life hangs by a slender thread in this area as it is.

Halfway down the Ridge at first light, I spied my magpie friends on a stunted oak and whistled to them as I passed. The dawn is glorious, the air filled with song, each bird proclaiming the new day. Was sitting on the stile fence watching the waves of colour seeping layer upon layer through the dark clouds when the magpie landed next to me – and then his mate also, a little way off along the fencing. (Though I say 'he', the sexes are identical, so I can't be sure the boldest magpie is the male. However, from its behaviour to its mate, I suspect it is.) He has a very pert, inquisitive expression as he examines the metal zip at the edge of my anorak that is lying on the wooden slat. Never realised magpies were so friendly until I got acquainted with this pair. His incredibly white underparts and wing patches make a perfect foil for his iridescent sheen of blue, green, red and purple. He is looking up at my face now, head to one side, soft little noise sounding in his throat. Then a lorry goes rumbling by on the Motorway above us and he launches easily into

117

space, his oddly long wedge of a tail and hoarse chattering laugh the last impressions I have as he sails effortlessly over the birches.

Wednesday 17 March
I went out again at 10.15 a.m. Bright sunshine interspersed with black clouds. Heard two green woodpeckers 'yaffling' their territories. The ponds are full and overflowing into every available hollow – a marvellous place to be. At the Main Pond, caught a newt in my hand, then four more and compared them. Markings vary quite a bit (three males and two female smooth newts); imagine this is due to incomplete breeding coloration – it's early in the year as yet. Put my hand on the pond's surface and watched them re-enter the water – rather sluggish. Their markings blend well with the dead leaves lying just below the surface.

Sat on the Ridge in the sunshine – everywhere there are leaf buds opening, catkins, birds and rabbits. A male green woodpecker probing in an anthill was confronted by another who flew down from a birch. Amid much aggressive noise, they faced each other, their black/red moustaches fluffed up, and swaying their heads from side to side, their head-feathers raised like crests. At the same time, they spread out their wings and tails in an effort to appear bigger than the rival, and made little rushes at one another. Eventually, the ant-gathering one flew off with deeply undulating flight, leaving the victor to 'yaffle' from his birch.

Friday 19 March
After several dusk and night checks, must conclude that whatever bird (little owl?) was calling near the Poplar Row last month has quit the area. The Long Field tawny hen is incubating her eggs and the male hunts for them both. Much contact calling between them – less territorially.

Had difficulty evading human activity tonight, both at the 'swap-shop' area and along the Wildflower Path – gets very irritating to say the least. I'm waiting for the night when two groups meet although, on sober reflection, I hope I'm not around then!

Old Joe and the Dump foxes are definitely not getting on. The badger seems to hang around the sett a fair amount, and tonight chased the dogfox who was approaching with his vixen's food. However, the badger was no match speedwise for the fox, even though the latter was hampered by the weight he was carrying. It's a curious situation, aggravated I think by the age of the badger and determination of the vixen not to move den. Wonder if her mate will stop providing for her and, later, the cubs, if Joe makes a habit of this?

Watched the moon's thin orange crescent rising slowly over Warby 3.30 a.m. Can imagine no lovelier place to be than here. A confused blackbird is singing his territorial challenge to the velvety night sky. The Main Road's amber lighting round the village must have something to do with this. Have noticed that the dawn chorus starts fifty to sixty

118

minutes earlier at this lighted side of the fields and woodland. Today, for instance, it has started at 4.20 a.m. here at the View, but I walked through these woods, sat and waited for it to begin at 5.10 a.m. on the Ridge and the fields bordering Briarmead where there is no blaze of lighting.

Saw a woodcock 'roding' above the trees just after the dawn. Have never witnessed this before; to me, a thrilling experience, not at all like their usual flight. 'Roding' is the bird's way of beating the bounds of its territory. It's a slow, meandering flight, accompanied by a kind of whistle, high-pitched and thin – must carry quite a distance. Had just decided I would try and get nearer when it passed above my head, this time croaking as it went. With its head and long bill pointing earthwards and so low in the air, I felt sure it must have seen me and wondered if the throaty noise was its alarm call. But evidently not, for shortly after, it flew leisurely back, whistling as before. Etched against the blood-streaked sky, its stumpy long-beaked silhouette and slow wing-beats appeared most strange.

[Discovered the woodcock's frog-like croaking is part of its territorial 'roding' and can only be heard at close quarters, unlike the whistling 'twisick'. This 'roding' implies it has a mate and, to quote the book*, 'occurs mainly between March and early July when the woodcock are raising their two broods of chicks'. The curious position of its eyes, high up on the head (which always remind me of the hare's eyes) give it all-round sight, i.e. 360° field of vision.]

Monday 22 March
Fine, breezy day with sunny periods. The poplars are looking their best and the pussy willow catkins are etched against the blue sky, more a promise of spring than the scattering of primroses and lesser periwinkle beneath. I watched yellow brimstones on the wood edge just above the Oak Dell. Wood anemones, sweet violets (both blue and white), white and red deadnettles, lesser celandine, are all in bloom now; daffodils are in bud inside the wood near Briarmead. Dandelions and coltsfoot everywhere – what bright splashes of colour they make. Which reminds me that the Prosser dogfox was biting off and eating the big, closed dandelion heads growing on High Ridge at first light this morning. Probably very juicy. Have not seen foxes do this before.

Wednesday 24 March
12.45 a.m. Chill, damp night, slight breeze and good visibility. Stayed in the Prosser dogfox's company for a while. High Ridge is a great hunting ground for a fox. The second time he fetched a kill back to the Wheatfield Copse, his vixen was above ground and greeted him enthusiastically – whining, licking his face and prancing round him, her brush waving. He was clearly delighted at being accepted back, as it were. Think she will

*Reader's Digest AA Book of British Birds (1980).

119

soon be leaving the cubs briefly to herself hunt near the den. (I have heard the whimpering of the Prosser and Dump cubs at both dens.)

Left them and wandered round to the Old Barn ruins. Hadn't been there long when the dogfox appeared, much to my surprise, and came right up to me. He seemed so pleased with himself that I tried stroking his back, which he allowed. By now, we were near the barbed-wire fencing at the lane top. A sudden, brilliant shaft of light shone down Briarmead. A car had been backed and parked just inside the wood there and now the headlights were switched on prior to starting. Although we were outside the beam, I was dazzled and looked away and down at the fox by my side. To my surprise, saw his eyes reflecting a blue/white glow (they generally reflect pink); have never seen them this colour before, but then never had these circumstances. Catching foxes in their headlights at night, drivers must frequently notice this. As the car slipped quietly down the lane, I saw its two occupants were police – and my fox had disappeared!

Walked slowly through the wood via the Ashtree and View Paths to the stiles. 2 a.m. and the Warby blackbird is lyrically singing his challenge – undisputed! Heard a loud, harsh croaking down near the Motorway. It stopped, then started again farther along, but the farmland between rises and falls, so I could see nothing. Decided to investigate and discovered Old Joe there, worming amongst the onion rows as if his life depended on it. There was no way of telling what bird he had disturbed.

Thursday 25 March
Lovely sunny day. Sitting under the pines at the Felled Logs Sett, watching and listening to the birds. Sitting here quietly in the sunshine at mid-day when the Dump vixen appeared from the View Sett just behind me on the slope. Some small birds are quarrelling in a tangle of a branch that fell to earth from a Scots pine during the January snows. The vixen is very intent on them and has sprung on to the far end of my log, ears forward, body poised to jump. She's very slender. The sunlight makes her coat appear pale by contrast. She springs, the squabbling abruptly terminates, and she's eating a bullfinch. Lightly she jumps on and off another felled trunk. For a moment longer, I see her large upright ears above the log before she's lost to view.

Made an odd discovery in the early hours of this morning. Watched Old Joe returning across the Motorway and he passed into the rows of onions very close to where I saw him yesterday. The ground at the foot of the hill just here is very wet. With the huge lorries thundering by a few yards away, it's very easy to come close to him under cover of the noise and ground vibrations, and I don't want my presence to perhaps inhibit him. He was worming for some minutes (quite on his own, of course), when he stopped, reared up on his hind legs – and gave a series of perhaps ten to twelve harsh croaking sounds! Dropped down on all fours, ran

parallel with the onion rows and the Motorway, reared up, snout skyward, and repeated the noise four times. Then he ran up the hill a little way, curving down after some yards, rose up and repeated it again. Finally ending near where he began, he made the sounds for the last time. Then he began worming once more. This was certainly the 'bird' noise I heard last night – it varied its position then. Why the noise? He's not listening for an answering call and couldn't hear one in any case with the lorries going by. He didn't wait for a lull in the traffic noise to make the croaking either. Too many onion-flavoured worms?

(Two 'night visitors' today, parked at the top of Briarmead lane from 9.20 a.m. until when I left at 1.30 p.m. Spoke to them, but didn't realise until this evening they were the 'swap-shop' contingent.)

Saturday 27 March
2 a.m. Thick fog, visibility four yards. Trees drip-drip with moisture. The Prosser dogfox found me along the Enclosed Path. His friendliness is flattering – but a warning to me not to get acquainted with his vixen again now she has cubs. Fortunately they hunt separately now, she around the Wheatfield Copse and he farther afield, so I can avoid her whilst still seeing him.

Arrived home at 7 a.m. The moment I walked into our warm kitchen, the smell of fox that I must have been carrying hit me. Liza took one sniff, yowled and shot out the way I had come in! Have never noticed it so strong before. Was wearing a plastic anorak, though (not my usual cloth one), and the mist had made it very cold and damp. The fox smell seemed to come from it, so I imagine that's the answer.

Sunday 28 March
Discovered three leverets on the Top Hayfield, Briarmead at dawn. Thick fur very wet and tousled, tiny ears flattened back against their bodies, noses very snub, almost set into their faces. Believe them to be new-born; partly because of their extreme appearance and also because I watched this field being sprayed yesterday and the tractor's tyre-marks, which are still clearly visible in neat 'lanes', go straight through the 'form' or shallow depression in which they were huddled. A mild, balmy sunrise, no frost or dew.

I have seen leverets before, but never so incredibly 'new'. Lighter fur around large, dark eyes. Can't tell actual eye colour as early light is deceptive, but imagine dark blue. Certainly nothing like that of the adults' eyes, which are distinctly amber. The three leverets could have nestled together in my cupped hands. Doubt if the largest weighed four ounces. Didn't touch them. Have read the doe gives birth to each in a separate spot, but would seem from this that, sometimes at least, she doesn't. Nothing to stop the mother later from carrying two away, to single 'forms'. Will remember this place and see what happens as the days go by. Wonder if they will survive – the foxes, tawnies *and* the kestrels hunt this field. To say nothing of the effect the sprayed grass might have on them.

[British Summertime started.]

Monday 29 March
7 p.m. and the day is slowly fading. Sitting on the buttressed roots of an old beech whose disembowelled trunk soars away above my head. Last year's rain-drenched leaves strewn on the mossy ground are vivid and glowing in this strange light. It's been a day of showers and sunshine and is trying to rain again.

The hare moved her young to separate forms an hour before dawn this morning and then fed and washed them. Have come to watch her with them before dark.

7.42 p.m. Waiting on the bank of the Top Hayfield, monocular in hand, having walked up Briarmead from the Chantry. The hare has appeared on the wood fringe near the entrance to the Ashtree Path. A rabbit that was browsing near by thumps and is gone. The hare is standing upright on hind legs, nose and ears aquiver – checking for sight, sound or smell of danger. Then she moves across the field like a diminutive kangaroo. Notice she doesn't make directly for a leveret, but seems to miss the form by yards, until suddenly she gives a tremendous sideways leap – breaking her scent trail? – and lands next to the youngster. She suckles, crouching low over her leveret in a similar attitude to that when grazing and with long ears low. Like this, hares

122

appear from a distance as flattened molehills or cowpats. Later the doe washes her offspring. Already there is a different 'look' to the little hares and their ears and noses are mobile.

This procedure is repeated with the next leveret, the doe again approaching its form with that great sideways leap. The three young hares are well scattered over the field. This evening, the mother moves the last one before feeding and washing it. She grips them either by the neck scruff or by their sides. Think I know why she has moved this leveret now. That field edge is very damp, and today's rain has extended the wet area. She has moved it to firmer, drier ground.

The moon's fragile curve is well above the trees to my left – the last daylight has ebbed from the sky, 8.45 p.m. Walking through these woods, there's a fabulous smell of wet undergrowth. Thought I would wait for Joe to emerge, unless he's gone already. Everything very quiet at the View Sett apart from the hum of Motorway traffic. Lights from the village below twinkle amongst the bare branches. Roosting birds make me smile – there's always one that can't get comfortable. A grousing and rustling from above, a piece of twig falls (at least, *I hope* that's what it is), a muffled complaint from a jostled mate, then quiet once more. Chickens in a hen-house bedding down for the night are nothing compared with this woodland dormitory.

Joe's out – my, he does like a scratch! Now he's rolling on his back in the hollow and gets up with old holly leaves sticking in his coat. He's disappeared round the cherry tree (think he's used the dung pit there) and suddenly he's returned, sniffing at the vixen's den. He's backed on to it and musked it. Stays a long while looking down into the hole and sniffing – seems loath to leave. He disappears along the Primrose Path in the direction of Little Chantry Field. It was sown and rolled today; even I can smell the fresh earth, just waiting for a hungry badger to worm in.

9.55 p.m. and I've nearly given up. Received my first gnat bites for 1982 (not sure whether that's a boast or a complaint!). There's a movement just inside the den entrance – a pair of large ears – the vixen looks cautiously out and the head is withdrawn. The minutes tick by as a moth blunders into my face. Then with one fluid, graceful movement she stands above ground, a silent, listening statue. She snaps – and the moth will blunder no more – looks round and back at her den, then glides noiselessly away.

Thursday 1 April
Cold, very wet night. Been raining steadily the past six hours, gusty wind, visibility good. Two leverets only remaining now in their solitary forms on the Hayfield. The Dump dogfox found the one nearest the bank and, having already had his fill of voles and blackbird, carried it back to his family. He had passed close by it four times as it was very near his regular 'route' round the field, but the wind was never in the right direction for scenting it. When danger threatens, the little hares crouch

remarkably still and, with no betraying movement or smell, they are safe. The other two are thriving. The loss of one of their number has caused the doe to move her remaining young to different positions. She attends them at varying times throughout the night, grazing herself round about, but the dusk and dawn nursings are the most prolonged. Have found that she 'lies up' during daylight in the thick undercover, five yards from the big ash tree.

At 3.25 a.m. I heard the astonishing sound that is called the badger's scream. Traced it to the headland over Great Chantry Field – and found Joe calling on the night air. Scream upon scream. Sure it was a challenge of some kind.

Friday 2 April
Misty start today, turning to sunshine by 10.30 a.m. Walked into Warby along the Main Road. In the lay-by, found an enormous dead black cat, struck by a vehicle and thrown on to the bank. It was so large that, as I approached I thought for a moment it was Joe. Always fear this will be his end.

Walking through Newby Meadows, saw a coot busy on the Bourne. The river runs clear and fast – many fish. A pair of sedge warblers on a partly submerged branch – tawny rumps, pale stripe above eyes and a rather harsh song. Here also observed two sparrowhawks soaring together in what I imagine to be their display flight; they are not at all common in this area.

Walked up Briarmead at 1.30 p.m. homeward bound. Where the bank divides the Top Hayfield from the Lower, and on the lane's surface, found two toads run over. Rather strange that one squashed individual was superimposed upon the other. Near the soakaway, saw what appeared to be a predatory hawk fly from that same bank to the woodland edge. Its pointed wings, however, didn't conform, so viewed it through the monocular as it perched. Long, grey, mottled tail hanging well below the branch, then it turned in silhouette and I saw its thin bill and barred underparts. The earliest I have seen a cuckoo. It was neither calling nor displaying. Will keep a look-out for it when I'm watching the hare with her youngsters.

Saturday 3 April
2.10 a.m. Mild, starry night. Excellent visibility. Was in the Prosser dogfox's company by the Old Barn ruins when he pounced on something amongst the broken slates, then let it go shaking his head. He ran his mouth along the grass, first one side then the other. Sat upright still shaking his head, opening his mouth and pawing at his muzzle. Spoke softly to him, wondering what he had tasted, and he came over to me – promptly rubbing his tongue against my trouser leg. Really, this friendship is going too far! Then his attention was taken by something else on the path verge, though he made no attempt to catch it. Suddenly,

I could see movement further along – toads. Have never seen so many all on the move. Very ungainly walking, not hopping. Some very big, some quite small – and slow. My fox sat watching, his 'tent' ears turning this way and that. Toads on the field too. If I hadn't witnessed this, would have found it hard to credit. One good thing, they were safe from Mr Fox; he came over to me, treading very daintily. Tried counting them and got up to forty-two when I saw something even more odd – a large toad with a smaller one on its back. Quite well balanced – the big character seemed unbothered at having a rider. Wonder if they are making for the woodland ponds or the Briarmead soakaway?

Saturday evening, 7.30 p.m. The toads have been making for the Briarmead soakaway throughout the day – it seems bursting with them. I haven't seen any in or around the ponds in Ashcroft Woods. This is interesting: the only obvious difference is in the depth of water. The soakaways are lined and very deep; the ponds, in fact, are not – even the Main Pond is quite shallow. Found two more sets of mounted toads and have realised why those I discovered run over yesterday on Briarmead were superimposed upon each other.

[From the AA *Book of the Countryside*:* 'The female toad is up to four inches long, the male only two and a half inches ... (they) emerge from hibernation in late March or April and make for their breeding pond ... (each toad) makes for a particular one, which may be up to a mile away and probably, like migratory fish, it returns to the spot where it was born, year after year. Common toads prefer deep water for spawning. They often pair on their way to the pond, the male riding on the female's back, and grasping her firmly with his limbs. Toads secrete a poisonous substance in their skin, which protects them against would-be predators. However, birds such as herons and crows disembowel them, and other mammals, such as the brown rat, skin them.']

Sunday 4 April
Both Prosser and Dump vixens are denning away from their pups now. Neither are far – the former has moved a few 'doors' away in the Wheatfield Copse, the latter in the Felled Logs area. Both hunt close to home, with their dogs killing further afield and fetching surplus back. Plenty of food about now – rabbits, rats, voles, maimed (shot) birds, fungi, beetles, worms (still very wet everywhere), moles (killed *and* eaten by the Dump vixen), and the small bulbs of the bluebells which are abundant under the trees. Often I hear tiny whimpers from below ground and sometimes the cubs are quite noisy.

Neither vixen sees her mate very often and may go several nights without meeting, since their fetching back rarely synchronises and the vixen may, in any case, be below ground nursing. When either couple *do* meet, however, there is much brush-waving and face-licking. The Dump

Book of the Countryside, Drive Publications Ltd, 1973, 1981.

vixen perhaps sees more of her mate as she tends to hang about her cubs' den. She has twice tonight warned off Old Joe and seems very edgy, pacing up and down. I'm surprised she doesn't move her cubs and be done with the matter. It's a brave – or foolish – vixen that stands up to a boar badger like this.

Tuesday 6 April
At 1.10 a.m. a clear perfect night with moon near the full. The Dump vixen was hunting at the 'dead tree' end of Long Field as I turned into the Primrose Path. Surprised she was hunting that far from the cubs, though she may be exhausting the View Sett vicinity, of course – fields and banks could be more profitable. Watched a stoat gliding along almost parallel to my little path; then, a short way ahead, it bounded easily across. Was unaware of me and seemed fixed on a scent trail.

All serene at the View Sett, the moonlight shining on the holly leaves' smooth surfaces. No unwanted food to be seen at this den – Old Joe mops up everything. Wondered fleetingly if the vixen had moved her litter the previous night. Then I heard them below.

The dogfox appeared over the rim of the hollow, something – a bird – in mouth. A low growling and everything seemed to happen at once. A head had emerged from the den entrance – not the vixen's, but a badger's. The fur round his jaws was all dirty as if he had been digging. Or eating. Something shot past me, across the den entrance, to land high up on the badger's back. Dead holly leaves and debris swirled through the clear air as the snarling, snapping foxes settled their cub account with Old Joe. The vixen had bitten deep into the badger's neck as her mate tried to dodge those dreadful jaws and close in. The boar snorted, then squealed in pain and fury – twisted and turned, but couldn't dislodge the torment on his back. I shouted and came forward within touching distance, but it seemed ages before they registered I was there. The foxes just melted away, slipping up the curve of the hollow to disappear over the top. Old Joe backed off, grumbling and grunting, his fur still on end. I found myself at the very bottom of the hollow, looking up at a badger who could back no further, now that he was stuck against the fallen cherry tree from which I used to watch him and his family years ago. I suddenly felt rather vulnerable and backed myself out of the way! And there we both were. The tragedy of the cubs was lost in the stupidity of the situation, but I was glad that for once I interfered. Worked my way backwards knowing the oak tree trunk should be just behind, and when I felt it, slipped gently to the ground, arms round legs, chin on knees, very small; to give him room and await developments.

They were some time coming. Joe, fur smooth now, watched me above him uneasily. He had to come slightly forward to reach the safety of his sett entrance. I could almost hear his mind working! Very slowly he did it, keeping a close eye on me – reached safety and disappeared below.

Surprised to find the time was only 2.15 a.m. but content to sit and mull over events and watch the shift of light filter further over the hollow as the moon journeyed across the sky above. By 3.45 a.m. I was getting stiff and damp (a dew falling, I think, as the sky still clear). A rustle to my left and the foxes had returned. The vixen went to earth, whilst her mate stood guard on the rim of the hollow. A pause and she was out again carrying a cub – it looked alive, too – very carefully. So at least one cub has survived Old Joe's meal. Then with the vixen leading, they quit the View Sett.

Waited as long as possible – till 5.30 a.m. and daylight – but they didn't return.

Wednesday 7 April
Have traced the Dump vixen to a den off Little Chantry Field. The cub resides in the badger twins' old sett.

Tuesday 13 April
Only one leveret now. The other, the smallest of the litter, quite dead and sprawled on its side in its form. No external injury.

Returning through the woods at 5.15 a.m., heard a tawny transfiguring the dawn chorus. For the first time, I realised that to describe the tawny's song as fluting is misleading – one thinks of a flute's glittering range. But this bird's voice had the quality of a mellow reed instrument, vibrant and warm, and it would have been in the lowest register of any flute. Standing near it in the half-light, I tried to gauge its pitch and

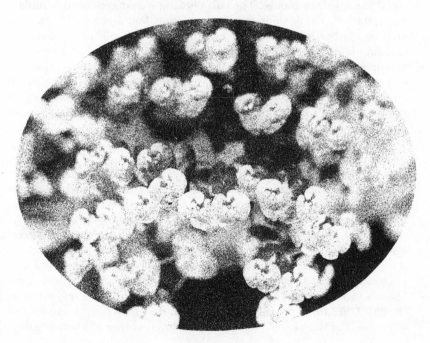

127

would say it was from the D above middle C up to, at most, top F in the treble clef certainly no higher than that. Was puzzled that I hadn't noticed this before. Have never heard a full tawny repertoire, complete with trills, sung against other birdsong. It left that dawn chorus standing – but then I'm tawny biased!

Wednesday 14 April
The single foxcub that survived Joe's onslaught is a very engaging little creature. The Chantry twins' sett is his new den. Strangely, he is bolder than the cubs of the Prosser vixen. He has already found that the thick stems of the clematis traveller's joy that hang from his tree-top like jungle lianas are very useful for hiding behind, getting stuck between – help! – or just chewing. The dogfox spends a good deal of time in his family's company. The two adults have been lying together outside the entrance this morning, with the pup 'climbing mountains' over their bodies; they are very careful with him. The father rolls slowly and gently on to his back and the youngster scrambles on to his chest. The soft baby-face gazing down into the adult's – the father's tail just stirring the dust as it moves to and fro.

The cub's belly is tight like a drum. Not only has the vixen been nursing him, but she also regurgitated a vole for him when she came in. This regurgitation seems to take the same form as I have observed in past years. A cub begins to lick round the mouth of a parent, who 'coughs' once or twice and vomits partly digested food, often something small like a vole or mouse. The cub's licking would appear to stimulate regurgitation. Today's pup is still very young, four and a half weeks old, and his mother helped him by holding on to one end of the meal, so enabling him to pull tiny pieces off. He's getting very sleepy now and whimpers as the vixen noses him over and vigorously washes his stomach. Above the dawn chorus, a twig snaps sharply. The vixen bounds to her feet, grips the back of her cub's neck, and carries him below. Her mate has vanished through the clematis stems. But for the birds, the place is deserted.

Thursday 15 April
Have been watching the remaining leveret feeding side by side with its mother in the field. Lively alert animal. Though it still suckles, it has been regularly browsing from Friday the ninth, when it was 12 days old. Now and again, it will do a few tiny bounds and a sideways kick, just for the joy of it. Though the mother still washes it after nursing, the leveret also washes itself quite energetically. Interested to see that this morning it has lain up with its parent near the ash tree, occupying the same form. It crouches at its mother's back, getting extra warmth from her furry bulk. Notice hares, like rabbits, practise refection during their lying up in the day. Our tame Flemish Giant, who had the run of the ground floor of our house, did this as she rested by the sitting-room fire of a winter's day.

A bit like chewing the cud, I suppose – the leveret is doing it right now.

This hare makes her form by turning round several times dog-like, usually in long grass. Then she nestles down, pushing her long hind legs behind her and spreading herself out. Within hours, the grass has taken on her impression or form. If I put my hand in the form when she leaves, it feels warm, even on a heavily frosty night. Like the fox, she faces *into* the wind and sleeps in cat-naps, eyes opening every little while, to close again briefly and then re-open again. Her large wide-open eyes have a glazed, staring quality; this is accentuated by the skin immediately around them, which is dark, and the fur beyond that skin, which is pale. I notice the leveret's eyes are changing colour – imagine by Sunday, three weeks old, they will have acquired the doe's amber. Indeed, the whole appearance of the young hare has altered. Probably, it could survive on its own now if it had to – much of its behaviour seems instinctive rather than taught. The mother has very hairy feet and her tail, which is white with a black streak above, has more the texture of cotton wool than fur.

Wednesday 21 April
Dull, cold, overcast night. Time 1.10 a.m., excellent visibility. Surprised to see my dogfox come to meet me as I walked through the tunnel. He's been too busy hunting for his growing family (still at the Wheatfield Copse) to have time to wait around lately. When I saw his shadow slip into the far end of the dark tunnel, I knelt down and called softly. He ran up, eyes glowing, breath smelling of fresh blood, and pranced round me, brush waving. He likes to be rubbed behind his ears and cheek patches – he's a great fox. Beginning to moult – strands of fur float gently away as I stroke.

On the very top of the Ridge. There's a wonderful smell of new growth – buds, blossom and unfurling leaves. My fox isn't inclined to hunt and has come to lie down and wash where I am sitting looking out over the landscape. My vision is very good tonight. *Vulpes vulpes* has finished grooming, so I'm covered in furry wisps. Foxes scratch even more than usual at this time of year. Not only their fleas to contend with, but the extra thick felty underfur that made them look well fed in winter comes away in wads when they groom and must be intensely irritating.

He's moved to the scree-top edge, sits back on his haunches, raises his muzzle skyward and howls. Think he's practising the fox's obligato – it's awful! I go over and stroke his back; he stops the racket and looks at me enquiringly. I listen, but there's no other fox sounding tonight. Think he was howling for the pleasure of it, like we sing to ourselves. I take a deep breath and try howling myself. He looks startled (or disgusted), big ears turning, tail waving. Then jumps to his feet, head raised to the night – and lets rip howl after howl. No, I have to hand it to him – he's a great howler!

2.45 a.m. Left him to it (eardrums shattered) and wandered wood-wards; had really come out to tawny-watch.

The vocalisation of the fox generally has a social significance, though I think the *meaning* of a sound may vary according to the circumstances. The Prosser dogfox was possibly enjoying the sound of his own voice but, on the whole, howling occurs throughout the year and can be a warning, threat or territorial sound.

The howl begins middle register with open-mouthed 'oooow'; then the sides of the mouth are channelled as breath is taken in; open-mouthed 'ooow'; narrowed again, all the while increasing in volume, hoarse and hollow; finally ending in an open, high 'ooow'. Like this:

I inadequately imitated it by starting with closed mouth slowly opening on a heavily breathed 'ooow', closing to breathe in slightly and opening again to repeat – but with hardly a break in sound. At a distance, the fox howl seems a continuous, rising cry, increasing all the while in intensity of banshee-like call. (Guaranteed to upset the neighbours if attempted indoors!)

Seriously, imitating a call gives the observer insight into how it is made by the animal. Fox barks and screams are produced as the breath is *heavily* expelled and the intake of air is so slight and slurred that often only at close quarters is the break between sounds noticeable. (The far-carrying vocalisations that can continue for some time – e.g. the 'wow-wow-wow' type of bark – are distinctive for their rasping breathlessness.) When I tried copying the badger's 'purr' (which is the nearest I can get to writing down the sound), I found it humanly impossible to reproduce accurately because I was making it from the throat. If I placed my palm on Jessie's chest when she purred, I could *feel* it there like the purr of a cat. This is what I mean by imitating giving insight.

Thursday 22 April
Warm, sunny day after misty start. Sitting amongst the trees trying to draw from memory the facial discs of tawny and barn owls (was watching the latter at Weldon last evening), when I heard a rustle just ahead. A fox was standing amongst the dog's-mercury and bluebells, but the movement of my head as I looked up made him turn to rush back through the undergrowth. Made the 'mmmmm' sound and called, 'Josh, Josh' – the name I call him now – but he was gone. Not surprised he was about during the day, they commonly are in spring and early summer.

Started to eat my apple when I saw he had returned. Spoke softly to him, whereupon he came right up – and gently took the apple from my fingers! Have never fed him before, unless you count the dandelion heads I pick and offer him to eat since I found he likes them, and the boletus, of course. Glad he ran away at first; shows he's very cautious of humans. Sniffed round my pocket that had contained the apple, but nothing else edible there. Then I saw a golden splash of colour too large to be lesser celandine growing amongst the wood anemones. Sure enough, a dandelion. Went over and showed it to him by moving it with my finger. His mouth went neatly over the flower top which was bitten off close to the bloom. He took no interest in other flowers there – just dandelions. Offered him a coltsfoot bloom last week on the Ridge; he sniffed it and turned his head away, so he knows the difference. (I believe they're very bitter, though haven't sampled them myself!)

Somewhere in the distance could hear a gun, but in this part all was peace. The birds singing. Scots pine and bluebells scent the air, so I continued my drawing and left the Prosser dogfox to go his way, 12.50 p.m.

Friday 23 April
Mild, warm, moonless night with clear, starry sky which by 4.20 a.m. had clouded over – wonderful visibility. I heard a distant click-clicking, and sure enough the irrigation machines were watering the sloping, sown field below Sleet House. The sprays move along a cable running the length of the field and parallel with the footpath. In the past have watched foxes at night (and, once, a badger) worming on this land when irrigation was in progress. The jets play upon one section for some moments, having the effect of a *very* heavy shower, before abruptly swivelling round with a quickened clicking. The badger seemed oblivious to getting saturated in pursuit of an easy meal, but have noticed that foxes will evade a heavy soaking if they can. As water floods the earth, worms emerge (possibly reacting to the vibration), and *Vulpes vulpes* times to a nicety the moment that the spray shifts. Then he can worm until the accelerated clicking minutes later warns him that the waterjets are returning. He is a faster animal than the badger, of course. As I know to my cost when the jets cover the footpath, you have to move quickly to avoid a soaking. But since a badger *can* move quickly over a short distance, I feel he isn't as bothered as the fox (or he is slower to associate the sound with the action?).

Spent a couple of hours tonight along the banks of the Bourne and, strolling up Briarmead pre-dawn, was greeted by Josh. Together we investigated a large, fresh, blood-covered area of tarmac near the soakaway. There were tyre skidmarks near it and the stain covered a third of that little lane's width. Whatever was struck lost a considerable amount of blood. Nothing dead anywhere on the banks or grass near by and no trail leading away. The dogfox smelled and licked the still-wet blood a long time, moving round the area, but not off the tarmac. If there *had* been a scent trail, he would certainly have followed it, so was the injured animal/human taken away in the car? Finally, he stood with legs slightly spread to urinate over it, then trotted up the lane after me as the sun's first rays touched the sky.

131

Monday 26 April
A badger has moved into my area and taken up residence in the side of the field adjoining that of the beehives. It's in a crater-cum-hollow amongst the rabbit warren there. Have only seen the badger once, but think it's a female. Too far over to come into contact with Joe, I suspect. Since his fox-fight, he seems very slow and ponderous. Wonder how much longer he'll last – ten is quite a good age for a badger in the wild.

The male Long Field tawny is vocal pre-dawn today. Hunting is good and his mate and their brood are flourishing. She covers them in the crevice of an old cherry tree where a branch has come away. In this woodland, the geans stand like pale ghosts clothed in their white blossom.

At 2.20 a.m. watched a bright beam of light moving over the barley of Great Chantry. Very like a car headlight, but unlikely to have been one. Too far away to check.

Wednesday 28 April
The $4\frac{1}{2}$-week-old leveret had a near miss just after dawn today. It was well out on the Top Hayfield browsing in clear light when the doe appeared close by me at the entrance to the Ashtree Path. She was reconnoitring on hind legs, long ears aquiver, nose twitching (in that attitude, they personify the expression 'a mass of nerves'). I could only see the youngster through the monocular when it moved, otherwise it merged beautifully with its surroundings. The mother made a far-carrying grating noise – with her teeth? Couldn't see what was bothering her. No fox in the vicinity; they stand out a mile in grassland. Next moment, she had bounded into the field herself, just as something plummeted out of the sky – the kestrel. A thin scream as a child in pain or terror, a screech from the bird and a flurry of feathers as the doe leapt with a tremendous kick that sent the hawk hurtling sideways before it could regain the air. The hares crouched in the grass a long while after the kestrel had flown away; so long, in fact, that I wondered if the leveret was badly hurt. Later, however, they moved slowly towards the concealing woodland, the mother leading, and went into the thicket near by.

Sunday 2 May
Cold, sunny morning with strong breeze. Cuckoo sounding off the Ashtree Path. Watched a lesser spotted woodpecker drumming. Elegant spikes of yellow archangel in bloom. Found fourteen eggs in a grassy scrape just inside the wood by the View. Very attractive creamy-fawn background mottled with brown. They were cold, so wondered if they had been abandoned, and watched out of sight to see. Eight minutes passed before their owner – a red-legged partridge – appeared from the field. It settled itself gently down over them, covering the clutch entirely

132

(no mean feat!). Looked very matronly, soft plumage so fluffed out that, by comparison the head looked quite small.

Tuesday 4 May
Bitterly cold. Bright, sunny periods between thunder, sleet and hail. Had the Water Meadows to myself this afternoon. Watched a grey heron stalking a meal through the shallows of this little river. Their great success as fishermen must surely be due to their enormous patience. When this one appeared to have given up for the day, it stood in the shadow of the bank, hunched up on one 'stilt', eyes apparently closed. Their hearing must be owl-acute. From this position, it lurched forward, stabbing into the overhang with its bill, and impaled a water vole. It raised its beak as it swallowed the prey whole. After a heavy hail shower, it quartered the meadow. Through the monocular saw it catch two frogs and then it passed out of sight.

Wednesday 5 May
Very cold night with clear skies, slight wind and deep frost. Ponds all ice-covered. Silent walking difficult as grass tends to crunch softly underfoot.

Watched the five Prosser foxcubs at the Wheatfield Copse playing King of the Castle on the remains of a dead rabbit their father brought in earlier for them. Already their appearance is more foxy. Their faces have lost the crumpled look of extreme babyhood, with their ears standing out more from their heads. Three little 'string' tails have small white tips; one has no white at all, and one has perhaps an inch and a half. It should therefore be easy to identify two at least. Interesting that even at this age − 7½ weeks − one in particular is dominant. In this instance, it isn't the largest (although often it is), but the quickest and most adventurous − the one with no tail tag. Though the largest of the litter tries to usurp his place, the tagless one by sheer persistence and aggression retains his position as 'top dog'.

Have noticed that pups can sound very much like adults in their bark at times. Just hear it now, when one tried to follow its father who obviously had no desire for a hanger-on and soon left its offspring well behind. The youngster ran a little way, then stood and barked at the dogfox's rapidly retreating figure, before returning to his litter-mates. Normally, however, they bark in a puppy-like way, growl, squeal and whimper. Very young foxcubs can sound like kittens, though these have passed that stage. When puzzled, the tail slowly drops and the head is cocked to one side. They were out on the path playing when the dog brought them the rabbit tonight. We had met up at the Enclosed Path, he carrying his catch. I waited behind as he went up the slope to the den and his family, not wishing them to become acquainted with me. From where I stood, I could clearly hear their high-pitched yaps of excitement and anticipation as they saw him coming.

133

The dead, fallen trunks and the stumps in this copse give endless opportunities for enterprising pups to jump on their unfortunate brethren from above – though the slope of the bank often means that the attacker ends up underneath. No real injury is done at this age, though, (except to pride and dignity) and when a cub submits by lying on its back with belly exposed, the scuffle is considered won and the victor goes off to find someone else to play with. Stick-chewing seems a favourite pastime with adults as well as youngsters, though you can bite off more than you can chew, as one hapless cub has just found when he and his outsize stick got wedged in the elm brush thicket here.

There's a movement at the bottom of the bank as the sow badger goes by, homeward bound – she seems to have come to stay in the hollow by the beehives. Above her, the little foxcubs stop their play, their ears laid back, tails held low in fear. Then hurriedly they scurry to the safety of their den.

Saturday 8 May
1.20 a.m. Never thought the time would come that I might try and lose a fox rather than get near one! Night of the full moon – it hangs a great orange sphere in a velvety sky. Bitterly cold nights all this week and tonight is no exception. Deep frost. Josh has found me on the Ridge, tawny-watching. The male tawny dive-bombed him, talons outstretched to tear at his head, so I've retreated into the woods. The dogfox is in a playful mood now, his breath smells of blood so he's probably full.

Stood for a long time gazing at the beauty of Briarmead and its surrounding fields lying under the moon. The lane stretches away in a silvery glimmer curving out of sight. Shadowy tree shapes reach far out on to the Top Field; the moon seems too heavy for the sky. Josh, doubtless bored by my inattention, tried to bundle me so we ended up playing on the tarmac. He stands up on hind legs, his front paws against my waist and 'laughs' open-mouthed as he tries to push me backwards. I nearly trip against one of the little posts behind me and end up sitting on it, laughing for real at myself and breathless; his paws are on my shoulders now, his face in mine. What is the fascination of foxes – how to describe it? Badgers I will always enjoy watching, but the fox ... long, fine muzzle, erect ears, yellow eyes with those strange, elliptical pupils – and just now the slender, incurving canines and tongue lolling as he stares into my face. The tawny is a perfectly adapted bird, the fox a perfect creature. I think Josh has decided he's won. Anyhow, I've given up – haven't his stamina!

Sunday 9 May
Full moon and frost, but not so cold. Avoided meeting Josh by following the Oak Dell Path and so to the View. Watched Old Joe worming on the freshly irrigated field by the Motorway. The Chantry is a magic place; the scent of bluebells lingers on the air. Saw the Dump vixen with her

134

cub in tow – he's growing fast and is larger than any of the Prosser foxcubs. She left him in the nettles at the Chantry edge and trotted out across the field to be swiftly hidden from view in a fold of the land. Time passed with the cub alert and silent until he turned his head at a movement below as his mother reappeared on the path. He stayed like a statue while she covered half the distance between them and put down her burden. The soft bark carried quietly on the frosty air, and the pup ran down to meet her.

Although vixens are said to teach their young to hunt, I've never actually witnessed this. Foxcubs play around the den and at first will sample almost anything ranging from stones, twigs, grass, pine-cones, to the scavenger beetles that collect under discarded food. Beetles are perhaps the easiest fox food that a cub *can* catch. Just as they learn by trial and error what is edible, so as they grow and co-ordinate their movements do they seem to learn in their own way the rudiments of hunting.

The Prosser vixen's cubs haven't, to date, accompanied their hunting parent. The Dump vixen often has her cub with her, it is true, but then she has only the one. He couldn't *see* her hunt over Great Chantry tonight, as the curves of the field hid her from view after leaving him.

3.20 a.m. Watched the Prosser cubs playing at the Wheatfield Copse. One cub's game of 'pick up and toss the stick' went on for some minutes until a fluttering moth caught its attention. Another cub now joined the moth-chase and soon the whole litter was involved, jostling and

135

growling. All at once the cub noise ceased. Over the woodland side of the field I could hear in the sudden quiet the first birds preparing to greet the dawn. Then the Prosser dogfox and his vixen were on the bank top, etched against the lightening sky, their pups eagerly swarming upwards through the brushwood to their parents. Enjoyed the sight of the family together as daylight stole through the copse.

Josh had disappeared from view, when I was suddenly aware of him at my side. Think he had wandered off along the bank and picked up my scent trail. As I touched his head, my movement was seen through the foliage by the vixen who hiccuped a soft warning to her cubs still above ground. (Adults will cough or hiccup a quiet alarm if very near their offspring, but at a distance will use a warning bark.) Now no cubs to be seen.

The vixen winds her way down the bank towards us standing together on the lower path. It's the first time she's seen me for some weeks. I've kept well out of her way recently and wonder what her reaction is going to be. She's still on the bank and we're face to face now, she at my level. Then she relaxes and looks towards Josh at my side. One of the pair whines softly and I'm accepted. Speak gently to her and decide to go – don't want her cubs to reappear and see me.

Saturday 15 May
It's been a mild night with clear skies, half-moon, and mist caught up in the hollows. Had the eerie experience coming here at 1.10 a.m. along the footpath of walking chest-high in swirling white, but with head and shoulders in the clear, silent air. Body and legs quickly became soaked – head and hair quite dry.

Went with Old Joe across the Motorway around 2.30 a.m.; he wormed along the verges of both the Motorway and the Main Road – quite a lot of fertile land here and the ground is very wet. On the way back, he came face to face with the Dump vixen and her cub – quite a sturdy chap now. The foxes carefully avoided Joe, making a slight detour to do so. He, however, took very little notice, just ambled on his way.

At 5.15 a.m. shooting started, so I'm glad Joe has retired. He's a sitting target, he's so slow and ponderous now. Although he *can* be very cautious when he feels unsafe, he's the noisiest wild creature I've come across. He grunts, snorts and wheezes as he reaches over his back to groom. Badgers must have very muscular backs – the fur (and therefore his skin) seems to ripple when he's cleaning himself. He enjoys rolling on long-dead holly leaves that have collected around his sett. This rolling is always accompanied by lots of noise. It gives him great pleasure – his equivalent of a backscratcher!

I'm very lucky this morning. A male lesser spotted woodpecker has now alighted near me on the dead cherry and is drumming. The action is so fast that head and beak are a blur. It's his way of joining in the dawn chorus. I've never watched one so close before, though the monocular brings them near, of course.

Tuesday 18 May
Yesterday, we had continuous thunderstorms throughout the daylight hours and torrential rains – the first of any real significance for weeks. The smell of wet earth, undergrowth and living things is most wonderful.

1.20 a.m. Successfully avoided human activity and now that the occupants of van and car have driven off, my friendly fox has quietly reappeared at my side – we like this wood to ourselves!

I've just startled a rabbit that's run from me, straight under Josh's nose – an easy meal.

Saturday 29 May
After nearly a fortnight's absence, have returned to find the countryside greatly changed. Encouraged by the heavy rains, deep green is the prevailing colour, with may blossom marking the hedgerows.

Met Josh – a cautious approach, then an ecstatic welcome. He has altered. Looks much thinner as his moult continues – accentuates his stick-up ears! Saw a quail at dawn feeding near the beehives; chunky, compact little bird.

Bank Holiday Monday (31 May)
9.15 a.m. Have been watching three badger cubs playing under the spindle trees at the Briarmead end of the Bank Sett. Since the sett stretches two-thirds the length of the Long Field and the bank is very foliated now, my chances of having an uninterrupted view were remote. Just luck that I was able to watch so well this past hour. Very hot and sunny on the fields, but beneath the trees on this bank it's beautifully cool – many insects, of course. Interspersed with the cubs' noisy playing, I could hear the purring of a turtle dove whilst a tractor sounded far out beyond the lane. Wonder when these young badgers arrived and from where – things have been happening while I was away. I'd like to see Old Joe's reaction – may give him a new lease of life. At least the sow should!

10.15 a.m. Had just finished writing the above and had started to walk slowly along the top of the Bank Sett, when I met a grey squirrel coming towards me. Our woodland squirrels aren't tame like those of urban parks and gardens, so I stopped and 'drummed' at him, i.e. touching the roof of my mouth with my tongue to copy his sound. He stood still listening intently, one fore foot raised – thought about it awhile, then unhurriedly climbed a sycamore to a little above my head and looked down at me. Walked up to him and drummed again. He let go the trunk with one small fore paw and looked into my upturned face. Close encounter; that's the nearest I've got to a wild squirrel when it's actually been aware of me. Very pretty little face, alert and curious. Orange sides to face, especially around the large prominent eyes. Orange on front of longer hind feet and orange each side of body where upper pelage meets white underfur. Claws of front paws long and curved.

My drumming attracted a small group of squirrels in the same sycamore and then a very young one on a felled branch below. None was frightened – cautious, yes, and inquisitive. Spent a long time experimenting with different sounds and enjoying my audience. Tried humming a tune softly, whereupon my first creature, all this while looking down from the self-same spot, made a gentle, quiet chattering sound apparently at or to me. Finally, I left the group and slowly continued to walk the bank top, followed at a distance by the young squirrel. He's not very accurate at jumping yet and clings on desperately on landing. Though this is doubtless due to lack of experience and co-ordination, his front claws, unlike the adults', are at present very short.

Old Joe has extended the small dug-out den on the Lower View Path and sometimes goes to earth there instead of the View Sett. A vixen with three cubs has moved into different chambers of the Felled Logs Sett which may have some connection with Joe's alternative accommodation. She appears to have come from the hilltop above Lester Lane and is unknown to me. She is hunting on her own for the cubs, but seems to be managing.

Found in a boundary ditch, an astonishing solitary fungus deep in leaf litter. It has a long, thin, white, hairy stalk with a small, dark-rimmed cap on top – think I'll call it Slim Jim of the Woods. It's proper title is *Coprinus lagopus*.

SUMMER 1982

Tuesday 1 June 1982
Very warm, close, cloudy night – excellent visibility. Watched Josh and his vixen hunting rabbits *together* on Barry Hains's cornfield. The little mother fox is fast – she can move like an arrow *and* twist and turn. She is in fact smaller and swifter than the male (this is only her second summer after all, she's a yearling), though Josh is fleet.

Interesting to watch this co-ordinated rabbit hunt. The warren starts in the hedgerow before the beehives, continues behind them, into the field corner and then extends a little round the other side. They have to graze far out in the corn as the nearer stalks are nibbled down to lawn height. Josh lay down under an empty hive, head on paws, ears far forward, hind feet under belly ready to push off – weight all forward. His vixen had gone; all was quiet as the minutes passed; the heat-laden air oppressive. A distant thud-thud and the rabbit colony was dashing for home – rabbits in the nettles, rabbits doubling back. Two rushed past

me, their staring eyes all unseeing, and gained the safety of a burrow ...
they were the fortunate ones. A squeal, a high-pitched scream. Josh had
gone after one that disappeared into the undergrowth – but just there
was a dead end, and not for nothing does the hunter know his territory.
The little vixen had done well, driving most of the conies to their warren
in the corner and chopping down one that doubled back almost under
her nose. I saw three dead rabbits in view and two panting foxes. Small
wonder their five cubs are thriving – none seems to ail. At 3.40 a.m., as
the sky was lightening, the vixen retraced her trail, back over the field –
to return shortly after with a plump, chunky bird in mouth – a quail!
Must have been run down in the general mêlée. I have never *read* of foxes
sharing a hunt, but if these do (as I've seen with birds roosting in the
Wheatfield Copse) this surely must be quite a common occurrence – and
the benefits are obvious.

Wednesday 2 June
Watched a lesser spotted woodpecker drilling out a nest hole on a great
branch scar of an old beech. *He* had two 'trial borings' (if that's the right
description) near by on the scar before selecting the third; then the
female took over the drilling. They have quite small beaks. [By the
following Wednesday, they were well advanced with yet another hole
approximately eighteen inches away from the others, slightly round the
curve of the beech but still on the branch scar. Will watch to see if eggs
are laid.]

Thursday 3 June
Stroking Josh in good light this morning well after dawn, was able to
have a careful look at his fur. Think foxes from spring to summer lose
most of their underfur – that dense, greyish, woolly layer that gives such
good thermal insulation in winter and causes the long guard hairs to
stand up, giving the animal an appearance of size. During the autumn, it
is replaced ready for the following cold months. Think the guard hairs
that give the animal its colour are replaced at a different rate, and,
having little underfur to make them stand up in the summer months,
seem duller by comparison. Never realised this before, but then I've
never had a fox I could treat so familiarly ... never brought home fleas
from Vicky either, like I do from Josh!
    (Watched Joe mate long-duration* with sow from the Bank Sett –
cubs nearby mildly interested.)

Tuesday 15 June
There was a breathless silence just before first light – nothing stirred. The
badger cubs I had been watching had gone to earth. No wind; each dark

*My idea of long-duration mating is fifteen minutes plus. This type of mating generally
leads to fertilisation and only occurs when the sow is in oestrus. Badgers also indulge in
rutting behaviour when copulation is brief and penetration not attained.

leaf etched sharp against a lighter sky. No birdsong; no beast; even the distant motorway noise seemed temporarily suspended.

Then a skylark began a tentative trill over the Long Field below me and, a moment later, from the depths of the wood, a badger screamed, unexpected cry upon cry. The sow badger in the sett below where I was sitting came above ground, turning her black-striped mask this way and that and sniffing the air. One cub came timorously up to its mother and she nosed it. Shortly after, both went back underground. I'm sure the calling/screaming was Joe – for calling is, I think, what the screaming means – a disturbing, eerie sound.

4.15 a.m. at the View, watching the half-moon disappear in a cloudy sky over Warby, whilst the sky above the treeline behind me was becoming streaked with the rising sun. Suddenly, a red-legged partridge strutted out of the barley and gave his self-opinionated version of the dawn chorus – 'chuka-chuka, chuka-chuka' – right in the middle of the path. Don't think he registered me as I was half-leaning, half-sitting on one of the old tractor tyres that mark the irrigation hydrants. To my delight, another partridge appeared, followed by eleven small and chubby chicks, sure-footedly walking on their longish legs as they pecked the ground, all the while cheep-cheeping quietly amongst themselves. Their overall body colour was cream with brown showing on the crowns of their heads, their backs and tiny wings. They had also a clear eye-stripe, but brown not black like their parents. As the family progressed along the path – father loudly leading the way, it struck me forcibly once again how remarkably well the adults blend into the landscape for such a colourful bird.

Wednesday 16 June
Heavy dew – constant drip-drip of moisture from the trees. The moon is in the last quarter; watched it rise over Crosshampton just before 2 a.m.

Sat on the fence at the bottom of High Ridge watching my magpie pair with their three well-feathered youngsters, though their tails are still quite short. Whistled, and after some minutes, first one adult then the other *and* the offspring came over. All finished up perched on my slat atop of the fence – got rather crowded!

Friday 18 June
Out with Josh who's very interested in the cut hayfield. Overcast night with strong wind. My fox seemed uneasy, but put it down to 'visitors' who turned up a little after midnight. However, at 1.25 a.m., we had a sudden prolonged roll of thunder that moved away briefly then returned with tremendous force – seemed to continue some while. No rain, and at first no lightning. Looked round for Josh – no fox, nor anything else in sight, come to that. Stood in the middle of the field, cut hay all around. The lightning began to divide the sky into jagged fragments – tremendously exciting, an incredible display, flash upon flash forking

141

out and down. The wind was by now bowing the foliage; the great tree that dominates the Ashtree Path was hurled this way and that. Then the rain descended in a torrent, bouncing off Briarmead Lane and soaking the strewn hay (and me) in an instant. Thought it best to find the shelter of the nearest holly, and there beneath its hanging branches I found I had been forestalled – by Josh! Curled up against the trunk, brush over muzzle, eyes reflecting in the gloom. Stood staring at him there, forgetful of the storm, as the scene jogged a memory. This had happened before – same holly, but the same fox or another?

Stayed until the storm moved away and the rain was just a pattering on the leaves. The tawny owl chicks could be heard calling their persistent 'ti-sweep, ti-sweep' through the woodland. Josh raised his head, listening, looked over at me and yawned. At the path edge, we parted. I would have dearly loved to have watched the owls and their fledged young, but had a feeling my companion was going to do just that. From experience, I can honestly say that foxes and tawnies don't mix.

[At home, checked back when I found a fox sheltering here before, or rather sleeping. On Saturday 21 March 1981. It quite probably *was* Josh, but I didn't 'know' him then, so have no definite way of telling. He's not a very young dog, approximately three years old. Certainly gives food for thought.]

Sunday 20 June
The Chantry is at its best in the early morning. Within its depths, all is dark, but since it stands on a promontory over the valley, the rays of the sun as it climbs the sky, stretch in and touch each trunk with gentle light. To sit at the headland and watch the dawn steal softly along the valley is an unforgettable sight. First it glints on the Bourne's moving surface, then on the wider waters of the distant ponds. Up here, the Chantry is in the midst of any storm that thunders its way across the ridge top; it feels the full might and strength of the gale that bends these tall beeches.

Been watching the Dump vixen hunting over Great Chantry Field tonight. She left her well-grown cub again in the nettles, but notice now he's inclined to do some hunting on his own account. He pounced on something that squeaked – missed it – nosed around at the field edge and then found it again; pounced and killed. Very long tail hanging from his mouth (wood mouse or yellow-necked?). Notice the young fox tried eating the tail as well as its owner, but nearly choked and spat it out. Has yet to learn to bite it off like the Prosser vixen. Later his mother appeared, approximately 4.15 a.m., with a squirrel which she let him have. Must have fed herself as she lay down, rolling and stretching in the furrow, then groomed. Much later, the young fox jumped on to a dead beech that came down in January's snow. He sat there looking very attractive and obviously enjoying his vantage point, the sun slanting across the field, giving a first warmth to the day. The vixen sat upright so suddenly that she startled her son, who nearly toppled off his log. Then she went bounding down the field side, crying and yowling, just as her mate appeared at the top of the Bank Sett. (Their hearing is fantastic; he didn't emerge from the undergrowth on the bank until she was well down the field. If he had barked, I would have heard. She must have heard him pushing through the bushes; unless he made a sound beyond human range, which is quite possible.) A short distance from him, she crouched down, tail waving frantically, inviting him to approach her. As he did so, she sprang up again, nuzzling him and licking his face. Foxes are never more dog-like (or dogs so fox-like) as when a mated pair meet. Together they ran back to the cub, bumping one another as they went, the male nibbling at his vixen's ear. The youngster was delighted to see his father and together the two dogs ran back and forth in the growing corn whilst the mother stretched out in the sun again below the log.

If the cub did but know it, these are his carefree months soon to come to an end. The summer months of plenty, with mice and voles in the hedgerows, rats and rabbits in the standing crops, birds and fruits in the woodland ways, and worms in the damp places. With the onset of autumn, he will go his own way, perhaps travelling miles from his birthplace in search of his own territory. But he is one of the lucky ones. As an only pup, he has grown big and strong, and barring the local hunt and the traffic which surrounds his little world, he has a better chance of survival than most.

Monday 21 June
Dull, overcast night. Have been watching and listening to the tawny owl family over the cut Hayfield, Briarmead. Once young owlets gain sufficient feathering to keep them warm, the hen tawny hunts as well as her mate. There is no nest as such, their home originally was a crevice in an oak where a branch had fallen away. Since tawnies hunt at night (the coldest time), the hen must stay and brood her young or they would soon die of exposure. Even when she takes prey from the male and shreds it for her chicks, she still 'cloaks' them with her wide wings as she does so; warmth is of primary importance. Now these owlets are fledged and could, in fact, begin hunting for themselves – but they don't, and they won't, until late July or early August.

It was Dr Southern who explained why this was so. Tawnies are extremely territorial. Therefore, the fledged chicks have to learn the limits of their parents' territory (from which they will soon be banished), and where neighbouring boundaries begin. This they are doing now, and if, as this night, they *do* stray across the borders, adjoining tawnies noisily confront them, driving the fledglings back. This flying about must increase their co-ordination and strengthen their wing muscles too – notice they are landing more accurately and are increasingly adventurous. The youngsters' persistent 'hunger' cries keep the adults very busy, especially round the Grain and Potato Dumps. With earthworms, beetles, rats, bank voles, wood mice and young rabbits on the menu, it's not surprising really that at times foxes and tawnies clash. I've noticed with Josh that the owl generally has the upper hand. If the harsh, resounding alarm 'wick-wick-wick-wick' doesn't warn him off, the sudden swoop with talons viciously outstretched, only to fly up and swoop down again from another unexpected angle, is enough to discourage much larger animals than a mere fox. Interesting that the tawny seems invariably to attack the head and the eyes. I've never yet had this unpleasant experience myself, though Josh's company nearly involved me once (see 8 May this year).

Whilst these tawny owls still have their fledglings, they will remain aggressive towards intruders. But from mid-August onwards, the youngsters will begin to disperse in search of their own territories. Their lives will depend on them finding their own which they will hold *for life* – their survival depends on this vital factor for, if not, they starve. The mortality rate of young tawnies is higher then than at any other time.

(Odd light again, this time near the beehives. Very much like a car headlight, but no car could get there. Next time, I'll try tracking it down.)

Wednesday 23 June
Ripe cherries litter the Wildflower Path and the Dump fox family were busily eating them after dawn this morning. To me, the gean fruit taste bitter and lack flesh, for though they are smaller than cultivated varieties, the stone is similar in size. [Wouldn't agree with that now – June 1984 – rather enjoy them!] However, foxes, squirrels and badgers like them, so obviously tastes differ. I've seen a weasel sample one and Wendy eat them too. See the old 'grandfather' cherry has dropped many about its massive bole – gathered some to try on Josh when I see him tomorrow night. Don't think his area contains any geans – will be interesting to see what he makes of them.

Was just thinking of returning home when a male hawfinch came down on to the path, 6.15 a.m. Began to crack cherry stones with that oversize in beaks – then its mate came and did likewise. Think they may have a nest in one of the tall geans by the up-and-over badger path.

[Josh does like cherries too! 24 June.]

Monday 28 June
Walked round the wood edge (unaccompanied!) at 3.50 a.m. The Lower Hayfield, Briarmead, has been resown and rolled, and after the past week of storms and rain, the grass-stalks stand well above ground. I happened to look back towards the lane's bank when I saw a sow badger hurrying across the width of the field in an effort to gain the safety of the wood. If she had been human, I would have said 'sneaking furtively with sidelong glances in the direction of my retreating back'! I quietly watched with amusement as she successfully reached what is the

144

outskirts of the Potato Dump crater, and scurried out of sight beneath a coppiced hazel. Stood out from the wood edge to check just where she entered the woodland. Felt fairly sure she was the badger that had come to live in the rabbit warren in the hollow round the far side of the beehives (26 April and 5 May); also had a hunch that she and Old Joe have got acquainted, though I haven't actually seen them together.

Stood there reflecting on this with the daylight getting clearer and birds all around tuning up, when another badger appeared crossing the field on the same route as the other and heading for the same gap under the hazel. Still at a distance, it spotted me and, changing direction, came speedily straight for me. Within a few yards, it stopped dead, raised one front paw off the ground a little, and sniffed the air. It was Joe. Not for the first time, I noticed how massive he had become – very grey, yes, but powerful. Stared at the width of him and the strength in that head and shoulders and marvelled how the Dump foxes could have ever dared attack him. All seems so long ago now – has the quality of a dream. I've a great admiration for him. He's lived so long, he obeys no law but his own – like some very old people. With the building of the Motorway, his world has changed but he has clung to the place he knows and refuses to alter. Perhaps now he has a mate, he'll forage on the fields her side of this wood and not the Warby side; I hope so, for his sake. His snout, jaws and lower legs were all muddy – plenty of worms in the wet places.

145

He looked over to the wood edge and the hazel coppice. I think his sow had probably returned to see what was keeping him. Then he ambled off, a big, shaggy, untidy-looking hulk gently swaying from side to side. At the trees, he paused, short-sightedly looking back. There was a movement just inside the wood and he lowered his head and went under the foliage.

The field seemed very empty when he'd gone.

Tuesday 29 June
3.15 a.m. A nightingale gave a fantastic solo performance pre-dawn chorus this morning. I was able to watch it singing from the top of a rose-covered bramble bush; they have a nest deep inside at the bottom. Beautiful outpouring of liquid notes slowly increasing in volume and intensity. When it finally flew down, it brushed my face where I sat looking up. It veered off across the field with a startled, grating cry.

This morning in good light at approximately 5 a.m., I checked the nest holes on the old beech (*see* 2 June). They are deserted. This tree is hollow though still very much alive and, standing inside the bole today, I realised why the lesser spotted woodpeckers abandoned their efforts. Woodpecker holes at first slope up slightly (to stop rain driving in), level out a short way and then drop sharply down. This pair of birds made four attempts, but reached the hollow and fresh air before they could complete any.

See at long last the fencing has been removed and the banks of earth levelled, on the gas pipeline route across the Top Hayfield, Prosser's Wood – but I think by an exasperated farmer, not by the contractors. It's been an eyesore since last August, but now both hayfield and pipe-line have gone under the plough. The damp earth smells marvellous!

Friday 2 July
Most of Barry Hains's cereal fields are wheat, a few are barley. It's ripening fast and glows in the early morning sun. Old Joe has become very friendly since Monday (I don't touch him); his mate is cautious, but tolerates me. One of these fields off Briarmead Lane has been planted with young cabbages and the badgers have been worming there in the wet, soft earth. I was happily watching their noisy 'spaghetti'-eating when a patrol car slipped up the lane. It was approximately 3.30 a.m. and light so, of course, they saw me and came to investigate. The badgers didn't wait to be introduced. Hung about after the police had gone, but realised the animals probably wouldn't return, with the men's scent fresh on the path – if they had stayed in the car, it wouldn't have mattered. Went up to the Dump edge and stood there enjoying the morning. A few minutes passed – then a fledged tawny flew silently up, softly round the field edge. (Their roosting stations are constantly changing at this time of year, no one place being used for long.) Another ten minutes and I heard a familiar noise of a badger moving none too

quietly, so called gently. Joe came up, but no mate – she's probably gone right round. Went with him into the wood, and so to the sett at the View.

Sunday 4 July
Mild, clear night – moon near the full, slight wind. The young Prosser foxes are beginning to wander at night, attempting to hunt for themselves. They meet up about this time, midnight, to groom and play, though their play is becoming aggressive. All five have survived and the tagless one is still boss (*see* 5 May). When very young, the runt of this litter was a vixen continually whimpering at the roughness of the others. At some stage, Tagless began to stand up for her in a casual way so that she gained confidence. In the shadow of her brother, she is now unmolested, and early on discovered that if she took and ate her food near him she could feed in peace – she is no longer a runt. It is the sequel that I find interesting. Just recently I've seen Tagless set upon by his bigger, heavier brother who has always been a rival. Twice the little vixen has joined Tagless and together they have routed the aggressor. This litter is now sixteen weeks old and, thanks to the hunting of Josh and his vixen, are fine young animals. The parents still hunt for their family, but no longer leave it at the den, but further away. In searching for what the adults have left them, the youngsters come across food for themselves. Never seen these cubs hunting with their parents either.

Hadn't seen Josh for a couple of nights so, crossing the fields at 1.45 a.m., I called him – three short barks from me usually gets an answer and he comes to meet me. The answer tonight, however, was rather a puzzle – the 'wow-pause-wow-pause' warning call, going on and on. Came from the Top Hayfield, Briarmead, where, due to the very wet weather, the grass still lies in swathes. Barked back at him on reaching the field edge and his warning came very urgently and close by. I jumped on to the tarmac and said 'Josh' quietly, then on to the Hayfield bank and there he was amongst the long grass, very agitated. Puzzled at his behaviour, I bent to touch him, just as tyres crunched on the gritty surface of Briarmead Lane inside the wood entrance, and a car, headlights now on, came towards us. Josh and I sped across the Hayfield, although the wet, cut grass was a hindrance. Zigzagged as I feared a shot, especially when a man shouted. Josh didn't leave me but kept close and since his speed is far greater than mine, this was surprising. A beam shone across the Hayfield – had they turned the headlights towards us? – but we were well out of it. A voice called again, not aggressive but reassuringly, and I stood there wondering if they could be a patrol. The car was unmarked, but certainly we were meant no harm.

Then my fox was gone, running back the way we had come. Standing just inside the beam he must have been clearly visible to the men. Josh gave one single bark to draw their attention to himself, then stood quite still and silent. There was a pause – could hear voices gently talking. He moved around the beam, edging closer – and barked. I called him loudly

147

by name and he came, effortlessly loping back to me at the wood edge. He covered the distance in great bounds, ears back, brush stretched way out behind all in a line with his body. He slid into the undergrowth and whined softly at me still hesitating on the grass. He whined again and I crept in and knelt beside him. Time passed, then the car turned quietly down the lane.

Looking back at the incident, two things stand out:

1) In parts of the countryside where traffic merely passes by, wildlife doesn't necessarily associate man with the motorcar. Here, however, people and their dogs go to and from their vehicles, so Josh has the man/dog association with a car even if nothing gets out of it and there's no manscent. Allowing for the fact that he is aware I distrust 'night visitors' as much as he, nevertheless he *was* warning me of my own kind. Which leaves me wondering in what light he regards me!

2) Why, when I hesitated at the wood edge, did he return and act as a decoy? Vixens draw attention away from their cubs and encourage dogs and humans to chase them instead. A fox will draw attention from its mate if it is injured or in whelp. Did Josh misinterpret my hestitation for tiredness? Very strange.

Monday 5 July
At 4.50 this morning on Corbett's land, I saw a hare acting most extraordinarily. Wondered if it had been affected by sprays. Watched it at first from a distance through the monocular, but it was so engrossed in continuing its odd pastime that I was able to come quietly very close.

It was standing on hind legs in the middle of the track turning round and round, its front paws dangling down. It wasn't regular in its momentum – sometimes it slowed, still turning, sometimes it gained speed. It never seemed to become giddy. No other hares – or any other animal – in sight. Just this solitary creature going round and round with birdsong coming from the woods and traffic noise from the Motorway below. Its black-tipped ears were conspicuously upright – almost rigidly so. I timed it (1½ minutes) although it was doing it when first I came by. When it did stop, in a little cloud of dust as the path here is sheltered by the wood edge and quite dry, it remained upright as if in a trance. Then started off on hind legs before dropping down on all fours and casually loping away. (I believe it's *not* unusual for a reconnoitring hare, i.e. upright on hind legs, to start walking in an upright position before dropping down.)

Scent of honeysuckle and sweet-chestnut flowers lingers on the air. Green woodpecker finding insects and calling from the dead trees of the Bank Sett near the Chantry edge, 5.25 a.m. Wild marjoram, toadflax, common rock-rose, field scabious, chicory and nettle-leaved bellflowers all decorated with fallen cherries on the Wildflower Path!

Heard the vixen at the Felled Logs area giving a 'single' bark and went to investigate, time 5.45 a.m. A shooter was looking around and

poking a branch into the den entrances that house her cubs. Know him quite well by sight [description given in diary omitted here]. Pleasantly persuaded him to leave the area and accompanied him, talking. Actually the vixen had been trying to decoy him away, but he didn't have the brains (or commonsense) to realise that.

Thursday 8 July
10.30 a.m. Walking to Warby via the Woods this morning, I met Barry Hains in his car on Briarmead. He asked me how the badgers were faring and what setts were occupied. The patrol hadn't contacted him about me being on his fields last Friday, though he was very interested that the police *had* been around. We both agreed it was a good thing for a variety of reasons. He remarked that there were strange people on farmland at night – present company excepted!

Told me that a stolen car had been abandoned in the middle of one of his wheatfields by the river. He had hitched a tractor to it and pulled it out before someone had the bright idea of firing it. Usually they *are* set alight when dumped, so he was lucky this time. The entire near-ripe crop would have gone up with it. He reckons he has most trouble from cars and motorbikes. Vandalism, arson and theft are constant threats to farmers. But he said, rather depressed, 'What can you do about it?'

Walking home much later along the Main Road, I had a good look at the flowering lucerne growing on the dry banks of the cutting. Though of Mediterranean origin, it has naturalised itself everywhere near the fields here where it was grown as a crop. It enriches the soil since its roots have the rare ability to fix nitrogen – it also makes valuable fodder. I first took an interest in it through Old Joe. It's one of his favourite greenstuffs.

149

Sometimes on *wet nights*, he seems to cross the Motorway just to eat it from this bank. He also enjoys eating red clover at the edge of Briarmead Lane.

Friday 9 July
Warm night, moon on the wane, stars showing, ground mist in the hollows – visibility excellent. Listened to tawnies over farmland near Madden Lane; they have two fledged young. I used 'red' torch – they definitely don't register it. Beautiful birds – very graceful, effortless flight.

3 a.m. At the Chantry, the badger sow and her cubs from the Bank Sett were foraging under the beeches. Youngsters very playful. One found a Coke tin with something hard inside. Made a fine, noisy toy to run around with, chased by the others. Anyone hearing and not seeing what was happening would wonder what was going on! These cubs use the fallen trunks in the Chantry to play on. Several dead trees are prevented from lying prone by the nearness of the living and are poised at curious angles, and it's surprising how high off the ground this badger family gets.

3.15 a.m. At first light, well before sunrise, I was sitting hidden on the Briarmead bank with tall grass and nettles way above my head, when a throaty croaking (like an outsize frog) and then a whistling over the hayfield in front of me came from the wood edge. Eased myself up gently to have a better look, and there etched against the moon still clear in the sky, was a woodcock 'roding'. Was a little further over to that seen in March, although probably was the same one. Its 'roding' was fairly brief today and the earliest in the morning I have known.

Monday 12 July
Mild, cloudy night with gusty wind – good visibility. 1.10 a.m., crossing Ingrims Fields, heard a tawny's alarm cry, very urgent. Then both adults were crying and swooping low over the barley a short distance from the footpath I was on. Had gone but a few paces further, when I discovered a young dead stoat lying on the bare earth with blood-stained fur. Continued quietly until my path met the wide tractor route that divides these fields; the owls were still calling and flying low over the standing crop. A large adult stoat bounded out and made to enter the barley opposite when a tawny swooped with talons outstretched. With a great leap the stoat spun round to face its pursuer, emitting a sound like a spitting bark, just as the bird attacked, missed and hit the ground. This left both creatures facing one another, and I supposed more evenly matched, since the owl's claws would be less of an advantage on the ground. I've read of creatures being terrified of stoats, but this tawny owl certainly wasn't. It rose up, spreading wide its wings and fluffing out its plumage as it hissed. There, I think, the matter might have ended, but for the other owl who came gliding in behind the stoat with lightning

150

speed. It not only flattened the musteline, but nearly did the same to its 'hooding' mate, such was the force of its attack, as, with talons embedded, the stoat was dragged some way along the track. A thin squeal and a strong musky smell – then both birds were tearing at the body. These owls have fledged young, although I didn't see them tonight. Wonder who started all this? Imagine there might have been other young stoats hunting with their mother and now concealed in the barley. Did they attack the owls or vice versa?

Returning at dawn along the same route, no sign of remains of either stoat.

Friday 23 July
1.10 a.m. Mild, overcast night; slight rain. Traffic noise very subdued. Treeline dark with breeze whispering through the ripe barley heads of Great Chantry. Briarmead lies quietly under the sky – visibility reasonable.

Met up with Josh on the Top Hayfield – he seemed very unsettled. Much later at 2.25 a.m., when I was in the Old Barn ruins, I saw him fetching back something and watched him follow the field edge and disappear in the wood. Wondered where he was going since his near-grown offspring were in the Ridge vicinity and *he* would eat on the spot. Thought about it awhile, then entered the woods at the point he had, where the spring runs out into the field. Followed to its source and there he was, standing just where the spring water begins to seep from the ground. A young rabbit lay amongst the grass and next to it another pair of eyes regarding me – his vixen, caught by her right front leg in a snare. I have tended to avoid her until very recently for fear the cubs would become used to me, so she doesn't know me in the way Josh does. She crouched there in great pain – the wire was deeply embedded to the bone. I had a great difficulty in freeing her and finally resorted to covering her head with my anorak and virtually leaning on her whilst I loosened the wire. As it was, she was snapping through layers of anorak, beside herself with pain and fear. Josh stood the while watching us – very quiet.

Saturday 24 July
There's something about acres of ripe grain stretching as far as the eye can see, with skylarks trilling over it as the sun rises. Can't imagine anywhere on this earth I'd rather be.

John Shaw's wheatfield by the beehives is in a very poor state, as weeds have taken over where the Brent geese in January grazed the young shoots. Normally, these birds just nibble down and the shoots will regrow although the wheat will stand shorter. But owing to the thawing of the snow, the ground was very soft, and the shoots were pulled right up, roots and all.

Old Joe and the two sow badgers (one of which has the three cubs) all seem to get on very well. The solitary female now lives with him at the

View, and the other sow and her family go to earth at the Bank Sett. (He mated with both females in June.) They have all been in the wheatfield halfway down Briarmead this morning, eating grain – running the ripe heads through their open jaws, then allowing the stalks to spring back into place. Only when you look closely do you see the grain is gone.

(The Dump foxes and their cub appear to have left the area. No trace of them anywhere here.)

Monday 26 July
The Prosser vixen's lameness prevents her hunting for herself, but Josh is fetching back for her and, to a certain extent, for the cubs. The latter, however, would survive on their own now by scavenging, if not by hunting, for there's plenty to be found in woods and fields. The cobnuts and beechmast that the squirrels bring down are readily eaten by the foxes and badgers, though not really ripe.

Friday 30 July
Tonight I found the answer to the curious 'car' light (*see* 26 April and 21 June). At 2.15 a.m., looking across Briarmead, I saw it brightly shining across the fields towards the Wheatfield Copse. (Have a theory about that light – many years ago I met a 'lamper' who worked these fields with his dogs.) Moved quickly from the Old Barn ruins round the wood/field fringe, in order to come behind the owner of the beam. Not

much bothered when sometimes the light went out, since I knew by now where it was and didn't wish to look directly at it in any case – that's the easiest way to lose my nightvision. I was banking on the light-holder's inability to see in the dark since to be behind a torch light or the headlights of a car is to guarantee bad nightvision. Soon I could make out one man and two lurchers – one animal by his side, the other running the beam – down on the path of the Wheatfield Copse. It was a lurcherman's lamp sure enough.

By day, rabbits feed close to their burrows, but under cover of darkness they graze well out from the concealing copse or hedgerow. This lamper was training his light along the wide, grassy space between copse and wheatfield, and the dog (very whippet-like, but taller) was catching rabbits with great agility. A good dog may catch many rabbits in one night. Lurchers are often run alternately, one resting while the other works. Sometimes this dog followed a rabbit well into the wheat. Barry Hains wouldn't be terribly pleased – it's getting trampled by children in their summer holidays as it is. If the dog went in too far, the lurcherman switched off his lamp.

At 4 a.m., pre-dawn, the lapwings are calling their sad 'peewit-peewit' over the ploughed, rolled field of lower Briarmead. They are by far the earliest birds to sound; in fact, they call and feed throughout the night. Watched them feeding amongst the badgers since, for both, the farmer's soft, prepared earth contains grubs, wireworms and earthworms that can't easily be obtained from the hard, dry ground elsewhere. One badger cub decided to chase the peewits as a diversion to food-finding, and soon all three youngsters were enjoying themselves. The birds were not much impressed, and simply flew up and along for a while, before wheeling gracefully back. Lapwings merge very well into these surroundings. Until they move on the ground, they are difficult to trace even with the monocular.

Sunday 1 August
Dull, overcast night and noticeably cooler. The water-pump by the Motorway that feeds the irrigation on Roger Johnson's land has been left on tonight to fill up the tank. It sounds loud from a distance away but, close to, it's deafening and makes the ground vibrate. A little way from the pump, I watched a hare drumming the ground. The doors of the brick-built shed in which the machine was housed were wide open and the animal stood facing them and was greatly excited. I couldn't hear the drumming above the din, of course – only see the action. I'm not sure whether it's noise or vibration that stimulates these creatures – probably both. Have read that they congregate near airport runways and motorway verges, though I've never seen this myself. They are, however, the only animals I've watched in this countryside that actively appear to enjoy an approaching thunderstorm. On the Top Hayfield of Briarmead a hare stood bolt upright – they seem to have the ability to stand and

'walk' on hind legs – watching the darkened sky. A prolonged roll of thunder and it drummed. Then in the rush of wind that precedes such a storm, it bounded round the field in a great circle, stopping to drum each time that thunder sounded. It continued so until the rain lashed down, whereupon it slowly passed into the undergrowth.

Old Joe and his cubless sow have been digging out tonight just above the den of last year's foxcubs. Wonder if they will settle here for a while? If so, it will be the first time I have known badgers in this, the Old Cherry Tree area, although these ancient workings were originally those of badgers. (There's a squirrel up in the beech tree on whose roots I'm sitting writing this at the Chantry and I'm getting showered with discarded mast cases! There's also a shooter down below me at the Bank Sett 5.15 a.m., so I'm not alone.)

The Prosser's Wood vixen's foot is healing well now. She puts it briefly to the ground, though she doesn't rest her weight on it. They are keeping closer together, she and Josh, mainly because she is sharing in his kills. Therefore I am seeing more of her now. The well-grown cubs only occasionally meet their parents and are finding their own food, plus the leavings of the adults. Food is abundant, especially the rabbits. There are rabbits of all sizes, from tiny ones that freeze at your approach and can be picked up in cupped hands to wily old 'uns, perhaps three years old (don't think wild rabbits survive much beyond that).

7.15 a.m. Patrol car came up and down Briarmead Lane though it did not stop. Soon after, I saw one of the Hainses checking a field further down. Some wheat already lifted although, in the main, these fields are still to be harvested – a great fire hazard in the summer holidays.

Friday 6 August
Thick mist lies over these fields and from inside the wood comes the constant drip-drop of moisture from off the foliage. Met Josh on the Top Hayfield, Prosser's Wood. His vixen is now coping on her own, though she still limps. Their cubs are quite independent these days and doing well; very handsome animals – the young vixen is sturdy too. This is the only pair of foxes I've been able to observe from pairing up and mating to independence of cubs. Next thing will be cub dispersal. And then the cycle begins again.

Traffic noise mercifully deadened with the mist. These damp conditions are paradise for badgers and foxes. Followed Josh along the last furrow of this wheatfield. I'm quite lost to view, being dwarfed on the one side by the bank and on the other by the standing corn. Josh is playful, having eaten his fill of worms etc. His coat is wet and so am I from the clinging moisture. A field edge is *not* the place to be bundled by a friendly fox – I've twice lost my footing and ended up in the long, wet grass. Think it's time I lost Josh!

4.35 a.m. A strong breeze has sprung up and the mist is clearing a little. Am sitting on a post writing this – on my tod! No birds, but then

August is a quiet month for them in their moult. Coming out of these woods by the Oak Dell Path at 5.20 a.m., I saw a quail family feeding amongst the lettuce rows where water is lying. Quails are shy, secretive birds – the chicks kept up a continuous soft cheeping as they diligently pecked the ground.

Tuesday 10 August
Mild night with gentle breeze. When I left home it was raining slightly, but has now stopped. Sky cloudy with fitful moon – visibility excellent.

Yesterday night was dry, no dew at all, and very warm. The badgers, Old Joe and co., were busy taking in bedding from the cut grass of the Lower Hayfield, Briarmead. Badgers much prefer hay to straw – they're not stupid! Joe and his sow are staying in the Old Cherry area now.

I'm leaning with my back against one of the field path's oak trees writing this and looking out at Josh and his vixen searching the cut stalks. It's surprising how many small, dead animals they find that didn't have a chance to get clear of the combine harvester. On a field lower down this lane, the badgers are doing the selfsame thing. It's 4.20 a.m. and will soon be light.

4.50 a.m. Ended up picking blackberries at the wood edge for myself – and Josh's vixen. She could eat a lot quicker than I could pick. The ripe ones were well beyond her reach – imagine she's helped herself lower down the bushes already. (I make it a golden rule never to pick for myself below my waist – the birds take the top ones, badgers and foxes the lower – though badgers also walk into bushes and weigh them down.)

Coming out of these woods by the Oak Dell Path, 5.10 a.m., I stand quietly watching the quail family again. Their calls are no help in locating them since they seem to be adept at throwing their voices, and, like the partridges here, are well camouflaged until they move. Should like to find out more about them; apparently not much is known.

A beautiful dawn, with the promise of a fine day.

Saturday 14 August
Cold, clear damp night with breeze. From 4.25 to 5 a.m., I have been *listening* to the tawny pair from the Old Barn ruins area of these fields and the Top Hayfield, Briarmead. Joint hooting for approximately ten minutes from stationary perches, then the 'kee-wick' call as one bird flew round the territory into the wood, round and out on to the fields, crying as it went for seventeen minutes. Later, renewed joint hooting. All this from first light to dawn. Plenty of small rodents amongst the stubble collecting the fallen grain, making easy pickings for owls and foxes. Seen yet again tonight that tawny owls *do* eat carrion, provided that it's fresh – a young rabbit and a mouse killed by yesterday's machinery, both eaten. Didn't have Josh with me tonight so indulged my tawny-watching – marvellous birds.

Earlier, at 1.25 a.m., as I passed the Scots pines on the Sleet House

155

footpath, saw movement in the orchard beyond the hedge. Went to investigate and found the badger family of that area in amongst the fallen apples. The fruit was never gathered and a strong cider smell hangs heavily on the air. The cubs, now nearly as big as their parents, ended their meal by playing ball with them. (Their parents mated – long duration – whilst the youngsters played.)

Tuesday 17 August
Pre-dawn is a fascinating time to be out – that short period between darkness and sunrise. As I came out of the wood on to the harvested wheatfield opposite the beehives, saw Josh's vixen with one of her grown cubs on the far path. She barked the warning bark as the youngster disappeared into the elm brush round the concealed hives, so I squatted down and barked back. We had a brief vocal contest, then she gave a yowl and ran towards me. (Her limp shows more when she trots. Going at speed, i.e. loping, it hardly shows.) Her brush was waving as she approached and met me face to face. She's very delicately boned, more so than most, long slender muzzle and thin face. She whined softly in her throat as I spoke gently to her. Then the youngster reappeared on the path, so I stood upright to frighten him and he made off again.

Tuesday 24 August
4.50 a.m. Sitting at the Chantry headland just before dawn, watching a bat hunting insects over Great Chantry. Its flight is slow compared with, say, the little pipistrelle, and not jerky. The dead and rotten trunks of the Chantry make excellent roosts.
    5.20 a.m. The sun has yet to touch the horizon but already its deep rays are diffused across the eastern sky, glowing redly through the dark clouds. Heard a fox bark within the woodland near the top of Briarmead and couldn't resist barking back as I was sure it was Josh (foxes give voice as individually as humans). Inevitably, it became a barking contest and – interesting, this – his barks became longer and longer drawn out, with me copying him as accurately as possible. Then he appeared on the wood edge.
    Thought at first I had upset him as he didn't advance, but stood stiff-legged, head forward and looking apparently through me. Then I turned and saw what *he* had seen – a patrol car drawn up under cover of our 'conversation'. So we both beat a hasty retreat!

AUTUMN 1982

Thursday 2 September 1982
Rain has ceased, sky slowly clearing. Near-full disc of the harvest moon glows orange in a glassy sky – very strange light.

Notice on the Ridge that the crickets' (or grasshoppers') stridulations (or 'songs') seem to vary, some a great deal. Feel this is probably from species to species, rather than individual variations amongst one species. Tonight, it sounds like a competition for the best/loudest signature tune. However, Josh soon upset things by pouncing at them in the long grass – he can't leave anything alone! Yesterday in his company, I discovered the dead body of one of his sons – shot through the head – at the back of High Ridge. Josh seemed uneasy, but not startled or surprised, so I concluded he had found it before. I deliberately went and looked at it again just now, as much to see his reaction as anything. The body is beginning to swell. Josh approached cautiously and stood by me as I knelt there. We turned our heads and looked at one another and I stroked the side of his face, feeling rather mean. When I stood up, he sprang round, eager to be off, and trotted by my side – usually he leads and I follow. He scent-marked neither the body nor the immediate area, although this is part of his territory. Nor did he yesterday.

All the badgers, including the three cubs, have been digging out of late in the Old Cherry area and are bringing in hay from the fields (ignoring the nearer straw) and bracken from the woods. It was the cubs whom I watched eating *plums* yesterday. Couldn't think where they had found them, then discovered it was from the two stunted old plum trees just in this woodland bordering the Lower Hayfield.

Waiting for pre-light and dawn at the top of Briarmead, I had a surprise. The first tawnies to appear and be vocal were not the adults but four fledged youngsters. Flew round and perched on the two field-path oaks, calling again and again. They remind me of very good student musicians, soon to turn professional. They will shortly be dispersing to find their own territories – this is the most precarious time of their lives. Glad Josh wasn't with me – perhaps this sounds fanciful, but he seems jealous of the interest I take in tawny owls and does his best to make them fly off. When he has succeeded, he makes a great fuss of me – never is he more dog-like than then. Very reminiscent of Wendy when I showed great interest in another dog.

I find the pitch of the young tawnies' calls varies from individual to individual (one especially sounds quite differently from the others), so even if I had not *seen* them, I would have noticed four separate voices. Their vocalisation ceased by 5.15 a.m., still pre-dawn. The Morning Star has risen well above the horizon – sun yet to come.

Wednesday 15 September
4.40 a.m. Sitting high up at the Chantry headland, I'm above the swirling mist of the Bourne valley, a tawny owl pair serenading behind me from an old dead beech, and ahead, clear, starry skies with a lazy crescent moon not long risen above the horizon, almost lying on its back.

At 5.45 a.m., I finally leave the tawnies still serenading one another to walk up Briarmead at first light. This little lane smells sweetly of the ripe damsons growing on its banks. The sun is unable to pierce the mist across these fields, but the moon appears floating in a pink haze.

Walking towards the Wheatfield Copse homeward bound at 6.10 a.m., saw two foxes in silhouette playing together on the burnt-off stubble – leaping, chasing and standing upright, face to face, with paws on each other's shoulders, brushes waving. I forgot the time in pleasure at their game. Then through the copse they chased and down on to the field below, so I quietly continued by, just as the rising sun broke the mist barrier behind the elm brush of the coppice. There was a dog-like growling from the undergrowth and, unthinking, I knelt down quite still. Another moment and, to my consternation, the tagless young fox and the little vixen, both Josh's offspring, emerged on to the pathway –

and came up. Never imagined they knew me that well, but how stupid not to realise they must be nearly as familiar with my scent trail as are their parents. Everywhere I go, they can smell me and know I've passed by. Stood up abruptly and moved quickly across the burnt-off stubble and so to the Ridge – didn't look back.

Monday 27 September
2.40 a.m. Old Joe and the cubless sow have been digging out at the Old Cherry Tree Sett – definitely seem to have settled here, all amongst the butcher's broom. After days of heavy rain and squalls, it's a clear, starry night with a half-moon and good visibility. Distantly I hear the calling of the Chantry owls high up on the further slope. My surroundings are dappled with moonlight shafting through the branches above. A bank vole has appeared from the gnarled roots of the Old Cherry and is nibbling a chestnut, seemingly unaware of the sow badger close by. She makes a sudden dart at the little rodent which jumps high at the unexpected movement and easily escapes. I make no attempt to hide from the badgers, there's no need. They are working their snouts through the wet leaves and finding plenty to eat. Every so often, one will make a loud snort amidst the regular snufflings, clearing the nose, I imagine – must get pretty congested amongst all that debris!

Friday 1 October
Clear, mild night with full moon. Met Josh at the foot of the Ridge –

surprised, as I haven't been in his area for some time. He wouldn't accompany me up the scree slope – seemed uneasy. Left him to continue up myself, only to hear him bark behind me as I was nearing the top. Turned to see him standing down below, then continued on my way.

First thing I saw by a clump of birches was a parked van. A few yards more – a tent. That explained my fox's unease – overnight campers. Continuing to the Wheatfield Copse, I was caught up by Josh who bounded around me whining his pleasure. He must have come through Prosser's Wood – glad he's cautious of humans (myself excepted!). Left him at Briarmead and so to the Warby side of these woods. All the fields have gone under the plough, so could see to the field edge – and Old Joe on the bank. Caught up with him right by the edge of the Motorway and knelt speaking softly. Juggernauts rushing by, dwarfing us, the noise and vibration deafening *me*, but apparently not bothering the old badger! I crept into the grass, encouraging him to follow. His big, muddy snout explored my face and hair – he's got bad breath! Couldn't persuade him not to cross the traffic lanes, however; he appears to cross when the vibration lessens. (Sound is odd on this stretch of motorway due, I think, to the gradient. I tend to think something's approaching when it's not – but Joe isn't fooled.) He always crosses in the same spot, near the overhead gantry. Followed him (with caution!) across the lanes. It's surprising in a sense that he chooses to cross just here, since the floodlit gantry casts considerable light – although it is perhaps fortunate for him that he does. Think it's the curved angle of the banks *and* what grows on them on this part of the roadside. This year, I have watched him eat lucerne, rowan and blackberries, and tonight sample elderberries and rosehips here. At this point, also, he is very close to the grounds of the big house and its dustbins!

Wednesday 13 October
First sunshine this afternoon after days of rain. Photographed bullace fruits with difficulty owing to gusty wind. Lovely sky with towering cloud formation. Badgers have freshly dug out Meg's Sett, including badger bones! Will have to see which animals are staying here.

Saturday 16th October
Mild, damp night with good visibility. Met Josh's vixen. In a quiet sort of way, we're very good friends. She's not boisterous with me like her mate – very gentle. Gives me an enquiring look with her lovely head on one side. When I squat down and speak softly, she comes right up.

It is the sow badger with cubs that is frequenting Meg's Sett. Old Joe comes along foraging at times – but he isn't denning with them. Foxes and badgers alike are finding more in the woodland now – a great acorn and chestnut year and the place is alive with the sounds of falling bounty. Many fungi too. The young tawnies are still around the parents' area, but less often. Hope they successfully become established elsewhere.

160

Monday 18 October
Wild, wet night – the wind in a fury. Briarmead at the Long Field edge has been under water these past eight days. It is already the wettest October on record.

The badgers are putting on fat for the lean winter months ahead. Where the fields are under water, there are worms galore, rising above ground to avoid drowning. Hornbeam and beechmast, acorns and chestnuts, crunch underfoot amongst the dark red haws. Old Joe had a pear bonanza in the Glebe's orchard – made a change in his diet. Slugs creep into the rotting fruit – added flavour! Along by the Poplar Row, the old badger came upon one of Josh's full-grown cubs freshly dead with its brush cut off. He quickly eviscerated the carcass, but left the rest.

Sunday 24 October
Clear, starry sky with moon in the first quarter. Thick frost in places, e.g. the foot of High Ridge; heavy dew in others, and swirling mist along the Bourne valley.

Aspen leaves that tremble gently in the breeze have the sound of pattering rain. The stand of trees that gives the Aspen Path its name have leaves of amber-yellow. The wild cherry trees seem aflame and vie with the hawthorns' vivid foliage. Met Josh and his vixen by the Main Pond. Much mutual grooming and play. She is a dainty lady; he, a big brash male, quickly put in his place if he gets too amorous! Was enjoying their company when I heard the crunch of grit distantly and *they* were

too engrossed for once to hear. I barked at them, and in an instant they had slipped away, and I too. The usual van, followed a few minutes later by the car going to the 'swap-shop' space. (Wonder if Ross's guess is right? He thinks the identical book-size packets contain drugs – or is that fanciful? – *see* 25 March 1982.)

Saturday 30 October
A beautifully mild, overcast night – visibility superb. Pair of tawnies very vocal at the Chantry. Much later, another owl from the Holmoak side of Great Chantry Field tried to 'gatecrash' their duet.

2.20 a.m. Two young dogfoxes screeching and screaming – having a trial of strength at the bottom of the Ridge – much vocalisation. The outcome undetermined.

Saturday 31 October
I came out this evening at 5 p.m., hoping to do a tawny count, but constant bangs from gardens at the bottom of Briarmead (Guy Fawkes Night next Friday) effectively keeping the birds silent.

Crossed Briarmead and walked the Two Oak field path towards the Poplar Row. Halfway along by the tumbledown shed, I noticed something sticking out of the long verge grass, but partly covered by a sheet of rusting metal. Walked past and nearly to the poplars, when something prompted me to return and look more carefully. One of the sow badger's grown cubs (the female), very dead, the face and head

blasted at close range. Happened some days ago, by the look of it, and deliberately hidden. Felt very sad going home – seems such a senseless waste – young Jessie all over again. No good telling the police – nothing they can do.

Friday 5 November
4 a.m. Mild, overcast night filled with the pattering of falling leaves. Find following Josh's little vixen through the undergrowth of the Chantry very hard going. So left her to make my own route through. Sitting at the Chantry headland overseeing the valley, find I have a dainty fox once more for company. A solitary tawny has been hooting near lower Briarmead – wonder if it's one of this year's fledged youngsters?

Earlier I watched the remaining badger cubs (and Mum) exploring an abandoned tyre from the large wheel of a tractor, lying on the path. At one time, both youngsters were inside it, hidden by the inner rim and clearly excited by the hollow sounds their noises produced – bedlam! Even the sow joined in for a while. Man's rubbish has its uses.

Walking up Briarmead Lane at 5.10 a.m., heard the sound of rain on foliage getting louder and faster, but no apparent rain where I was standing on the tarmac. Then quite suddenly it was upon me. Was soaked in a moment, almost before I could zip up my open anorak!

Thursday 11 November
Mild, gusty night with dark scudding clouds through which the just-risen crescent moon struggles to shine. Can see easily even in the depths of this woodland, as most leaves are now earthbound.

Met my foxy lady on the grass verge by the Motorway tunnel tonight; by accident or design, no way of telling. Soon joined by Josh who bounded up to me, standing upright on hind legs, brush waving. He pawed at me, chewing my sleeve, I laughing as I tried to keep my balance on the rough scree – until a low growling stopped us both short. Josh dropped down on all fours and backed off. His vixen is jealous or, rather, possessive. Spoke softly to her as she fussed round me, then stroked her head, but when her mate attempted to come near again, she silently showed her teeth. So left them and walked up through the whispering trees to the View over Warby. Sat on the stile there, listening to one of the Chantry owls fluting – cadence upon cadence, surely the loveliest night music – and gazing at the little village below.

4.25 a.m. Heard this woodland's other pair of tawnies dueting amongst the trees behind the Old Barn ruins, so I crept very close – in fact, under the male owl's tree. Notice that tawny owls, when dueting, have a definite sequence of calls. The male hoots – a pause – then he gives a short 'prompt' note prior to a sustained hooting. When he starts the latter, his mate joins in to make the melodious tremolo, so ineptly described as 'tu-whit tu-whoo'.

163

Thursday 18 November
The last three days and nights have witnessed gales and sudden gusts of wind at great speeds – nevertheless, very mild. Tree trunks and boughs litter the woodland rides – some held precariously upright by their deeper-rooted brethren. Beautiful night sky; stars seem to glitter, the moon a delicate thin curve. No animal seems to like wind – they cope with rain far better; the owls very silent. The wind is parting Old Joe's fur. They hate this – the blast gets to their body.

Picked some creamy, sweet bullaces coming here, and offered them to the old badger. A cautious snuffling, then a quick gobble. I've never fed him before. Sat down on the ground and laid the last four in my lap. A little hesitation and that india-rubber snout poked out and found them. The nose of a badger can lift right away from the jaw, allowing the teeth to gently take them. He nosed my half-open anorak, then my sweater – then looked in my face. We were both on a level – he, a very large badger; me, a very small human, and sitting down at that. Like an old dog, the once-black parts of his face are flecked with grey. One of his eyes is very watery. The stiff, black hairs round his snout seem very long for a badger, but if indeed these are to help him gauge the width of an opening, possibly then Joe's *would* be longer.

Sunday 28 November
1.20 a.m. Deep frost, biting wind and clear, clear skies. The rows of cabbages are frozen humps, hugging their granite field. Passing through the woods at the Warby side, I heard sounds towards the Motorway – two male foxes having a war of nerves. If I hadn't *seen* them, I would have said it was a fox and cat fight as some sounds were very cat-like, i.e. yowling. Have noted this many times before and think many reported cat/fox fights are in reality fox/fox. (In all my years of night-wandering, I have witnessed a) cat/fox friendships; b) cat and fox warily avoiding each other; c) cats fighting cats; d) foxes fighting foxes. Have yet to see a fox fight a cat – not sure what this proves, though maybe it indicates cat/fox fights are rare.)

At first in tonight's fight there was no actual physical contact and neither would submit. Then one leapt at the other – who stayed his ground. Then the leaping one hesitated – and thereby was lost. The other screamed, its hackles raised and legs stiff, making it seem taller and larger. Its opponent turned and fled, hotly pursued by the other, and both disappeared towards the Motorway bank. A few moments passed; a movement in the shadows, and another fox stepped into view. It sniffed around the area of the fight and stood awhile looking after the others. All was quiet. Just the wind in the treetops as it blew upwind past fox and myself standing close to the hedge.

3.45 a.m. and the tawnies are serenading from the Briarmead side of the Chantry. I crept through the undergrowth to just below their beech

164

overlooking Great Chantry Field, but was unable to move quietly as it was frozen, even under the sheltering trees. One bird swivelled its head and regarded me solemnly, pausing a fraction – then continued its quavering refrain. Their singing carries a great distance (as do other sounds) in these weather conditions. (Regretfully, the traffic noise also carries. Find it impossible at any time to tape the owls here without the recording being spoilt by motorway sounds.)

WINTER 1982–3

Thursday 16 December 1982
2.05 a.m. Very mild, breezy night with occasional violent gusts that send debris flying. Was with Old Joe in the Briarmead side of these woods when the top half of a birch trunk parted company with the rest and came thundering earthwards. A little too near us for comfort, so we scattered. When the dust had settled, I returned to look at the fallen trunk. Lesser spotted woodpecker holes – three in all. Bark peeling away; bracket fungi (*Trametes confragasa*) looking like a series of neat shelves, and two flat and pure white examples of birch bracket (*Polyporus betulinus*). The whole section was rotten and insect-ridden – a wonderful haven for all kinds of life. Moments later, discovered I had badger company again as, turning, I saw Joe moving slowly along the log top, tearing off strips of bark as he went and snuffling up the grubs beneath. He sampled the *Polyporus*, but without much enthusiasm, and soon reverted to his bark-tearing.

Everywhere is very waterlogged – light reflects on each puddle and runnel and the woodland paths are streams. No moon, few stars, excellent visibility – light clouds blown fast high above. Haven't been out after dark for ten nights and now the scents and smells in the damp, moist atmosphere are intoxicating – it's another world.

Trailed a musky, weasel-like odour along the Briarmead bank and down on to the tarmac. Felt sure the owner wasn't far off and, sure enough, saw it right in the bank edge nibbling at something held between its front paws. Presently the weasel dropped what it had been gnawing and appeared to be listening, still on hind legs. Then it sprang, up and under the drooping grass-edge and disappeared. Was interested to find that it had been eating an oak-gall – one of the curious ones which, up to recently, I had been unable to identify, but which I find have no English name as yet, the Latin being *Andricus quercuscalicis*.

Wednesday 22 December
Met Josh and his vixen as I walked the field path to the Poplar Row. A great and noisy reunion – this time no growling (*see* 11 November). Stroked them both simultaneously and got knocked to the ground for my pains! Two very excited, silly foxes – worse than dogs!

My foxes have accompanied me down the scree slopes to the foot of the Ridge. Josh high-pounced on a half-formed molehill – a squeak, and he had the mole in his jaws. He chewed once and tossed it up in the air. His vixen picked it up, then dropped it. Left them both there, nosing about in the freshly dug earth – two shadow shapes just beyond the lights of the Motorway tunnel.

Saturday 1 January 1983
Dull, windy, overcast morning. Stood watching a flock of waxwings – twenty-two birds in all – feeding on hawthorn and dogrose berries on Cullen Rise. Unbothered at my presence, so was able to get very close. Distinctive call – very attractive birds. Also heard and watched a woodlark there.

Friday 7 January
Bright, breezy morning after frosty night. Poplar and whitebeam buds very big and full – hazel catkins well formed but are not yet opening. Many branches felled in the woods, but the grandfather of cherry trees still stands in spite of all the gales of the past week – long may he remain so. From the undergrowth the green blades of the grey iris gleam brightly – bulbs are pushing upwards everywhere. The tiny white flowers of butcher's broom just opening; the honeysuckle has its new leaves and the flowers of the white deadnettle toss in the gentle air.

Wednesday 12 January
Mild, soft night with moisture in the air. 12.52 a.m.: Josh and his vixen

mated – seemed unbothered by me there. Prolonged mating; returned to same area at 2.35 a.m. and found them still in position but facing away from each other (*see* entry for 11 January 1981).

Watched one of the badger cubs (I'll have to call them yearlings now) worming amongst the cabbages. Lines of water gleaming between the rows – moisture everywhere. Wind getting up. Tawnies vocal at the Wildflower Path at 4.55 a.m.

5.20 a.m. Saw Old Joe snuffling round the base of the discarded tractor tyre still on the same path (*see* 5 November 1982), but moved further down into the woodland during the Christmas holidays. He looked up and regarded me for a time, then continued his search for slugs and grubs. Perched myself on the other side of the tyre to enjoy this wood at night. Very quiet everywhere – no owls now, no rustlings – just the snorting/snufflings of my foraging badger. Having explored the outside, Joe clambered (nimbly for such an apparently ungainly creature) on to the top and down into the tyre's inner rim. Water collects there and the sounds of lapping were clear. A pause, then more snuffling as the ground that side was examined. Something touched my side and long, curved claws were gripping the tyre top, a face near-sightedly gazing up. A movement – the claws slipping a little on the curved rubber surface – and my companion was next to me on the tyre top.

Sunday 16 January
Mild, damp, overcast night. Josh and his vixen keep very close together – much mutual grooming and play. They are the first pair of foxes that I know beyond any shadow of doubt to have mated for two consecutive winters. Foxes are stated to be promiscuous – these certainly are not – though in greatly disturbed districts, where there is sheep rearing, for instance, paired animals must often get split up and find their territory too 'hot' to return to. I know one of Josh's cubs (last year's) was killed; the little vixen cub and her brother Tagless are together and will certainly mate; I have been unable to trace the last two cubs of the litter since late autumn – these young dogfoxes have probably dispersed in search of their own territory. This is the most vulnerable time for foxes and many are shot, snared, hunted or run over in unfamiliar country-side. My two foxes – Josh and his vixen – are lying up by day in the shrubby fenced-off area round the disused well on Corbett's land.

2.02 a.m. Held up for a time when a car, then a van, were driven into these woods – way beyond the ponds area and past the top of the Beech Path. Car finally burnt out and van driven off.

Owls dueting at 4.45 a.m.: there are three pairs of tawnies here now. Dawn very lovely at 7.25 a.m. with dark sky pierced through with vermilion and gold. Have been asked to do a bird count and, with that end in view, I walked the Warby side of these woods with Corbett's fields on my right. Here, to my delight, saw nine red-legged partridge bob-bobbing out of the woods (reminded me of school children!) on to the field where they began to feed. Stood some minutes enjoying these bustling little creatures when something gently touched my trouser leg, and I found myself looking down into a pair of elliptical eyes! Had a sneaking feeling that Josh's appreciation of partridge was gastronomic rather than aesthetic, when he left my side and stole up the slope towards the group, his long lean body hugging the ground; I had to smile for I knew he had no chance of catching one that way. Partridge are sharp-eyed and see the slightest movement. Sure enough, they seemed to flow across the field – always keeping together. Just as the birds reached the shelter of the hedge, a red streak darted out – Josh's mate. The red-legs scattered, all but one, and rose into the air calling 'chuka-chuka, chuka-chuka' in alarm. By now, Josh had reached his vixen and lay down watching her quietly as she began to eat her kill. After a time, she looked up, then moved aside. Whereupon, the dogfox finished off the partridge while the other groomed herself.

The advantages of a shared hunt are obvious – so often this past year have I watched this 'co-ordinated' hunting that it cannot be a) coincidence or b) peculiar to this pair of foxes. Indeed, it must be commonplace.

8.27 a.m. Shooting started in these woods (around the area of the Wildflower Path), so continued the bird-count with caution! A great branch has been torn off one of the ash trees at the Bank Sett. It has left a raw scar and exposed an old woodpecker nest. Hazel catkins are pollen-laden. A badger has been recently digging out at the old sett just inside these woods by the Wheatfield – it was dug out by men seven years ago. I think the fresh badger activity may be one or both of the yearlings – must check.

Watched eleven goldfinches feeding on lesser burdock seedheads on Little Chantry Field. No wonder a group of these pretty birds is called a 'charm'. Their song is a liquid twittering interspersed with tinkling bell-like calls.

(Altogether, counted 3 tawny owls; 2 jays; 2 green woodpeckers; 1 lesser spotted woodpecker; 3 *woodcocks*; 5 pheasant; 110 wood-pigeon; 32 collared doves; 11 carrion crows; 9 red-legged partridge; 9 hawfinches; 2 bullfinches; 5 blackbirds; 9 skylarks; 2 great tits; 5 blue tits; 1 treecreeper; 3 chaffinches; 11 goldfinches; 5 bramblings; 1 greenfinch.)

Saturday 22 January
Mild, breezy, overcast night – excellent visibility. Watched Joe and the young sow digging out along the Bank Sett. An ideal night for it, as the earth is damp but no longer waterlogged. It took me a while to realise there were two badgers at the task, as I only saw the old boar for a long time. However, whenever he emerged pushing earth backwards and away from him out of the hole and stood snout raised in the night air to rest and check for danger, sounds of another animal digging came clear from underground. Think, all being well, the sow should soon produce

cubs. It could be any time from the end of January to mid-March, but more likely to be the first two weeks of February here.

Something neither badger had noticed, since both were underground at the time, was that a van and car went up Briarmead with several people in them. But they were both above ground at 3.45 a.m. when the vehicles came slowly down. The two animals froze until the red glow of the vehicles' rear lights disappeared from view and all was quiet once more. Then both began to groom their fur with pauses every few minutes to listen, snouts raised. Presently, Joe began to groom his sow's face and neck – who was making the 'purring' it is difficult to say – then it was the old boar's turn to be washed.

In daylight, I returned about mid-morning to look at something the sow badger had dragged up from deep inside one of the tunnels. No wonder she had difficulty bringing it to the surface as it was about broom-handle length, lightweight, hollow, but strong (her teeth had barely dented it) and made of tubular metal – steel? I felt uneasy about it, but couldn't think what it had been used for – must have been pushed into an entrance and accidentally dropped.

Wednesday 26 January

At 12.32 a.m., a mild clear night with half moon; by 2.20 a.m., overcast with slight rain. Have been checking just where my badgers have settled. The twins (yearlings) are denning at the Wheatfield Copse with occasional days spent sleeping at the old sett just inside the wood on the other side of this field (*see* 12 January). The twins' mother is living at the

View Sett; Old Joe and his sow are still at present at the Bank Sett. I have found out what the hollow metal tube (*see* last entry) was probably used for, having, coincidentally, been given a photocopy of an article from the *Sunday Times* on present-day badger hunting. Tonight, checked the tube's measurements and condition. It is five feet long and fast rusting – one end particularly so. When I looked at it on Saturday, there was no rust except a little at this end, which indicates it hadn't been left long in the sett tunnel. It would appear to be a metal probe or listening device. It is fortuitous that the badgers weren't living there then. I can't be around at dawn this time of year, except at weekends (during the week I have to be home by 6 a.m. to get to work), so can't keep an eye on the badgers here at the crucial time.

7.45 a.m. Misty, occasional rain, but went out in daylight to check the entire area. An entrance of the Old Cherry Tree Sett has been dug out with *spades*. Had no badger occupant – one of the yearlings dug it out three weeks ago, but then rejected it; badgers often dig out several setts before selecting one. If later disturbed at the chosen one, it may return to one of those previously dug.

At 8.25 a.m. in the wet bracken at the back of High Ridge, spied a fox slowly quartering the ground, scent-marking as it went – too pre-occupied to notice me standing there. I'm almost certain it was Tagless, but visibility poor. Wet bracken and fallen leaves are the only back-grounds that camouflage a stationary fox in winter. Everywhere else, the animal's lovely colouring stands out like a sore thumb. Tagless was slowly moving and it was the movement that attracted my attention.

Saturday 29 January
1.10 a.m. Full moon, clear skies, slight wind – a beautiful mild night. Old Joe and his sow are firmly established now at the Bank Sett. Five of the entrances and a great many passages have been cleared of accumulated debris. That badgers are now living here is all too plain to see; even at a distance, the piles of fresh earth on the bank show clear. Just hope the people who used the probe to listen for badgers – and found none there – won't return to check again. I can at least watch at weekends, both here and at the other occupied setts, although the Wheatfield Copse where the twins are denning is at a distance from the Bank and View Setts, which should give me plenty of exercise!

The Chantry owls are hunting over Great Chantry and the Bank Sett. Their wingspan seems immense under the moon; its rays give them an ethereal quality that their silent gliding flight only enhances. It shines, too, on each smoothly curved surface of moist earth the plough has overturned. These neat rows stretch away from me and over the brow of Great Chantry. This field is at its loveliest now lying under the great white moon.

Both badgers are collecting leaves for bedding! Leaves are *not* the easiest things to collect in a heap, bundle under your chest and beneath your chin and walk backwards carrying them to the entrance. Though their jerky, shuffling movements are comical, however, they nevertheless move surprisingly fast – and are very accurate considering they don't look round to *check* the direction of their route. At one time, the sow was growling and grumbling at Joe and for a while I couldn't think why. I've finally concluded it's the beech leaves from the Chantry she prefers (they don't seem to rot, but rather stay smooth and whole). Her mate was lazily collecting ash and oak from just around the Bank Sett itself – the journey up the hill to the Chantry beeches and back doesn't appeal to Old Joe. Now he's opted out, leaving *her* to bustle to and fro. So he's come to me as I sit here on the dead log, writing. I've grown very fond of him – though I keep well clear of his sow. (His breath smells so fetid that I imagine he has rotten teeth – especially noticeable, as now, when he pushes his face shortsightedly into mine!) Nevertheless, he's a great character.

6.50 a.m. The badgers went to earth an hour ago. The sky is beginning to lighten in the east in front of me, whilst at my back a blackbird sings from a leafless gean on the Wildflower Path – and the moon still clear in the sky has moved to stand on the very tops of the trees there. Slowly, very slowly, pink light is stealing over the edge of the field ahead of me and softly touches the long-dead heads of teasel on the Bank. I sit, and watch, and wait until 8.30 a.m. as the sun climbs the hillside and floods these woods with light. Then, walking home, I check the other setts – all quiet, serene and untouched – the air filled with birdsong.

Sunday 30 January
Fine, clear sky with full moon and strong wind, which by 4.30 a.m. had increased and clouded over the sky – temperature dropping. The Bank Sett has been the scene of much badger activity tonight – mainly on the sow's part (she's *still* bringing in beech leaves), though Old Joe has helped.

7.10 a.m. Don't think there will be a dawn as such – it's beginning to hail and the wind is biting. Partly to keep warm, have walked all round these woods and then to the Wheatfield Copse. No sign of badger trouble – although bird shooters have parked their cars on the Grain Dump path well hidden from the lane. However, the hail and wind have deterred them and they are sitting in their cars. Getting very chilled and wet and feeling I'm wasting my time, but nevertheless will walk round to the Bank Sett once more, just to see everything's quiet.

8.15 a.m. and the wind-driven hail was stinging eyes and face. Coming out of this wood on to the Wildflower Path, thought I saw figures over the Long Field on the Bank, but the visibility was awful – eyes painful with the hail. Head down and pushing against the roaring wind, I seemed to hear a dog bark, but probably imagination. Reached the foot of the Bank in time to see a terrier run down – see me – and run up, at the same time a man's voice shouting against the wind. Began to pull myself

172

upwards by the springy branches, then near the top stopped dead! Three men with their backs to me, one kneeling by an entrance, one with a spade, one holding a dog (not the dog I first saw). The kneeling man looked up and saw me, just as the nearest turned, shouted and thrust the spade at my head. Luckily, the intervening branches deflected it and it merely brushed my shoulder, but in ducking away I lost my footing on the wet bank and fell backwards on to the field below. Half stunned by my contact with the frozen earth, I seemed to hear voices and running feet for a long while above me, though was rather vague about time. Think they could have had a terrier below ground. Can't say for sure which way they went, but almost certainly to the Main Road, via the View. Hail turning to blizzard and later, to snow – took an age getting home.

Thursday 3 February
1 a.m. First quiet night after days of gales, sleet and rain. Mild now with clear skies and half-moon. Think Joe's sow is near her time – she's keeping very close to the sett and is increasingly aggressive towards him. Crossing Long Field and entering these woods near the Old Cherry Tree, found I had the old badger for company. One thing, it's an ill wind that blows nobody any good – he's found two dead birds. He had to dig under a fallen branch to rake out the thrush with his long claws – the jay was lying in the undergrowth. Badgers seem more fussy about feathers than

foxes and will carefully tear down the body and turn it inside out rather than eat the whole thing. Badgers certainly have more dexterity with those long claws.

Then a surprise. At the View stiles and just outside this wood, a hibernating hedgehog rolled up in a ball and doubtless washed out of some cranny by the surging floodwater that earlier this week turned the paths to fast-moving streams. Extending his claws, Old Joe batted it over slowly, then, finding the 'join', dug down with his left paw and unrolled the hedgehog (using the right paw) flat along the ground like unrolling a tiny carpet. He had some difficulty; would the muscles of a hibernating animal be set and stiff as in rigor mortis, I wonder? No sound from the victim. Joe cleaned the skin carefully, snout checking every inch of it, teeth pulling the last vestiges away. He bit off and swallowed the feet one by one – and finally the face. He left no blood, no morsel of flesh, just the skin quite camouflaged amongst the dead leaves – a curling oblong strip, spines towards the ground. [First saw him do this in June 1980.]

Noticed as I walked along with Joe that he has established dung pits at the boundaries of his home range, as usual at this time of year – but only *up to* the Motorway. Does that mean he no longer looks upon the land on the Warby side as his? Is he content to stay this side with his two sows and the twins, or would any more territory be too great for him to maintain?

5.02 a.m. Sat on a fallen log at the side of Little Chantry Field listening to the tawnies 'fluting'. Joe climbed up and ambled along its length, then back to me. Not much food for a badger here for the bark has long since disappeared, though a beetle scurrying out of the rotten wood was eagerly chewed and swallowed. He jumped down, then looked up as I spoke to him softly. He seemed to stare up at me for so long that I gently slid off the log, my feet touching the ground. His gaze transferred to my boots – and turning round, he backed on to them and musked them. Hope nothing bad happens to my old badger – have become very fond of him.

Tuesday 8 February

Think Joe's sow has had her cubs. Bitterly cold these past two days and nights with snow showers and overcast skies. Plenty of food still about, though, for foragers. There was a shoot here last Sunday and among the birds lying scattered around were a woodcock and a tawny owl (to say nothing of siskin and a robin). Makes me wonder just what they took home with them? I watched Josh eating the robin and wondered about lead poisoning – the same goes for any other predator, of course.

Was under the Scots pines by the Main Pond with Josh and his robin when the vixen appeared, 2.30 a.m. She slowly approached him, whereupon he lay down amongst the cones, his waving brush gently shifting them to and fro, his head resting on his forepaws. She smelled

174

the spot where her mate had eaten the bird, then pranced up to him and nipped his ear – invitation to a game! Next moment they were chasing in and out the pines and, forgetful of my surroundings, I followed them laughing. A crunch of grit and a car appearing round the bend in the path caught us momentarily in its headlights as it swung round into the 'swap-shop' clearing. Realised too late where we were – three shots were fired in rapid succession and the diminishing sound of the foxes running through the undergrowth, down towards their old well and home. At least they didn't *sound* injured to me as I crouched down amongst the bracken. The car was driven slowly round the clearing, its headlights searching the perimeter. I, feeling very much like Brer Rabbit, lay low, wishing I was his size! Two men sat in the car talking softly (*see* 25 March and 24 October 1982), the headlights now dimmed. Again the sound of tyres on grit, and the van entered and came gently to a stop. Suppose I should have tried to move closer and memorise vehicle numbers – but bravery is *not* my strong point! So remembering the shots, I stayed put and watched the transfer of packages. Have never been so close before and hope I never am again.

About 3.40 a.m. when all was quiet and with large, dry snowflakes turning the world white, I walked down across the frozen field to the bushes around their den and 'barked' up my foxes. Gleaming eyes in the flying whiteness and there they were, no worse for their fright – and a lesson for the three of us for the future.

Friday 11 February
Everywhere is white with snow tonight – it crunches frozen underfoot. Slight wind, cloudy sky and, as always in a snow landscape, marvellous visibility. Doubt if anyone will be trying to dig out badgers from this frozen ground.

Two days ago at home, I came across Wendy's old, red, solid ball, and, out of curiosity to see my foxes' reaction, have brought it with me. Neither the two badger sows nor Old Joe have been abroad during the past forty-eight hours of snow and ice: no prints around their entrances at all, apart from birds and rabbits. I'm sure now that the female badger at the Bank Sett has her cubs – and am undecided whether the View one was pregnant. Some years they skip a pregnancy; not certain why.

Both Josh and vixen sniffed the heavy ball for a while (it has a strong smell) but their interest soon waned. On the snow-covered ground, there was nowhere to bounce it but, seeing a fallen tree trunk, I bounced if off that and caught it repeatedly. The vixen's big ears turned as she watched with bright-eyed enthusiasm – then she sprang and caught it in mid-air. After that it was a case of which fox could take it from the other. Josh finally went with it under a yew tree (where the snow had hardly penetrated), and tried to chew into it. Each time he turned his head to grip it in his carnassial teeth, they failed to get a purchase on its round

175

surface, otherwise he might have succeeded. Don't know what happened to it finally – probably lying in the undergrowth somewhere.

I am still finding dead birds in these woods, most of them shot, including the male tawny owl from the Gully area – that makes two tawnies shot.

Thursday 17 February

Have been out every morning this week from after midnight and returning by 6 a.m., my deadline. No more snow has fallen, but since it has stayed bitterly cold, the snow still lingers. Deep frosts at night.

Tonight, walked through a frozen, snowy landscape with clear, starry skies, 1.10 a.m. Watched the Holmoak tawnies; regurgitating the nightly pellet always seems something of a struggle. At first, it is soft (like a newly laid egg), but once in contact with the air it hardens very quickly as the mucus around it dries. Owls (and grey herons) stand on one foot when it's cold, tucking the other into the body feathers – just as we keep one hand in a pocket, whilst using the other.

The female tawny hunts alone over the Gully and High Ridge. Her lonely 'kewick-kewick' is unanswered now; a phantom shadow slips over the snowy ground – the broad, rounded wings glide effortlessly through a birch's twiggy branches – 'kewick-kewick'. Never till tonight did I think

176

the sound mournful. The call goes unanswered as she flies back and forth. These birds mate for life. Now that the male is shot, any eggs she lays will never hatch, for she will have to leave them uncovered in order to hunt for herself.

Picked up fresh badger prints by a broom bush that was weighed down and frozen with snow. The badger had startled a hare, then crossed a fox's path, before continuing up and over to the back of the Ridge. Was so busy concentrating on my badger tracks that, following them parallel with the Poplar Row, I nearly walked into their owner! It was one of the yearlings still living at the Wheatfield Copse – foraging under the trees where the ground was free of snow.

Monday 21 February
Ground no longer frozen; snow fast disappearing from the woodland hollows and fields. This morning, I walked through these woods to Warby, to check on the setts in daylight and to do a bird-count.

Old Joe was out tonight in the Felled Logs area, with the sow who dens at the View (she hasn't had cubs) – they used dung pits by a heap of logs; dug up and ate bulbs, also chestnuts etc. A Scots pine trunk has been used as a claw-scratching tree.

(Someone has attempted to dig out vacant badger sett.)

Sunday 27 February
1.10 a.m. Somewhere behind these clouds, the full moon is shining. Mild, damp, showery night – visibility superb. Moths are blundering into my face. Over Ingrims Fields, foxes are barking and yapping.

Came out very cautiously tonight as had a recurrence of the ear infection causing vertigo and nausea. In Prosser's Wood, Josh and his vixen found me, and I walked slowly after them to the Wheatfield Copse. Sat down with my back against a stump feeling very giddy and ill. My foxes were clearly puzzled at my unusual behaviour – was neither playing nor running with them – my relationship, particularly with Josh, is generally rough and tough. Now he stood a short way off, looking at me and whining softly. His vixen pushed against me at ground level with her nose. Tried to stroke her muzzle but couldn't speak. Felt my temperature rising and sweat breaking out over my head and body. Aware that Josh was 'yipping' at me – that curious fox sound I have occasionally heard before. His vixen, who now was lying head on paws by my side, raised her head and looked up at the noise – then lay down again. Josh finally tired of his efforts – to rouse me, or her? – and slowly wandered off.

Time passed and my world began to revert to normal, my soaked body to cool, but I had no desire nor strength to get to my feet. The vixen had disappeared.

Much later, walking in the woods, I saw that the Council men had cleared the Wildflower Path. Everything completely razed and large

177

areas burnt, from young whitebeams to bluebells and grey iris – think they call it conservation. Pity they can't remove the tins, broken bottles and rusty wire exposed by their clearing. Is this then what the County Preservation Society meant when they spoke of their 'management plan for the area which, we hope, the District Council will put into operation'?

The full moon, finding a gap in the clouds, is pictured on full ponds. 4.55 a.m., aware of a movement near by and the Prosser vixen is with me, head on one side, eyes agleam. Bent down and stroked her as she fussed round me – think she senses something's amiss, or is that just my fancy? Foxes seem very dog-like – or dogs fox-like – at times.

Should wait to see that my badgers are safe, but feel too cold and ill to do so. Dawn won't be until 6.15 a.m. – home seems a lifetime away.

SPRING 1983

Friday 4 March 1983

Damp, mild, windless night – moonrise very beautiful. Josh and his
mate are still denning together at the well on Corbett's land. Josh
followed me round the hillside until we nearly reached the stiles by the
View. Warby was bathed in moonlight, stars in a velvet sky. Left my fox
nosing around in search of worms and slugs on the wet ground.

2.25 a.m. Sitting at the headland of the Chantry, enjoying the quiet of
the place and the beauty of the valley below, when to my left I heard the
startled cry of a bird at the Bank Sett. A moment later and a badger was
walking – with strange care – along the top of the bank. The odd angle of
its head aroused my curiosity. A careful look through the monocular
partly solved the mystery – it was carrying something in its mouth,
away from the sett. It was the sow badger moving with her head held
well up, not along the narrow, concealed path that winds through the
undergrowth on the bank, but out in the open. Couldn't see what she

179

had, but felt sure it was a cub. When she finally returned half an hour later, I was much nearer and watched the transference of two more cubs, carefully held, kitten-like, by the scruffs – have never seen this before so close to. Their eyes were closed – heads and bodies covered with fine fur, their facial marking suprisingly clear at this age, and quite long tails. Why was she home-moving? No signs of digging out by badger-baiters. Must be a strong reason, though – dogs sent down? or probes? I've been out of action all this week, and feel I'm badly neglecting these badgers. Just getting here at present seems such an incredible effort.

6.15 a.m. Had a desire to look at the Bourne. Was gazing out over the river deep in thoughts of how best to protect Old Joe's offspring when a flash of blue skimmed low upriver. Hardly a wingbeat gave the impression of a bejewelled arrow – how tiny a kingfisher is. Moments later, it was back and, alighting on a twig sticking out of the riverbed, gave a burst of song. The trill seemed to echo between the banks – the bird listened, head cocked, as if to the beauty of its own voice. Once more it trilled. A swoop of blue and another kingfisher was on the twig with its mate. I could see no difference between the two – each was a mirror image of the other. The morning sun rising above the bank caught the magic pair in a glow of light. The first bird flew upriver, leaving its mate on a perch preening. Next moment, it was back with a fish (stickleback, I think) in its bill. Alighting by the other it offered the fish – headfirst – and it passed to the beak of the female and was swallowed with ease. A pause, and the fisherman mounted its mate. The sun, rising ever higher in the sky, cast the scene in a rosy glow – all the birds along the valley seemed to be throbbing with song.

Sunday 20 March
Old Joe's sow has moved her cubs to the Wheatfield Copse, and has remained there in spite of the human activity all around her (John Shaw's men are busy clearing the dead wood). One of the twin males is denning further along the copse – the other is living the wood side of the Wheatfield. These twins were the previous year's cubs of the View Sett sow; she has had no cubs this year. I haven't seen the other sow's new family yet apart from when she moved them; whether she has more than three and whether they all survived the move, I don't know. Too early for them to come above ground yet.

It has been a dry, warm night and the mother has brought up the bedding to air. It's a good thing that badgers prepare more than one sett for occupation in the autumn – a precaution against moving. The bedding hay is spread out all around the entrance to the sleeping-chamber (tell-tale wisps left uncollected are what the badger-baiters look for as a sign where to dig). It's 4.35 a.m. and she's appeared from below ground and has begun scraping it up into a bundle against her chest. Then with the aired hay held carefully by her front paws and chin, she has moved backwards into the sett. It has taken four more journeys before the hay is restored to the sleeping-chamber and even then she has left some lying about.

Met Old Joe worming amongst the rows of young lettuce on Corbett's irrigated land. Stroked his back, then his head and ears. He's a massive animal – old boar badgers have been known to weigh 27.3 kg (60 lb). Although they generally lose weight in the winter (when they live on the summer/autumn accumulation of fat), Joe seems to have easily found food, as the weather has been relatively mild.

Easter Sunday 3 April
Once more a world of white; everywhere snow perfection – branches, twigs, a fine white tracery against the grey sky. On the windward side, trunks have a build-up of snow two inches thick. No sign of badger activity – neither twins, sows, nor Old Joe have been above ground all night.

Found Josh at the Grain Dump (a fresh heap of grain has been deposited here recently and is sprouting). It is riddled with runs and is a haunt of bank voles (the longer-tailed, chestnut-coloured vole), wood mice, and field voles (the shorter-tailed vole so popular with foxes). He was digging into it with great success, killing three small rodents and a nest of young. The tawny owls do well here in snowy weather, when mice and voles grow rash in their quest for food.

The snow on Long Field is three inches deep and is dotted with rabbits digging down to the shoots of corn. Over on the far bank, the snow-laden trees are alive with birds and squirrels whose activities send small flurries of soft flakes earthwards. A shadow moves at the bottom of the bank, gliding along the drainage furrow that runs the field length. Now it is gone, but I know it is still there and wonder fleetingly where the other fox is? A pause – the glare of this clear, cold, snowlight hurts the eyes. A movement near me and there, crouching by the cherry branch, is Tagless's little vixen – belly hugging the earth, elbows protruding up above her back, head held low and straight, ears cocked forward. Rabbits are streaming towards us as the sun, reaching the brow of Great Chantry, touches the lower field with light. Tagless slips easily behind them – shepherd dog herding his sheep – watches for one to break away from the bunch and guides them towards his hidden mate. The nearest two dart for the 'safety' of that cherry bough lying largely in the snow. Their fate is sealed as, with an ease born of practice, the vixen chops down the nearest, leaps the branch after the other and traps it in the twiggy depths. Rabbits stream past me – some very young – one stumbles over my boot, its eyes staring with terror as it runs with a final burst of speed into safety under the geans.

Tagless is out in the middle of Long Field, eating his kill in the snow. He tugs the body over and tears into the stomach – sometimes pausing to look around, then over at his vixen still by the cherry and eating too. The sun is well up now and people will soon be about – time to go home.

181

I haven't seen any signs yet of toad migration (3 April last year). I wonder if the spell of cold weather has any bearing?

The two pairs of foxes – Josh and vixen, Tagless and vixen – seem to have overlapping territories. Or, perhaps more accurately, they aren't excessively territorial. Tagless's vixen is denning in the Chantry with her cubs; Josh's vixen is living at the well. It is interesting also that the yearling pair are not only brother and sister, but also son and daughter of the older pair. I think the reason for the mutual tolerance is not the relationship, however, but due to the abundance of food.

Beautiful sunny afternoon. Took the bridlepath to Crawford's Farm – snow all gone. Horrified to find that yards of hedgerow have been grubbed out, including much of the hedge path which was an animal 'highway'. True, there were some dead elms in it, but many thriving trees and shrubs also. (Although I don't altogether subscribe to the current theory of hedge-dating, nevertheless this hedge was old and, in the main, thriving.) Mr Groom was so enthusiastic about the wildlife on his land – I'm glad he's not here to see it. The whole look of the landscape here is altered. The farm is one long sweep of field going from the Motorway to Bancroft Lane. The place has a bare, open look – the new farmer will have problems with the wind and possibly soil erosion on this hillside.

Saturday 9 April
Tonight I have been watching Old Joe's mate who moved her two cubs
(the third has evidently died) back to the Bank Sett last Wednesday. The
activity at the Wheatfield Copse has just proved too much for her
although, sadly, now it is all finished and the dead elms cut into portable
lengths. The men *did* begin the work in mid-February, a good fortnight
before she moved home on 4 March. The other badger (the yearling twin)
moved out of the Wheatfield Sett two and a half weeks ago and is now
living on the far edge of the 'grandfather' Cherry Sett (which was dug out
by humans on 20 March).

Watched and listened to the female tawny owl at the back of High
Ridge at 5.40 a.m. Sloe and damson blossom opening. Met a toad as I
walked down Briarmead just after dawn (I've met a lot worse on that
little lane!). Hunted along the verges and found fifteen more, so the
Great Migration is well under way – if a little later than other years.

Have been examining the great pollarded tree that contains the
badger entrance in its bole. The sett runs almost the distance of the bank
– that part not occupied at present.

7.05 a.m. Have seen greater and lesser spotted woodpeckers within a
few minutes' walking in these woods and, simultaneously, I can *hear* a
green woodpecker 'yaffling' a short distance away.

Tuesday 12 April
Cold, rainy night with high, gusty wind. The two badger cubs made
several brief appearances at the sett entrance. Their mother no longer
sleeps with them but farther along the Bank Sett. She goes in to nurse
and groom them at intervals. Her mate, Old Joe, has been accepted
back, but is not permitted anywhere near the nursery. Not that he's a bit
interested – in his long badger life, it's all happened many times before.

9.20 a.m. Sunny periods, but still very windy. Wish the Council
wouldn't coppice guelder rose – it's only a small tree at the best of times
and coppicing does *not* improve it.

Thursday 14 April
Cold, frosty night, much of which has been spent in Old Joe's company.
At dawn on the second hayfield along Briarmead just above the
'grandfather' Cherry Sett where he is denning at present, I watched the
woodcock roding so they must be trying to breed again. My badger was
mildly interested. However, he was much more enthusiastic over some
fungi I discovered in the meadow, much to my disgust. As fast as I
spread back the grass to examine a cap, Old Joe was swooping forward
and eating it up – you can go off badgers! I hunted around for some more
as I still hadn't identified it properly. Finally found a last specimen only
to have that snapped up too by my gastronomic opportunist!

So gave up and started to walk into the wood and down the slope to
the sett, followed at a distance by the still-munching boar. Suddenly was

183

aware of two men just below me – it was well light now at 5.50 a.m. – with spades (apparently no dogs). I stopped in my tracks so abruptly that Joe bumped into the back of my legs, moved round me and continued past – then gave a loud snort of fear as he saw the men. They in turn registered him before seeing me (bad luck that, they *know* for sure now there's a badger actually there). They ran down the slope and along the Wildflower Path. To my horror Joe dashed along the little woodland path that also comes out on to Briarmead. He could be trapped in the lane if the men saw him, so finally I caught up with him and stopped him just inside the wood. Knelt down and held him all the while speaking softly – it struck me for the first time just how old he is.

Friday 15 April
Old Joe is still denning at the Old Cherry Sett, and the yearling badger at the far end of the same one. Saw this morning that some of the dug-out earth of yesterday has been thrown back into the hole. Could be children, of course – still the Easter holidays – but why? Feel very uneasy about the whole business. Each badger sett is so widely situated from the next – some on the field banks, some in the wood itself.

Reported yesterday's digging out at the sett to the police after some thought. Was told, among other things, that there had been a similar occurrence in the Newby area quite recently – that's interesting.

Sunday 17 April
1.55 a.m. Very warm night with occasional light rain – visibility good. The Bank Sett sow's two cubs are lovely little creatures just ten weeks old. Their mother is worming on the field just above as they explore the bank and path immediately round the nursery chamber. Their whickering is punctuated by snuffles and the odd whimper. They are still very small and easily frightened by a sudden noise or the fall of a twig from above. Their movements are more co-ordinated now, although the steeply sloping bank isn't the easiest of places on which to play. The sow has just appeared along the path and lies down on her side, her back against an old log. Her 'purring' as they suckle is reminiscent of a mother cat. They jostle one another for a place, and presently she half sits up and begins washing the nearest, who whimpers a protest.

4.20 a.m. All quiet – the badger family have gone to earth. From this bank, the blossoming cherry trees over the Long Field on the Wildflower Path are ghostly white; the fresh stumps of the coppiced trees like open wounds. Am watching the only *pair* of tawnies left in this woodland after the shooting earlier this year. The female has nested in a cavity in one of the birches, and is calling softly to her mate for food.

6.05 a.m. Two people (with a dog on a lead) examining the entrances of the Old Cherry Sett. Seen them do this at different setts many times in the past few years, always very early morning, often in bad weather. Occasionally see the man on his own in the day. [Diary description of the

184

couple – a man and woman – and their dog is omitted here.] I used to wonder why they came up here so early and in such bad weather conditions to walk a little dog that was never off the lead. Never liked the way they poked about the entrance holes, but until last winter, I've never suspected them. However:

1) the best way to see if a badger is denning at a sett is to wait until it rains – when the earth is softest – and see where digging out has occurred;

2) few people except shooters are in these woods so early – who have their own reasons for casting a blind eye – and they seldom venture out on wet, cold mornings;

3) up to last year, I would reckon on there being evidence of badger-hunters perhaps twice in twelve months. This year, it has been four times in four months; the first and last times I actually witnessed. Looking back, I seem to have seen this same couple just prior to evidence of badger disturbance, though I never kept a record. But this year I saw them just before the 30 January trouble with the men and dogs, and again in March, and two days before I discovered a sett entrance dug out with spades. Feel the man and woman are local and will pass on the information; that this is well-organised and involves several groups prepared to dig out badgers – whether for baiting or for the pelts, I don't know. Whether they suspect there is a sow with cubs in the vicinity or not, they *do* know Old Joe is around, who is an exceptionally large boar at that. So it's only a question of time before the badger-hunters try again.

Wednesday 20 April
Cold night with clear skies. Thick frost on the open fields, but muddy and wet in the woods. By 4.30 a.m. a mist has drifted over the farmland and lies like a scarf along the valley.

4.50 a.m. and the sky is lightening – Joe, sow and cubs are all below. (Old Joe musks me more than ever now when we meet.)

5.05 a.m. A blackbird sings at the Briarmead edge, and another challenges from inside the wood. I've been having a rough and tumble with Josh – he has hunted well this night for himself and his vixen. Now I'm sitting where I can see both setts in case of trouble, but the sweat is cooling on me and I can't stop shivering. Have decided to walk round the top of the Bank Sett to keep warm – my breath vaporises before me. By 5.30 a.m., every bird has joined the dawn chorus. The mist is lifting off Long Field as the sky glows red in the east. Have to leave the area by 6 a.m. – takes an hour to walk home from here; hope the police *do* patrol, but have no way of knowing.

Came back here in the afternoon to check the setts and to call on Barry Hains as I wanted to find out who reported the badgers being dug out in the Newby area to the police – there's only Barry at Newby Farm, his father at Burr Lane, and the people at Newby Manor. Neither of the Hainses has reported the badger-dig.

[26 January 1984: Steve Hammond of the R.S.P.C.A. told me it was the owner of Newby Manor.]

Sunday 24 April
Mild night, clear starry skies with moon near the full. Had a surprise tonight: was with Old Joe on Corbett's land (he was worming as usual along the rows of young lettuces) when we heard a series of high-pitched noises and the sound of movements coming from the wood. Kept at a distance whilst the boar investigated, and moved round by the path from the stiles in time to see him come out of the undergrowth and meet his sow and cubs. It probably was his first real encounter with his offspring, now eleven weeks old, and his curiosity was clearly tempered with healthy respect for his sow. He stood there, head submissively lowered as the mother slowly circled him, the young badgers huddled together on one side, the situation tense. Then the atmosphere relaxed and at first tentatively, then with more confidence, he began to groom the side of her face. Joe made no attempt to go up to his cubs, but wisely let them come to him. He looked immense towering above the tiny creatures, now very muddy and bedraggled from their long trek.

The family must be moving home again. Wonder if she is staying within my area, i.e. Ashcroft Woods-High Ridge-Prosser's Wood and the immediate farmland; or going back whence she came last year (26 April 1982). She had no cubs with her then or mate, whereas the other sow that appeared also last year (31 May 1982) had three youngsters. Two of these have survived and are the yearlings now of this place – the third I found

186

shot on 31 October last year. Badger life is very hazardous and there's no way of proving just why those two sows moved. They must have felt threatened, however.

[This family is now living at Meg's Sett near the Oak Dell.]

Tuesday 26 April
All the badgers, except Old Joe, have moved house and the foxes also – rather like a game of Musical Chairs. Tagless's vixen and cubs are now at the Bank Sett, just over the field to Josh's mate who has gone from the well to the Cherry Sett. The two families of cubs have quickly got themselves acquainted (as children will!) and there is a mutual coming and going across the width of Long Field and up the slope through the bluebells. I like to sit on my coppiced stump just inside this wood, writing up my notes and watching the passing cub traffic. Lots of gruff, tiny barks, occasional yelps and high-pitched 'tch-tching' (the latter reminiscent of the blackbird's alarm cry). Now about six weeks old, they have chubby little bodies, dark marks on front of legs, ears more pointed, tails not so string-like. It's quite a long journey to go and play with your friends and, puppy-like, they move in short bursts of speed, sitting down with a bump every so often, but spurred on by the sound of playing from the other family.

Thought they had all gone by this morning, when I saw a tiny face bob-bobbing over the rows of corn, and an also-ran turned in at the big human-made path (interesting that these young animals don't yet use the undergrowth for cover when travelling, like adults), stopped to look at me as he briefly defecated, then hurried on up the slope to the game being played (he's missing out!) under the 'grandfather' Cherry, just a few yards past Old Joe's entrance.

Friday 29 April
Mild, clear skies – full moon. Pre-light starts now at 4.30 a.m., just when the male tawny was calling the bounds. First birds begin singing at 4.40 a.m. – skylarks over the open fields and blackbirds from the woods.

5 a.m. the pheasant sounds from near the Bank Sett and at 5.20 a.m. a cuckoo calling amongst the dawn chorus.

Tonight one of Josh's cubs found a hedgehog as it searched for food amongst the leaf litter around the Old Cherry's great bole. At first, the young fox was frightened, but spurred on by the excited squeaks and barks of his den-mates, he grew bolder and soon the four little cubs had surrounded the unfortunate 'urchin' and, with bottoms skywards and tails wagging, proceeded to play Teasing the Stranger. The hedgehog didn't bother to curl up, but merely continued foraging, until eventually one cub came too close and had his nose pricked for his pains.

Saturday 30 April
Mild, overcast night with slight rain. Old Joe has dug out extensively

187

tonight – the sandy earth shows bright and clear on the bluebell-clad slope. He was with me until a few minutes ago, 6 a.m., together with his cubless sow.

We have two nightingale couples on the wood edges this year so far. One pair is almost in the same place overlooking Briarmead as last year, only a bit nearer the Grain Dumps, the other where coppicing was done in 1981. They seem to like nesting where the undergrowth and topwood is less dense and where bramble is well established – therefore, two- to three-year-old coppicing or wood edges suit them best. I am keeping a watchful eye open for nightjars, but it's somewhat early as yet. Birdsong, bluebells, wood anemones, primroses everywhere – in spite of the rain, this is a glorious place to be.

Spent some of the night watching the badger cubs at Meg's Sett. There are some campers in the Oak Dell near by. The green tents blend well and are not visually obtrusive. Avoiding the campers, Mum and offspring went along the Beech Path to the ponds area. Every hollow is full and overflowing here and the pickings were good. I was suprised to see the sow actually swimming – body submerged, long head held dog-like along the surface. Finally, she clambered on to part of an old wooden door floating in the middle, shook herself vigorously, and began to groom. The cubs paddled about at the water's edge and didn't immediately notice where their mother had gone.

One cub picked up a twig and was chased by the other along a land jetty sticking out towards the pond's centre. Then, jostling together for ownership of the stick, the sow cub overbalanced and fell in. The depth wasn't great but instantly she set up a frightened cry. The alerted parent stopped her grooming and gave several short, high-pitched sounds, 'kaak-kaak'. The youngster struggled to reach her mother and was actually swimming dog-like in a panicky way. She reached the raft but couldn't clamber on to it, whereupon the sow grasped her none too gently by the scruff and hauled her aboard. Funny how quickly animals recover from a fright. Within minutes, the youngster was investigating the new land and barking a challenge at her dejected little brother all alone now at the water's edge. No amount of barking would induce him to attempt the journey, however.

I suddenly noticed that the adult was watching something intently in the water. Next moment, she had slipped silently back (surprisingly silent for such a large animal) and again was swimming around. This was why she originally took to the water – there was something here that she wanted. Then the badger disappeared momentarily – a flurry – and back to shore with her catch, a grass-snake. I've watched them swimming here and so has Sam Mercer when he has been bird-ringing, but I never thought I'd see a badger catch one. Slow-worms as well as snakes are good swimmers and come here for the tadpoles, newts, frogs, etc.

The little badger left on the door set up a great whimpering when it saw the other two eating on the bank, but no way would she chance the

188

water again. Taking her time, the sow finished most of the snake. Then leaving her cub to battle with the tail end, she leisurely swam back to the other sitting miserably on the edge of the raft. At first, it wouldn't come and merely whined as her mother nosed her. Finally, she re-entered the water – almost on top of the sow – and swam with her the short distance to the shore.

Sunday 1 May

Notice Josh is well into his moult now; the loosening fur irritates and he tugs it as he grooms. Presently he has a ball of pale undercoat or felting between his front teeth, which he spits out. This curry-combing results in a wad of fur containing two indentations spaced a little apart – left by his canine teeth. Before I really came to know foxes, I would find these results of grooming and wonder what caused them – now I know! Ran my fingers through his thick shoulder fur, pulling gently, and got rid of a fair amount that way. Might have known it would end up as a game, however – trouble is, he never knows when to stop! Later on, when I was standing under a beech tree listening to the nightingale singing from a thicket, Josh suddenly sprang at me; my foot slipped on the wet moss round the tree's roots and I fell on my shoulder. I cried out – the nightingale flew off – and a very subdued dogfox stood nuzzling me and whining as I tried to stand up in a haze of pain.

Dull, wet dawn with slight mist. Waited until 7 a.m. to see that the badgers were safe, then made my way home. Pins and needles in my arm and can't seem to use that hand – sometimes I go off my boisterous friend!

Bank Holiday Monday 2 May

The tawny chicks in the old birch are growing fast. Their mother tears into digestible pieces the prey that the male brings to the nest. Nevertheless, the chicks waste a lot and the area directly below the nest hole gets very messy and flyblown with discarded food. However, badgers are known to be opportunists and one of the foraging yearlings has cottoned on to the tawny-food-potential and checks here as he returns home to the far end of the Old Cherry Sett each morning. There is nothing 'pretty' about tawny chicks – they are big, untidy bundles of off-white fluff with glaring red-rimmed eyes and are capable of making a lot of noise, especially at feeding time. The food-call of the hen tawny is rather like a radio bleep made repeatedly. They are beginning to flap their as-yet useless wings. One will start, and soon all three are flap-flapping – strengthening the wing muscles.

7 a.m. All quiet, no shooters or dog-walkers, just birdsong all around. Was standing near the Old Cherry amongst the bluebells when I saw movement below to my right. Where the View Path joins the lower track, a fox appeared – very streaky looking in its moult and carrying what looked like a white plastic bag in its mouth. This didn't seem a

189

heavy burden, for it walked with ease and grace, turning its head to look and listen as it went. I wanted to move nearer without being seen, so edged hastily along the upper animal trail that winds through the bluebells.

It was Tagless's vixen – which was strange in itself – and it *was* a white plastic bundle she held. Before I could make out more, she had disappeared into an entrance of the old badger sett almost next door to her mother. Stood awhile wondering where she had picked up her find when I noticed a white patch – not unlike rice pudding – on the heaped earth that falls away from the entrance. Back-tracked the vixen to the View, then over Corbett's land – sometimes just guessing the general direction of her path since I've trailed foxes now for so long – but every so often finding these little blobs of white to confirm the route. In fact, the substance was very high cottage cheese which could have almost walked by itself! Finally, it led me to a hole in the garden fence of one of the houses which back on to the fields. The mystery solved – another fox likes dustbins!

Saturday 7 May
Fine crescent moon above the treetops; very mild night with showers. The twin yearling males are back together again at the felled Wheatfield

190

Copse. It seems strange with no trees or undergrowth there, but badger instincts for former homes are deep. I just didn't expect it to be reoccupied so quickly.

Josh has been too busy hunting for himself and his family to want to play. Which is perhaps just as well, since I'm still getting over the effects of his last game! Both vixens *are* denning close together and seem unbothered whose cubs they feed – nor do the youngsters appear to mind from whom they suckle. Both mothers are trying to wean the cubs by lying down on their teats when the cubs try to nurse. The males, as they fetch back, are wary of each other should they meet, but it isn't often that their visits synchronise. Six of the cubs (the seventh is very puny and won't survive much longer) bundled Tagless just now. Because of his moult, his coat is looking like tatty carpet – two cubs even hung on to his brush. When he decided enough was enough, he shook himself vigorously to rid himself of his shiralee and bounded down the slope – family life can get a bit much!

First light and dawn getting earlier. The beauty of this wood is impossible to describe. At the Old Cherry Sett the ground is a carpet of rich green moss and foliage, vivid bluebells, white fallen cherry blossom and wood anemones, and here and there a still bright primrose clump. Birdsong and drumming woodpeckers – flower scent hangs on the air.

Joe's sow, complete with their two cubs, has moved to the Old Cherry Sett close by her mate. Not surprised, since someone has been pushing sticks down the entrances of Meg's Sett – also filling the holes with earth and stones. Now at their new home, she has just finished re-digging out the entrances that her cubs and she are using. With all the recent rains, the earth is easily worked. Unfortunately, the bright, sandy heaps among the bluebells on the slope are very obvious from the path below.

Have walked round wood and farmland carefully checking each sett. At 4.50 a.m., I first heard, then saw, a male cuckoo and a male tawny *both sounding together* on the Damson Bank! Looking over the landscape, the fields of oilseed rape are bright splashes of yellow.

Returned to the Bank Sett at 6.45 a.m., in time to see a woman walk up Briarmead and along the Wildflower Path, turn in at the Old Cherry Sett and disappear from view. I moved closer as I was almost certain she was the woman with the man I saw 17 April. Same dog on the lead. She carefully examined the dug-out entrances to the cubs' new home, then straightened up, walked back down the slope and straight out of these woods, again via the View Path. Determined to follow her as I'm sure that couple are local and are connected to the badger-hunters. I quite easily trailed her and she never looked behind to see what her dog was looking at.

Sunday 8 May
Observing young animals at play is interesting. Just as foxcubs watch the movement of a playmate, then spring, so badger cubs will pick up a

191

leaf or wisp of grass and back a few paces with it until their attention is distracted – forerunner of the activity of bringing in bedding in later life.

Old Joe's two surviving offspring are growing fast and quite often accompany their mother on foraging expeditions. Young foxes have difficulty coping with their first worms, so do these little badgers. The female caught a worm just now almost by accident – it was wriggling along on the surface. With it held halfway along its length, she tried swallowing it whole, choked and spat it out. The worm beat a squirming retreat, only to find a small paw pressing it down. This time, the cub took an end between her teeth and sucked it up spaghetti-like – she must have seen her mother and the other adults eat them this way. Unlike them, however, she didn't bite at intervals along its length – or better still, bite and swallow – so ended up as at the first attempt with too large a mouthful to cope with. Again she swallowed, very nearly choked – then stood for a while rather quiet!

Hope these young badgers survive. Dull, wet morning with heavy showers. Stayed until past 7 a.m.; no sign of trouble.

Monday 9 May
Clear skies, mild and damp. First light 3.45 this morning. Tawny male sounding and hunting well into daylight, 5.10 a.m., for his growing family. The tawny chicks venture out along the branch from the nest-hole – much wing flapping.

Old Joe's other sow is now denning at the Old Cherry Sett. So now at one end by the great tree itself I've got the mother badger and her cubs; at the other, Old Joe and sow; whilst in the middle, two vixens and their cubs (six foxcubs now). Rather congested, but at least it's easier to watch over. Easier for the badger-hunters too – they can't go wrong here now, wherever they dig.

Tuesday 10 May
Joe's cubs are very entertaining – Rolling Down the Bluebell Slope is a favourite game, as is Climbing the Old Cherry Trunk as Far as You Dare. Their mother and Joe do it too, only in their case it's for slugs and beetles, etc. hidden in the deeply fissured bark. This area round their new home has great play potential for the young badgers, but the bluebells are looking a bit limp! The foxes have moved out to the Felled Logs Sett, but aren't far away – the vixens are denning near by. I've never come across this situation before, though have heard of it happening – that is, vixens sharing cubs and territory quite amicably. In this case, they are mother and daughter – and their mates are father and son.

Sunday 15 May
Very mild night, cloudy skies, no rain. Corbett's men have been ploughing the field at the View, and it is there that the badger family have been foraging tonight. The smell of wet, freshly turned earth carries

a long way and badgers are adept at following their snouts. As I was returning from the field about 2.30 a.m., the sow mother went into the View Sett briefly, emerged, but didn't dig out. However, she took in bluebell bedding by the chinful, that is, tucked between chin and chest and carried in backwards. (N.B. Not the flowers, but the green leaves bitten off close to the ground.) The twins, full of excitement, took their little bits in too. The cubs were squeaking and grunting with delight; pushing and shoving themselves and Mum; slipping in the deep mud of the Primrose Path; falling over the dead wood and trailing lianas of traveller's joy and generally driving the adult mad. She finally gave up, leaving them to carry in bedding and, sitting back on her haunches, groomed the field-mud off herself. From below ground came the sounds of a cub quarrel, but this was clearly a case of 'Let them get on with it'.

Notice Joe gives his son and daughter a wide berth – he nearly makes an audible sigh if he sees them coming at night. Can't blame him at his age. He has been digging out the entrance in the bole of the giant pollarded ash at the Bank Sett – a long time since any animal has touched that. He also dug out in the hollow at the Chantry – very old badger workings here, too. Huge clump of primroses near by, and everywhere are the pale green spathes and deeply purple spadices of the wild arum. The Chantry still holds its mystery and allure for me; it has the largest groundcover of yellow archangel in these woods; vivid yellow against green leaves, the purest of colours.

Sunday 22 May

I think young animals will try eating anything. A foxcub has just successfully caught and eaten a large moth. The fox families are growing fast and becoming very handsome and adult-looking; they have quite lost their baby appearance.

Over the past week, we have had storms and heavy rain. This wet weather is good for foxes and badgers. With plenty of easy food, the cubs are doing well. The tawnies hunt well into the morning, causing some consternation amongst the daylight birds. The young owls are now safely left 'uncloaked' whilst the hen bird helps in the quest for prey to meet the ever-increasing demands of their growing family. The youngsters' feathers are appearing through the down, giving them an untidy look.

Last Friday morning at 5.30 a.m. I spoke to a police patrol in Briarmead Lane and they asked me how the badgers were faring – all quiet on the badger front at present. I've seen the police around at 5 a.m. several times, so know they are doing all they can.

Nightjars are attempting to nest in Ashcroft Woods again – in the bracken area of the ancient boundary ditch which runs from Main Path to the Silver Birch Path. I enjoy watching the strange nightjars that perch along a branch, not across it as other birds do. During the day, they rest on the ground, merging with the dead leaves and general debris

193

that litters this woodland floor. Their silhouette in flight is unmistakable, as are their pointed wings and (male) white wing spots, their sudden whip-cracks and their 'churr-churring' bike sounds.

7 a.m. Shooting started, but not a lot – imagine it's just one person.

Monday 23 May
One of the badger cubs, the little female, has injured her foot, leaving a trail of blood through the bluebells, and is obviously in a great deal of pain. Her mother licked the paw, then grunted abruptly and stopped. She showed no inclination to have another go and neither did the youngster who just stood whimpering and lame. Any weight applied to it caused a fresh outbreak of cries, so after a while I decided to have a go myself. Joe's mate is well used to me, though I normally move away if the cubs approach. I made a fuss of the little cub at first, talking softly to gain her confidence and calm her down. Could feel her trembling and shivering – blood everywhere. Difficult to see what was causing the trouble as the blood flow was unceasing. Sat with her held firmly between my knees and felt gently over the pad – only to cut myself! No wonder they weren't anxious to clean it themselves; a piece of glass was embedded there. The pad covering is hard, almost rubbery, but underneath the area is soft, sensitive, and bleeds freely. (Unlike a dog's pad, a badger's is a continuous covering spread over the bottom of the paw.) The cub was very good about the whole affair, offering very little resistance, though this was probably due to her mother standing near by. Had nothing to grip on without cutting myself again, so I used the fine blade of my fungi penknife to ease out the long glass sliver. By now, I was sticky with blood. The cub sniffed her paw, then looked up as I spoke to her, the white of her muzzle reddened. Then I had her little snout feel curiously over my face. Sat with her on my lap as she showed no inclination to clamber off. Think this night a relationship has been forged that won't easily be broken.

There's an irony here. I have very mixed feelings about allowing wild animals to get too used to me – and have never deliberately set out to do so. Yet in this situation, had I not known these badgers through Old Joe and his musking of me, I could never have removed the glass.

Tuesday 24 May
Tawny hunting and hooting well after dawn. Old Joe has been investigating the old sett near the Motorway on Corbett's land. Must ask the new manager's permission to come here at night. Have only just discovered the original man who allowed me here left a long time ago. One of the foxcubs barked at me (the warning bark, could have been an adult, but not with quite the carrying power), then caught my scent; it advanced, still stiff-legged, then relaxed. I watched the nightjars for an hour. Their flight is almost silent, twisting and turning in their chase for moths and insects.

Young 'un's paw is still open; hadn't realised what a cavity the glass had made – it goes at an angle, deep into the foot.

Friday 27 May

Watched a grass snake this morning at about 5 a.m. as I kept vigil over the Old Cherry Sett. Sat near the edge of the Wildflower Path (surrounded by gnats!). The snake was gliding through the nettles and bracken – its tongue darting in and out. Its length as it passed back and forth seemed astounding, though just an impression, of course. Then the flower stems ceased to move, and it was gone – but I had the feeling it wasn't far away. A bank vole ran over my coppiced stump – there was a movement, and the snake had gripped it from behind. With the head and torso protruding from its gaping jaws, the reptile slowly began to swallow the plump little rodent which struggled at first, eyes protruding, squeaking repeatedly. The snake's mouth dislocated to take in yet more of its prey; the back-pointing teeth secured a firmer grip and the dying vole twitched momentarily. Wonder how long a meal of that size would satisfy the predator before it need hunt again?

Gnats by now are having a meal of me so it's time to go home! 5.35 a.m.

Saturday 28 May

The field below Briarmead was turned under yesterday and since it is a showery night, the badgers have made full use of their opportunity! All seven (including the yearlings and the cubless sow) are worming there. Stood watching them with great pleasure – am determined to continue to come out each morning and see they are not dug out again. Hope all goes well with them from now on.

It's 5.25 a.m. and well light; the tawnies are still hunting. They find the vantage point from the Old Cherry's sloping trunk very useful as it overlooks the badger spoil heaps at two of the sett entrances. These mounds of earth cover wide areas among the bluebell greenery which are crossed by small mammals in their quest for food. A shrew has just made its final darting run across the bare earth. The ever-watchful owl swoops effortlessly, talons outstretched. She takes her kill back to the ancient cherry and – interesting, this – rips the shrew in half. Then, having swallowed the head and chest, she silently glides back to the nest-hole leaving the rest of the shrew lying on the deeply fissured trunk. Foxes kill shrews but do not eat them since they are distasteful. Notice, however, that tawnies will eat them, but reject the lower part of the shrew's body.

10.30 a.m. Walked round to Colts Farm to ask Pete Williams, Mr Corbett's new farm manager, if I could go on his land at night to keep an eye on Old Joe – gave his consent.

Monday 30 May

I have been accompanied by a little friend for the past hour, so am

195

keeping the mother sow in sight. Her daughter – young Limp-Along-Lesley – rather enjoys having her paw checked, which I'm doing regularly in case of infection. Can't help seeing a parallel in Jessie and the splinter of wood that caused the abscess which later became infected. I'll watch the cub's wound until it eventually closes which, at present, it shows no sign of doing. The joint above the foot is stiff and painful and she seems unwell in herself. Have found that the easiest way of examining her paw is to roll her gently on to her back and tickle her tummy. Her pads then are facing me and I don't have to turn the injured foot to look at it and maybe hurt her in doing so. This, of course, has become a game which her brother joins in to be tickled too! The mother has fully accepted me mainly because, prior to visiting her, I make sure either Old Joe has musked me *or* I've stroked and fussed him so that my hands smell of her mate.

Walking down the scree slope of the Ridge at 5.50 a.m. when one of the magpies flew overhead. Whistled to it and, sure enough, it came round and alighted on a clump of flowering broom! Sat on the fence by the stile to see if it would come over to me as in past years, as I'm certain it was one of the same pair of birds. Moments later, it perched on the top slat, bright-eyed and inquisitive. At least this suggests they keep the same territory. Wonder how long they live?

SUMMER 1983

Wednesday 1 June 1983
A storm started at 1.10 a.m. as I walked up the Ridge – torrential rain, sheet lightning illuminating the clouds. Lasted an hour before passing; then the rain ceased. I no longer heard thunder, but flashes lit up the distant sky. I was anxious to see the cub, who is far from well, but knew until the storm ceased that the badgers would be below ground. They emerged about 2.30 a.m. It was immediately apparent that little 'un was very sick – unable to put the paw to the ground. She made no attempt to forage for herself, though worms were everywhere on the surface.

The mother left the field edge and came over to where I was standing near her cub. She let something drop from her mouth that fell at the youngster's feet – a worm or piece of one. The cub sniffed at it, taking very little interest – then ate it almost reluctantly and stood there as before, with her head down in a dejected sort of way. Some while later, however, the sow returned again to her huddled offspring and repeated

197

the action. This time, the cub took no notice, but her brother came bounding forward and gobbled up the worm himself, pushing his sick sibling out of the way and nearly over in his eagerness. His sister whimpered at the rough treatment – the knock had forced her injured paw to the ground. But the boar cub, in his desire to get more such food, jumped excitedly up at his mother's face and began, puppy-like, to lick around her mouth! The adult turned slightly away but her boisterous cub still persisted with his licking. She began to heave, coughed, and brought up partly digested worms – a great heap of them. Could hardly believe what I was witnessing – I've never connected regurgitation with badgers; since much of their food is soft, it would normally be unnecessary. The boar cub pitched in with great delight but his sister appeared uninterested. On an impulse, I lifted her up and set her carefully down on the opposite side of the regurgitated food, well away from her brother. She ate – true, it was slowly, but a fair amount none the less.

The mother began to groom herself, when we were made aware of the returning storm as a great roll of thunder came nearer and nearer, and the trees bent in the sudden wind. The young boar fluffed up, then bolted across the Wildflower Path and up the bluebell slope to home, his sister hobbling wretchedly behind. The adult started after them, looked back at the worm remains lying on the field edge and hastily finished them off! Then as lightning and thunder exploded simultaneously overhead, she galloped up the slope after her cubs. Rain lashed down once more and, still soaked from the earlier deluge, I turned for home. Only 4 a.m., but no one could dig out badgers in this and I had an hour's walk ahead.

This afternoon, went to the Barksham vet and explained the situation. He has given me hydrogen peroxide to pour into the open wound – says it is good for any external wound. As it seeps away, it takes pus etc. with it – that's interesting for future use – and is easily obtainable at a chemist's. He has given me antibiotic in capsule form – one a night. I can either empty capsule contents into a tasty morsel of food, or give it whole. We both agreed that if this doesn't work and her condition worsens, it would not be right to take her from her surroundings. Her mother would almost certainly reject her, besides being a terrifying ordeal for the cub. But he said to come back and discuss the situation if it doesn't improve.

Friday 3 June
These past two nights, I have been visiting the badger family at the Old Cherry Sett. Everywhere is very muddy, so I lay my anorak inside up on the ground and turn the sick cub on to that. She accepts what is happening to her without protest – an indication of her illness. The problem has been rather with her brother who naturally enough crowds round, even treading over her in his determination not to miss anything. His robust health is in marked contrast to his sister's and a reminder of

how she was before the glass incident. Just now, however, the mother has herself chased him off, so her influence is greater than mine! She is probably concerned at little 'un's whimpering.

I clean the foot up (pus everywhere), then pour hydrogen peroxide into the cavity. Have found, as with Jessie, that muscatels are acceptable, and the capsule wedged between two of these raisins is swallowed whilst she is still on her back. I keep her there for some minutes (to let the liquid seep well into the wound), stroking her face and behind her ears. Then gently set her on her feet again.

The honeysuckle is in flower. Its long streamers trail from above, scenting the night air. I like to stand absorbing its sweetness, the blossoms a ghostly paleness in the woodland depths. To me, the scent of honeysuckle always seems stronger at night, and maybe this isn't just my fancy. I've been watching hawkmoths alighting on the protruding stamens.

Monday 6 June
Last afternoon and evening, we were again hit by storms which have left flooded areas and high winds. The injured badger cub is still very sick, although the foot itself appears to be healing. The wound is no longer discharging, though still open. Difficult to get her to eat; she hasn't foraged for herself these past six nights and is very weak. I believe these cubs are weaned. Haven't witnessed the mother regurgitate again although it's possible she has been doing so. Have seen her several times drop morsels in front of it. She is keeping close to her sick cub and now, at 2.35 a.m., is grooming her. Apart from giving the cub a capsule between raisins, I'm keeping well out of the way as it's vital that the mother's interest continues – I don't want the cub rejected. Not using the peroxide now as I fear it may prevent the wound closing. Lost a capsule in the mud tonight – fortunately, I carry a spare on me for just such a contingency.

The nightjars here fascinate me. They share the incubating of the eggs (two eggs seem to be a nightjar's limit, at least for Ashcroft Woods) which have been laid where an old piece of branch is slowly rotting into the bracken of the ancient boundary ditch. They build no nest and are beautifully camouflaged in these surroundings. Since I have been spending so much time lately on the Briarmead side of the woods (both tending the sick cub and guarding against the badgers being dug out), I have noticed that the nightjars fly over and frequent the field where Barry Hains's cattle and horses graze on the other side of the lane. Imagine with livestock there, they may well find more insects on the wing – their staple food. They also hunt the moths feeding from the masses of honeysuckle flowers – badgers aren't the only opportunists! In a quiet way, nightjars are most beautiful birds.

I feel it is significant that, since the police have been regularly patrolling Briarmead Lane, the early morning shooting that other years was so prevalent and disturbing to wildlife here has largely disappeared. This is a welcome and unexpected bonus of the badger-hunting situation.

Tuesday 7 June
Mild, clear night with thin-edged crescent moon. The high winds of yesterday that have helped to dry out the wet earth are gone. Found Joe and the cubless sow from the View Sett worming round the large stretch of water below the Motorway on Corbett's land. He hasn't dug out any more at the Motorway sett. I explored it at first light, 3.10 a.m. – very old badger workings in the chalk. Amazing the tons of earth and heavy flints generations of these tough animals have moved. No badger has lived there this year and there are no animal trails through the perfect deep green carpet of ivy and dog's-mercury above. Ashcroft Woods look darkly mysterious from my perch high up on this bank. The distant sky above them is faintly flushed with pink, so it's time to leave and watch over the occupants of the Old Cherry Sett.

3.20 a.m. Have just seen the sow badger regurgitate without any prompting licking from either of her cubs. This happened in front of the injured cub, who ate with a will. Her brother soon realised he was missing out and came to eat also. The family went to earth at 4.10 a.m.

Wednesday 8 June
Went back to the vet today as the badger cub has finished her capsules and is still far from well. Discussed her condition and mentioned that the young animal's nose or snout, usually so flexible and rubbery-like, has assumed a rigid, odd appearance. I wondered whether it was infected (her snout and sense of smell is of vital importance to foraging etc.) or if, dog-like, their nose was indicative of their general health. Neither of us very sure on that point! However, have been given a further eight capsules – one a night, as before – and hope these will get her back to normal.

(Had a frightening experience going to the badgers at about 3 a.m. Someone repeatedly tried to run me down in the Motorway tunnel. The young male passenger who was laughing and encouraging the van driver I've seen before with badger-digging groups in the woods.)

Saturday 11 June
The badger cub, Limp-Along-Lesley, is fast returning to normal. After feeding her the capsule-cum-raisins tonight, I had my fingers playfully nibbled! My stay in her company now is very brief – restricted to giving the antibiotic, and then leaving; I want her life to revert to normal as soon as possible. The injured paw sometimes touches the ground now, though little weight is put on it. The cavity in the pad will be slow to close as it's such a size and depth. However, it's drying up now and will probably heal slowly from inside. She plays with her brother, though not

200

for long, as naturally he is too rough and strong for her weakened state. Nevertheless, the desire and interest is there and she's finding food for herself once more. Stays closer to her mother than the boar cub.

The past three days have been hot and sunny, though the early mornings tend to be dull and overcast. The mud and wet places are drying up fast, but this doesn't affect the badgers in my area who simply go on to the stretch of water like a lake below the Motorway if they want to drink. It's not only the cubs that like a splash-about there; the yearlings do too, and even Old Joe isn't averse to getting his tummy wet. Badgers look very comic when they emerge from water. The wet fur clings to their stocky wedge-shaped bodies, and with a stomach full of worms ...! And their greyish, wispy tails resemble tatty bits of wet dishcloth.

Sunday 12 June
Watching over the badgers these past two months, I've rather lost touch with my foxes – indeed, I've tended to avoid fox encounters since I didn't want to carry fox scent to the badgers, especially when seeing to the cub. The vixens have moved their joint cubs several times and now they are living at the Felled Logs Sett. They have grown greatly and attempt to hunt for themselves – beetles, moths, etc. It's surprising what a foxcub can find to eat as its co-ordination improves through play; its ability to pounce accurately and interpret the tiny rustlings and squeaks that come to it through those large ears. Young birds fallen from the nest or learning to fly are within a foxcub's grasp.

At 6.20 a.m. it's a dull, windy morning. Met a squirrel in the

201

Briarmead Gully and clicked at him. He ran up a young oak until level with my face and rose up on his hind legs, one front paw raised. He began waving his tail up and down, up and down, as my clicking became louder and faster. It would be lowered below the branch on which he stood, then raised up until rigidly upright. Did the down/up movement with great speed and then held it upright for a few moments before repeating the action. When I stopped clicking, he stopped his tail waving but, unlike other squirrels I have done this to, he did not click back. Have noticed before that they have this visual signalling with their bushy tails, but haven't had one do this to me before. Wonder what the action signifies? Come to that, I'm not sure what the clicking means, though feel it could be a challenge. At no time did this grey squirrel seem nervous or frightened – curious and interested, yes.

Thursday 16 June
Mild, dry night with moon in the first quarter. Between the woods and Madden Lane, a hydrant used for the irrigation sprays has been left partly turned on. Sufficient to say, all seven badgers have made the most of the situation, worm-wise. The cubs looked as if they had been having mudbaths. Gave Limp-Along-Lesley her *last* capsule sandwiched as always between two fat raisins. Had little muddy pawmarks all over my trousers and anorak, and a little muddy snout investigated my hands, face – and then pockets! How many badgers have explored my pockets over the years – Jessie, Old Joe, and now his daughter. Their long, narrow snouts and sleek heads are certainly made to fit into small places! Those neat teddybear ears don't get caught up either – makes one realise how ideally they have evolved. Lesley's evolution, however, didn't succeed in finding her anything edible in my pockets, though she *did* try to convince herself that tissues are tasty!

I had just decided to move on and that this must be my last meeting with the family now all was well with the cub, when she suddenly backed on to my boots and musked them, turned and smelt her musking, then re-musked. Obviously hadn't done it to her satisfaction the first time.

Sitting writing this whilst guarding the Old Cherry Sett at 4.45 a.m. when I happened to look down the slope in time to see something whitish disappearing along the lower path. Hastily put my notes away and ran down the slope in time to see a man dressed in [description omitted] and carrying two large containers, rapidly walking along the path to the View. Sure it must have been the same man as on 17 and 20 April, although I never saw his face – just the [description of action omitted]. The steep undulations of the path lost him from view, then I saw him once more (either his burden was heavy or awkward or both), then he was gone. At the View itself, he had a choice of five routes. I checked he didn't go down the wood side to the end of the lane; he could have gone the opposite way round the wood edge, but the outward curve of the trees obscured the view. But there are three other paths within the wood

202

he might have taken. Was uneasy about leaving the Old Cherry Sett too long – always feel I could be decoyed away and the badgers dug out in my absence. First checked the Felled Logs and View Setts – all quiet – and returned to write this and wait until 5.30 a.m.

(This evening, I discussed with Ross what the man might be doing. Ross is inclined to think his activity either has nothing to do with badgers or the badgers are a sideline to delivering things for collection by a third party; or, just possibly, the setts and dens are hiding-places. We both agreed he's not merely dumping, since you don't need to walk *through* a wood to do this, but would just dump on the outskirts or even on the edge of the lane. Alternatively, of course, he *could* have been carrying gas cylinders.)

Friday 17 June
See the Top Hayfield of Briarmead is already baled – it's good weather for haymaking. Am sitting at the Old Cherry Sett, watching and waiting over the badgers here, as always. The dawn chorus is more subdued now the birds are moulting, but none the less very enjoyable. At 4.40 a.m. became aware I was not alone, and there was Old Joe back again, peering at me from round the fallen trunk. Surprised he had re-emerged and wondered why. Think he was as surprised to see me; probably doesn't realise I stay around after his family has gone to earth. Spoke to him softly and he came right up – first resting his chin on my knee, then the front half of his body with his fore legs dangling over. And there we stayed – my left arm round his shoulders and both of us gazing through the foliage down the slope. The humour of the situation struck me and I had difficulty not to laugh – were we both watching for badger-diggers? If they had appeared, don't know who would have had the greatest shock – them or us! (Notice that the patch mark on the boar's flank, due to different fur growth, has completely disappeared now he is very old and his coat lightening with age. It was the result of an injury and distinguished him from other males when I watched badgers here years ago.)

The two sows have been fetching in fresh bedding tonight – there's nothing quite like the smell of newly mown hay to get a badger going! Little Lesley hardly attempted to help. With the use of only three legs, she has enough effort getting herself along; carrying hay in backwards is beyond her at present. Her brother helped, however – i.e. got in the way. I never cease to marvel how patient badger mums are – they put their human counterparts to shame. Telltale wisps of grass are caught here and there on the brambles and bluebell seed-heads. The other sow at the View Sett had much further to go, but this didn't deter her. Their favourite bedding seems to be hay and will tempt them quite a distance, even if the going is rough.

5.10 a.m. and Joe seems to be falling asleep across my knees. Have to gently push him off as he's such a weight that my legs are going to sleep too! Don't like him being above ground so late either. Watched his shaggy body ambling back along the path. As he turned to go into the entrance, his black and white, grey old face looked up a moment to where I still sat. Wonder if I've really done him much good, knowing him so well. But I'm afraid the damage, if damage there is, has been done and there's no turning back. Shall miss him greatly when he dies – and it was his musking of me that saved little Limp-Along-Lesley.

5.45 a.m. Walking back along the path to the beehives, I saw in the distance the Prosser vixen, Josh's mate, carrying back a rabbit – she didn't see me. She put it down twice to get a better grip on it, for a grown rabbit is quite a weight for a fox to carry very far. Watching her through the monocular, it struck me how well a *moulting* fox's coat blends with ploughed earth.

Tuesday 21 June
Dull, grey morning with slight mist. Steady drip of moisture from the trees above. Found the Old Cherry Sett sadly altered – sticks left poking from entrances, bottles and plastic wrappers strewn about. It was glass from such a bottle that caused the badger cub's injury. The small fallen trunk Joe and I sat on last Friday has been broken up – the pieces thrown down the slope.

Wednesday 22 June
Everywhere is very dry; no rain for some time and what moisture there is soon evaporates during the day. The sow and cubs have left the Old

Cherry Sett and have moved in with the other sow at the View. I say moved in, but they're not actually sharing a nesting chamber as there is plenty of room. This is a curious sett. To the casual observer, there are five entrances very close together, under and around an old holly bush and cherry tree, situated in the bank of a hollow. Search the area, however, and you find as many more entrances at a short distance in the undergrowth. This View Sett also links underground with the Felled Logs one which, at present, has the combined foxcub families, so in fact there is far more room here than appears at a glance.

Old Joe stubbornly remains at the Old Cherry Sett – in spite of the badger-diggers of 14 April and the interference of last Sunday. I hope his obstinacy doesn't cost him dear.

Saturday 25 June
A mild, overcast night. Have been watching the bats and nightjars catching insects on the wing over Long Field and the Wildflower Path. Have established that the former roost in the cracks and crevices of tree-bark here, especially of the geans or wild cherry trees which become deeply fissured with age. The night air seems alive with insects; the moths, particularly, tend to blunder into one's face. The two young nightjars are flying now, but are still fed by their parents. Catching airborne insects must require considerable skill, and though the fledglings are attempting to hunt their own, they also beg for and receive food from the adults. Though nightjars have quite small beaks, their gape is wide – the lower jaw opens out surprisingly. This is very apparent with their young who have just landed on the path and are gaping at their parents.

Friday 1 July
4.10 a.m. Whilst guarding the Old Cherry Sett this morning, I watched a wood mouse (formerly the long-tailed field mouse), near Old Joe's main entrance. Mice and voles appear to have regular runways, so it is by no means the first time I've seen this little chap. One burrow entrance is at the base of a tree stump to my right and it always seems to go home with a sudden sprint from the thick vegetation near by. This dart across the ground, then a pause to examine something, is characteristic of these mice. Yesterday, as I sat here, it ran along a fallen tree near by, then sat back on its haunches and proceeded to wash. Like the rabbit, this wood mouse first licked its front paws, then wiped them down its muzzle, face and behind its ears very quickly. Next it cleaned its body, and lastly its tail. It picked up the long tail and ran it through its mouth, licking it clean. This grooming is performed at lightning speed – yet very thoroughly. But then wood mice seem to do everything at a gallop! I've read that it is doubtful whether they live beyond the end of the breeding season following that in which they are born – seeing them in action, I'm not surprised!

205

It's been a mild night with clear, starry skies and a half-moon. Everywhere very dry. The foxcubs are reduced to five and are growing fast. Both sets of parents are leaving food further away now. In searching for it, they find their own food too. This encourages them to explore and get to know the surrounding land; it also teaches them to forage. Cherries are a popular choice, mainly because they are easily found, I imagine.

Sunday 3 July

Lesley found me tonight, as I stood watching the family from the shelter of the wood edge. On reaching me, the young badger musked my shoes. Sat on the hard-baked earth of the field path to be on a level with her. Let her explore me and my clothing. Pockets are interesting, even if empty; the zip-end hanging from my jacket was vigorously chewed (remembered this later on in the morning when it wouldn't do up!) and my watch was snuffled over. I had one ear washed, then my hair carefully examined. Made the mistake of playing with her by pulling my jacket over my head, then making myself appear again. At first she just sat back on her haunches, staring – but the third time I did it, she pounced on me with great delight, dragging at the jacket with her teeth and emitting little squeaks and barks of excitement which, of course, attracted her brother. Found to my cost that even five-month-old cubs have sharp claws and struggled to my feet in sheer self-defence – in time to see, a few yards down the sloping field, Old Joe in the act of mating with their mother. Rather surprising this, considering the noise we were making. The cubs, on finding they had 'lost' me once I was on my feet, and very excited by our play, tried to continue the game with their parents. Joe swung round at them growling formidably, and they bolted back to me – two very subdued youngsters. I sat down between them, with a hand stroking each, and was able to have a quiet close look at Joe's offspring. The male cub is noticeably bigger and heavier than Lesley, though at the time of her accident they were of a size. Already his face is broader, his cheeks fuller – he has the teddybear look of the male. His sister has a longer, narrower head – flat rather than domed between the ears – characteristic of the sow. In spite of her smaller size and slight limp, she is now as lively and alert as her brother.

Wednesday 6 July

A much cooler night with a thick mist. Constant sound of moisture drop-dropping through the foliage. Not enough moisture, however, to soften the earth for digging out or worming. These badgers would be hard hit if it weren't for the irrigation on Corbett's fields – they are foraging there now. Old Joe went off on his own about 2.45 a.m. and I followed him slowly, more for something to do than anything else. Stopped to examine the sweet-chestnut catkins; their scent is very cloying in the damp air. Was aware of Joe standing at the path corner looking back at me –

waiting? – so caught him up, until eventually we arrived at the bracken slope between High Ridge and the Gully. I lost interest in his snuff-snuffling up and down the slope, and climbed on to the great fallen beech that blocks the path. The upturned bole is higher than me and the trunk and branches stretch far out on to the Ridge – a great bridge across the uneven ground.

Was suddenly alerted to what the badger was doing by a furious buzzing and a cloud of wasps rather too near for comfort. I've never moved so quickly; gnats this time of year are bad enough, but I draw the line at wasps! Worked my way round and up the slope until I was above the scene. Using the monocular, watched Joe eating the nest, quite oblivious of its owners or their stinging. Badgers are very partial to the grubs as well as the adults and a large amount of the nest gets eaten as well. Sometimes he would look up and chop at a group of insects still flying around, the sharp sound of his jaws mingling with their buzzing. Later on in the morning I passed here, homeward bound, and saw that the nest had been built into a cavity between the roots of another beech growing out of the steep slope. A few wasps were crawling over the debris of their former home. Joe had dug down to it at an angle – earth and pieces of nest lay strewn about the slope.

First light late – skylarks didn't begin singing over these fields until 4.10 a.m., then stopped for a while until the woodland blackbirds started at 4.30 a.m. A police car on Briarmead at 5 a.m. – glad they still patrol here.

Wednesday 27 July
Full moon, warm night, clear skies and good visibility. Everywhere a dustbowl except for Corbett's fields. In many areas, badgers are not finding enough food and their cubs are starving. Here, thanks to Pete Williams, the farm manager, and his irrigated, quick-turnover crops, my badgers are healthy and thriving. Foxes haven't the same problem, being more agile – besides hunting, they eat an abundance of insects in the summer months. The young tawnies are flying well, though the parent birds still bring them food. Enjoy watching their silent, gliding flight over the fields here – graceful ghosts. Sometimes the owlets call one to another; this I define as their contact call and is quite different from that of the adults. They also have a hunger call, which is most persistent in the summer months. Tawnies, too, like foxes, are great insect eaters. One insect both creatures shun, however, is the gaudy burnet moth which frequents the Wildflower Path and is locally common. Once when Josh was foraging here, I offered him a burnet and his reaction startled me. With a growl of alarm, he jumped back and stood regarding me uncertainly. Puzzled, I advanced slowly with hand outstretched, whereupon he hurriedly trotted off. Quite recently I have read that burnet moths produce poisons: one totally unknown poison protects the eggs; another, found in the eggs, the caterpillar; and the moth itself is

prussic acid. Since fox parents don't, in my experience, 'teach' their cubs, I imagine that Josh had sampled the unpleasantness of burnets for himself. Did his sense of smell warn him (prussic acid smells like bitter almonds), or vision (most toxic insects have vivid coloration, though not all gaudy insects are toxic)? Moreover, having studied foxes so long now, I'm convinced they are *not* colour-blind, though I doubt if they see colour quite as we do.

Tuesday 2 August
Dull, overcast night after twelve hours of storm and rain. It has been the hottest July this century. Many trees already have autumn tints and leaves litter the ground. I have been taking water to my area each night I come out, as some of the eighteen trees I planted this year have wilted in the dryness. I take water to those round the Briarmead area, for the Main Pond is very low, but find I can fetch it from a hydrant to the others. In the woods, I have planted four hornbeam saplings, two beech, four oak, two willow by the pond and two wild service; and in the hedgerows, two gean and two wild service. The willows were cuttings from that pollarded at the Cottage site; all the rest were seed from these woods. Noticed back in June that some of these young trees were being nibbled, but solved the problem with a large canister of cat-pepper that I hid in an old tree. A circle of the powder around each sapling seems to deter rodents as well as felines! Badgers aren't keen on it either. Little Lesley and her brother were taking an interest in the canister one night and came too close when I was using it – they left me to myself with great disgust!

When first I knew these woods, they contained many mature and many dying or dead trees, but little young growth. That which did spring up naturally was either nibbled away by rodents or burnt by the many 'accidental' fires. So over the years I have planted trees from seed collected here, grown and tended at home and brought over the young plants before they became too large to carry. Then watered regularly – that's the difficult part – in their early years. I have kept careful count of those that survived to grow untended – 528 to date. If you count trees in a wood, you will quickly find that the number is very few.

It seems to me that the landscapers of the eighteenth century who planned the estates and parks we enjoy today were incredible people. To plant trees, not for your lifetime or your children's, but for those two centuries ahead, and to see in your mind's eye what a place would look like in that time, requires humility and vision. To always be aware that you are merely the instrument by which these things are done – never the creator – requires humility. To plant a tree is one thing, to create a life-force is something different, and to see it grow is a small miracle. One can merely plant with a sense of vision and hope that vision will live on and flourish.

208

Friday 12 August

Clear, starry, warm night, but now at 4 a.m. a mist hangs over the
countryside. On the Top Field in front of the Old Barn ruins, I was able
to get very close to the lapwings. The barley here has been cut, a
firebreak ploughed around the field edge, and the stubble burnt off. The
burning destroys the weeds but doesn't affect the sun-baked earth.
Lapwings feed extensively at night and seem less fearful of man during
the dark hours. Burnt-off stubble is uncomfortable to crawl slowly over,
but when I ended up within a yard of these fascinating birds and sat
arms round knees watching them, any discomfort was amply rewarded
by further lapwings flying down all around. Thus at first light, 4.40 a.m.,
I was sitting amongst a flock of lapwings at least 350 strong – no gulls.
They scrape at the soil with their feet and turn up hard cases of insect
larvae, grubs, etc. Certainly plenty of food here – they must be the
farmer's best friend.

I spied Josh creeping up on the unsuspecting flock, quite unaware of
me in their midst. Guessed the little vixen was near by and, sure enough,
she was approaching from behind. She jumped at one as the birds rose
with their plaintive 'peewit' sounding on all sides, then stood, bird in
mouth with its wings thrashing her face, staring at me in surprise. Her
grip hardened and the bird was dead; a few feathers floated to the
ground. Thought she would have eaten it and perhaps allowed her mate
something. But instead, she let it fall. Best describe Josh's attitude as
sheepish. His vixen was less restrained – looked at me, then slowly came
up and put her face into mine. There's no living creature more beautiful –

209

to me – than a fox. After Josh ate the lapwing, I shared blackberries with my foxes.

Whilst sitting on one of the little posts of Briarmead writing this, a shrew appeared from the grass verge opposite and busily darted about on the tarmac surface, this way and that. Rustled over a crumpled paper bag, gradually worked its way up the lane, to finally disappear in the long grass at the top post opposite. I continued writing for a while, when the shrew darted out and picked a worm up almost at my feet. Holding it in its front paws, the tiny creature made short work of quite a big meal!

Wednesday 17 August
Slight moisture falling, strong breeze, lowering sky. This parched countryside cries out for rain; the wayside foliage lies covered in a thick dust. Looking at Ashcroft Woods by day, the trees at a distance have lost their deep green and appear freckled.

Stayed at the Chantry for some of the night, watching the tawny owls hunting at the field edge. Both Great Chantry and Long Field have barley waiting to be cut; the bent heads rustle drily at some small creature's passing. Later, I carried water to all eighteen young trees (usually I tend nine one night and the others the night following). Took me an hour and a half, but I'm determined they'll not die. This is the first summer in all my tree-planting years that I've needed to tend the young saplings for so long.

Just after first light, came through the undergrowth on to the lower path from the stiles at the View, in time to see a man with his back to me walking quickly away. As I hesitated, he turned and saw me. It was the same man as I saw in April and on 16 June; he had a large container in each hand. He dropped what he was carrying and ran towards me as I jumped back up the bank. Luckily, he tripped, which gave me a start or I would never have got away. Ran through the undergrowth on my foxes' path which is only just visible in broad daylight and certainly was not apparent then. Could hear him crashing behind me – thankfully I'm small and light. Dived under the green hanging curtain of an old holly tree and crouched behind the great, grey trunk within. Heard him go past and fade into the distance – felt like a hunted fox myself.
[Re-reading this – have not seen him since.]

Monday 22 August
I had a careful look at the rabbits feeding in the early morning, as there have been local reports that myxomatosis is on the increase again, believed to be due to the prolonged drought. However, only a minority here seem to be suffering from it; no more than usual.

From Briarmead at first light, heard the high-pitched 'nick-nikking' of young badgers at play, and traced the sounds – very far carrying – to the second hayfield, that is, the one above the Old Cherry Sett. It's still half cut, and Lesley and her brother were using a mown 'lane' on which

210

to play Chase Me Charlie. When she caught up with her brother, she simply gripped his tail with her teeth and stopped running – which, not surprisingly, brought him abruptly to a halt! Badger tails seem like tatty dish mops at the best of times – his looked a wet, worn-out one, due for renewal. Wondered where their mother was, but at 5.30 a.m. she had probably already gone to earth.

Sunday 28 August
Clear half-moon, starry sky, warm night. All the corn is harvested now and the stubble burnt off. One of the Josh/Tagless cubs barked at me near the ancient boundary ditch. I barked back to stop it running away, then knelt and spoke softly to it. It came right up and I let it smell my hands and face. Handsome dogfox – lovely coat. The near-grown cubs look in better condition than their parents, since the adults are still in process of growing new coats, but the youngsters don't moult in their first year.

Spoke to a patrol on Briarmead. Some while later, was with Josh at the Grain Dump just inside the wood. He was after rats – and I, rather bored, happened to look out on to the field. Patrol car still at the top of the lane, at the wood entrance, headlights off.

You learn a lot about light and reflection if you are a long way from habitation regularly at night. A distant light can appear to be moving if foliage is between you and it. A plane light can appear to be stationary then 'go out' when, in reality, it is moving away fast. A shielded light is quite different from an unshielded, held the hand. Never look towards headlights or your night vision is temporarily affected, perhaps when you need it most.

AUTUMN 1983

Thursday 1 September 1983

Had rather a surprise a short time ago – about 2.40 a.m.? Was shot at whilst on Pete's land above brightly lit Warby. I was watching the badgers worming, and was standing leaning against one of the giant hose-reels (and in its shadow), Lesley's brother at my feet chewing my shoelaces. A noise startled the badgers who rushed off down the field and, without thinking, I stood upright and looked out from the hose. Two men going round the wood edge – one turned, saw me and raised his free hand. I've seen that gesture too often not to recognise its meaning. Pulled myself hastily back just as something smacked into the metal of the reel. The gun had a loud report and was small in his hand – revolver? Only had a fleeting impression of the couple before they were hidden by the hedge. I wonder what they were carrying?

Fine crescent moon in clear skies. Watched the male nightjar flying low over Long Field hunting insects, 3.45 a.m. They will soon be making their journey south – shall miss them. (Notice the owls and nightjars given one another a wide berth.)

[Reading this entry later: were these men collecting something left by the man seen on 17 August? Possibly not as that was fifteen days ago.]

Wednesday 14 September
Wet, cloudy night with slight rain; warm, visibility good. 1.20 a.m., met Josh on the Ridge. Had a rough and tumble with him and nearly won this time – must be getting tougher! We went together to the top of Briarmead where he caught a frog and a field mouse. I was picking blackberries at the wood edge – a very impatient dogfox whining for more – with my back to Briarmead, when a patrol came up, swung round at the entrance, paused briefly and went down again – 3.15 a.m.

The arc of his headlights didn't quite reach us. I was very pleased with Josh's reaction; he just stayed very tense and still at my side. Foxes are intelligent, but they cannot reason. If a fox sees another creature at night, he assumes that creature (if he is out in the open as we were) can see him. Therefore, the fox will run away. What Josh cannot understand is that most humans are unable to see in the dark very well. To stay still, he is less likely to be seen – to run is to court disaster if the human has a gun. However, he's learning fast!

4.45 a.m. Old Joe has appeared – Josh has disappeared! He musked me and, when I stroked him, he first smelt, then licked my hands – blackberries, of course! My badgers are digging out now autumn is here. The twin yearlings (males) will leave the area, I think; they seem restless and quarrelsome. Joe is still very much the boss in spite of his years. Lesley and her brother tend to stay above ground well after the others have gone to earth. Rather like human teenagers keeping late nights.

Saturday 17 September
The badger-hunters are back. Was at the Old Cherry Sett with Lesley snuffling about at my feet, and heard some hooting sounds that puzzled me – like a tawny owl with laryngitis – sure it wasn't a bird. A while later (4.15 a.m.) thought I heard men's voices from the Chantry direction (sound tends to travel from hilltop to hilltop), but the wind high up in the trees made the noises indistinct. Lesley raised her head though and stood, snout raised towards the Chantry, scenting the air. Whatever it was made her uneasy, and shortly after, she disappeared below.

Was sitting on the curious tree-seat behind the Old Cherry at about 4.35 a.m. when two Jack Russell-type dogs ran up the slope. Leapt to my feet as the foremost disappeared down Lesley's entrance. Grabbed the other by the scruff and picked it up with my free hand. It snapped and snarled, trying to turn its head to bite, with me holding on – think I had bitten off rather more than I could chew! Other dogs appeared as I saw three men indistinctly through the foliage, at the bottom of the slope. One carried a light but it must have been shaded as, although it was

213

large, it wasn't very bright. (It was still dark, of course, and even darker under the trees.) I shouted to them to call their dogs away, which they did – by hooting! The dog I held renewed its struggles at the sound. One man called up, asking what I thought I was going to do with his dog – good question, since I wasn't sure myself. I answered, 'Hang on to it.' They talked together quietly on the path below, then began to walk back the way they had come, towards the stiles at the View. I sat back, speaking softly to the terrier and gradually released its fur to stroke round its ears. It only struggled once again and that when the hooting came from the distance. In the quietness, sat thinking about that sound. Far better than a whistle or a shout, yet sufficiently unlike a tawny for the dogs not to mistake it for the real thing, since these owls commonly hoot around dawn and dusk. Why not use a dog-whistle, though – they are usually above human pitch?

After a while, I began to walk along the path taken by the men – still carrying the dog, tucked under my arm and getting rather heavy. Stood beyond the stiles, trying to decide which way they had gone. Remembering I had first heard their voices from the Chantry, I wondered if they would return their spades and equipment there – could have been collecting them earlier. Set the Jack Russell on the ground and watched it sniffing along the edge of the field. It didn't seem bothered about its master, so I left it lapping from the puddle and went across Little Chantry Field just as light was beginning to touch the sky. I walked the width of the Chantry listening, and came out on to the headland overlooking Great Chantry and the valley. They could have had a car parked at the foot of this field off Briarmead, or nearer to Warby. At that moment, I heard the hooting again in the distance and realised I should have stayed on the other side or, at least, held on to the dog. Ran back through the Chantry and down the side of the hill in time to hear a car drive away below me.

Sunday 18 September
Raining hard with a strong wind. At first light, checked all the setts, including those on the fields. All untouched, nobody around. Kept one eye on Briarmead hoping to see a patrol – nothing. Searched part of the Chantry but it's like looking for the proverbial needle in a haystack – could find nothing. Feel sure the badger-hunters wouldn't risk being seen coming to and from this wood with spades and tongs. Wonder if this group uses probes; certain that the man whose dog I held was the one who struck at me with his spade on 30 January. Can't be sure about the other two. Yesterday was the first time I have seen men carrying tongs – which is not say they haven't had them before, of course.

Didn't leave until well after 9 a.m. Still raining.

Saturday 24 September
Quiet all week; no sign of the badger-hunters. Had hoped to see a patrol

on Briarmead, but at this time of year I have to leave before dawn during the week to get to work, so yesterday, I reported the incident at the station. Searched the Chantry again for any sign of their equipment, but without luck. Twice I had Josh, my dogfox, with me and rather hoped *he* might turn up something. However, his mind is more on food than metal!

Sunday 25 September
6.15 a.m. Watched the dawn above Ashcroft Woods whilst the yearling twins had a dig out at the Motorway bank on Pete's land. The traffic above us on the Motorway has been busy this past hour, but it doesn't seem to bother them. Some of the passages must go far under the road itself. One of these male badgers has been taking an interest in young Lesley, but think they will soon be ousted from this area, as Old Joe is getting very aggressive towards them. It's been a mild, warm night with few clouds, visibility excellent.

Spirals of mist are rising smoke-like from the stretch of water below the Motorway. I walked round it in good light at 6.45 a.m. and examined the prints left in the mud. The badgers drink here (as do the foxes), then go up the bank and forage along. Two clear trails in the long grass – the overhead gantry just above. This is where Old Joe used to cross the Motorway and come down the other side to the big house in Warby.

The moon is still bright above the badgers' bank though it's 6.55 a.m. and the sun is climbing the opposite sky. Came back to the Old Cherry Sett soon after to check all was well. See that badgers have been digging out entrances there. Fresh mound of earth at the entrance above that where the men dug out last April. Also one close by. Could be Old Joe, or the sows.

All quiet but for the whisper of leaves falling earthwards – lovely autumn morning, 7.25 a.m.

Monday 3 October
Bright, mild morning after day and night of rain. Fungi on every side – parasol mushrooms in large groups where Great Chantry meets the Bank Sett. This field has been replaughed, and I walked about collecting sherds of old tile, most of them Roman, but some medieval. Found a large piece of the former with the peg/nail hole in it. The difference in the firing and texture is interesting.

Checked my saplings this morning – all doing well, especially the wild service and willows. Below the Main Pond, the wet beech leaves colour the ground in burnished copper. Squirrels are very noisy in the treetops. (Two men were shooting here at 7 a.m.; I saw them by the Oak Dell firing across the footpath.)

The badgers have been digging out at the Old Cherry Sett; at the View Sett; the Folly (cubless sow); at what was the Wheatfield Copse (a yearling) – best call it the Wheatfield Bank now that the trees are gone.

215

Lesley has dug out Meg's old sett (helped, or hindered, by her brother). She's a bossy little badger and very much in charge! After they had got themselves thoroughly muddy in the wet earth, they decided a game using me to clamber over was on the cards – oh well!

Wednesday 12 October
Mild, clear night. Water still lying on the fields from the recent rains. I was with Old Joe on the Top Hayfield at 1.25 a.m. when a car came up Briarmead, turned left, crossed the bottom of the field and entered the wood. Some minutes passed, then a van followed suit. The badger was uneasy and moved off gaining the shelter of the undergrowth near the Ashtree Path and disappeared from view. I walked slowly round the field edge to within a few feet of the entrance used by the vehicles as I had the feeling they were the package people, not using the 'swap-shop' area this time. Sure enough, when they came back some thirty minutes later and re-crossed the field, I saw that they were. (Remembered that the burnt-out car still blocks the path by the Main Pond – their regular route. Though somebody has tried to push it out of the way, it has got stuck fast in the chestnut scrub on the bank edge.)

Walked through the woods and down to the stretch of water below the Motorway on Pete's land. Five badgers – including Old Joe – were busy foraging there. Interesting that badgers and foxes roll/rub slugs against a convenient object (or the ground) to reduce their slime intake. However,

216

since slugs produce large quantities of this substance, especially when pierced, the predator must still swallow a fair amount of slime.

Joe's two sows are digging out and mounds of earth show bright around the entrances. Falling leaves should soon hide the give-away signs – I hope!

Friday 21 October
1.10 a.m. Clear skies, full moon, frost. Met Josh on the Ridge – the foxes are beautiful now in their winter coats. He caught a small rabbit in the bracken at the field edge behind the Ridge. I stood out from the trees but hidden in the deep shadow cast by the moon, and saw movement halfway down the field towards the footpath. Barked softly once – twice – and his vixen came up to me; had thought it was her. Knelt down so that our faces were on a level. Of all the foxes I have known, this one is my favourite.

The leaves are falling fast, and the woodland paths grow wider as foliage and undergrowth die back. The burnt-out car that blocked the route at the Main Pond was moved last week – the package people will soon return.

Spent the remainder of the night at the Grain Dump just off the Top Hayfield, and watched the tawny owls hunting here. Both caught themselves a rat – the pickings are easy. Then the hen bird flew calling over the moonlit field, her black shadow stealing alongside. Her mate followed suit – heard their answering calls for a long time coming from the Old Barn ruins area.

Walking homewards across High Ridge, had a magpie for company. It would fly a little in front, then alight on a branch or fence until I was nearly abreast, then fly leisurely ahead once more. Curious to see what would happen at the tunnel under the Motorway at Madden Lane. It merely flew through and waited, head on one side, bright-eyed and watchful, waiting for me to catch up. I stood a short distance away and spoke softly, then clicked my tongue. It turned round on its perch, presenting its back to me, then, facing me once more, scratched its face with a long claw. Walked up to it still sitting on the fence – they really are gaudy birds close to. This, of course, is one of my regular magpies from the Ridge. Left it still there and walked homewards, dawn light touching the sky behind me.

Sunday 23 October
Very cold night, −2°C. Thick frost, clear skies, glittering full moon. Puddles lying on the fields reflect the stars in their frozen surfaces. The foxes very vocal – always seem more so in these conditions. I found a young fox shot on the Ridge (one of this year's cubs); its brush cut off.

Crossing Johnson's land on my way to the woods, I saw a hedgehog rooting amongst the windfalls under the trees. A very strong cider smell hangs over the orchard. They enjoy not only the sweet apples, but also the slugs, worms, etc. that creep into them. Have noticed this year that the nightjars can do a 'helicopter' landing, that is, land vertically. To do so, they must hover. Apart from kestrels, what other birds can do this, I wonder?

[British Summertime ended yesterday; this makes dawn now about 6 a.m.]

Thursday 27 October
Clear night skies all this week; waning moon; grass crunches underfoot. Both yearling male badgers have now moved out of the area – Old Joe is still boss here in spite of his years. Lesley was very playful tonight. She chewed my shoelaces undone, then tried to run off with one – tugged and tugged – something had to give and it did – one broken shoelace! She has a habit of putting her mouth gently over my wrist but doesn't bite or hurt me. I think it's her way of drawing attention to herself, and she does it especially when I'm quietly sitting watching the badgers foraging on the fields. If I take no notice, she then pulls at my wrist. When it happens to be the left wrist, my watch invariably suffers. She has dug out the old Chantry Sett and has extended it. It's in the side of an old hollow and near to a mature beech that grows on the fringe of Great Chantry Field. Her father, Old Joe, has been taking an interest in it – and her – and now they seem to den there together. Funny arrangement, perhaps, but it seems to suit them. The two sows are together at the Old Cherry Sett and Lesley's brother also. Their digging is very apparent; the fresh, sandy earth shows at a distance. Only the Chantry spoil heaps are hidden – the fallen beech leaves copper the ground.

[28 October: Was told that a badger had been killed by traffic in Crosshampton. Investigating, I found it was the larger of the yearlings.]

Saturday 29 October
These woods are filled with sounds – the fall is aptly named. The ground is strewn with chestnuts, acorns, beechmast, leaves, seeds and berries. By day, the fields are richly green, the trees aflame.

I'll have to call young Lesley the Chantry badger – this is clearly going to be her winter home. Father has been helping her by bringing in leaves and dry bracken for bedding. He seems very anxious to please his little daughter. He backs in with it and, moments later, emerges and goes down the field edge for the next load. Lesley is below ground – probably chewing it smaller and spreading it on the floor of the sleeping chamber. After several such journeys, she emerges with him and grooms his face and ears of bits of bracken clinging to his fur. He nuzzles her and 'purrs' loudly. I think he will probably mate with her – have to laugh – Old Joe seems to go from strength to strength. Next February, he'll be twelve! They went to earth about 5 a.m. I left the area after dawn, approximately 6.15 a.m., as felt very sick and giddy, and it takes an hour

218

normally to walk home. All quiet – beautiful morning sky. Grass crunches underfoot.

3.15 p.m. Returned to these woods in the afternoon as had promised to look for suitable collage materials for a neighbour's youngsters. Was horrified to discover that, since I left earlier, the Old Cherry Sett had been dug out with spades – straight down into the bedding chamber, dogs' pawmarks everywhere in the turned-up earth. And at the Chantry – Joe's bracken mixed in with the debris shovelled into the bottom of the hollow. The men must have waited for me to leave. Cursed myself for not staying – I could have done as it was Saturday, but felt so ill and cold. Feel stunned – it's such a clean sweep. Wonder how many of the badgers they took. Will doubtless find out tonight.

Sunday 30 October
Went out at midnight – bitterly cold – frost sparkles in the clear air. I saw a little shape moving along the wood edge above Warby and called. Lesley hurled herself at me crying and tugging my wrist – this time it hurt! At least there's one badger the men didn't get; perhaps the others are safe also. She seemed very agitated, whimpering unceasingly. When I got up to walk, she nearly tripped me up, as, cat-like, she tried to wind herself round my legs. She musked my shoes repeatedly between bouts of jumping up. I ended sitting on the ground and cradling her in my arms until her chunky body stopped trembling. Was thoroughly 'groomed' – my ears, face and neck washed and my hair nuzzled. Her warm body soon heated my chilled one. Sat a long time there, holding the young animal in my arms, my first feeling of relief turning to unease at her reaction to me. What *had* happened to the others – and Old Joe?
4.25 a.m. Spent the rest of tonight searching and calling the badgers – I've never needed to call them before, they always found me. Have a great sense of loss. Bitterly regret returning so early yesterday – they must have waited for me to leave the area and then simply moved in and dug. Stood deep in thought at the Chantry Sett, now gaping open and empty, at the bedding so recently and painstakingly collected and fetched here by Old Joe. Remembered their pleasure in one another – the way she had groomed the bracken fronds off his face. I looked at her now, standing miserably nosing at the spadefuls of earth thrown into the crater. How had Lesley escaped? Dog prints everywhere. I imagine the great boar had put up a fight. An elder had been snapped off halfway up the trunk – dried, dark blood on the bare ground. Had she crept deeper into the sett under cover of the noise and confusion? I'll never know now.
Didn't go home until well after dawn, simply because the cub wouldn't go underground. Tried to get her to go into the View Sett – nothing living there – but she would have none of it. Worried about her fate. Badgers are very sociable creatures who like one another's company, and form strong relationships. She's on her own here now and

219

barely nine months old. Finally, I persuaded her to go to earth at Meg's old sett that she and her brother had dug out earlier this month.

Phoned the station sergeant at Oakley on my way home, to put them in the picture – nothing they can do, of course. The men must have had two vehicles. I know they leave their equipment here somewhere, but dogs, men and four badgers would have taken up some room. I think two groups must have done this because of the distance between each sett and the areas dug out; time would have been too tight for one group working at both. I asked if the patrol had seen anyone parked around here between 6.15 and 7 a.m. yesterday, but no. As far as the sergeant knew, nothing reported.

Wednesday 2 November
Warm, overcast night with slight mist. Watched glow-worms in the woods amongst the dead leaves, just off the View Path. Couldn't decide whether they were female adults or the larvae, as both rather similar, so tried to pick up one for a closer look. The first that I touched, promptly 'switched off'. The next I put very gently on the palm of my left hand whilst I drew it in my notebook; it continued glowing all the while and still did so after I placed it back amongst the leaves. There were four insects all told and the light emitted was *very* clear.

[From *Field Guide to the Insects of Britain and Northern Europe* by Michael Chinery: 'All stages of the life history, including the eggs, give out light but it is the adult female that emits the strongest light. The light emitted is a pale greenish blue ... the function of the light is to attract males and the females merely sit in the grass and raise their abdomens.' My glow-worms were larvae.]

Tuesday 3 November
Each night this week I have been greeted by the young badger. Even now, when I have Josh and his vixen in tow, she still approaches me, though clearly she dislikes their presence. If Lesley were a mature badger, they would quietly slip away, but instinctively they know she is young, confused and unsure – and alone – so stay quite close, boldly watching her. In the end, I ran off calling her, and so together we left the foxes' company. Then in the undergrowth above the Oak Dell, I trod on something hard and round and discovered the solid ball I brought here for the foxes earlier this year, on 11 February. Lesley sniffed it, not much interested. I rolled it down the path and on to the field, ran after it and threw it back up the path. Of course, it rolled towards me once more – but a small, excited badger reached it first!

Saturday 5 November
Mild, misty night. I'm not happy where Lesley is denning. She has returned to the Old Cherry Sett and been digging out there. Seems to me the safest place is at the Wheatfield Bank between open fields. The elm brush has grown up somewhat giving a little cover, and in all but fog conditions it is in clear view of Glebe Farm; it's never been dug out by badger-baiters yet. So I persuaded the young badger to follow me and tried to interest her in it. I found a rusty piece of metal on the ploughed field below and, digging into one of the entrances with it, cleared away old debris that had collected there. Lesley took over after a while and set to with a will.

Nothing haphazard about a badger digging; their wedge-shaped bodies, short, powerful legs and long claws, have evolved for the job and for a life underground. Digging with the front feet, the long fore claws soon amass a heap of dirt beneath the body which arches up with each backward push. When enough is excavated, the animal backs away from the entrance – some earth being pushed by the body and the rest dragged backwards by the front legs hugging it to the body. (Rather reminiscent of bringing in bedding!) Lesley's earth collection showed up too bright amongst the elm brush for my peace of mind, so I took it down the slope and spread it on the ploughed field. As she went deeper into the sett, so the excavated earth became more interesting. Spreading it on the field, I found – not surprisingly – empty wheat and barley husks; also chewed blue chunks of plastic fertiliser bag – young Jessie had a liking for these at this very sett. The tiny front 'hands' of a mole joined by a withered stretch of befurred skin. But the strangest find of all, covered in dirt but still quite recognisable, was part of a sawn-off shotgun, the shortened barrel with teethmarks upon it. Had it been pushed down an entrance to hide it, and a badger taken it further down, or had the owner forgotten its exact location? By the look, it had been there some time. The young badger dug out three tunnels in all before first light touched the horizon behind her.

221

Provided I remove any fresh earth she excavates, the last of this area's badgers may have a chance of survival.

Tuesday 15 November

12.25 a.m. Cold, very frosty night; half-moon and clear skies. This is the night of the fox; at the Ridge, Josh was having a war of nerves with a young male (possibly one of his grown cubs) – Josh won. There's always a great deal of sorting out of territory at this time of year. Didn't see his mate until past the Wheatfield Bank, when suddenly I had an escort. Stroked her head and together we went to the ruins of the Old Barn. Stood a long while there watching my vixen hunting in the long grass.

Though young Lesley has accepted the Wheatfield Bank as her new home, I wouldn't say she is settled there. She seems to haunt the Old Cherry Sett, and, after sniffing around the entrances and musking two, has come to where I'm sitting on the horizontal chestnut that grows out of the slope there, and has scrambled on to my lap. Together we look out over the dug-out entrances, down to the path below. This was the cubs' home where, in the main, they grew to adulthood. True, they moved around in their very early days when disturbed, but at one time all the badgers were living here in different parts of this ancient sett.

I hope the badger-baiting group that operates in this area think they have taken all the badgers – a bit optimistic, I'm afraid. The frost that was sparkling on the young badger's pelage is melting as she snuffles about on my lap.

4.20 a.m. The tawny owls are vocal over the Long Field. The male bird of the Chantry pair is hooting his boundaries – distant challenge from the

gardens at the bottom of Briarmead. The Chantry male continues to call at well-spaced intervals, until the other male ceases to answer. Then the hen tawny from the Chantry begins a slow, gliding flight – round and round and above her mate as he sits on the dead, barkless tree at the Chantry entrance. She calls 'kewick, kewick' until he answers her with a long, tremulous fluting, then perches above him, and softly sounds the contact call. Silently he stretches those wide wings and, leaving his branch, alights next to her. I left them at 5.10 a.m. – the tawny male gently preening the feathers of his mate's facial disc.

Friday 18 November
Mild, damp night with slight mist over the waterways. Lesley *very* playful. I'm not sure where she keeps the rubber ball but after greeting me – and musking my shoes – she generally disappears and returns shortly after with it held dog-like in her jaws. I think she must leave her sett each evening with it, drop it whilst she forages, then retrieve it before moving on. The game is for me to try and take it from her. She trots off, I following, then I pretend to lose interest. She sees something edible and drops her ball, whereupon I snatch it. Bouncing it off the nearest tree trunk and catching it excites her. She tries unsuccessfully to jump and get it back – unless I drop it – and ends up bundling me. I go home with my anorak covered in a complex pattern of muddy pawmarks. Sharpness of sight is not one of a badger's strong points, but this game certainly has alerted her. At first, she couldn't register the ball leaving my hand and returning (after the bounce), but there's not much she misses now.

Tonight on Long Field, I found one of those curiously curved pieces of metal that the plough turns up occasionally. I used to think they had come from some old type of farm machinery, long since obsolete and forgotten, but discover they are oxen shoes or 'kews'. Unlike the horse, the ox's feet splay into claws that grip as it walks. So two of these half-moon-shaped plates went on to each *front* foot – one kew being nailed on to each half of the cloven hoof. Their hind feet went unshod. In many areas, oxen were not replaced by horses till well into the 1800s.

The tawnies were very vocal. I watched the female hunting with her mate round the overgrown bushes of the abandoned garden at the top of the lane. She flew round and round a bush 'kewiking' and, apparently clumsy, kept brushing the branches. Whereupon various small birds fluttered from their roosts and were easily caught by her and her mate. Have not seen this done before.

Tuesday 22 November
Bitterly cold night, −4°C. Hoar sparkles on every side, full moon. Tawnies very vocal; also foxes; I met Josh and his vixen at the back of the Ridge and left them hunting there.

The young badger has been digging out at the Wheatfield Bank, so I was kept busy taking earth from the spoil heaps down to the field below. I am determined to hide the evidence and so protect here. Wonder if she could possibly produce cubs in February? She's young, but I've known it before at her age.

Everywhere very beautiful – a glittering world of white, no wind, a petrified landscape. The frost has deftly touched each straight furrow; each stiff row of next year's corn shines under the radiant moon. Far colder than snow; have to clench my teeth to stop them chattering. Lesley appeared briefly at an entrance to greet me as I was moving the freshly dug earth and – sensible creature – retreated to her warm bed. When I'd finished disguising her work, I followed her example and went back to mine!

Sunday 27 November
2.30 a.m. Very mild and wet with strong gusts of wind. It has been raining since yesterday – the first real rain for a long time. I've been treated to a fantastic welcome from young Lesley – bronchitis has prevented me from coming out since Tuesday. She runs round me giving little barks interspersed with whickering, only stopping to listen with one paw raised when I have a bout of coughing! Now she's found a new game – jumping up and hanging on to the bottom of my anorak with her teeth. Was startled to see the size of the spoil heaps she has created on the bank whilst I've been away. I can never move these or disguise them – there is simply too much earth which the rain has turned into mud. I've certainly got a problem now; it's plain to see that a badger is active here.

I am very concerned that the head of Oakley police is reported as saying he is not convinced that badgers are being dug out in the area (as the digging appears too shallow). Wrote to him but have little faith in my efforts to 'convince'. I'll tell the next patrol I meet on Briarmead where Joe's daughter is denning and ask them to keep an eye on it; they seem to have more interest in protecting the badgers here than their Inspector; however, I haven't seen a patrol since September. If, after a week, the Inspector is still indifferent, I'll write to Ernest Neal, tell him of Old Joe's death as I promised, also the manner of it and the official apathy to the situation, and ask his advice, for he has proved a good friend.

WINTER 1983–4

Saturday 3 December 1983

Two nights ago, I discovered young Lesley has a companion. Of the two male yearlings that left the area in October (*see* 27 October), one was run over in Crosshampton but the other has returned and is denning with Old Joe's daughter at the Wheatfield Bank.

2.10 a.m. The two badgers have been roaming round the woods. There is plenty to eat in spite of the frozen earth – chestnuts, acorns, etc. and bulbs. Lesley had a dig-out at the Old Cherry Sett, then stood looking out over the slope for a long while – until her mate began washing her ear. She promptly turned playful and together they chased in and out the trees like a couple of cubs – which is all she still is, really. Very glad for her. Will avoid meeting her now when possible as I don't want her dependent on my company – not a good thing for either of us.

3.20 a.m. Prolonged mating (19 minutes) at the Wheatfield Sett. Feel she's not too young to produce cubs in February. [The badgers also mated on 4 and 5 December, long duration, pairing preceded by play, loud 'purring' and tail-raising.]

6.30 a.m. First light has touched the frozen countryside; a thick, white shroud covers the land. 7 a.m. Stood on top of the Wheatfield Sett and watched the sun turn the horizon to blood over Crosshampton. The badgers are asleep somewhere below me. Death hasn't come in this dawning – but it will. I have never heard from the Inspector – feel that time is running out – Lesley's dig-outs in the woodland make it clear that a badger is still in the area. But I'll fight for the last of these creatures, come what may.

Wednesday 7 December

1.10 a.m. Deep frost crunching underfoot, so silent walking is impossible – dead leaves crackle at the slightest pressure. Clear skies, icy wind.

Suddenly sensed I wasn't alone so 'barked' softly. But it wasn't Josh's vixen, as I had expected, but Taglass's little mate who crept nearer! A movement beyond the shadows, and the dogfox himself appeared. I began walking along the side of the Oak Dell, up through these woods to the hayfield above. However, since the vixen decided to accompany me, so did her mate. Though December is the height of the rut for foxes, their vixens won't permit coupling until they come into heat – generally about the second or third week of January around here. Tagless was busy scent-marking on any – and every! – conspicuous object along the route. Felt he would probably come to grief if he wasn't careful as, strictly speaking, this is Josh his father's territory, not his. Had hoped to tawny-watch at the Chantry tonight, but with two foxes in tow I would be wasting my time. So led them out on to Long Field where the rabbits were browsing on Barry's corn.

Left them there watching a potential meal whilst I slipped back across Little Chantry Field and so into the Chantry itself. I love this place and its beeches that have grown tall and slender in their struggle upwards to the light. Seem to see Joe everywhere here – it was one of his favourite haunts. How *could* the Inspector say he was not convinced the diggings were to extract badgers, when the sett lies open and silent here? He has answered my letter at last, and to my request to be allowed to explain why some spadework is shallow and some deep, merely states, 'I have no wish to know more [about badgers] than the law requires me to be conversant with.' In other words, get lost. Sat the remainder of the night under the tree canopy there, the coppery leaves hiding the raw earth of the old badger's last home and the tawnies calling and serenading each other in the star-studded branches above.

Saturday 10 December

I took Dick Barling of the County Preservation Society round Ashcroft Woods this afternoon to view the main badger setts. As he told me abut his work, I realised for the first time that his is not an easy job.

Walking back to Briarmead, we met Barry Hains. I asked him to let Glebe Farm know that the badgers are denning on the Wheatfield Bank; it is in clear view of the farmhouse. Nothing else I can do now, unless Ernest Neal has any suggestions.

Sunday 11 December
Bitterly cold night, deep frost, clear starry skies. Avoided the badgers as I wish to have as little contact now with them as possible – just sufficient to know they are all right. Watched the rats that frequent the Grain Dump just inside the wood. One sickly rat has been harried and finally killed by another. The victor nosed it, then left the body and, sitting back on its haunches, began to wash itself. Shortly after, another found the corpse and began to eat it; in a few minutes, others were doing likewise – much pushing and squeaking. Surprised to find the bones were eaten too, just the end portion of the tail left. I saw something tonight which I have twice observed before amongst these brown rats at the same place. I don't know the reason for the action which once occurred during eating and twice during grooming: the animal is supported on its hind legs while the front ones, which are about to be used for eating or washing, begin to shake very quickly.

Brown rats have quite heavy-looking, 'ringed' tails (have heard them described as 'scaly', which is a bad description as they are, in fact, ringed). Like other animals, they stand on hind legs to sniff the air when first emerging from their burrows. The first animal out takes much more care over this reconnoitring. The next rats pause briefly before emerging.

Thursday 15 December
Mild, damp night with gusts of wind and clear skies. *Very* windy on the Warby side – there the trees have a mighty voice.

2.05 a.m. The package people here again, beyond the Main Pond – business seems booming for them as well as the badger-diggers. I'm beginning seriously to think Ross's guess may be correct – that the packets could contain drugs.

Saturday 17 December
Started out under a starry sky with moon near the full – very mild. By 5 a.m. steady rain. Badgers been digging out at the View Sett. Had to smile – young Lesley decided to start a new entrance under the last beehive at the far end of the Wheatfield Bank. Fortunately she changed her mind before the hive ended on top of her. It's got a distinct list to starboard, however – what a badger!

8.30 a.m. Still raining with water running down Briarmead. Watched pied wagtails busy on its gritty surface. These birds seem to be more common in recent years. Observing them, John Clare's rhyme sprang to mind – trotty wagtails, how apt. The lapwings still frequent the fields here at night and early mornings – their plaintive cries like lost souls hovering above the earth. When the tawnies begin calling before first light, the peewits will sound on all sides, like a dirge to the dark.

Wednesday 21 December
1.05 a.m. Rain which has been falling continuously for three days has ceased for a while, full moon showing clear as clouds move away. Wind still gusty, but very mild. I am seriously considering whether to come out less at night as the two badgers find me so often. I don't want this attachment; it's bad for them. It has only just dawned on me why I am unable to steer clear of them – they are picking up my scent trail and tracking me! It seems to be a 'race' who can reach me first – the yearling 'wins' almost as often as Lesley. They have plenty of time for play now with all this wetness about, as they don't have to forage long for food – worms, their staple diet, are everywhere on the surface of fields, paths, etc. I watched the tawnies here bounding along the ground to catch and eat them too. Their worm meals seem to go on a long time – as long as the worm, in fact!

All seems quiet badger-diggers wise, which is just as well as the police no longer patrol Briarmead at dawn. Ernest Neal warned me to stay well into daylight 'on Boxing Day morning – a traditional time for this'. I shall be here.

12.30 p.m. Came here this afternoon to check things in daylight – I'm so rarely here during the day in winter. Discovered Meg's Sett has been dug out with spades – all three entrances. Very recent (almost certainly at dawn this morning) as the rain hasn't had a chance to smooth down the particles of excavated earth. No sign of dogs' prints on the soft earth. No other setts touched. I wasn't too bothered at first, since Lesley and mate are denning at the Wheatfield Bank – or are they? In my efforts to avoid their company, I haven't seen them go to earth for some nights; she has dug out several times at Meg's Sett recently – they could have denned there. The spades have gone very deep. Phoned the R.S.P.C.A; also the County Preservation Society and spoke to Dick, who will ask Pete Williams if he saw anyone drive on to his land and will also inform the police.

Thursday 22 December
Wild night with sleet showers, strong wind and thunder. Would the badgers be above ground (if they had escaped the diggers) in such weather? Sleet and thunder had stopped, however, by the time I reached the Ridge. Wind and wet on the overhead electricity cables was deafening. Water lying on the fields and running down the paths.

I stood on top of the Wheatfield Sett bank; visibility good yet no sign of my badgers. Called, but the wind tore the sound away. Walked along the top of the bank where they would most likely see movement – if still about. Stood above the beehives – wind, cold and dread gnawing at me. Heard a sharp bomp – another – and, glancing down, saw a hive at a curious angle, apparently on the move! Lesley at it again and this time helped by her mate. A pair of *very* muddy, breathless badgers having a marvellous dig-out. Sat amongst the wet nettles; dirty snouts exploring my face; earth-caked paws clambering over my lap; arms round two soaked little bodies – the relief indescribable!

Before going home, I tried to straighten the hive. Had no idea they were so heavy. Or that it had some occupants although, fortunately, very torpid! Eventually, got it level once more on its stone base, a mildly interested duo washing themselves near by.

Monday 26 December
6.15 a.m. Still dark; mild, very windy morning. I checked the Wheatfield Sett and walked on to Briarmead via the Two Oaks field path, meaning to check the Old Cherry Sett. No vehicles or people in sight, but I was uneasy, so walked up the lane towards the Briarmead entrance, whereupon a car parked inside went further into the wood. Followed it up and round past the Main Pond and, in the near darkness, knelt and felt the rear number plate. As I moved back into the tree-cover, the driver (its sole occupant) turned his head sharply – so obviously he had seen me. I stood in the undergrowth and wrote the number down, letting him see me do so, then walked along a little and came out on to the path in front of him. He switched his headlights full on, but I was out of his range. Continued through the wood as I still wanted to check the Old Cherry Sett. As I did so, heard the car go quickly back the way it had come.

At the Old Cherry Sett, everything quiet. The badgers have been digging here, but I'm not sure whether they denned here this morning or in the Wheatfield Sett. Suddenly thought I heard a car door shut quietly, so ran down the slope on to the Wildflower Path just as *the* car drove away towards Briarmead with four men inside, 6.40 a.m.

Wednesday 28 December
Lovely night – mild, clear skies, crescent moon. I was musked by Lesley and her mate; the first time the young boar has done this. Plenty of food here for the badgers – everywhere very moist. Both *very* playful. Young Lesley appeared with her ball! Had forgotten all about it; what a bossy little character she is, but great fun.

No cars parked anywhere in or near these woods yesterday or this morning. I am still anxious about Monday's car and its occupants. Feel they were after the badgers, but have no proof of course. Will keep the car number [number entered in diary omitted here] and await developments.

Dawn is now about 7.15 a.m. (though later if it's cloudy). Standing on the Wildflower Path I watched the rising sun over Great Chantry Field gently transform the dead bracken next to me into a blaze of colour – literally setting it afire. The beauty of this place hurts.

Friday 30 December
All quiet on the early-morning badger scene. Lesley and her mate have been digging out at the Old Cherry and View Setts. They are denning at present at the former. In his last letter received on Wednesday, Ernest Neal writes: 'I find here the mild weather following the cold period has brought forward badger activity and they are digging setts like mad ...' This certainly applies to my badgers, too, although I feel a sense of insecurity is also encouraging the young sow to do this in order to have an alternative home in an emergency.

Later in the day, was here with Dick Barling of the County Preservation Trust. We were almost at the entrance to these woods by the Oak Dell when a woman and dog went by on the path below – the woman and dog who sometimes accompany the cylinder-carrying man. How easy it must be to dog-walk round the area, checking setts for any evidence of badger activity as you go.

Monday 2 January 1984
Badgers dug out an entrance and renewed bedding at the Old Cherry Sett, then went to earth there 5.55 a.m. Walked round the woods checking for cars and reached the top of Briarmead at first light, approx. 7.20 a.m. It's been a mild, dry night with clear skies – tawnies very vocal an hour ago. Followed the wood edge to return once more to the Old Cherry Sett via the field above.

I was still some distance away when a man carrying a rifle appeared from the tree-cover at the path above the sett, and stood watching the lane. Thought at first that he was an early-morning bird-shooter – but if so, why the vigil? He turned and saw me walking towards him, looked back into the wood, then raised his rifle and fired at me. Stood watching him a moment, took a deep breath, and came on quickly just as he fired again. Felt sure he was both warning someone below him on the slope that I was around, and also trying to frighten me off – so I started to run in order to shorten the distance between us. He fired a third time, rather too near for comfort, then disappeared into the wood. Seemed an age reaching the path – the grass of the hayfield was long and wet. Sure I heard a dog bark once, then again, above the noise I was making through the bracken. Reached the Wildflower Path in time to see a car turn off the field on to Briarmead and disappear down the lane. Back as well as front seats occupied – three to four people. Much too far away to distinguish its number.

Returned to the sett to check the entrances. Dogs' prints in the fresh earth dug out by the badgers tonight, but otherwise undisturbed. Seems they got as far as sending the dogs down, then I came along. What can save the badgers when I return to work next Monday and can't be around so late? If only the Inspector would have his men patrol Briarmead two or three times a week at dawn as they did in April to

August last year. There was no trouble here at all then. The sight of the police is a far better deterrent that I can ever be.

Monday 9 January
Lesley and mate are denning again at the Old Cherry Sett. After the recent rain, their heaps of sandy earth show clear on the slope from the path below. Ironically, she has made a fresh entrance to the sett just above the one that the men dug out with their spades when they successfully took her mother, brother and the cubless sow. Her mate and she have also re-dug two other entrances in the immediate vicinity.

I'm still wondering if Lesley may have cubs this year, in which case there would be little or no delayed implantation. It is well known that although badgers may mate and be fertilised at almost any time of year, cubs are born at one season only, due to delayed implantation. Often late January/early February in the south of England and generally later as one goes further north. The big question has always been – what triggers off implantation then? Different theories have been put forward, but none proved beyond all reasonable doubt. [N.B. The time from implantation to birth is seven weeks, give or take a day or two.] In the case of Lesley, however, she might not have cubs at all as *stress* can delay implantation or perhaps even prevent it happening. So we'll see.

Tuesday 10 January
R.S.P.C.A. Inspector Steve Hammond came this morning and discussed the badger problem. Shortly after he left, Dick Barling phoned. He is

231

hoping to arrange a meeting with Steve Hammond, himself and the police. Both he and the R.S.P.C.A. Inspector have promised to ask Oakley police to patrol around dawn on Briarmead Lane two or three times a week. Dick has heard locally about recent badger-digging in these woods – just how fresh, we are wondering. Could it be Meg's Sett dug out on 21 December and only now discovered, or what?

Wednesday 11 January
Steve Hammond came today from a meeting with the police. He had previously told me that he would arrange to come out with an R.S.P.C.A. friend one Saturday or Sunday morning with me in the hope of catching the badger gang at work and thereby securing a conviction. Unfortunately, other convictions secured for similar offences have only resulted in very small fines like £40 – nowhere near the maximum of £1,000. However, as a result of the police meeting, Inspector Hogarth has arranged for one of his men to operate a radio 'from the nearest farmhouse' next Sunday morning. Another policeman with portable radio is coming with us. The equipment has to be collected from police headquarters first. I suggested the most unobtrusive place to leave their cars is at the badger-diggers' favourite spot – amongst residents' vehicles in the lane just off the Main Road. I'm to meet them there at 4 a.m., take them to a sheltered position at the Old Cherry Sett and leave them while I go my usual walkabout and check for parked vehicles round the woods. For once I'll not do so worried that the gang will move in whilst I'm gone; as in fact they did on 2 January. (It will seem very strange to have other people with me – friendly ones, that is!)

This weekend will be as good as any since Lesley and co. have dug out for all to see. (They are denning there also, though I must check this tomorrow.) I am staggered that Steve Hammond has been so successful – and very grateful. I never expected such co-operation and interest from anyone. I only hope someone comes to dig the badgers out and their vigil isn't wasted. I don't think Steve will be too bothered if they wait in vain – he is used to such situations. But Inspector Hogarth will want results for the use of his manpower and equipment – which I can understand. If nothing turns up, they hope to try again the following Sunday. The R.S.P.C.A. Inspector is the first person to actually achieve anything practical as opposed to just talk. And he's willing to share in the dirty work. I hope for his sake as well as the badgers that he gets his conviction – he deserves to. He has also told me that magistrates at Totnes in Devon fined a man £1,000 yesterday on eight charges of killing or cruelly ill-treating badgers. Perhaps this will encourage other magistrates to be tougher.

Thursday 12 January
Left home at 12.10 a.m. Mild, damp night after evening of heavy rain.

Skies clearing fast – visibility marvellous. Met Josh and his vixen on the Ridge. Know they have already mated by their attitude to one another. No obsessive trailing and snapping – just quietly sure of themselves; keeping close together; face-licking and mutual grooming. Both circled me, then jumped up. Stroked them, one hand on each as I knelt between them. I remembered the vixen's possessiveness with me in the past and don't want to upset her now. Walked along that part of the field edge that follows the Enclosed Path, my foxes keeping me company and foraging on the way.

I was standing by the entrance to the Ashtree Path at 1.40 a.m., the foxes further out on the ploughed-up hayfield, when a glow appeared over the hump of the lane and a car drove up into the woods; seven minutes later, another did likewise. Looked very like the package people: they seem to use two cars sometimes now, not always a van and a car. Twenty-five minutes later, first one emerged from the tree-cover and drove away, followed some minutes later by the second. Only the driver in each car.

Which reminds me that two weeks before Christmas, a small, double-trunked tree was felled, right on the corner by the Main Pond. It was sawn at a very steep angle, the raw wood facing down Briarmead – very conspicuous at night. It is on Barry Hains's woodland, so C.P.S. wouldn't have done it – neither would Barry himself. No other trees near by have been touched – this one wasn't in anyone's way. Cars that go into the 'swap-shop' area at night must take care not to take the left-hand turning too soon, as the earlier one goes a short distance and ends at a bank. Now they don't have that problem as they take the sawn tree turning that shows up clear in their headlights.

3.10 a.m. Both foxes digging into the Grain Dump. The vixen cornered a brown rat that leapt at her face and hung on to her above the right eye. She dashed it to and fro in her pain in an effort to dislodge it. Josh bit deep into its back, whereupon it loosed its hold on his mate. I very gently took it from his jaws – his bite had severed the vertebrae. I looked up from the rat to see Josh licking the wound on her face. Neither seemed interested in the 'kill' so I laid it by the pile of grain. Rats are said to leap upwards and bite into the throat, but I think they bite at any part presented. They do tend to leap upwards though, when attacking. Years ago, Wendy routed some feeding rats that fled in all directions. One jumped and sunk its teeth deep in my leg above the kneecap – it didn't loosen its hold though I hit it repeatedly.

Lesley and mate *are* denning at the Old Cherry Sett. Had a great fuss made of me by two excited badgers! Interesting that both can almost *run* up the cherry's sloping trunk – partly in play, but also in search of slugs and insects that creep into the deep fissures of its bark. It would be marvellous if they did this when the men are here on Sunday. If they stay very quiet and still, they could have a good chance of watching them. Depends what time they arrive and settle down. The badgers at

233

this time of year go to earth about 5 a.m., and I'm due to meet Steve Hammond and companions at 4 a.m. If I can stop three big pairs of boots from touching the badger trail back to the sett, the men might see what they've come to protect!

Sunday 15 January
12.10 a.m. Windy with flurries of snow after an evening of high winds and sleet. Visibility excellent. Tracked Tagless and vixen but didn't show myself, as obvious that her oestrus is near.

Lesley found me on the Top Hayfield, Briarmead. Tiny flakes of frozen sleet lie on its rough-ploughed surface. Only the top of the furrows are frozen; beneath is muddy. Very hard to negotiate in these conditions. After greeting and musking me, she moved slowly ahead foraging along the upturned turf. A lark has risen too late from its resting place within the furrow, probably torpid in the cold air. The little badger, darting forward, caught it with ease. How many times have I seen this – and caught one myself – yet never thought to tell Ernest Neal.

Sat on the horizontal chestnut seat at the Old Cherry Sett as, at 3 a.m., it was too early to go down the hillside and meet the men. Lesley chewed my boot, then scrambled up on to my lap. Was startled to feel her body taut and solid beneath my hands. Felt gently and carefully to confirm she was in cub and surely near parturition.

Was at the meeting place in good time and waited in the shadows until a car's headlights came out of the gloom and swung round as it parked. Stood up to approach when I had moment of doubt – just as well, as it was a couple of residents coming home late, 3.45 a.m. For a moment, thought the woman would see me in the shadows when she looked directly round at me. Stayed quite still – and they went up the path as a dog began barking indoors. Could imagine them dialling 999 to say that someone was lurking around!

Half an hour later, the arc of headlights swung round as a car quietly turned and came to a standstill. Stayed in the shadows to be quite sure I had the right occupants this time. Then the car doors opened and the four got out. Have rarely felt quite so small – there seemed to be an awful lot of them. One detached himself from the group and walked up to the path to where I stood, hands inevitably in pockets. Steve explained we had a Rural Constable, a Special Constable, and his R.S.P.C.A. friend. The latter walked up the hillside with me quietly talking, the others just behind carrying the equipment and radio. I found my unaccustomed company rather embarrassing so was glad to have someone to talk to as we walked along the path to the edge of Long Field. Pointed out the Chantry to my companion as we passed and explained that I thought the badger-diggers left their spades etc. somewhere there. All the men carried torches, but I was relieved to see they didn't use them. Hate artificial light as it tends to spoil my nightvision. Took them up the slope of the sett, along the winding badger path, to the old once-coppiced chestnut at whose side I'd cleared a space. Left them saying which path I'd return on and approximately when, but not before I'd noticed they seemed to have a remarkable amount of equipment.

I went in search of my other foxes, Josh and vixen. Moved into their territory and barked them up; they found me! She's a dainty vixen, delicately boned, a beautiful head – my foxy lady. Made the soft contact bark, very gently – and she answered equally so, bringing her face up to mine. Josh decided there was too much going on between us and not enough of him in the conversation (typical male!), so jumped up, trying to push me backwards, his jaws open, tongue lolling. But two can play at that game and I gave as good as I got. He's like an undisciplined dog, but I know his Achilles heel. If he gets too much, I blow in his face – how he hates that – and I'm the victor.

6 a.m. Checked round the woodways for any parked vehicles or people – accompanied by my foxes. Nothing except two men with guns moving noisily through the bracken. Watched Josh and mate slip like shadows along the ancient boundary ditch and so on to the fields below.

Returned at first light along the promised path and walked silently along until I made out their still shapes amongst the trees. Stood awhile watching the dawn steal gently across the the field below and enjoying the feeling of comradeship never before experienced in my lone dawn watches over the sett. How boring and cold it must be for them. It's different for me – I'm committed to the place most dear to me. Came quietly closer to the little group – and was horrified to see that Steve appeared to have on *white* trousers, showing up clearly. I hadn't noticed them at the meeting place where there had been road lights, and in fact they turned out to be light fawn. As he approached, I hissed, 'Steve, your trousers!'

'Don't *you* start about my trousers,' he groaned. 'I've had it already from the others. Anyway, look at those trees,' nodding to some barkless trunks near by, 'and those birches.'

'Yes, but no way do they resemble your legs,' I retorted, and looked up to see we had a very amused audience, one of whom told Steve to 'Get them off!' This embarrassed him not one whit, but did me for starting it! The others joined in with great delight and suggested a black plastic bag they had previously been sitting on would make a more suitable garment if two holes were torn in the corners. Steve, not surprisingly, declined the offer, me grinning from ear to ear. I was invited to have some soup or coffee – they certainly believed in keeping the inner man going – but shook my head. Couldn't verbally refuse for laughing. These constables had been on duty since the previous evening. This was the 10 p.m. to 6 a.m. shift running well over time.

Waited until well after the usual time. Dave Jones, the Special Constable, was very cold, but seemed to have loads of enthusiasm and said he wanted to come again. He asked me about the badgers and the wood itself as we walked up to look at the Chantry. At first, the men were

235

inclined to feel they would quickly find anything there in spite of my saying I had divided the place up in sections and systematically searched each portion. However, as we walked through the Chantry and out on to the headland, I noticed they were rather thoughtful – there's an awful lot of wood here! Steve and his friend said they would return in the afternoon and have a thorough search of the place.

They offered to give me a lift home, three squashing into the back of the car and me sitting next to the Rural Constable who was driving. 'No one booked,' he said. 'Never mind. I don't think the present badger-digging hysteria in the media has helped. They may be lying low. Better luck next time.' The car drove along the Main Road towards Oakley, when a voice sang out from behind us. 'Hey, she's not wearing her seat-belt. Book her!'

'Right,' said the Constable, laughing. 'Consider yourself booked!'

Wednesday 18 January
1.20 a.m. Full moon, thick frost and freezing wind. How I wish I could take photos of this wood by moonlight; tree shadows blackly stretching across the ground; birch trunks transfigured in the silvery brightness. All to a background of tawny 'parleying'.

A mature birch has been uprooted in the recent winds. Their roots form shallow spreading 'mats' and easily come away. Its fall has partly flattened some lesser trees in its path, and it is suspended horizontally a few feet off the ground. I clambered on to the trunk followed by the badger pair and walked slowly along its length. It snowed earlier tonight – flakes glitter upon its rugged bark. Lesley disappeared, but I didn't notice for a while. Too preoccupied gazing at the starry sky seen through the swaying branch pattern and listening to the owls in the oak just behind me. The young boar was tearing long pieces of bark away to nose for the grubs beneath. It wasn't until I jumped down that I saw her rump with its tatty tail showing from inside the depression made by the uplifted roots – digging out, of course, what a lass!

Walked the length of the Ashtree Path and looked at the deep hollow near the field edge there. Badgers love those old holes either to forage in the dampness or to roll about amongst the debris that collects in the bottom – nothing quite like a good roll, scratch and clean – and, of course, to dig setts into! The View Sett and that at the Chantry are both deep hollows. Given a diggable soil, the badgers' greatest problem is dampness which leads to subsidence; this is why they so love banks. A hollow is a bank in miniature – with one very special advantage. A bank has dug-out entrances all along but, apart from joining up, your home goes in one general direction. Such hollows can be dug into from any direction, entrances can join up underground just the same – but your potential for home extensions is almost unlimited. And, let's face it, badgers *do* like digging out!

236

Watched Lesley's mate grooming himself whilst lying on his back – you can get at all the awkward little places on your tum so easily in this position!

Sunday 22 January
12.10 a.m. Cloudy night – visibility good. Met Lesley foraging on Long Field. With her cubs soon due, she is finding food close to home now. Stroked her face – she's a gentle, inoffensive creature. I never dreamt last June when I treated her festering leg all that was to happen to her. And she's not a year old until 7/8 February. Hope she's not disturbed any more.

The pair of tawny owls in this area are roosting together now. The pattern and quality of their calling alters in January. The male's hooting is often disjointed when he 'parleys' with his mate – her voice has a wailing, banshee quality. Know from past years when I did the tawny survey here, that their hunting night begins with his ritual courtship feeding and soft contact calls on her part. This gentle calling by the hen and disjointed hooting by her mate also occurs pre-dawn – or later – as they settle down to roost together. Reminds me of a human couple talking quietly together before going to sleep!

Started snowing about 4 a.m., by 4.30 a.m. it was lying thick. The fallen birch looked great stretching outwards – the branches and lesser trees are holding its crown well off the ground. On impulse, I climbed on to the bole and walked slowly upwards towards the crown, to see how near the top I could get. Strange to walk up a tree; like a giant's causeway rising gently out of the snow, its bark deeply fissured with age. Nearing the top and moving cautiously lest it shift suddenly, I found I had a companion following me along – Lesley's mate. Probably feels lonely now she has sent him away from the Old Cherry Sett they shared. He's denning not far from her at the View Sett, but she won't let him too near now until after the cubs are born – and even then he'll have to watch himself. He ran ahead of me into the branches and the trunk gave a slight shudder. His extra couple of stone on top of my seven was a bit too much, so I hastily jumped down.

Stood with my back leaning against the birch just enjoying the snowy scene, when I heard a chittering in my ear and felt a playful snout snuffling my hair. Turned laughing, scraped some snow off the ground and threw it at him. He blinked, sneezed and barked at me, whereupon I threw some more which landed on his head. That did it – a game was definitely on the cards. He scampered down the trunk, jumped off, ran round the roots in a flurry of snow and back up on to the trunk once more. Stood up there and barked again, whereupon I pretended to throw another snowball – only couldn't as I was laughing too much. He promptly repeated the performance, but this time as he raced round the roots (badgers aren't really built for racing!) he nearly fell down the hole left by the toppled tree – then up on to the trunk. We both ended up sitting on the birch together; me out of breath from laughing – he from racing. Badgers are the greatest clowns.

Returned to the Old Cherry Sett at 6 a.m. in case of trouble and stood looking out over the snow-clad slope. First light came reluctantly with no dawn as such, just the whiteness and the strange silence snow brings. Waited until 8 a.m. (the tawnies still sounding), then walked up Briarmead, the wet slurry very treacherous underfoot. Near the Two Oak field path, a car passed me, sliding and slipping across the lane. It turned at the top and came slowly to a halt by me. Inside was Ralph, a friend of Barry Hains. He offered to dawn-watch with me – provided I give him a couple of days' notice – if I feel any time there might be trouble. He wouldn't give me his number, just said to ring Barry.

Tuesday 24 January
12.50 a.m. *Very* mild night after frosty evening. Wonder when Lesley will have her cubs? She and Sam mated 3/4/5 December. If there's no delay in implantation, it could be any time from today. Stood with one hand on the bark of the Old Cherry Tree when the little sow appeared from the sett entrance, came over purring, and musked me. She sat grooming herself for a few minutes, then went to earth.

Last Sunday's snow nearly gone, but the Main Pond is still deep frozen. In winter, the sun's warmth never touches this sheltered water, so once the ice is thick it may stay so until the spring. Beginning to snow at 4.30 a.m. and turning colder.

Steve Hammond called this afternoon. Has agreed with police Inspector Hogarth on a repeat performance of dawn-watch at the sett for next Sunday, but will let me know details later this week. Steve has a way of bringing things into the conversation very casually – but they're never casual at all! However, that suits me fine. I'm at ease with him since we speak the same language and he's a go-between for myself and the police. The latter, I instinctively feel, have always regarded me as an oddity, i.e. that woman who goes out on her own at night. 'A nutter', as Steve would say. Steve doesn't (now!), though he says he had his doubts when first he was told of me.

I find I can talk of anything regarding that wood at night and even if he doesn't fully understand, his army and animal experience allows him to meet me halfway. For example, talking of the mystery car on Boxing Day, he queried the colour. I said it was still dark, so although the vehicle was a *light shade*, I couldn't say more than that. Now most people think that because I can see in the dark, I should be able to distinguish *colour* in the dark. But I can't – nobody can. Steve knows this because he has nightvision also. I mentioned that the hollies afford good protection from the bitterest frosts in the winter for myself and my foxes. He has sheltered similarly in Germany where he had to spend the night alone in a forest, before finding his way back to base the next day. So there's no

awkward explanations between us, no doubting looks. He's also a good listener, which helps!

He said that the men last Sunday week were relieved that I came back to them via the little path as I said I would, and not from any other direction, so avoiding confusing them in the half-light. Said he'd like to know more about badgers. I mentioned the setts, some of which he doesn't know. He 'casually' brought up the 'night people' I'd talked of a while back, who use the clearing by the Main Pond, and asked if I would show him the clearing as well as the setts.

We agreed that he would collect me in his van from work tomorrow and go straight to Ashcroft Woods. I have to work this Saturday, so asked if he could take over from me around dawn. He said yes immediately – he really is terrific. Felt a weight lift off my shoulders.

Wednesday 25 January
I'm keeping a close check on the young sow badger. I know exactly *her* birth date, so hope to learn that of her cubs – it would be of interest to Ernest as well as myself. No sign of her at all tonight – significant, I think.

Steve was waiting for me dead on time. Gave him my copy of Ernest Neal's book *Badgers* to read. He told me that they searched the Chantry last Sunday week without success. Either the spades etc. were very well hidden, or they had been removed. He also told me that the same afternoon, whilst they were checking, men were caught in another area

239

attempting to dig out a badger sett. They had with them a van *rigged out with cages.*

A beautiful afternoon – sunny, mild, birdsong everywhere. He drove straight up Briarmead Lane, entered the wood and so to the Main Pond. Pointed out the sawn tree stump guide-marker (*see* 12 January); told him to turn left and then left into the clearing further along. He said he couldn't get his van in – I said I knew he could, so he backed it to take the curve and smoothly drove inside. Brought the van round in the large space, stopped – and just sat. After a while, I suggested we look at the setts and we began to walk along the path to the beech, turning in order to get to Meg's Sett, now, of course, dug out. I felt his heart wasn't in it – his thoughts all on the 'swap-shop' clearing. I showed him the fallen birch on which I had played in the snow with Lesley's mate, then up to Meg's Sett. He suddenly decided he must go and check his radio, so we returned the way we had come. Answered his radio, then asked if I wanted a lift home. I shook my head, inwardly smiling. Knew he wanted to be alone – perhaps explore a little without me around. Said goodbye and walked homewards in the sunshine.

Thursday 26 January
Raining hard – high winds. Lesley came to greet me as I sat on the chestnut bough. She *smells* of milk, like Wendy did in whelp; had forgotten what a strong smell it was. Watched her grooming to confirm she is lactating. This dates her cubs as 24/25 January. Seems *very* pleased with herself. Fussed around me, musked my boots, then my hands when I put them on the ground to steady myself! Very affectionate – nuzzled my ears and hair. Funny how badgers seem to like human hair. Imagine that to them that's the only bit of fur we have!

Sunday 29 January
Wet, mild night. Met Lesley's mate on the fallen birch where last Sunday I snowballed him. Sat there talking softly and scratching behind his ears. Unlike the fox, badgers are capable of moving their ears only slightly. He is missing his mate. For my part, I am keeping well away from her now I know the cubs' birth date. I hope motherhood will make her less dependent on my company. Will try and steer a middle course between staying clear, yet keeping an eye on the family's well-being and knowing immediately should they move. This latter will be the tricky bit for I must always know where she is denning if I am to protect her – or ask the men to protect her – that's vital. But she will have to stand on her own feet now. I don't want her cubs to get familiar with me, though when they eventually come above ground they will inevitably pick up my scent. Can't avoid this. And if Lesley makes a fuss of me, she will carry my scent to her cubs. Who knows – perhaps the cubs born of Old Joe's daughter may re-populate this place in time.

4 a.m. Watched a flock of geese flying overhead – Canadas – long

necks and deep, deep wingbeats most distinctive. Calling one to another as they flew northwards. Ten minutes later, another flock followed – then a few frantically calling stragglers – every species has them!

Walked down the hillside and arrived a little before the men. Took the number of a transit van parked in the cul-de-sac, although I think it probably belongs to a resident's visitor. Engine cold. The men arrived just after six and were immediately interested in the van. They were the Special from last time who had said he would come again, a constable and Steve. We took the same route as before and then I left them at the Old Cherry Sett and went walkabout, checking for cars. All quiet. Met up with Josh and his vixen above the Oak Dell. They are denning together at the Well den near by. The only car was Ralph's coming up Briarmead – he asked how the badger situation was. Felt awkward as I haven't mentioned to him or Barry Hains that both the police and R.S.P.C.A. are helping me.

Met up with the dawn patrol at the sett – all quiet, nothing seen. They're very good about their wasted time; don't seem put out at all. (Whether they come again or not, I don't think I'll ever feel as vulnerable here as I did at Christmas, now I've had their backing.) Steve has told the police about the package people. Relieved, as I felt they should know in spite of Dick Birling saying they were aware of it. As we were leaving, one of the constables picked up a spade(?) handle lying at the pathside next to the Main Pond. Steve said the police will leave the area alone for a while now – he'll keep in touch. Said goodbye and walked the Briarmead route home. Sun shining, birds and squirrels busy – lovely morning.

Friday 3 February
Checked Lesley on Wednesday – she's fine – but apart from that, have kept clear. Wrote to Ernest Neal today sending my records of badger long-duration matings that he wants in order to amend his graph for his revised book. Told him of the young sow's cubs – herself two weeks short of a year old. This is proof positive of something he wrote in his last letter: 'It is is possible that a successful mating in December (of a sow born that year) could lead to immediate implantation – no delay at all. This, if proved, would be extremely interesting.'

Sunday 5 February
The young mother sow is foraging close to home whilst her cubs are helpless. Plenty of food here – everywhere wet. She has been digging up bluebell bulbs growing on the sett slope and *eating them* (she's very selective about this – only one in three she actually eats, though she carefully smells each one). There are still chestnuts to forage for and eat. Keeping well out of her way and watching with the monocular.

Went down to the lane to check for strange vehicles amongst those of the residents – none. Walking back to check the bottom of Great

Chantry Field, a wind sprang up and it began to hail violently, stinging my face and eyes. No cars anywhere, but someone has fixed birch saplings across the path by the Main Pond that leads to the clearing.

5.55 a.m. Settled down to watch at the Old Cherry Sett, soaked to the skin. Hail had ceased – temperature dropping fast. Feel sick with cold, but determined to stick it out. Just such a morning as this would suit the diggers best. Beautiful first light – all clear-cut and glittering in the iciness. A squirrel darting about amongst the leaf litter has reached my left boot; runs a short way up a chestnut coppice, and scolds me from above. Try to click back – but can only shiver. 7.45 a.m. and the sun's great orange disc clears the curve of Great Chantry straight ahead. Lesley and cubs safe for another day. Struggle upright, preparing to leave – home seems a lifetime away.

Wednesday 8 February

Mild, clear night. Everywhere very moist. Lesley musked me on Long Field. Very sedate – taking great care of herself – good badgers are scarce! Watched her grooming the belly fur and washing her teats. The fur is getting pulled away and quite clear areas are apparent round each. She seems to have plenty of milk; was secreting and tasting it herself as she washed. She seems to be in good condition to care for and maintain whatever cubs she has. Very compact little body and looks the picture of health.

Notice sticks have been pushed down the entrance under the chestnut bough. Wish people wouldn't do this.

Saturday 11 February

7.30 a.m. Sitting on the chestnut bough after my dawn-watch writing this, and watching the squirrels – their tail-waving intrigues me – I must find out more about it.

Lesley met her mate tonight. He approached purring, and she let him groom her face. He was obviously very interested in her new smell and tried to nose beneath her which made her growl. He, very abject, backed slowly away. Wonder if this is the first time since the birth of the cubs that she has allowed him near?

Just looked up from writing this as I heard a noise. See there are five squirrels now – three on the Old Cherry's sloping trunk and two on a chestnut coppice – all tail-waving and churring at me! Have a feeling I'm not wanted. Tried clicking back but that has made them worse. I'm being ganged-up on, so think I'd better go!

8.30 a.m. and birds as well as squirrels busy now. Dull, misty, damp morning. Each hazel tree is a yellowy green cloud of catkins. Those at the wood edge, especially, show to advantage. Many primroses in tight bud; found three open flowers – delicate, lovely, harbingers of spring.

8.50 a.m. Saw Barry Hains's car coming up Briarmead and waited to speak to him. (Police patrol has just come and gone.) I told him that

Steve Hammond did my Saturday watch when I had to work on 28 January. (I would like these two to get acquainted, so if I'm in the company of one and the other turns up, I'll introduce them. They have a common interest, after all.) He doesn't know who put the barricade at the entrance to the 'swap-shop' clearing – how strange, the mystery deepens! One morning recently, he came up here just as a vehicle piled high with logs passed him and went down Briarmead. He found later that one of his oak trees near the pond had been felled!

Monday 13 February
Lovely, starry night with slight wind and deep frost crunching underfoot. Something strange happened earlier at 12.35 a.m. I was with the boar badger just inside the woodland path nearest the foxes' Well den, when I heard a trumpet-like honking and looked up as a group of Canada geese came flying in low over the treetops. A thrilling sight; seven of these majestic birds against a background of the moon two-thirds to the full. Oh, to take photos by moonlight! Left Lesley's mate foraging in the frost-free undergrowth, and walked up to the 'swap-shop' clearing as I thought the geese might have landed there as some did once before (20 November 1981). Sure enough, there they were, preening and very much at home.

Approached very slowly, talking to them quietly. Think, as before, this is a family group. Strange how geese seem unbothered by humans at night. I stood amongst them – stroked one's wing that it was washing, then its long neck. Its beak passed over my head, then my anorak, neck, face and hair. Didn't hurt – just the preening action. Another came from behind me and did likewise. Spoke very softly to them – was thrilled at their acceptance of me. It seemed very crowded with eight of us in the clearing. They made gentle noises amongst themselves; one sampled the dead bracken.

Had been there some time when a light appeared from my right as I stood facing the entrance. I probably could have disappeared, but the great birds would have needed time and care to make an effective take-off and clear the trees. So I stayed where I was, one hand on each Canada by my side. Thought it might be a patrol checking the clearing, but no, it was the first car of the package people. It swung round with ease in the entrance – and stopped! Next instant, the dimmed headlights were blazing and the Canadas, that until then had been quite peaceful, panicked. I wonder what the driver thought? Swan-like, they rose up high, flapped their wings, necks outstretched – the noise they made was indescribable. Then I think the driver panicked, but I couldn't see as I was blinded by the headlights and was knocked to the ground by those great wings. Above the birds' noise, I heard branches rasping against metal, the engine stall as it tried to reverse and take the sharp corner. The driver was used to driving in and turning – then driving out again later. Think it knocked against trees as it reversed past the Main Pond;

243

the footpath winds there. With the blaze of light gone, the geese were calmer, the wing flapping eased. At this time of year, a car light at the top of Briarmead is clearly discernible; the ground is also on a downward slope. The first car now facing down the lane met the second coming up. Both sped away a great deal quicker than they came. Wonder what the first driver said to the other when eventually they stopped? Bet they don't come up here again in a hurry!

Have a feeling the Canada geese are used to coming to this clearing quite apart from the other time I saw them. Left them some while later when they seemed quite calm again and looked as if they were going to rest the night away. Wonder where they are destined? [The next time I was speaking to Sam Mercer, I mentioned the Canada geese. He said that the men fishing tend to feed them – also the greylags – hence their tameness.] Moon changing from silver to deep orange as it goes down, 4.20 a.m. Tawny vocalisation is altering – February is an interesting month owl-wise. The hen's gentle 'oo-wip' contact call is becoming more frequent. Both perch together and mutually preen before roosting. Dr Southern's own words best describe it: 'a formal parleying of disjointed hooting by the male and a mixture of contact and soft calls by the female'.

Saturday 18 February
Full moon, no wind and deep, deep frost. Everything glittering in the clear air. Met Tagless and his vixen near the Poplar Row. This little vixen – once the runt of her litter – is the swiftest fox I know. She had caught herself a rabbit and, having taken her fill, was graciously allowing her mate to finish the carcass. Lesley's mate has dug out some entrances of the Wheatfield Sett earlier tonight. Thursday last, he reopened that at the Lower View Path in the woods.

5.20 a.m. Checking for parked cars, discovered a [description and number omitted here] with its engine still slightly warm, cleared windscreen fast freezing again, tucked away at one of the entrances to the woods. I went straight to the Old Cherry Sett and stayed there out of sight.

6.30 a.m. Heard a rustle, and saw a terrier moving round the old tree's leaning trunk. I ran forward to stop it entering the sett and met a man holding a rifle. The little dog darted into the entrance beneath the chestnut bough just as another man and a dog came up the slope. I told them to get their dogs away. One stood looking at me, the other walked behind me. [Description of men and dogs omitted here.] Both carried guns; but there was no sign of spades etc. They called up the dogs and left by the path going towards the View. Didn't follow at first as I had the car number, but changed my mind after a few minutes and started after them. Saw they hadn't gone very far, though they hurried their pace more when I came into view. Suddenly felt uneasy and retraced my steps. Came back and round on to the lower path again in time to see a

244

man with a spade at the chestnut bough entrance and another with a spade and a terrier on the slope just above. They saw me returning and ran up to the hayfield, just as another dog emerged from the same entrance and followed them.

By now it was 6.55 a.m. Stayed at the sett as I had a car number after all and couldn't risk the cubs. Was relieved that neither dog had emerged with one as, according to Ernest Neal, 'There is no doubt that for the first few weeks, the cubs are buried in a mass of dry bedding which is an excellent insulator, so the heat from their bodies is retained. This is likely to be increased at intervals when the sow returns to suckle them. However, she does not usually remain with them during their first few weeks, but lives in a separate part of the sett during the day. This explains why dogs sometimes enter setts and bring out very small cubs without being molested by the mother.'*

Stayed until 8.15 a.m. when the sun was well up. Walking down Briarmead to see Barry at Newby Farm, I noticed car tracks in the frost of the Great Chantry drive-in. So a car has been parked there too.

Phoned the police, but the car number is foreign so unable to check it out – just my luck! Phoned Steve's office, too.

Friday 24 February
Mild night, damp and overcast. Lesley full of energy and playful. She is friendlier towards her mate, although she won't let him near the sett. They have both been worming together in the muddiness of the lower path.

Very uneasy about the badger situation here – men are around. Two odd happenings this week:

1) Tuesday morning I came down to the lane to check cars. One parked a short way from the stile hastily drove away. Time 5.15 a.m. (first light now about 6.10 a.m.). Didn't get number, just X–X; not a resident's car, as those accounted for, but could have been staying with residents, of course.

2) This morning, I walked round checking before going home. Felt uneasy so returned to Old Cherry Sett once more, although late. I saw a light on the sett slope; couldn't possibly have mistaken it for anything else. It went out abruptly, and dimly saw two figures going off. I hung about there for a while, but no further developments.

There's obviously something afoot here and, from past experience, it's going to get worse as Easter approaches – Easter is always a bad time. I don't think the group here has realised yet that I have to leave earlier during the week. I always choose a different route by which to leave these woods and often return several times to the Old Cherry Sett before finally going. This not only keeps me from getting too chilled when it's

*From *Badgers* by Ernest G. Neal, Blandford Press, 1977.

below freezing, but also makes the badger-diggers unsure whether I've really gone or not. However, it's only a question of time before they realise.

Saturday 25 February

I went out late this morning, but in plenty of time to dawn-watch at the Old Cherry Sett. Was stopped by a patrol along Holmoak Lane about 4.40 a.m. They were interested in the badgers, so I showed them the sett and stood on the lower path there for a while discussing the situation. Two-way CB radio was suggested, which has a three to four mile range. Wonder how expensive it might prove and whether the range would be great enough, but it's worth looking into. (However, they also said I would need to be careful using it as so many people listen in.) They mentioned a badger had been run over in the area of Rendcombe. They left me about 5.30 a.m. – very glad of their interest.

Sunday 26 February

12.10 a.m. Tonight began bitterly cold with snow showers. Now at 3.20 a.m. it is mild with slight rain. Lesley is in great form; decided to play 'pull' with a pocket flap of my anorak! She also had designs on its furry hood – she's a little tearaway, but very endearing. Had my face washed – and my left ear! It intrigues me how she is able to 'groom' me and purr at the same time (though I must admit the purring gets a bit bubbly when she does this!). Her chunky body glows with warmth and vitality. She smells strongly of sweet, warm milk. She and her offspring are well worth protecting.

Running my hand over her rough fur, I thought suddenly of yesterday's patrol. One constable in particular, Len Watts, had been really interested, not merely polite; wished he could have seen her now. No words can describe an animal that you've only seen dead on a road. How can you imagine affection, playfulness, the warm and the living, when you've only seen the lifeless, crushed and grotesque?

When she went to earth about 4.20 a.m., I heard distinctly in the quietness, a high-pitched trilling, the young cubs' greeting to their mother. Then, unbelievably, sounds of suckling interspersed with the softest purring – Lesley nursing her young. Laid my head on the wet earth and had the sounds magnified. No doubt about it. Know now for sure which is the nursery entrance – they can't be far below ground either. Hope a terrier doesn't find its way down there.

Tawny male sounding his territory at 6.45 a.m., it's now quite light. Walking homewards through the woodland, see many primrose buds opening and dog's-mercury is all in flower. The sleet has changed the dead beech leaves underfoot to burnished copper and the bracken is all aflame. A green woodpecker keeps pace with me in the branches just above and 'yaffles' as he goes – spring is nearly here again.

Sean Cooke came to see me this morning. He is a lecturer at our local college. Sean walks in Ashcroft Woods in his spare time and we've known of our mutual interest for some months now. On Sunday 29 January, when the police and Steve were here with me, I came back to these woods in the afternoon and met Sean struggling along a mud-covered path. Inevitably, we talked shop – stand types, wildwood, ancient pollards and earthworks. Told him how disheartened I became when engaged on my tawny survey (out of five pairs of these birds, only one and a half pairs survived the shooters etc. after six months). Also told him how helpful Ernest Neal's contact, Dr Southern, was and how dearly I would have liked to do a proper small mammal survey here, but lacked transport and the Longworth traps to do so. Told him how interested I am in the food chain caused by the Grain Dumps in Barry Hains's part of the woodland.

On the strength of this, Sean has spoken to an acquaintance who is finishing his PhD and is looking for some 'light relief'. He can use his college's Longworth traps and has transport. They will start when the weather is warmer and let me know how things go.

I looked at Sean standing there, smiling – don't know who felt more pleased, he or I! Must remember to ask Barry's permission, though, since part is his woodland.

SPRING 1984

Thursday 1 March 1984

Quiet all week at the sett – ominously so. After the trouble on 18
February and the odd happenings during the following week, there's
now been a weekend and week conspicuous for its peace. Have to work
this Saturday so will need to leave the area by six. Phoned Steve's office
last Monday and left a message asking if he can take over from me (will
check out car numbers before I leave the woods on Saturday), but I
haven't heard from him. I hope he can spare the time because it will now
be too late to ask Ralph to step into the breach as *he* needs a couple of
days' notice. (I hate asking people to help – much prefer being
independent, but these days I have no choice.)

The badgers are thriving and together much of the night although
Lesley still won't let her mate near that part of the sett occupied by her
and the cubs. I keep well clear of them, but use the monocular to check

they're all right. Meet up with boar or sow about once a week just to keep in touch.

(Ross has checked prices and range of CB two-way hand radio suggested by the constable last Saturday. The cheapest £27.50 each (two required), minimum range one mile, maximum three to four miles according to wind, mist, atmospherics, etc., so would be no use at all as, at best, it would be almost out of range. The next kind would be fine but quite out of the question pricewise – range up to twelve miles, £80 each.)

Saturday 3 March

Very exciting night – gale in progress. I went out just after midnight. Owing to this wood's peculiarity of growing along a hill ridge, the Warby side was taking the greatest force of the wind, whilst the Briarmead region was merely very wind-tossed. I find gales exciting. To discover which animals did or did not mind gales and storms, I once went out in every such condition for a year, and recorded what I found. Badgers and foxes didn't mind gales; owls and squirrels did (both are very vulnerable at such times and the squirrel mortality rate was quite high). Badgers and foxes don't care for thunder and lightning; owls take it in their stride; hares are stimulated by it and will drum well before a storm reaches them.

No rain accompanies tonight's gale. High wind in the treetops is evocative of a storm at sea. The badgers were competing in a mopping-up operation – farther over, so were Tagless and his vixen. A surprising number of birds and squirrels find their way to the stomachs of such gastronomic opportunists.

It was not cold at all and by 4 a.m. the wind had eased. Went walkabout checking for cars later on, but nothing to report. Steve Hammond contacted me yesterday, so I came on to the Wildflower Path about 6 a.m. to see his van coming up Briarmead, dead on time (I *do* like people that can arrive when they say!). He said I could let Barry Hains know now about the police doing a dawn-watch here in January; rather relieved at this, since Barry might hear it from another source which could be embarrassing.

I had a phone conversation this evening with [name omitted and conversation reconstructed, omitting the give-way parts yet keeping the sense].

X: ... but there's more of everything these days – badger-baiting, dog-fighting, ferreting, cock-fighting. And more dogs! Never seen so many lurchers – and terriers – in this area. Just a few years ago, a lurcher was almost a rarity here.

CF: Have you any idea who is responsible locally?

X: I *know* who Mr Big is locally, but I'm certainly not prepared to say.

CF: I know how you feel – you want to be sure.

X: It's not that – I *do* know – but he's a dangerous man.

CF: Dangerous? How do you mean?

249

X: Just that. Dangerous. I'm not saying any more.

(All this from a man normally calm and unruffled. He has a young family and is very uneasy. In so many words, he can no longer help me.)

Sunday 4 March

4.40 a.m. Surprised to see thick frost on the residents' cars in the lane. Had thought it a mild night! Clear skies, no wind. All quiet at the sett. First light approx. 5.40 a.m., dawn 6.10 a.m. *Beautiful* sky over the Bank Sett. I stood in amongst the cherry trees on the bank of the Wildflower Path – just where I waited for Steve's van yesterday – and went back through the undergrowth at intervals to check all was well at the Old Cherry Sett.

6.40 a.m. I had just walked to the Briarmead end of the Wildflower Path when I saw a vehicle – no lights – come quietly round the curve of the lane where the banks are high. Thought in surprise, 'What's Steve doing here again?', although the lack of lights did seem odd. Then I realised it was a car. Driver was looking to his left and away from me, waiting for the space between the trees where you can look down on to the fields; left hand guiding the cruising car, right hand resting on the open window. No other occupants. He turned his head, saw me standing there in the half-light and sped off down the lane. I was so taken aback that I only took in the first three letters of the car number. I have seen this man before in the wood, walking about in the dark during the week of 20–24 February. [Description omitted.]

I continued on down the lane for a way, then back to these woods via the bottom of Great Chantry and up through the Chantry itself, coming round in a circle and back along the lower path leading to the Old Cherry Sett. Saw someone on the slope, so stood behind a tree, watching. (7 a.m. and now quite light though a dull, overcast morning.) He walked along the sett path for a way (around where I used to leave the men in January) and back, looking all around. He carried a rifle held horizontally – interesting, as all that morning I wasn't to hear a shot – and laid it down whilst he walked about on the slope checking the used sett entrances, twice kneeling down to do so. Eventually, he picked up the gun and came down the slope on to the path, still looking carefully around. As he came abreast, I stepped out and challenged him. He made to bring up the rifle, but I was far too close for him to use it in any way – face to face, in fact. He was badly frightened; turned and ran up the slope. [Description omitted]; have never seen him before.

I stayed at the sett after that for quite a time, then walked the length of the sett path until nearly at Briarmead. Had almost decided to go home when I heard a car come up the lane and drive on to the Wildflower Path. Walked quietly down Briarmead and up the bank to where the same car was parked! It sped away as before – same solitary driver, but now I had the full number [omitted]. He was obviously trying to pick up his friend. The first registration letters coincided with the car in the lane (*see* 24 February). Got to the lane as quickly as possible – and there he was, the car tucked neatly next to those of the residents, only facing towards the main road entrance! I let him *see* me take the number – again – before he raced off. Doubt if he'll come here any more, but I must let Steve know as he'll probably turn up somewhere else.

Monday 5 March

4 a.m. Mild, damp night. Stood on Briarmead Lane watching a little owl flying back and forth catching insects. It was aware of me and Josh, but unbothered. Bounding flight – stocky little bird. Perched on one of the dead damson stumps that line the bank. Its 'keeoo-keeoo' call is far-carrying. Wonder if a pair will nest here?

Friday 9 March

The badgers are fine. Have been keeping away from Lesley, but was found by her mate when tawny-watching at the Main Pond. Teased him by pulling his tail. He loves a game and needed no second invitation. Ended up with me chasing him round the water edge. Sat on the path to get my breath back and he's run off with one of my gloves. A few moments later and he's back again, glove in mouth. Every time I go to take it, he backs away just out of reach – wants me to chase him again! 5 a.m. He's finally gone to earth with it at the single-entrance sett on the Lower View Path – serves me right.

Saturday 10 March

Mild morning with slight rain. At 5.55 a.m. and pre-light, standing in amongst the geans watching Briarmead and Long Field with a tracery of branches almost in blossom above my head. The most perfect moment, neither night nor day, when time seems suspended. Birds not yet singing, no squirrels move in the treetops – the very wood holds its breath.

A tawny flew silently past my face, then wheeled effortlessly round as I softly used the contact call of the hen owl. I sat on the little bank there, still calling, raised my left hand towards it, the thumb lying flat above the clenched fingers. And just like my injured tawny of that Easter morning so long ago, this one took my thumb in its talons, perched there facing me, and stared intently into my face. Close to like this, they're beautiful birds. The large, brown eyes set forwards in the apparent flatness of the face give them a superficially human resemblance that their slow-blinking eyelids do nothing to dispel. The mottling of this bird is almost red-brown and its pale breast is darkly streaked. The mottling seems to vary a great deal amongst individuals. This one's feathering is touched with white on its back and head – some have no white at all. The mottling on wings and tail becomes bars when either are spread. The extreme softness of their feathers and the comb-like edge to each wing tip make them quite silent in flight. These tawnies – and the nightjars that bred here last summer – are beautiful birds, and however much I watch them, they'll always fascinate me.

251

I saw its mate had landed near us on the muddy, rutted path and, after a moment, it began searching amongst the tufts of grass (they enjoy earthworms like the badgers and foxes here), although looking in our direction with interest. Sat for a long time in that position until the weight of the bird on my thumb became unbearable and I had to let my hand slowly drop. Then, quite unhurriedly, it spread those lovely wings as its mate scrambled clumsily up the bank. They're rather comic birds on the ground! Then back they flew, the way they had come, along the Wildflower Path under the geans and into the wood below the Old Cherry Sett, calling as they passed – time now 6.15 a.m.

(I found my glove at the Chantry before I left at 8.15 a.m., rather the worse for wear!)

Sunday 10 March

I believe both my vixens now have cubs. Josh's vixen still dens at the Well; Tagless's mate dens near the old dug-out sett that was Tossy's first home. A lone vixen in cub moved into the area recently and is denning at the Wheatfield Bank – she has now littered. This, of course, was Tagless's territory and caused a certain amount of female vocal aggression. With a plentiful food supply, however, no physical contact occurred though both vixens are very wary of one another. Tagless, wise fox, kept a low profile.

I find it interesting that it is the dog who first quarters, scent/scat-marks, defends a territory from autumn throughout the rut into January. After mating, this declines in the male, but the vixen begins to do the same with a smaller area around her chosen den within his territory. She will continue thus until her cubs begin to venture above ground. Then, provided there is no real shortage of food, these strict territorial boundaries begin to break down. In a year of abundant food, there may even be a sharing of dens – and of cubs – as I found last year. There is plenty of *room* here, as well as food. I imagine there would be a very different situation in, for instance, a confined, urban area.

Wednesday 14 March

Met up with the Canada geese again tonight. Snowing earlier in the sharp wind, but by 2.30 a.m. much milder, misty and the wind has dropped. Found Lesley and mate round the waterlogged field edge near the Old Barn ruins. It is always very wet there owing to the spring that rises just inside the wood. Plenty of worms etc., both badgers very playful amongst themselves and with me, and I ended up looking as if *I'd* been foraging in the mud! Lesley decided to accompany me as I went cross-field, so I passed the beehives thinking to cut across Briarmead and so to the sett, for her benefit – since I guessed she was coming my way to feed her cubs – does not like to leave them too long. Then heard honking in Barry Hains's field above Newby Farm where he keeps his mare and her grown foal. Sure enough – five Canadas. Very friendly. Certain that at least three were of the group seen on 13 February in the clearing. Lesley made off in the direction of the sett – isn't that keen!

Met up with her again later at the Old Cherry Sett when she emerged from the nursery entrance. Groomed herself, then decided I needed a good wash too – my hair always comes in for a lot of badger attention! Could hear the cubs playing below ground and twice I saw a tiny face fleetingly within the darkness of the entrance – they are seven weeks old now.

3.40 a.m. Left her and went across Pete Williams's fields as I wanted to look at the stretch of water below the Motorway there. Turned very cold again and misty the Warby/Crosshampton side of these woods. Swirls of smoky mist writhing above the glassy surface. Something eerie about mist rising from water. The traffic just above is muted and seems much farther away. The illuminated gantry is here – I can never look at this place without recalling Old Joe and the times we crossed the Motorway here. Still miss him. His death and manner of dying will always be on my conscience.

Did the usual check before going homewards. All clear at the lane; thick frost again on the cars. Came on to the main path above the Oak Dell at 5.10 a.m., well before first light. Saw the headlights, then rear lights of a car as it backed close to the fence and stile there. Stood uncertainly in the middle of the path, just as a man came up it. He didn't at first see me. Still dark and darker under the trees and he wasn't being cautious; obviously thought he had a clear field. Then he was running back the way he had come and shouting a warning to someone else. The car was moving away as he reached it and went at speed down the rough track, bumping as it did so. Dogs in the back – lot of white – bobbing up and down as they passed over the ruts. Tried to make out the number, but with the fast-increasing distance and jerky ride, I couldn't. Watched them turn left on to Madden Lane, then ran up to the Main Pond and the clearing in case it or another car should come along. I stayed at the Old Cherry Sett until the sun was well up and too late for anyone to move in and dig.

(I have seen, not very clearly, and heard distinctly, the man before this morning. Realised where and when this afternoon. At the Old Cherry Sett last September 17. He was the man who called up the slope asking what I thought I was going to do with his dog.)

Monday 19 March
12.25 a.m. Moon just past the full. Sitting halfway up the trunk of the Old Cherry watching the squirrels. They are often very active on moonlit nights, especially in spring and autumn if there's no wind. It's surprising what noise they make in the trees and, of course, amongst the dead leaves littering the ground. The oak is a particularly good food tree – they will eat the oak catkins even when unopen, likewise leaf buds, young leaves and acorns when available. This Old Cherry makes an

253

excellent vantage point. I'm only about eight feet off the ground, but the steep incline of the earth brings me higher up to the trees growing below.

A favourite action of these squirrels is to hang head down from and under a branch, and tear at the bark of the trunk with their fore paws. I've only observed this with oaks, though that's not to say they don't do it with other tree species. I watched one through the monocular, doing this just now; it didn't appear to want the bark – so I think it's taking the sap. But whether it rises more freely from below a limb or whether the bark is easier to tear at that point, I don't know. (This accounts for the reddish marks just here on the oaks, left by the scratching of their long claws.) I don't think I'm going to do much more squirrel-watching this night, as at 1.15 a.m. Lesley's mate has appeared and picked up my scent trail. I now have company on this trunk and his presence has attracted the squirrels to me. Oh well, it was good while it lasted!

Since this badger took my glove the other night, he's always trying to do so. They're really gloves inside mittens and come off readily, so he sneaks up on me when he thinks I'm off my guard! He is just above and behind me as I sit here. On the pretext of washing my ear, he has leaned over my shoulder and tried to snatch one from my hand. Have promptly clenched my fist, but with his teeth well embedded in the material, that's started a tug-of-war! Finally wrested it from him and now have one glove rather longer than the other – I wonder when badgers grow up?

Wednesday 21 March

Mild with good visibility on the ground, but high mist blotting out moon and stars. Over Ingrims Fields, I heard the cries of geese flying above the mist. Seemed to be circling round for some while. I couldn't make out from their 'aang-ang-ang' calling what they were – not Canadas. Walked on, crossed Holmoak Lane and on to Roger Johnson's land. Near their farmhouse, the same thing occurred; the birds circled for a good time and then passed on.

Met Tagless on the Ridge. He briefly put down the rabbit he was carrying to make contact, then gripped it round the body again. Together we passed through the back of the Ridge coming out halfway along the Enclosed Path. Went our separate ways at the wood edge – he to his vixen's den, I on to the open fields. I thought to go down to Barry's meadow again like last Wednesday, when I met the Canada geese, but I never arrived there, however, for not far down the sloping fields that border Briarmead, I found a flock of Canadas with other, rather smaller geese amongst them. I think they must be greylags – compact with heavy bills. All the geese were feeding on the young corn shoots. The greylags were more cautious of me at first, but I soon found I could stroke their long necks. Feel rather shattered – they make pigeons look non-starters. 3.20 a.m. Something has disturbed the geese who have started to hiss, some taking to the air and circling round (heavy flight, same call as before). Glebe's farm dog barking; think I'll get going. Have just seen the cause of their discontent – Josh, fancying goose dinner!

4.50 a.m. Checked for cars – all quiet. Mist has descended wet and clinging. Had previously decided not to wait round the Old Cherry Sett this morning, as feel I'm seeing too much of Lesley. For some reason, I changed my mind after checking that no vehicle was hidden at the Great Chantry entrance off Briarmead. Walked along the little sett path from the lane when I heard the young sow calling cry after cry as she did when I tried to leave her that morning after the other badgers were taken. I pushed through the undergrowth towards the sound and there she was, caught fast by wire among the deadthorn and butcher's broom. It took me a while to discover it was a snare, but not one set just here. Tight round her neck – her long, sleek head must have passed through in a moment – had probably been set on a trail, hedge-gap or up-and-over path. And most likely for a fox; would be secured more stoutly to keep a badger tethered. The loose wire was caught up in the undergrowth and also round her left front leg. Thankfully, ever since her paw injury as a cub, she's always trusted me. Even so, I was a long time easing the tension on the wire and releasing her. It had cut deep, her white neck and head were all bloodied, her front legs slippery with blood. She wouldn't stop to let me check her properly, but stumbled to the nursery entrance and disappeared. Wondered how long she had been like that, and away from her cubs.

3 p.m. Went back to Ashcroft Woods after work to make a start checking the area; there must be other snares. Lesley doesn't forage far from the sett at present and I know her favourite places.

When I released Josh's vixen from a snare on 23 July 1982, I later found others placed on trails in the neighbourhood. They were secured strongly and wouldn't have been intended for foxes at that time of year and were in quite the wrong position for rabbits – which left badgers as the logical alternative. Up to mid-April, fox pelts are good; after that, their moult begins.

Checked the whole of the woodland round the sett that is bordered on two sides by fields and on the third by Briarmead. Also the Chantry. Nothing. Found two snares at the spring, one behind the Old Barn ruins and another in the woodland just round the corner edge of the field there.

When I got back, I phoned Barry Hains and asked him to look out for snaring. Mentioned the Canadas and greylags are feeding on his crops at night. Suggested keeping the birdscarer on at night, but apparently the scarer's not his, but belongs to his neighbour, John Shaw.

Thursday 22 March
Found Lesley and mate on Pete's land, where his men have been preparing the fields for the new season's crops. The young sow is in a fair amount of discomfort. She has cleaned up the leg well – no problem there. Considering their bulky bodies, badgers – especially sows – have

255

surprisingly narrow heads and longish necks. The wire noose had passed over the vocal-chord area on to that part equivalent to our collarbone; possible she was moving at speed. There is little flesh here, just skin and fur, so the bone is exposed. I imagine her mate is responsible for cleaning round her neck, but the cutting above her chest is still bloodstained and messy. No way could she clean it herself. I had brought the hydrogen peroxide with me and let her smell it. Her reaction was interesting. She looked up at me, then down at the plastic bottle – sniffed it again and pushed at my face with her snout. She recognised it as something she had in the past associated with me. To say more than that would be pure hypothesis. I cleaned the wound with one hand whilst stroking her head with the other and talking softly all the time. Suddenly, I felt a slight push from behind and a snuffle; her mate was feeling neglected!

Just before dawn saw a woodcock roding and whistling – first time this year.

11 a.m. Returned to this place and spent the afternoon searching for snares. Found five more which, counting that which Lesley 'found', makes a total of ten. Am reasonably satisfied there are no more, and by their placing and securing were intended for foxes.

Saturday 24 March
High winds have given way to heavy rain – the first real rain for a long time. Holmoak Lane and Madden Lane flooded. I found Lesley with her mate on Long Field happily worming – how badgers love the wet! Knelt on the path to clean her throat and was bundled from behind by the boar! Ended up as muddied as they. The young male seemed to think the whole affair a great game, galloping off across the field, then circling round to bump me again. He's become quite a hefty fellow – I feel I'm on the receiving end of a battering ram. Eventually Lesley snapped at him, which solved the problem, and I was left in peace with her. Shall leave the wound for a few nights now to see if it will close.

Still raining hard at dawn – all quiet human-wise. Tawny pair sounding together near by, each seeming to outcall the other. Stood under the Old Cherry's steep sloping trunk that gives some protection from the wet until at 7 a.m. it was safe to leave the sett for another day. Walking through the woods homewards, saw Josh just off the Main Path, hunting in the bracken round the scrub oaks. Rarely see my foxes in *full* daylight, so was surprised to note how *black* his coat appears when soaking wet. The guard hairs are flattened to the body and the dark felting of the underfur shows through. His cheek ruffs stand out from the sodden head and only the cylindrical brush seems unaltered.

Sunday 25 March
1.25 a.m. Mild, windy night with showers. Flood water has gone down now that it has been absorbed by the dry earth. I had a surprise at Holmoak Lane – a toad migration in progress. The lane itself appeared

to be on the move, so covered was it. A week or so early this year; has the sudden rain after a dry spell had any bearing? Couldn't walk on the footpath or lane, so went round on to the field for fear of treading on them.

3.20 a.m. Am sitting on the sloping ground above the Old Cherry Sett, watching Lesley with her $8\frac{1}{2}$-week-old cubs through the monocular, as I don't want them to know me in the way their mother does. Still can't say for sure if there's two or three, as they're timid and pop back and forth into the entrance a lot. Too young to be very steady on their feet yet, and keep close contact by nosing one another. The nursery entrance is rather curious as it's part of the sett that the men dug out last October. Their spades went straight down exposing a tunnel, where presumably the terriers had one of the three badgers then resident here at bay. Thus the tiny cubs are moving about (can't call their actions 'play' yet) in a shallow, oblong pit. This has rather the effect of a play-pen, although it won't restrict them for long! At a very early age, their facial markings are clearly defined. When I watched Lesley's mother moving her cubs in March 1983, they were $3\frac{1}{2}$ weeks old and their stripes showed then. These little cubs like the sound that their movements make amongst the dead leaves and debris that lie in the pit. After a while, the sow went to earth, hastily followed by a lone cub left outside. Heard its anxious whimper as it sought its mother. The place seemed very empty when they had gone.

British Summertime starts today (in theory), so dawn is an hour later, 6 a.m. Black stormclouds obscuring the rising sun; the steady drip of moisture and subdued birdsong the only sounds.

Returning along Holmoak Lane at 9 a.m., I found many toads crushed in the lane. Lost count after 47 and, in any case, many bodies superimposed on others. This is a quiet lane, especially at night, but just one car could account for this.

Wednesday 28 March
Everywhere is very wet – heavy showers since last Saturday. The badgers are fine. The young animals are becoming steadier on their feet – have established there are two cubs only. Lesley lay among the leaves of their play area for them to suckle. When they had their fill, they clambered over her body – she washed each carefully, especially their bellies and anal regions. Does this help them digest and defecate?

Earlier tonight, I met her worming on Long Field and checked the wounds round neck and leg caused by last week's snare. Both are dry and closing so can leave them alone now.

The hour difference means I have to leave the area before dawn on weekdays. Am uneasy about this especially as, after rain, badgers tend to dig out and advertise the sett is occupied. Crossing Ingrims Fields about 6.20 a.m., I happened to look back. The morning sky was streaked through with shades of blue, red and orange – droplets of moisture on the growing corn sparkled in the clear air.

Saturday 31 March
Josh accompanies me nowadays when I check for cars before dawn – don't quite know why. He keeps very close to me and doesn't scent-mark or forage. It's mainly the only time of darkness that we come out of cover and into possibly human-occupied places. It's having interesting consequences. Three times in the last fortnight we have been together on the Briarmead verge when a patrol car has passed by. Each time, like me, he has merely kept quite still and we haven't been seen. This morning, at 5.20 a.m., was the nearest we have been to one – just three yards away. Surprised though that the driver didn't spot my fox's highly reflective eye-shine; white to blue if seen head on, or pink at a lower intensity when not looking directly at the source of light. Josh has learnt well. The first time this happened was 14 September last year. Like this, I could even let him come with me to the Bourne or Warby at night, instead of pushing him back when he tries to follow. Let him know I was pleased with his performance when the patrol had gone. It doesn't matter with the police, but could be life or death to him with a different occupant – especially up here.

No trouble here this morning. Dull, damp dawn but not cold. The

258

spring flowers of the woodland are splashes of colour under the trees. Wood anemones are scattered like white blossom. Golden lesser celandine in masses; its smooth and shiny green leaves a perfect foil for the brilliantly burnished flowers. *Prima rosa* is still holding its own and the few wild daffodils are in bloom.

Sunday 1 April

Strong gusts of wind, sleet and snow showers. Lesley's mate found me in the Gully, at the side of High Ridge. He's rather good at this. He often crosses Madden Lane now and forages on Pete Williams's land between the road and the Motorway above. Low-lying Madden Lane is regularly flooded in wet weather, in spite of a deep ditch on the Motorway side. Lesley's mate (have to give him a name – Sam is as good as any) can get enough worms in $2\frac{1}{2}$ hours from this wetness to last him the night through. Notice he has broadened out this winter; at two years of age, he's a fair-sized badger and mature.

4.20 a.m. Nearing the Well den on Pete's land, I was met by Josh. He came dancing up to me, waving his brush, tongue lolling and, forgetful of the badger, I put my hands out to him, laughing. Next moment, there was an angry snort as Sam rushed forward and attacked him. At times, both badgers and foxes can sound like cats when fighting – a yowling, spitting din. At a distance, however, this wouldn't be apparent. (I can understand the stories of foxes and badgers being heard attacking cats, though myself I think this would be very rare in the case of a badger and hardly ever in that of a fox. Have, of course, known friendly cat/fox relationships. Should think as far as aggression goes that the cat would be the aggressor – except if the badger or fox had young cubs.) Normally, Josh would have retreated in the face of an angry badger, but he stood his ground tonight, both creatures snarling at one another. Sam made a sudden rush, but the fox was round the back of him in an instant. For a heavy animal, the badger was a quick mover, but the fox was quicker. They circled round, each looking for an opening, then as the fox tried to run in behind the other, the badger swung round his head and with a sideways swipe, bit him smartly in the flank – and that was the end of the fight!

5.30 a.m. All quiet at the sett. The sky has cleared briefly and the pre-dawn space above Great Chantry field is red. Dark clouds moving in again, so no sun to follow. 6 a.m. Snowing hard.

Monday 2 April

The first day of the Easter vacation! Went out at 9.30 a.m. in radiant sunshine – a perfect day. Sat on the Ridge watching the kestrel pair hunting for $1\frac{1}{2}$ hours – and could have stayed until the sun went down. At the Old Cherry Sett, 12.30 p.m., I found Lesley had dragged out her bedding and that of the cubs to air in the sunshine – fluffed-out heaps of hay and chewed-up bracken – terribly obvious, oh badger beware! Sat there awhile in the warmth; must be the loveliest day this spring. Watched the squirrels high up in the overgrown coppicing, several sunbathing on branches with their give-away tails hanging in space! Everything green from the recent rains, green upon green. Even the tree-trunks have a mossy-lichened look. All's right with my world.

Evening. Today, have found out the name and address of the man said to be at the heart of the badger trade locally. Details are: Don Francis of Bourne Place [names changed and full address omitted]. Involved in badger-baiting and dog-fighting. Used to snare for badger and fox pelts. Breeds dogs for fighting. *Keeps badgers at Bourne Place overnight.* Francis himself drives a van [description omitted], and takes a dog [description omitted] with him to check setts in the area. (I see that van sometimes parked on Briarmead, most recently on 22 March when I was searching for snares. At one stage when I was actually detaching a snare, I saw a man watching me but just ignored him – thought he was being nosey. The irony of this is that it was almost certainly Francis himself come to see what was in *his* snares and I was busy getting rid of them! He couldn't very well have asked for them back as it's illegal to snare there.) Doesn't do the actual dirty work himself (though he enjoys snaring!); employs others. Doesn't take kindly to snoopers around his big house – once quite a fine place, but now rather run down.

What I find so interesting about this is a) it ties in completely with the other stories of 'Mr Big' (*see* 3 March); b) his keeping badgers overnight. It isn't an easy thing to do, especially with a fully-grown animal. You need space and either a cement floor or a heavy-duty cage – a badger can dig itself out of anything else, fast. Have often wondered since my four badgers were taken last October what the men did with them until they were used. Perhaps I know now. My O.S. map doesn't actually show outhouses at Bourne Place, but maybe I could go there at night and investigate. If Lesley and family are dug out, they could be held there briefly until killed. Better to know the layout beforehand.

Another point to which I've given a great deal of thought. Police, R.S.P.C.A., County Preservation Society, etc. talk of badgers being taken to the city to bait, but when I start asking how they know, I find there's no proof of this, just a general opinion. Badgers fighting can make a fantastic noise – squealing, snorting, snarling, spitting and, eventually, screaming. Two people who heard a dug-out badger screaming not so far from here thought it was a woman being murdered. That's not a bad description of an adult badger in mortal pain or terrified. A pub with cellars and a disco blaring above would be ideal.

Wednesday 4 April
Beautiful night with deep frost and clear, starry skies. The ten-week-old badger cubs playing in their pit are much more steady and co-ordinated in their movements. It's surprising how many typical badger actions are inherent rather than taught. Even at this age, one little cub has picked

260

up a dead leaf and carried in backwards for a brief moment before discarding it. I notice that Lesley still noses them back into the entrance before she goes off to forage.

Quiet, lovely dawn with no problems, but then a patrol car has been parked the Briarmead end of the Wildflower Path this past half hour! Stayed until well into the day.

Monday 9 April
Mild, damp night – fine rain falling. Lesley has been digging out the sett entrances she and her cubs use. As fast as she excavates it, I have been moving the fresh earth some distance away. She's so used to me doing this (first started to at the Wheatfield Bank last November) that when I paused just now, she came backing out of a hole with an earthload tucked between body and limbs, to find the last earth still heaped up. A look of enquiry was turned my way – mustn't sit down on the job! Both adult badgers have begun their moult. Always seems to be the shoulders that lose it first, and always the underfur.

Sam has dug out one of the Chantry Sett entrances, also the one-entrance sett on the lower View Path, and a couple on the Wheatfield Bank. He's not really settled anywhere, but wants to get back with Les at the Old Cherry Sett. However, she won't let him at present as he tries to dig close to her and the cubs. If he excavated one of the farther entrances, I don't think she would mind. He has been feeding on wild arum corms in the Chantry. Their bitten-off greenery lies on the beech leaves there.

Was on the highest Briarmead bank at 1.10 a.m. when the package people went by. Usual interval between the two vehicles and the same time (20/25 minutes) before they came back down again. Obviously, the Canadas and I on 13 February didn't put them off for long!

At first light the rain has finally ceased. Jotted down the first few members of the dawn chorus to sing: skylark (from the fields); woodcock roding and whistling; crow; turtle dove; pheasant; female tawny; then male tawny; blackbird; thrush.

Tuesday 10 April
Mild, dry night. Set out for Bourne Place and took the route across the fields that is shown on the OS map. Have never been over this farmland before and was curious to see how my nightvision would serve me on totally unknown terrain. No problem at all. Though the sky was overcast, my visibility was excellent. I saw a fox foraging a short way off and facing me, so I crouched down small and yipped to it. Quite forgot my destination. The dogfox regarded me, it seemed, for ages, then curiosity got the better of it as I softly made the contact bark. We ended up face to face, two yards from each other. Thrilled that I'd been so successful with a strange fox on unknown land – then I recalled the

reason I was here and continued on to Bourne Place. [Description of house and other buildings omitted.]

Slipped through the fence and moved towards the house as dogs in nearby buildings began barking. Moved between some cars and saw one which must be the van I've seen on Briarmead. Just then a light went on in the house – dogs barking in there now, roused by those outside. Thought to allay fears of intruders by doing my fox act and heard a fox (probably the one I'd encountered earlier) answer my barking from beyond the fence. Realised, however, that I'd come unstuck when another light came on in the house, and the door opened to let the dogs race out. This fox got back over the fence a lot quicker than she came in! Waited a while for the barking to quieten, but finally decided I'd get nowhere by remaining.

Returned to the Old Cherry Sett just before 4 a.m. Spent three-quarters of an hour moving and hiding the earth Lesley has excavated. Whether this *does* disguise the fact that a badger is in residence here, I know not. Also tossed dead leaves in and around the used entrances, after she and her twins had gone to earth. The little cubs can scramble out of their play-pen now and scamper amongst the bluebell greenery. They're engaging creatures – their small world is one of discovery, each twig, leaf, stone, a potential plaything. They move in little bursts of speed. One tried to scratch its back this morning, but leant too far and toppled over with a squeak of indignation. Then turned on its sibling and nipped it! Some playmates get the blame for everything!

At first light, the Canadas feeding in Barry's meadow above Newby Farm prepared to fly back to their daytime haunts. Restlessly, first one then another raised its head, honked loudly, spread and flapped its wings once or twice, then settled again. Eventually, one succeeded in rousing the grazing flock and, honking loudly, they rose one after another with a great noise of wings, and flew towards the river, still calling.

10 a.m. Returned to Bourne Place by the same route to try and take some photos without arousing suspicion and see if I can learn any more about the place. Took some pictures at a distance but, nearing the place, two men came out of the house and stood talking. A number of dogs, including a tan-coloured Labrador cross, began barking, which attracted the men's attention to me, so had to walk on past the house and down the road.

Saturday 14 April
Sam is denning now at the Old Cherry Sett and some distance away from his mate and the cubs. Very cold, frosty nights since Thursday with beautiful, sunny days. Full moon and glitteringly starry sky. Steve arrived very early to take over from me this morning. Before I left, we discussed amongst other things Bourne Place and its implications. He has agreed to come and look at it with me one day next week. I'm anxious that a search warrant can quickly be obtained when badgers are

next dug out in the area. No good arranging to search when nothing is there, but speed will be vital when the time comes. If only I'd known of this place when Old Joe and the others were taken in October. (Steve shook me rigid by saying in conversation that baited badgers have their hind legs broken before being put to the dogs. This is to give the dogs a more equal chance. My thoughts have always shied from my favourite badger's death – he was too dog-like in his affection. But now in my mind's eye, I saw Old Joe maimed and fighting for his life – dear God, it hurts.) Steve has heard it said that a fully-grown badger is worth £1,000 and added, 'So if a magistrate *did* fine the maximum of £1,000, they only need to dig out one more badger to pay their fine.' That's a sobering thought.

Sunday 15 April
Another badger family has arrived in my area – sow, boar and at least one cub (though there could be more). The sow has taken over the one-entrance sett on the lower View Path; her cub is clearly younger than Lesley's twins. The sow carefully scent-marked the entrance and an area round about. This female has two identical areas of injury on her body where fur and skin has come off leaving long red weals. There is one on each side of her body directly behind each front leg, starting halfway up the body and running upwards for about six inches. Looks as if she has caught herself in something and pulled clear – rather odd. Her boar is denning at the View Sett. Sam was vocally very aggressive to the new boar and they scuffled briefly when he came upon his new neighbour digging territorial dung pits round the View Sett area. Don't quite know how this will turn out, but there's certainly room enough for the two families food-wise. Wonder where the strangers came from – and why?

Cuckoo sounding at dawn this morning – also a chiffchaff thirty minutes later. Many trees in tiny leaf. Primroses everywhere amongst the wood anemones – early dog violets and fragrant sweet violets litter the ground.

Thursday 19 April
Mild, dry, overcast night – visibility excellent. The balsam poplar trees' young leaves are unfurling on Roger Johnson's land – the scent of incense lingers on the air.

Three setts are now occupied in my area; 1) the Old Cherry Sett with Lesley, Sam and the terrible twins; 2) the View Sett with the new boar – he dug out a badger femur there yesterday; 3) the one-entrance sett with his sow and her *three* cubs. All adults have been digging out and bringing in bedding, the latter consisting of, in the main, bluebell greenery so plentiful here, plus some dead leaves and bracken. Lesley's cubs thoroughly enjoy fetching back bedding, running alongside, squeaking with excitement, getting in the way, picking up their own little pieces, backing with them and generally having a marvellous time! What patience badger mums have.

I'm sure Lesley's cubs are two females. At twelve weeks, their heads are narrower with no teddybear cheeks. They dig their own little dung pits and back on to them to defecate. However, their aim is none too good at present – a case of hit or miss! Sat high up in the Old Cherry watching them playing round Lesley. All went to earth at 5.05 a.m., just first light – a bitterly cold and frosty morning, haven't felt so cold since January. Just about to leave my perch and go walkabout to get warm when Sam appeared heading down the slope and went to earth. Looking down from my tree, I saw that the nursery entrance was steaming in the cold air. Like my breath vaporising from my mouth.

Saturday 21 April
5.10 a.m. The quail are back! Was sitting idly on the dirt path waiting for the sun's disc to touch the distant horizon when I heard a movement as the growing corn parted and, to my great delight, a pair of these dumpy little birds stole forth, looked carefully about them and began to peck the vegetation at the wayside edge so close I could have touched them. Doubt if they were more than seven inches long; never realised before just how much white their streaked plumage contains. Felt a deep affection for these shy birds. They took insects from the grass stems and seeds of a downy dandelion clock.

The past five days have been warm and sunny but yesterday (Good Friday) had the heat of a summer's day. Clear, starry skies with bright half-moon. Tonight the badgers have been worming on Pete Williams's land the Warby side and also that bordering Madden Lane, as the irrigation is turned on daily and the earth is always soaked there. Elsewhere is very dry.

Les and Sam appear to have accepted the strangers. The new sow's injuries are healing fast. Spoke to Steve about this when he came last Wednesday to arrange a visit to Bourne Place – he confirmed her injuries are consistent with those caused by tongs; stupid of me not to have thought of this before. Of this sow's three cubs, one is somewhat smaller than the others.

Easter Day 22 April
This spell of unusually hot weather in April is causing the four adult badgers to forage for worms on the irrigated fields; on the whole they seem to have adjusted to one another very well. None of the cubs are mature enough yet to forage with their parents. They play around the setts a good deal and Lesley's cubs, being older, are more boisterous. Doubtful if they will be weaned while the weather stays so dry. Where there is no irrigation, cubs may find their mother's milk dries up if no worms are available – this is the most common cause of death in badger cubs.

264

The orange/red sky at first light was very beautiful – promise of another sunny day. Sam has just dug out four young rabbits from their nursery stop at the field edge. Ate them from the vent end, turning the fur back and leaving it lying there, inside out. An adult rabbit's head would have been left with the skin thrown back over it, but the heads of these tiny offspring were simply crunched up. Sam has made his entrance to the sett much larger in spite of the sun-baked earth. He couldn't enlarge the roof as it's under a chestnut bole so he has clawed away the entrance floor, and the long marks are clear in the dry dirt.

Skylarks over the fields and a turtle-dove from the wood foreshadow the dawn chorus. Now the tawny and his hen are parleying – call-answer-call-answer. Next, a pheasant is claiming his territory. Watched squirrels these past few nights feeding by moonlight.

Tuesday 24 April
10.10 a.m. Steve and I went to look over Bourne Place this morning. He had taken the R.S.P.C.A. stickers off his van and wore casual clothes. Parked his vehicle just off the lane.

Another lovely day – the view across the folding fields indescribable. As we neared the grounds, a transit van moved out of a side entrance there, with two occupants. The driver asked if he could help me, but I said we were just out for a walk. Steve confirmed this, remarking on the weather, and the van continued on its route, that is, the way we had come. Steve asked if I knew the driver and though I said I thought not, a twinge of doubt crept into my mind.

265

Bourne Place looked quite deserted – disappointingly so. No dogs, no people – nothing. Had a terrific sense of let-down and felt I had wasted Steve's time. He didn't say much but noted one or two things that to his experienced eye seemed odd. He is used to investigating outbuildings etc. which was why I had wanted him to come in the first place.

3.45 p.m. Steve called to say he has checked out Don Francis at Oakley police station. Seems my informant was correct – he has a police record and his photo shows him as the driver of this morning's van. The police will think out some excuse to search as and when the time comes. (Have remembered where I've seen the man before, driving up Briarmead one morning nearly four weeks ago. Josh was with me on the high bank that gives a good view of the lane. The man stalled the van as he saw me with my fox and just sat there looking up at us. I felt annoyed at being seen with Josh, so turned and walked back into the undergrowth.)

Wednesday 25 April
Just after dawn, saw a male nightjar fly in from Long Field and perch along the branch of a sweet chestnut near the sett. It wasn't vocal and I didn't see a hen bird.

Ernest Neal came today. Marvellous to talk with him face to face – so much to discuss. Took him to Crosshampton via Ashcroft Woods. Still beautiful weather with clear blue sky and not a cloud in sight. Met Barry Hains on Briarmead and introduced them.

Friday 27 April
At first light, 4.35 a.m., the cuckoo is calling and displaying as the tawny sounds his boundaries, whilst the other birds are still preparing for the dawn chorus. Really that term is very misleading – the chorus is *before* dawn.

Coming here, I see the fields bordering Madden Lane are being *nightly* irrigated now, and all the adult badgers are worming here tonight. Discussed this with Ernest Neal as we passed en route for Crosshampton. Good feeding, especially in such dry weather as now, plays a large part in development – and, in the case of cubs, early maturity. When they begin to forage for themselves, the cubs in my area have no problems with drought. Indeed, damp conditions for them are guaranteed. Early maturity in captivity with a plentiful food supply has been known to lead to early oestrus and cubs born within the mother's first year. We don't feel this is all the answer, but it could explain it in part. It is, however, still very unusual according to Ernest – that's interesting.

All very quiet on the badger front. The Easter vacation is nearly ended and I return to work next Monday. Will still, of course, guard here, but I won't be able to stay beyond 6 a.m. on weekday mornings. I'm determined to try and protect the badgers here – just hope I'm around when the diggers turn up.

266

Tuesday 1 May
The pale windflowers' drooping heads are closed against the night and
the scent of bluebells lingers on the air. They grow in dense masses here,
carpeting the ground. Found just a few marsh marigolds yesterday,
lighting up a damp and shady place, and photographed the best plant.
Can remember twenty years ago they were quite common here. Has been
a warm, clear night and dawn; there are four pairs of nightingales this
spring on the wood edges.

6.45 a.m. Photographing ash flowers off the Wildflower Path when I
saw a man and dog approaching. He stopped when he saw me – Don
Francis and his tan-coloured hound, so I slipped the camera over my
shoulder and came to meet him. He said, 'I thought I might find you
here,' and unthinking, I used his words to me when Steve and I met him
near Bourne Place – 'Hello, can I help you?' He looked taken aback for a
moment, then smiled a little and answered as I had answered him that
day, 'No, thank you. We're just out for a walk.' I started to laugh and
bent to stroke his dog. Then slowly he said, 'Yes, you can help me. Tell
me, what's your name?' Looking up from the dog, I shook my head and
continued along the path. But for my pre-knowledge of him, would have
found Don Francis a likeable man.

It's a pity he saw both of us last Tuesday. He now knows two people
are interested in Bourne Place. Also, where he can find me. The badger-
diggers have been quiet around here for some time; Bourne Place
appeared empty last week, and he's not likely to keep badgers there now.
So where will he keep them when the time comes?

[Have been told today – 4 May – that Francis has guessed my
companion was police/R.S.P.C.A. Not surprising it's felt that badgers
would be taken direct to (name of district omitted), where Francis
has connections, for safe-keeping now, as Bourne Place is known.]

Wednesday 2 May
One pair of nightingales is nesting in the blackthorn trees that border
part of the Briarmead edge. Have been watching them on the tarmac
finding insects – they and the little lane are all bathed in the early
morning sun. Don't know why the bird books describe them as shy, and
I think their appearance is quite distinctive with that bright chestnut
tail. They are perhaps an inch longer than the woodwarblers – another
favourite of mine – and have pale, creamy underparts with brown above.
The blackthorn blossom is very lovely lining the lane; the grass and
Barry's fast-growing barley, a vivid green in the sun.

Saturday 5 May
I brought some cobnuts left over from Christmas to the woods yesterday
and scattered them about on the slope of the Old Cherry Sett, thinking
the squirrels might eat them. However, the badger family have found
them first. Sam and Lesley crunched them up thoroughly rather as they

do chestnuts and acorns; the cubs merely played with them. About 6 a.m., a nuthatch flew up into the Old Cherry with one, wedged it into a crack in the twisted bark, and hammered vigorously at it. He has finally broken the shell, pecked out the kernel and flown away. Just a piece of shell left fixed in the fissured bark to tell the tale. The squirrels are having some, however! They take up a nut and turn it in their paws as if testing for weight and, therefore, soundness. Then deftly, the more pointed end is bitten off and the shell split neatly in two.

Behind the Old Cherry is the flattest part of the slope, once a spoil heap now worn smooth and bald as it's the twins' play area. A few bluebells did attempt to flower here, but have since given up the struggle as the cubs grow more boisterous. The rest of the slopes are covered in these flowers with tracks running from entrances to the footpath below.

Looked at the View Sett before I left this morning, and at Old Joe's elder tree in front of the main entrance. Discussed this business of tree-scraping with Ernest Neal last week. Have noticed that a) only boars do it; b) some more than others, that is, dominant boars; c) it could be to clean the claws, but seems to leave the tree looking very *white*, especially when it is an elder. We both agreed it was probably a *visual* sign of boar supremacy within the territory.

All used entrances of the three occupied setts here have been re-dug in spite of the dry weather. Bluebell leaves for fresh bedding have been taken in.

Sunday 6 May
1.10 a.m. Dull night with slight rain. Met up with Josh fetching back a rabbit, so went with him to the Well den. Stood in the tree shadow there and watched as his vixen came to greet him, her brush waving and making little noises in her throat. Both adults are hunting for themselves and the cubs, and unless their visits here synchronise, they may go some nights without seeing one another. She licked one side of his mouth and he dropped the rabbit. It lay on the ground between them whilst they stood quite still, nose touching nose. Then Josh made a sudden crouch-down movement, rump in air – invitation to a romp. But, at that moment, five of the six cubs appeared and came forward sniffing the carcass. These little foxes are nearly weaned and growing fast. The area round the den is becoming very messy – I imagine their mother will move them before long. Slipped back into the woodland whilst the family was preoccupied. Two pairs of foxes are quite enough to know intimately – don't want these cubs to get used to me, too.

5.42 a.m. Have just seen a stoat come bounding out of the standing barley and kill a rabbit that was browsing on the Wildflower Path. Except when it's a hedgehog, their prey is always killed with a bite into the back of the neck which breaks the spine. Noticed before with a large kill such as this that the stoat clings on, gripping with its front legs whilst clawing with his hind. *Heard* the stoat lap the blood coming from the neck wound. (Just realised this is exactly the spot at which I saw the quail pair on 21 April.)

Standing on the Old Cherry slope after dawn, watched the male tawny hooting the boundary of his territory just here, mobbed by the blackbird pair whose territory this is also! The tawny hen has chicks and the blackbird hen has eggs, so both males feel it is imperative to continually reaffirm territorial boundaries – felt rather sorry for the owl all hunched up on the branch above my head, but still defiantly hooting!

Bank Holiday Monday 7 May
Lesley's cubs are playing with the last few hazelnuts. One has just run round the base of the Old Cherry on whose trunk I am sitting, with a nut in its mouth, hotly pursued by her sister. (The bluebells are finding life rather a strain!) Neither youngster is interested in nuts to eat – playing with them is more fun. They regularly go off now with their mother to worm with her under the sprays that water Pete's crops.

Checked for cars at 5 a.m. after the badgers had gone to earth. Feel much more relaxed about their safety here – both families doing well and no sign of potential badger-diggers for some while. Was sitting above the bole of the Old Cherry at 7.05 a.m. writing my notes and with 'snow' blossom floating all around when a head appeared at the edge of the chestnut 'seat' and there was Lesley re-emerged from the entrance and looking up at me. As she crossed the bare 'playground' between us, I could hear her purring. She put her front paws up on to the sloping trunk and peered up at me sitting there, notebook on knee. Old Joe's daughter has grown into a lovely badger. Long, sleek head and neck; the white so white and the black stripes so exactly drawn. Spoke gently, telling her to go to earth. The long snout quivered, then smelt upwards towards the toes of my boots. She turned round, her back to me, all fours on the ground, and I thought she was about to go back. Instead, she slowly did a neat handstand, hind legs up the trunk, and with deliberate care, musked my boots. Got down again, then, head first this time, reached up and sniffed her musking. Decided she hadn't done the job properly, so did another handstand and repeated the process. I promptly had a fit of the giggles – she doesn't look nearly so elegant from the rear end! Next moment she was beside me, nibbling my ear, then went behind me and used my shoulders for a front paw rest as she did a look-out over the area. (Noticed as she stood above me like this that the twins have kneaded all her fur away round her teats – she's a very bald badger underneath, not that they have a lot of fur there at the best of times!) I patted her paws that were on my shoulders with my notebook, and found I had started her off on an ear-washing and grooming session of me! Her grooming is none too gentle as badgers draw their snouts back and nibble their tatty bits, and clearly Les thinks my hair very tatty!

269

Wednesday 9 May
Left home at 2.50 p.m. to do some photography in the woods. A tractor came on to Long Field and stopped below the sett. The driver came running up, then came more slowly and apologised. Said he didn't realise it was me – saw a woman there and thought I was a look-out for someone sending dogs down. Thanked him for his concern for the badgers and had a long talk on animals, farming techniques and ancient field names! He is one of Barry Hains's men, Alfie – very glad of his interest. Said he keeps an eye on the sett if he can, and has warned off people with terriers – not recently, however. The badgers here undoubtedly have enemies, but they certainly aren't lacking in friends!

Friday 11 May
The package people came at 1.10 a.m. Used the clearing but could have gone further along any of the paths here now as the wood edge has been cut back a great deal to make rides. This encourages the butterflies and insects but also, I'm afraid, the cars – four in the past fortnight have been stolen and abandoned in these woods.

Have unfortunately come to be known by Lesley's cubs. Yesterday, their mother with them in tow found me in the Chantry. Think she must have picked up my scent trail. Then tonight, I saw a cub playing with something that glinted, and took it from her – a piece of broken bottle glass. Luckily, it hadn't cut her. Afraid now I have two little mates – they are fifteen weeks old and perfect young animals. The whole family, including Sam, are in lovely condition, although the adults are well into their moult now and looking somewhat patchy. The other badgers here are settled and healthy; their cubs are two females and a male.

4 a.m. Heard the Canadas on the meadow above Newby Farm and found four of them feeding amongst Barry's horses. Have made friends with both horses and geese. The grown foal used to be nervous, but now is the first to greet me.

Saturday 12 May
Tagless's vixen has moved her cubs to the earth under the broom near the bottom of the Ridge. The adult foxes of my area look very streaky now in their moulting coats. Watched the cubs playing there when I left the badgers worming off Madden Lane about 3.50 a.m. I say left them, but Sam decided to follow as I walked through the woods. By now, the eastern sky begins to lighten at this time of year; a few more weeks and it will be the shortest night.

Coming out on to the tarmac of Briarmead, I saw the geese again, this time on the Top Field eating the young shoots of the spring-sown barley. They looked up from their feeding as we appeared from the wood and made those odd little noises amongst themselves, impossible to describe. Noticed they looked intently at Sam as he came with me – rather too intently, I thought, but he continued on to their field – or *his* field – quite

unconcerned. Then the nearest goose ran a few paces forward, spreading those wings and stretching out its long neck, hissing as it did so. Its companions lowered their heads almost to ground level, the necks snake-like, their chin-patches like the badger's facial stripes, very distinct in the poor light. Too late, the badger realised his mistake and, turning, galloped bear-like for the nearest woodland fringe. He gained safety with all seven Canadas following on behind, trumpeting as they chased – the little bounding figure in marked contrast to the big birds in hot pursuit!

5.25 a.m. The Canadas are just leaving, sounding as they go. Daylight seems to have little bearing on this. Every morning they leave about this time, whether it was just pre-light as some weeks ago, or very good light as now.

7.15 a.m. I was sitting amongst the bluebells in the undergrowth beyond the Old Cherry Sett watching a cuckoo, when a tan-coloured hound came up to me. Stroked its head and spoke softly to it – have done so before. Wondered where Don Francis was. Watched it wander off towards the ridge, then disappear down the slope. Moved further along until I came to a spot that gave me a good view of the sett slope. On the path below, there they were – man and dog. Francis stood there some time looking upwards and round. Finally walked towards Briarmead.

Monday 14 May
Mild, clear night. By 5 a.m., mist stealing over the landscape. Crossing

271

Little Chantry Field saw high up in the beech at the Chantry entrance a squirrel confronted by a weasel. Watched this so many times before. Sometimes the squirrel retreats to a branch end (always over a space as now – the open field), and jumps or falls to its death. Or faces the weasel, and is attacked and killed. Or like today, screeches and clamours – jumping up and down on the branch, attracting the attention of other squirrels who gang up on the weasel which runs off.

All very quiet in the Chantry when they had gone. Never have its beeches seemed so tall; their smooth, straight, slender trunks soaring upwards like the columns of a cathedral – the sky above, a finely etched lattice of new leaves and old 'mast'. Walked through just as the rising sun touched the headland outside, sending a shaft of light that poured into the dimness. Stood spellbound; my eyes straining to see beyond its brightness and dazzled in its beauty. In that moment, past, present, future became as one, and I knew the spirit of the place.

Thursday 17 May

1.10 a.m. It has been raining gently since yesterday afternoon – already the vegetation seems to have grown. It's been a long drought after a very dry autumn and winter. The badgers at all setts have been carrying in bluebell greenery for bedding. Sam has taken sticks in too, quite deliberately. Three he managed to take right down, but the fourth became wedged just beyond the entrance. He struggled to free it until 4.40 a.m. and light, then lost interest and squeezed past it to go to earth. Don't know why they like to take sticks into the sett (neither did Ernest Neal). There's a theory about sticks keeping bedding off the damp ground so keeping it drier – however, that's just a theory. Not all badgers do this by any means.

Josh's vixen has dug out under the prostrate trunk of a barkless tree and has moved her cubs there. Since their new home in the bank is in clear view across Long Field to the Old Cherry Sett, I can foxcub-watch through the monocular whilst keeping vigil over the badgers! Notice the twin sisters of this sett appear rather interested in the young foxes playing. Noise carries at night on the still air, and the badger siblings stand on the bluebell slope listening to the barks, yaps and occasional yelps of the youngsters over the way.

I think this is going to be a good quail year. Have seen *pairs* of these birds in nearly every field round the woods. They should be nesting soon, so will try and locate a nest and watch the young – have never attempted this before.

Saturday 19 May

1.10 a.m. Jumped down from the Old Cherry where I had been sitting with Les. Slipped in some gunge on the rim of a cub dungpit and fell headlong down the slope! Sat up gingerly at the bottom and said some home truths about badger offspring in general and Lesley's gruesome twosome in particular. Their mother, after peering over the trunk at me for a moment, disappeared discreetly into the gean's foliage above.

The twins weren't there as it happened, since earlier they had gone to play with the five little foxcubs over at Long Field – the sixth and weakest is missing since the move. The young foxes were uncertain of the others at first, but have found out for themselves now that five small agile foxcubs are more than a match for two larger but slower young badgers should the play get too rough. Favourite games are Chase and Tag and Stopping Your Playmate Running by Hanging on to His Tail. Using the fallen trunk is a good spot for King of the Castle, and Let's All Bundle One of the Badgers is understandably a favourite with the little foxes. The noise is incredible and can be heard the length of Long Field. Haven't seen the police here since 4 April (which isn't to say they haven't been about, of course), but if a patrol came up Briarmead tonight, they'd have great entertainment! When Barry Hains and I were discussing his barley ten days ago, he said Long Field was the best, although the part nearest the fox den is getting rather flattened with cub-play; fortunately, Barry is very tolerant.

All my adult foxes are fetching back many rabbits for their respective litters. There are so many here, they remind me of flocks of mini sheep as they browse on the fields. Interesting how such a 'flock' will often graze field edges in a half-circle, rather as a tethered horse or goat. Have seen only *one* rabbit this year with advanced myxomatosis; a few have lumps at the base of the ears. Again, it has no apparent effect on their feeding. In past years, even blind and deaf rabbits with this disfiguring disease appear well nourished. The baby rabbits skip about in tiny bursts of speed and are very pretty to watch (good job Barry isn't likely to read this!*). They crouch down low in the grass if alarmed, so are easy to pick up and examine in my cupped hands – none of these young ones have *any* signs of myxi.

I watched the View Sett badger sow last night dig down into a nursery stop, and turn up a rabbit litter. She did this three times in an hour, letting her cubs have their share. I'm sure they locate them by smell as well as hearing; rabbits here rarely burrow deep underground. Her cubs were very interested in the digging-down procedure. Won't be long before they, too, will be doing the same.

Sunday 20 May
This morning, at about 3.15 a.m., the tawny male came and perched on my thumb again (*see* 10 March). He and his mate are hunting now for their chicks. As the growing leaves develop and darken the woodland floor, they will hunt further out where the light is better, over the fields and hedgerows. Therefore, what they catch alters too. Up to now, it has been voles, mice, etc. Tonight, a rat and two very young rabbits were

*Ah well ...

273

brought back to the fledglings' hole in the hollow tree. I picked up a tawny primary on Long Field – the softest of feathers, gently barred like the veins of a leaf; shades of cream, buff, fawn; the end smoothly rounded. Perfection of flight.

Josh has brought in a hen pheasant for the cubs. This may seem generous of him as they aren't so often caught, but he's eaten *all* eleven eggs she was incubating. And coupled with the wood-pigeon he caught earlier, he's feeling rather full. His vixen was away hunting when he brought it in. He sheared off the wings with the bone of the shoulder attached, for the cubs, but, unlike their mother, made no attempt to tear up the carcass for them. All five fell upon it, growling. Then one more dominant cub stood on it, daring the others to challenge his right. Josh, who had been looking round for his mate, promptly tipped the aggressive youngster off the prize with his muzzle, then trotted along the field edge at the bank bottom, keen eyes searching, upright ears turning to detect the first sign of her.

Much later, when the foxes had gone to earth, one of the badger cubs came looking for her friends and found instead a sheared pheasant wing lying on the field. With great care she carried her prize back to the bluebell slope (I was watching through the monocular from high up in the Old Cherry). Together she and her sister had a fine game of chase with it until, at 4.50 a.m., they disappeared below.

Went my round of the setts as always, and there, forgotten by the chestnut seat, lay the pheasant's wing. Wondered if anyone from the villages out walking later this Sunday morning might think the badgers had caught themselves a pheasant in the night.

Came on to Long Field from the Primrose Path in time to see a Landrover backing into the wood, one man standing, directing the driver. The latter looked up along the field and saw me. The other jumped in beside him as the vehicle hastily moved off towards Briarmead. Impossible to note registration number or see faces owing to distance and visibility, but did note type of Land-rover.

Wednesday 23 May
5.10 a.m. The loveliest morning has dawned after hours of rain. The sun warms as it climbs the sky and, from the far bank, tree shadows steal across the velvet barley. A pheasant's 'korr-kok' challenges the air, harsh above other birdsong. Near the stand of wild geans that line the path, the tawny soft-calls a muffled note that halts halfway. These woodlands, fields, banks and hedgerows have become to me the dearest place on earth. Yesterday was driving rain and flailing wind and still I loved it. Today is a morning to store in the mind's eye. Faint moon-curve fast fading in the blueness; tracery of blossomless cherry stalks, promise of the fruits to come. The far villages a mere suggestion in the misty distance and, over all, the skylark's bubbling song. Just myself and solitude ... and yet ... Something stirs behind me, whisper of a

274

movement and Josh's little vixen is standing at my side. Kneel to be near her, one hand to stroke her head, together we keep vigil over this sunlit place.

Saturday 26 May
2 a.m. Rain and more rain with Holmoak Lane flooded.

4 a.m. Found a quail's nest! For some days, I have been watching this pair of birds through the monocular as I sit on top of the gate at the side of Briarmead – a lovely vantage point provided a car doesn't sneak up on me! The quail's nest – a mere scrape between the rows and lined with blades of wheat – contains nine eggs. In the poor early morning light, the colour is difficult to determine, but the eggs aren't white. Their background is probably beige/buff and the blotches and spots I imagine to be brown. Didn't want to examine too closely in case the hen, on returning to the nest, should detect an intruder. Now I know *where* and *how many*, I'll watch mainly through the monocular so as not to disturb them. The hen is back on the nest now. Her mate is always close to, almost guarding her. I wonder if he acts as a decoy if she is threatened – I know so little about quail. He has an unusual cry, not easy to describe – a wispy, haunting call that is quiet, yet sounds through the other birdsong all around. Once heard, it's not easily forgotten and is like no other bird note that I know.

I was told today of a man who takes his dogs badger-digging. He has started in a small way, but is being very successful. Did have a Land-rover the same type as seen on 20 May, but may not still have it. Clearly he is small fry – his contacts could prove interesting. Will try and find out what pub he frequents; Steve would be interested.

Bank Holiday Monday 28 May
Has at last stopped raining for a while. On Holmoak and Madden Lane, the flood warnings are out. Briarmead is not yet under water. Badgers very lively, if a trifle bedraggled. Sat on the gate at 4.30 a.m. watching the quail. When not at rest, they seem forever hurrying and pecking at this and that. The female only appears to incubate the eggs, leaving them briefly to feed. Close to, quail make a curious low-pitched double sound – very quiet – that has little carrying power. These bustling mini partridges are beautifully marked (the female less so), their stripes blend wonderfully into the background.

Tuesday 29 May
Package people at 1.15 a.m. Damp morning with rain showers. Badgers at both setts have dug out all the main entrances. The Old Cherry Sett has eight holes thus. Holly trees in flower, may blossom's musky scent is very cloying.

3.40 p.m. Sunny afternoon. Went to Ashcroft Woods after work. Found two of Josh's cubs shot dead at the den entrance – had been shot

275

since I left this morning. They were probably out playing in the strong sunshine between showers; the bodies are all wet now, but they wouldn't have come above ground during daylight if it was raining.

Wednesday 30 May

12.25 a.m. Warm, mild night with clear skies. Saw the badgers foraging on the fields, so slipped by undetected to climb high up in the Old Cherry and watch the squirrels. Sean Cooke asked me the other day what caused the oak catkins, complete with twig tips and leaves, to litter the ground in places. Was able to say that it was the work of squirrels in *certain* trees only. Squirrels like oak catkins even when unopened, but these are quite untouched. First one will start to nibble through a twig end, often clinging on with all four feet to do so; then others will follow suit. Notice the raw end near which they are clinging will be carefully licked, so is it sap they are after? Within an hour, a mature oak will have the ground beneath strewn with their work. A month earlier, they were doing this to aspen catkins.

Have seen a female squirrel moving her young ones to another nest again – watched this last spring also. This time, the original home was waterlogged. As before, the mother carried them one by one round her neck, as it were; she grasping the youngster at the side where the skin seems loose, whilst it clung tightly to its parent's fur, its tail curling up round her neck. She carried each very carefully, making no attempt to jump from branch to branch. Instead, she came down the trunk, across the open ground with many pauses to watch and listen, still carrying her burden. Then up the trunk of another tree, head held high to avoid injury to the nestling.

There seems to be a fair amount of fighting in the spring amongst grey squirrels, most of which is noisy with little injury sustained. Something happened around dawn this morning, however, which came as a complete surprise. Two squirrels chased another and finally overtook it on the main trunk of the Old Cherry. Now this trunk divides into three large branches, one lower and flatter than the other and it was this I was sitting on. The squirrels came racing down another branch and caught their victim just below me on the trunk. They fell upon it, biting until it moved and twisted no more, then they began washing themselves. Meanwhile, the male tawny who calls his boundaries about this time flew across to state his claim at a chestnut calling station near by, and immediately the squirrels were still. When he had flown off to repeat the performance nearer the Briarmead edge, one squirrel ran down the Old Cherry's trunk and disappeared amongst the fading bluebells. The remaining animal began grooming again, then stopped, approached the body – and broke open the head, for all the world as if it were breaking open a nut (the same action). Nothing was eaten. Did the sight of the head trigger off the nut-opening action? Then it too ran down the trunk and into the bluebells.

Walked round to the View Sett to check all was well there, Josh accompanying me. Then out again to the Wildflower Path where a heavy dew lay over the barley field, millions of tiny water droplets giving to it a paler, shining sheen. Josh left me and walked through the standing crop to his cubs' den in the Bank Sett and I saw his passing had left a perfect 'bruise' trail there. When a fox or badger walks thus, its passing shakes the stalks causing the dew to drop off the grass heads which become their natural, darker colour again, so marking or 'bruising' the way. Once the sun's warmth reaches the dew, it quickly evaporates and the trail is gone. Must bring a camera to photograph a bruise trail.

Thursday 31 May
Came out late this morning, 3.25 a.m., but with plenty of time to guard the setts. The moment I entered the wood, I sensed I wasn't alone, but was not concerned as at this time of year when the sky begins to lighten at 3.30 a.m., people are sometimes about early.

Checked for cars and, at the same time, the quail nest also. Fine, dry, warm morning with lovely dawn. Passed the Old Cherry Sett but didn't linger and continued straight to the View Sett. Everything fine, the woodland seeming filled with birdsong and a nightingale fluting at the field edge. At 5.30 a.m., I returned to the bluebell slope and stood by the Old Cherry there, one hand on the trunk, looking down the slope and enjoying the place. Suddenly remembered why I had brought the camera – the bruise trail I hoped might be visible again on Long Field.

Started down the slope just as three shots rang out behind me and something narrowly missed my head – not a shotgun or air rifle. Continued on to the path below and looked up the slope trying to see movement – nothing. Took a deep breath and ran back up, keeping the old tree's great trunk, I hoped, between me and the shooter. Stood behind the trunk trying to see who had shot at me. Then remembered that Mick Anderson, who works for Pete Williams, could be walking past here at any moment on his way to the farm and realised in horror that he might walk into something not intended for him. Ran down on to the Wildflower Path and along towards Briarmead. Then commonsense told me he probably wouldn't start the irrigation yet as the earth was still fairly wet. Had a tremendous feeling of relief. Walked to Briarmead, then quietly round to the little path that leads back to the Cherry Sett. No one. The shots might never have been, though I knew they had – nearly to my cost. But who?

SUMMER 1984

Monday 4 June 1984

Sometime between 7.30 a.m. when I left yesterday morning and 2.30 a.m. when I came here tonight, the Old Cherry Tree fell. It lies *across* the slope as one would expect and won't roll or move as two of its three branches (each the size of a mature tree) are steady on the ground. The great trunk is sunk into an old spoil heap with some of its roots still anchored in the ground. Provided enough nourishment can be obtained through the remaining roots, this giant of its kind may still continue to live. Be interesting to see if its tiny, green cherries swell and ripen. [No, they didn't; eventually shrivelled and dropped 29 August.] I've been carefully examining the trunk. The branch on which I sat doing my squirrel-watch last Wednesday has split, revealing the reddish-brown wood – lovely smell. The great tree makes a wonderful seat; a classroom of children could sit on it.

Walking up Briarmead at 4 a.m. to begin to check for cars, I had two pipistrelles for company. They flew round the damson trees hedging the lane, back over my head and on to the barley field opposite in their quest for insects that the damp warmth had brought forth.

Steve Hammond came this afternoon. Has had complaints and has inspected the smallholding of the man I heard about on 26 May, but not in connection with badgers. Has never found anything out of order, although Steve has suspected and challenged him with badger-digging. Man admitted to doing so before the Act. Steve interested that what I had been told confirms his suspicions. He has warned the man off, so he would be very foolish if he continued to dig.

Steve spoke about terrier shows. He was told that one is being organised soon locally. 'Business' is sometimes arranged privately at such events and though he knows the venue, he doesn't know the date. Will see if I can find it for him, but couldn't promise. (It's useful knowing someone like Steve – he gets me thinking along different lines!)

Friday 8 June

1 a.m. Sam found me at the Chantry tonight as I was sitting on the roots of a beech looking out over the valley. Very wet and warm after yesterday's heavy rain and everything smells marvellous. Both tawnies were busy hunting from the wood edge – earthworms and a baby rabbit carried back to the fledglings on the bank of Great Chantry Field. There are two owlets and they spend much of their time on a branch near the nest-hole, wing-flapping to strengthen their muscles for flight. I notice badgers have a good forage round such trees, as young owls are messy feeders. Scraps that go overboard are never wasted here. Sam waits until the parent birds go off hunting, however. He may have been attacked in the past.

3.10 a.m. On the Old Cherry trunk with Sam amongst the foliage that hangs down the slope when Lesley and the twins appeared from the field above. After greeting and musking me, Les had a dig-out of all six entrances used by her and the cubs, which triggered off the urge in her mate to clear his two. One of their youngsters scrambled on to my lap and began chewing a sleeve of my sweater. (I had hung my anorak on a tree when I came into the wood.) I tried to pull the material from between her teeth without it tearing – forlorn hope! From the young badger's viewpoint, this was a new game, especially when her sister joined in. I pretended to get cross, but that simply made them more persistent as they growlingly shook and worried at the sleeve. I might have stood up and pushed them away if we hadn't been perched on the prone trunk high off the ground which sloped steeply away below us. Finally smacked a snout rather hard, and a *very* offended young sow went to find her mother. Her sister took the hint – let go, and scrambled on to my knee, where she looked into my face. You can forgive a badger anything, even a wet and shapeless sleeve! Making herself at home, she began grooming on my lap, using me to lean back upon as she washed her chest and belly. My wet jersey soon collected a covering of hairs and, with the gnats taking an interest, I decided it was time to look at the quails before checking for cars. The young badger was of a mind to accompany me, but I pushed her back as, at 4 a.m., it was quite light. Only a van from Ireland staying overnight, otherwise nothing.

Sun a great orange disc breaking through haze – has the promise of a lovely day. I had great difficulty remembering where I had hung my anorak hours earlier! Hadn't realised there were so many trees in Ashcroft Woods.

Saturday 9 June

Am sitting on the Old Cherry at 5.10 a.m. writing up my notes. See someone has pushed a thick chestnut branch far down a sett entrance. Dragged it out with difficulty. Yesterday was hot and sunny; from the litter, a picnic took place on this old tree and, inevitably, the sett was of interest. Too large a branch for children to handle. Would have been teenagers or adults.

9 a.m. Went to see if the Hainses had returned from their holiday. In conversation, spoke of the quail's nest. Barry very interested, but worried when he realised where it was as the wheatfield should be sprayed – a fungicide. Told him its position as near as possible, but I had the impression he was reluctant to spray at all in case a slight wind should spread it. Wished I hadn't told him; it's his livelihood, after all. Pointed out that quails aren't common, but neither are they rare.

Wednesday 13 June

Warm night, beautiful full moon. Skylark high over the barley, singing, at 2.50 a.m., although it was quite dark. The grass ley above the Old Cherry Sett has been cut and the hay tedder has stirred the grass in the long swathes to dry – great badger country! Found Lesley and one half-grown cub worming under Pete's new irrigator, which was watering the crop *and* badgers. I spied Sam also a short distance off – but no sign of the other cub. The young twins generally stay together, so I felt something was wrong.

Thought I'd start searching from the sett and work my way round to all the likely places she might be. Didn't have to search far. A net had been pegged to one of the largest sett entrances and the cub was well entangled, tired and sweating. The single peg had been driven into the hard earth up to its hilt and I had a job myself to pull it out. Nylon net so no amount of chewing would have freed her. As she had pulled and struggled, so the drawstring had pulled up and tightened.

Two points puzzle me over this: 1) typical rabbit/ferreting net, but this was over one of the largest sett entrances, and this sett is one of the best-known badger setts in the locality; 2) how did the young animal come to go into it? Rabbits see the net, but with a ferret just behind them, choose to run into it rather than face the mustelid. A badger – cub or adult – emerges very cautiously. A ferret may face a fox, but not a badger, and the five-month-old cub wouldn't have feared such an animal. There are plenty of other sett entrances; unless of course, it wasn't a ferret that was chasing it ... Why wasn't it taken away by the person who owned the net? Were they disturbed – I know a runner goes through this wood about 8.30 p.m. each evening, and in the summer people come here until nearly dark. They would have had a job to free her if they were after an adult animal rather than a cub. Young badgers can give good account of themselves.

3.40 a.m. Saw the hen quail was off the nest, so crept over and had a look. Three tiny chicks, one with a large piece of shell still sticking to its rump! Of the remaining six eggs, one had cracks radiating from a central point. Didn't stay for fear of being discovered by the mother. Chicks were well covered with damp down; again, early morning light makes colour misleading, but I imagine the down to be an off-yellow with darker lines here and there, reminiscent of the parent birds. I sat on the wet gate a little later and watched the mother quail return to her brood. Morning sun touched the dew-drenched meadow just as a pair of partridge walked out of the hedge and settled comfortably down together very near the two horses. Many insects about – birds and bats busy in the clear air.

Thursday 14 June
I have to make sure neither of my foxes is accompanying me when I check the nest in Barry's wheatfield! Five chicks now; they peck around already – very pretty.

Met Josh's vixen quite late, 4.35 a.m., and walked behind her on the trail through the high barley at the bottom of Great Chantry. At one time, she stopped so abruptly just ahead of me that I nearly tripped over her. Her moult shows the true contours of her body. Foxes are built like miniature greyhounds and weigh little more than a domestic cat. On impulse, I bent down and encircled her back and belly with my two hands. My fingers touched beneath her, my thumbs touched above – her body neatly fitted within my hands. The vixen's head turned enquiringly at such unusual treatment, so I gently released her and put my face into hers.

At the Old Cherry Sett, Les has been digging out beneath the roots of the fallen tree. Earlier, the badgers were nosing along the swathes of cut grass on the field above – not quite dry enough yet for them. Another sunny day or two and they will be fetching in bedding. I love watching them do that. Even after all these years, it's always a thrill – and a small miracle – how they carry their bundles backwards to the sett and, so often, from a distance.

Met Mick Anderson on the path going to work at 5.15 a.m. The vixen nearly walked into him – she a little ahead of me – but she realised in time someone was walking round the corner.

281

Friday 15 June
Mrs Quail has nine healthy chicks keeping close to her as they move through the grass of the horses' meadow, peck-pecking as they go. Now, with their downy covering fluffed out, they look a lot larger than when I first saw them. Father feeds a short distance from the family.

Earlier, about 3.20 a.m. and light, Lesley and her cubs returned all muddy from worming under the sprays and found me climbing about along the Old Cherry. We had a great game amongst the branches suspended over the slope, the youngsters whickering with excitement. I had a thorough going-over by all three ladies. My bossy badger mother has finally met her match in her two daughters. If I used to think Lesley was a tearaway, well, these two leave her standing! I've had the toe of my boot chewed until it will probably let in water, and my hair 'groomed' – I'm sure *I've* got some bald places now – and the knee of my jeans musked. I'm covered in mud from their snouts and paws, so I'm feeling a very scruffy human at present.

(I phoned Ann Hains at 8.30 a.m. to let Barry know the quails were off the nest, so he can spray if it's not too late now. I wonder how many farmers would put a wheatfield in jeopardy for the sake of nine quail eggs?)

Saturday 16 June
Lovely warm night and morning – all quiet on the badger front.

7.20 a.m. I was photographing flowers along the Briarmead border when Josh jumped out of the damson hedge from the hayfield behind, a large rabbit gripped in his jaws. He saw someone standing there in the sunlight and, not scenting me, rushed off down the lane, his head held high to stop the rabbit dragging, and his claws click-clicking on the tarmac. I barked and he turned his head abruptly, the carcass swinging. Then he dropped his burden and ran up, tongue lolling. As he sprang up at me, a car appeared over the hump of the lane and stopped short of the dead rabbit. We both stared in surprise at the vehicle's unexpected appearance, then Josh turned and in one great leap cleared the bank and was gone. I ran down to the car and, picking up the rabbit, made to squeeze past, whereupon the man sitting next to the driver opened the door, effectively barring my way. His companion jumped out and clambered up the bank, but I knew he would see nothing but the field of waving barley – Josh was safe.

Why are people so anti-fox? Is it man's predatory instinct? Noticed both the car's occupants had guns, so they were coming here to shoot. They began questioning me about my fox. Was it a tame one and, if so, where was it going? One man caught hold of my arm and, as he did so, I remembered the rabbit. He tried to take it from me just as another car came up behind. He let go my arm and I squeezed past the cars and down the lane. I hurried along the path that separates the fields; the rabbit was surprisingly heavy – no wonder Josh looked so uncomfortable carrying it. Looked back and saw that both cars had gone – whether into the wood or back down the lane, I didn't know.

I was determined my fox should have his kill returned. At the beehives, I knelt and barked him up and, sure enough, the nettles parted and Josh leaned forward to smell his property dangling from my hand. I laid it on the ground between us and stroked his head. His brush waved as he inspected the rabbit. For a moment he regarded me, his cat's-eyes mere slits against the sun. Then gripping the rabbit carefully around the body and shifting it a little to balance, he turned with his burden into the tall nettles that closed behind him.

Tuesday 19 June
Julia Dougal came this evening; she is doing a flora survey of the woods – started last Tuesday. Has found what she believes to be a baiting or holding pit. She took a police constable to view it, but he said he needed expert opinion before he would comment. I'm curious as to what she has found, so I've agreed to meet her tomorrow to look at it. After she had gone, I thought of the Well shaft, dug to approx. twelve feet and never completed – wonder if it's that?

Wednesday 20 June
Met Julia and she took me to the old dug-out camp by the boundary fence. Not, of course, anything to do with badgers, but she wasn't to know. She is well used to woods and badgers, but finds our wood rather strange. I remember someone once described Ashcroft Woods as evil. How odd people are – how can a wood be evil? I don't think Julia is very keen either. This place *has* seen violence through the years but what town isn't without its murder or violence? We don't class them as evil. Talking to Julia has made me realise how much I take for granted here. The lone man who lived in the Chantry so long, the shelters and pits that folk have temporarily inhabited.

Thursday 21 June
Clear night with crescent moon. Lovely morning. The hay has been baled, stacked and taken away. The fields round about Briarmead are very beautiful – the long whiskered barley has a golden tinge. Honeysuckle hangs from the woodland trees – its scent lingers on the air. The badgers have been bringing in *their* hay. Sam left some caught up in the brambles and butcher's broom. I pulled it clear and offered it to him. He carefully bundled it under his chin and inevitably took it in backwards. Just before he disappeared below, he looked at me kneeling there and chittered – his eyes above the hay shining from the darkness of the entrance. Have become very attached to my badgers.

Monday 25 June
Had a day's leave, so was able to stay out late. Fox and badger cubs no

longer play together – both too big and have gone their separate ways. One of Lesley's daughters had a snapping contest with a former playmate at the edge of Long Field about 4.30 a.m. Rather sad really, but inevitable, I'm afraid. This woodland echoes with the continuous calling of the tawny fledglings; a persistent, penetrating sound.

Whilst guarding the setts these past weeks, I have also observed the grey squirrels. I say grey, but the term is more true of their winter pelage – now their coats are nearly russet in some individuals. Mating chases are very common in the early morning, several males pursuing a female along the tree-ways. Usually the female will play hard to get, but this morning I may have witnessed a reversal of this, when one took up a position in a chestnut coppice high above the slope, flicked her tail as she crouched along the branch, and began click-clicking. The sound started fast, then slowed and became a hoarse wail. She had repeated this three times, when another squirrel appeared in front of her. Both rushed off, however, as the tawny swooped towards them en route for his hooting tree. Whether she was calling a mate, I can't say – but it's a possibility.

I watched the sunrise over the Hayfield. These nights are so warm that I need no anorak or jersey. The freedom to run so with my foxes or merely climb about here is one of the assets of summer, but how I miss the long hours of darkness. The night is my friend; the ability to see well at night, my advantage.

8 a.m. Barry Hains drove up Briarmead Lane. I thanked him for not spraying the Wheatfield. He looked rather embarrassed and mumbled that it probably wouldn't have been necessary anyway. Changed the subject by teasing him for growing the opium poppy (*Papaver somniferum*) in this field, suggesting the wheat was a cover. He was rather startled until he realised I was joking.

Tuesday 26 June
Thin sliver of a moon in a velvety sky. I took some of Karen's young frogs, plus daphnia, common water crowfoot (*Ranunculus aquatilis*), frogbit (*Hydrocharis morsus-ranae*) and great ram's-horns snails (*Planorbis corneus*) to the stretch of water on Pete's land. This little lake is quite unpolluted and has great potential. I was going to wait until I saw Pete Williams before doing this, but the frogs are already too well developed for Karen's aquarium, so will speak to him as soon as possible and ask his permission to plant cuttings from the woodland's crack willow (*Salix fragilis*) and marsh marigold (*Caltha palustris*) that I have been offered from a local nursery on the mudflat there. Unlike the pond in Ashcroft Woods, it is little disturbed, as few people except the farmworkers know it exists.

Both families of badgers have been worming under the irrigators. Lesley's two cubs were *very* interested in my containers and my precious ram's-horns nearly became a badger snack! The other badger family is getting used to my presence and will forage within a few feet. Ernest

Neal was wrong when he said it was difficult to know badgers as I do – it's simply familiarity. I'm around every night and they eventually accept me. Anybody can do it and, indeed, I expect they do. I could get to know this other family really well but have no wish to – one group of badgers is quite enough!

Was looking at the packing station near by; the lettuces are packed on the field and taken straight to market. Turned round to find that Lesley had followed me on board and had taken hold of the loose end of the roll of plastic bags which, in consequence, was steadily unrolling! I hastily tore off the nearest to stop them all doing the same, rolled them up again, then went after my tearaway badger, anxious that she shouldn't swallow the rest. The more I tried to take them, the harder she clamped her teeth. Nothing is straightforward with Old Joe's daughter – she has his perseverance and stubbornness. In the end, I pretended to pick something off the ground and eat it – a favourite trick. Lesley immediately dropped the plastic and snuffled my hand, which saved the situation.

Badgers seem to have a liking for plastic. Old fertiliser bags, discarded gloves, carrier bags and bottles are often turned out with their bedding here, and show evidence of being well chewed. Have also found pieces in their dung, blue fertiliser bags being predominant!

Someone has interfered with the cubs' entrance of the Old Cherry Sett. It has been carefully blocked as if they were testing to see if it is occupied. The young badgers have cleared it. This was the entrance over which the net was pegged. There are ten well-used entrances at this sett; would this save the diggers time – putting their terrier down the most used entrance?

Friday 29 June
Everywhere is moist after yesterday's rain; fungus, especially stink-horns, in evidence. Bright, sunny morning. Someone is testing the twins' entrance at the Old Cherry Sett again, to see if it's actually occupied. A thick piece of branch, also sweet wrappers and leaves, pushed right in. The cubs dragged everything out and, on returning home at 4.15 a.m., had a glorious dig-out. Whoever did it now knows it's well and truly occupied. It's a secluded entrance hidden from the path below. I wish the police would patrol Briarmead as they used to, but short-staffed with the miners' pickets, they are deployed elsewhere.

Afternoon: Steve came in answer to my phone call, and we discussed the disturbed entrance. He goes on holiday tonight; Ralph (Barry Hains's friend) is already away and, with the police short-staffed, I will be on my own. I had decided that if anyone turned up this weekend, I'd let them dig for a while in order to incriminate themselves and thereby perhaps help to secure a conviction. He doesn't want me to, however, in case things go too far and can't be stopped, so will take his advice.

He asked me about Julia's baiting pit; no one had told him that it wasn't. Conversation led to survival holes and camps. Young men (ex-army or otherwise) often dig these, which are later abandoned and last like this indefinitely. That in Ashcroft Woods is used by lads sometimes in the summer and is so deep they have a rope tied to a tree to help them climb in and out.

Saturday 30 June
1.10 a.m. Lovely warm night. Took pondweed and water-snails to Pete's lake, accompanied by the twins. These young badgers are very interested in everything I do. Like human children, they want to be involved and quickly lose interest and misbehave if not allowed to. Like children, too, each vies for my attention and pushes my patience to the limit. Their reactions to a scolding are quite different one from the other, though. The largest cub goes off – her sister tries to make-up, peering into my face and chittering softly. Am determined to protect them and the other badgers here from the diggers, come what may.

Lesley, Sam and their cubs play together a great deal. Have never known a boar badger join in so much as Sam. The whole family are very young. Les is a yearling, Sam only two years old, so this could account for it.

4.05 a.m. at the Old Cherry Sett. Birds' alarm calls, so know the owls are around. Sure enough, tremulous hooting and answering. How fearful are the little birds.

Sunday 1 July
Wading in the Main Pond, accompanied by the twins, found my left boot *does* let water in through the top of the foot. That's what comes of

badgers chewing it! (*See* 18 June.) Retreated hastily with a wet foot. After they had gone to earth, I climbed into the Old Cherry's branches that hang out over the slope. Some while later, as I was writing up my notes, Lesley reappeared, musked my jeans and scrambled on to my lap as I sat there on the branch. She soon smelt my apple that I had left in a crevice of the cherry bark, and tried to take it. I make a rule not to feed my badgers or foxes (except when getting Les to take her antibiotic capsules last year, or picking blackberries with them). This apple was destined for *me* – hours out in this wood, I tend to get thirsty – and a piece for each of Barry's horses in the meadow. So a rather disgruntled badger went below in disgust.

4.55 a.m. Heard someone moving on the little path behind me. They stopped and there was a pause of some minutes. Then the sound again and a man appeared who looked carefully all round – but not up – then stepped out into the open. As he turned to motion another man to approach, he caught sight of me sitting amongst the foliage above and to his left. Stared scowling at me. Carried what at first I took to be a long stick but was, in fact, a painted metal rod approx. five feet long (half an inch in diameter?). The men looked at one another, nodded and walked up the slope towards the field above. As they went, the second man turned – saw me still watching them – and spat. I decided not to try following them as they wouldn't lead me to a car, too wily. Didn't want to leave the setts too long either, in case they doubled back. I had just jumped off the tree, intending to check for cars in the direction from which they had come, when Les reappeared. I told her sternly to go back and, tucking my apple for safekeeping under the tiny elder growing against the Old Cherry, I ran down the slope to look for vehicles in the immediate area. Nothing, however, so returned to make sure both the View Sett, then the Old Cherry were untouched.

I saw and heard no more of the two men and at 7.15 a.m. decided it was safe to leave. Planned to walk down Briarmead to share my apple with the horses. However, no apple was there – vanished without trace. Had a sudden thought and looked at Lesley's entrance with a grin – some badgers *are* pigs!

Wednesday 4 July
Lesley found me sitting in the Chantry tonight, but after musking me, she wandered off and dug out her father's old sett in the hollow near by. Watching Joe's daughter, I recalled them making a home together in this place last October. She's lovely badger.

4.20 a.m. A length of grey mist is snaking out of the hollow of the horses' meadow and into the wheat. The rising sun has banished it elsewhere – just this creeping swathe remains. As it moves, so the horses come into view and, seeing me, trot up in greeting as I slip through their wire. The nightjars have been busy this morning here in their quest for

287

insects, also the bats. I regret I haven't observed the former as I have other years, but guarding the setts each morning now takes up much of my time – and energy. And the badgers must come first if they are to survive.

Friday 6 July

Thick mist envelopes the land, though in the wood it is clearer. I think sometimes that the dense foliage makes a living wall which holds it back. Came down the sett slope at 4.40 a.m. to see the two men of last Sunday – one with his metal rod just beyond an entrance, looking at the ground, the other by the Old Cherry's trunk as if on guard. I challenged them and the younger man advanced towards me brandishing the rod (which I saw was pointed at one end). His companion remonstrated with him. Then both strode away down the slope, the aggressive one turning round as he went to shout a warning not to follow them or he'd smash me. When they had gone, I had a quick look along the wood edge in the opposite direction as, again, I didn't feel they had been going towards their car. Wondered what significance the rod had apart from being a weapon. The thin end solid for a probe (see 22 January 1983).* Several points about this encounter are worth noting:

1) When challenged, the man made no attempt to appear innocent;

2) I was soaked from the heavy mist. Hair, pullover, jeans, all very wet. The younger man, when he approached me, was scarcely damp which indicates he was either very local or, more likely, had only just got out of a car;

3) I feel certain they were checking the sett before calling in others. A car could have dropped them and continued up Briarmead and so to the Main Pond area, but it's too far to check quickly.

Sunday 8 July

Watched three young wrens on the Wildflower Path being fed by their mother. Barry's men have deposited a load of old grain at the dump, so I took a handful and spread it on the surface of Briarmead Lane to see what it might encourage forth while I sat on the gate. Rabbits!! What price Watership Down! The young ones did little sideways skips and were very playful until a handsome cock pheasant came sauntering out of the barley of Long Field loudly proclaiming his ownership and scattering them all.

At the Oak Dell, found Tagless shot and dying, time 9.15 a.m. Knelt at his side until he died, nothing else I could do. If people must shoot, how I wish they would do so cleanly. Fortunately his agony was soon over – but not soon enough. The sunlight filtering through the foliage dappled

*28 October 1985: Reading *Death of a Badger* sent to me by Sgt C. Parkes, Derbyshire Constabulary, 'The presence of metal bars or rods ... bars are used to trace the line of a tunnel.'

288

his tawny body as it lay in the dust. I put him in the undergrowth and went home across the sunlit fields.

Monday 9 July

Mild, warm night with half-moon clear in the sky. At 5.45 a.m., saw a squirrel raid a crow's nest on the bank between Long Field and Great Chantry. It ran off, leaping from tree to tree along the bank, the mother bird calling and diving at it. It tried to dodge the parent and find somewhere to eat its victim, but the crow wouldn't let it be. Long after the squirrel had disappeared with its prey into the hollow trunk of a dead ash, the crow was still calling as she flew round outside.

8 a.m. Barry Hains drove up Briarmead and stayed talking. Asked me about the badger situation. Both he and I have noticed the same thing – that this year there are far fewer ordinary people frequenting the wood of a morning. Barry feels they are nervous of encountering antagonistic badger-diggers. Strangely, one of my Warby contacts said the selfsame thing last week – but as a statement of fact, not opinion. How sad that such a lovely wood should not be enjoyed at the best time of the day. My contact had added, 'Should anyone hear you in trouble, they would probably rush home and phone, but they'd not go to your aid. You would be on your own. There's just too much fear both of being hurt and of reprisals.' I think, then, that rumour is worse than reality. After all, it's not that bad up here.

9.15 a.m. Went to call on Pete Williams at his farm office. He gave me permission to stock the lake and plant the mudflat below the Motorway provided I accept that at any time his boss, Mr Corbett, or the Council, might decide to drain it. I said that was fair enough and thanked him. It appears there is a culvert beneath the lake which is blocked (as well as that further along), and sometimes it causes flooding in Warby. The Council drained it two years ago and should, in fact, do so every six months.

Pete asked me about the badger situation; he was interested in the effects of irrigation on the badgers.

Tuesday 10 July

I carried two plants each of white water-lily (*Nymphaea alba*) and yellow water-lily (*Nuphar lutea*), plus some more water-snails to the lake tonight. Had seen them in the nursery when I collected the marsh marigold and couldn't resist them. I planted them well before dawn in spite of my 'helpers'. These badgers are like puppies, viewing the whole affair as a game. As I remonstrated with one of the cubs, I heard a crunching sound and turned to see Sam with his snout in the snail container. Took it from him and held it high out of his reach, whereupon he jumped up at me so that I lost my balance and sat down with a splash in the water! The remaining water-snails dropped to freedom into the safety of the lake and an excited Sam ran up and down the bank barking.

Wednesday 11 July
Planted marsh marigold in the lake; also young willow, spindle and bullace at the far end. Had avoided the badgers, so worked without mishap.

There is always traffic noise and sometimes voices from the Motorway, so I didn't at first register someone calling me. Then looked up to see three men sitting on the barrier above! They asked me where the badgers were this morning, then came down the steep bank to talk. They are long-distance lorry drivers, two are English, the other foreign. They must have left their vehicles on the hard shoulder, I imagine. It seems that one has been aware of me on these fields a long time, and he asked what had become of the 'great big badger'. Old Joe, of course. This is worrying, so I asked them to keep it quiet. Think they probably will as they seemed very concerned when I explained the dangers of publicity.

Friday 13 July
Went out at 1.30 a.m., fine night again – full moon, very beautiful. Came across a man carrying a hold-all on the Sleet Path; couldn't avoid being seen owing to the moon, but occasionally see people on warm summer nights so didn't think too much about it. However, changed my mind when he produce a knife. (Don't think he'll try it again, though!)

Met Josh and his vixen on the Ridge, just as it began to rain. It's been dry so long that I'd given no thought to an anorak – just T-shirt, jeans and the inevitable boots (long grass is nearly always dew-laden in the hot weather). The encounter with the man made me unsettled, so I went and checked the dug-out camp, as last weekend it was occupied. No one there, however, so climbed down into one of the holes. Neither fox would come down, though, the vixen whining uneasily from above. Didn't like it much myself – there's a suffocating, trapped feeling to such places – so climbed out and went with them to the Yewtree Grove. Remembered telling Steve last time we met of the oblong pit dug here fifteen years ago, that within a couple of days was filled and disguised (*see* 2 July 1981). Tried to decide where it was – the rain now heavy, but quite dry under these ancient trees. Fifteen years is a long time, though, so can't be sure. What a store of secrets this wood hides.

Sunday 15 July
The falling of the Old Cherry has left a large oblong of sky, clear of foliage. As all living growth here struggles upwards towards the light, so the dormant elder, cherry and chestnut seeds have sprouted and begun their skywards journey. The play area that the badger cubs once used is now moss-covered with invasive bramble creeping over. The deep fissures of the great tree's prone trunk are drinking places for the birds. Guarding this sett is far from boring, and now that both badger families (except for the sub-dominant boar) are together here, I feel I can stay longer without passing to and from the View Sett quite so often. This

290

morning I've seen the hawfinches drinking here; also cracking the cherry stones that litter the ground. The flesh of the tiny red fruit is ignored – it is just the kernel inside the stone that they eat.

7 a.m. Watched a short-tailed vole busily searching for food below me as I sat on the Wheatfield gate in the sunshine. It disappeared under a tussock of grass off the path. Butterflies and bees moving amongst the dogrose and wildflowers. Lovely summer's morning.

Thursday 19 July
Heard that Barry Hains has had his hay barn destroyed. It could only have been arson. Wondered who – though not, of course, why. Think he has four hayfields in all – and he brought it in under ideal conditions, so it would have fetched the highest price. What a loss.

Doing the rounds with Josh. The wild gean's cherries are surprisingly sweet when ripe. Birds, foxes and badgers enjoy them, and so do I! Josh and I are competing for the best as we walk along the Wildflower Path. Eyes down scanning the ground for the red/black fruit, we have twice collided head-on as we go for the same one! All quiet and peaceful at the setts, time 5.45 a.m.

Friday 20 July
1.10 a.m. Had a marvellous romp with the badger twins tonight. A good game is hiding from them behind a tree. As fast as they spot me, I run to another, dodge round it, then away up the slope; their Old Cherry trunk is home. When they are full from foraging like this morning, I can make rings round them. They chase after, puffing and squeaking their indignation. Then seated on the ground, they clamber all over me. These sturdy young animals are already two-thirds grown – and strong. They feel like small battering rams when they cannon into me. I enjoy rolling myself into a ball, head in lap and arms tight round knees. Whining, they frantically scrabble at me, trying to find my face. Then a snout is pushed down past my ear until it finds my cheek and jaw. Its owner pushes and pushes until I lift my head, whereupon the 'winner' grooms me, purring as she does so. Fortunately, they don't use their claws much when we play, or I couldn't do this. What is a mere scratch to themselves, furred and with that almost rubber-like skin, is a ripping of flesh to me. They are wild animals, after all, and have no notion of the wounds they could unwittingly inflict now that their digging claws are fully developed. Lesley trusts me completely with her daughters, and Sam invariably turns up too. I have never had such joy with badgers.

It is incredible to think that in June 1983 their mother, herself a cub then, was so sick that the vet and I discussed putting her down if she didn't improve. Such a short time ago, yet so much has happened in a year. This little family is young, healthy and full of life and energy. Feel I am very privileged to know them. Watched the Wheatfield boar go to earth. Think he would come up to me if I didn't move off so abruptly

291

when he appears, but I don't feel it is wise to know any more badgers. His family have moved to the Old Cherry Sett. There would be plenty of room for him too, but Sam is dominant there and won't permit it.

At 4.50 a.m., returned to the Cherry Sett and walked straight into three men, two of whom I have encountered before on the first and sixth of this month. Two carried spades; the other (who on a previous occasion had threatened me with a metal rod) carried a rifle. Two terriers and a larger dog accompanied them. I was completely unprepared, although they were obviously not surprised to see me. The whole situation very tense. Told them to move off, which they did, but not before the armed one had pushed me backwards and down with the butt of his weapon, kicking me where I lay. As they went down the slope, I was warned not to follow. Had an idea where they might be going, so I gave them a few minutes, then slipped back up the slope and went diagonally through the undergrowth on my foxes' trail. Waited, and sure enough they appeared on the path below. Followed with ease at a distance, until suddenly the large dog gave voice and I was discovered. The armed man fired over my head and shouted that the next one would be through my skull. One of his companions – the older man seen previously here – told me to turn round and go back or his friend would shoot me. The one with the rifle seemed almost hysterical – very voluble and abusive. He threatened to come back and 'fix' me – wonder if he will? (*See* 25 November 1984.) With regret, I took the man's advice and returned to the sett.

Stayed until 7.45 a.m. then went to sit on the Wheatfield gate since Barry Hains was due by at about 8 a.m. Told him what had happened earlier, then discussed the firing of his hay barn. It was first seen at 11.45 p.m. last Thursday. His new equipment stored there went up in the blaze with 400 bales of last year's hay and 6,000 of this. He seemed quietly resigned to the fact – felt very sorry for him and his family. Discussed the possibility of these fields being fired; I feel this is less likely to happen of an early morning, though I always keep a look-out when the harvest is ready and everywhere dry. Think myself it's much more likely to happen in the late evening. He said things are quieter up here in that respect since the Motorway was built; not so many odd people hanging around. Interesting, that.

Sunday 22 July
2.15 a.m. Warm night with clear crescent moon. On the partly harvested barleyfield at the Briarmead edge, Lesley and her daughters have been gleaning the dropped grain. They have also played in the swathes of cut straw and are now very dusty. They sit in a group on the tarmac, scratching and washing. I stand on the bank watching the headlights far below me on the Main Road. The badgers twist and crane to get at the awkward places, sometimes nibbling where a burr is snarled into the coat. Three together doing this are comic; now they are mutually grooming each other's heads and ears.

292

Alfie, one of Barry's men, has ploughed and rolled the hayfield opposite and left the roller here. One cub scrambles on to it, King of the Castle style, and barks at her sister. The other tries to get up too, is pushed back and runs round 'nik-nikking'. She sees her sister's tail hanging down one side and pulls hard. Major disaster area – there is a yelp as one cub falls on the other. Les has gone downfield in disgust to some fresh molehills on the rolled surface. Digs down swiftly. A quick twist and the mole is thrown clear in the air. The badger pounces as it lands and chops it briefly.

3.40 a.m. I leave them and walk down to the Wheatfield gate and sit there quietly as a soft trail of pink shows in the eastern sky. Many, many insects over these fields; bats and nightjars busy. The bats seem to prefer the hedgerow near my gate and the Wheatfield itself. The nightjars hunt over the horses' meadow. Certainly neither appears bothered by the others. There's a movement on the lane and Les is there, her white mask with its black stripes still showing up with startling clarity though the sky is becoming lighter. She has followed my scent trail and I'm amused to see that she's lost it at the gate. It's a high six-bar metal one so I'm a good way off the ground. She squeezes under, then casts round in search of my scent the other side. Back she comes, picks my trail up – and loses it again. I whisper, 'Les' and she looks up, then stretches on hind legs towards me. Satisfied all is well, she yawns largely, showing a fine set of teeth! Then a very full-up badger settles herself in a ball in the tangle of traveller's joy that descends from the gate-post – and goes to sleep!

A few birds are stirring; the skylarks over the fields (no owls – July is a quiet month vocally for tawnies) and a crow caws suddenly from the wood edge. My short-tailed vole (*see* 15 July) appears again from under its tussock of grass off the path. It is almost under Lesley's nose when it seems to sense danger. Then two things happen simultaneously. The agile vole darts back home and my not-so-agile badger dives after it. Quickly her snout digs into the superficial runway and her jaws close over the owner. Just a small conical pit and the tussock is cast aside to tell the tale. I feel rather indignant – I liked that little vole. But so then did Lesley!

5.10 a.m. The badgers had gone to earth and it was quite light. Walked up to the View Sett where I surprised some men round the back entrance of the hollow. But the holly tree obscured my view and they moved off into the far undergrowth. Checked the boar's entrance quickly and saw it was untouched, but they have attempted to drag clear the dead trunk that partly hides and protects it.

Went back to the Old Cherry Sett – all quiet; then walked up the slope to the ploughed and rolled Hayfield (where the cubs played this morning). Beyond Briarmead on the skyline, I saw a figure walking through the cut barley. It stopped and looked all around as if searching for something – or making sure the coast was clear! Through the monocular, saw it was [description of man omitted]. Now in the centre of the field, he gathered the straw into a heap, then took something from inside his anorak. I saw a flame jump – and I shouted with all my might. He stood up and looked down the lane. I ran across the field and on to the Briarmead bank opposite. He must have wondered where I had come from as he was only visible to me from the wood edge high up, and now, of course, from the lane. The flame, I think, must have been a lighter. He hadn't lit the straw. He turned and ran back the way he had come as I came on to the barley field. Followed him a short distance to see which path he would take. After saying to Barry only two days ago that I thought early mornings were safe from arson up here, how ironic. Looked at my watch, just 5.45 a.m. Had to return to the setts in case of trouble there, but came and went via the wood edge too, although I didn't think the arsonist would be back – today.

Sunny morning. Blue sky with wispy fluffs of cloud. Stretching to the horizon, field upon flaxen field of barley blowing in the wind with Paddy's cottage nestling amongst it. A beautiful scene that could turn into a nightmare – by the careless drop of a cigarette stub or the deliberate flame of a lighter. No hydrants here. Once under way, a fire with this wind would have swept towards the farmyard, consuming hedge and field after field. Once under way, nothing could stop it.

When all seemed safe, I walked to Newby Farm and told Barry about his ill-intentioned visitor. Promised to keep vigilance each morning and to phone from Mick's cottage if there's any trouble. Left a very worried farmer standing at the gate – wish I could do more.

Friday 27 July
Ernest Neal wrote to me today: 'The badgers here are suffering badly
from drought. Cubs have died of starvation and adults have been seen at
all hours of the day foraging. We've hardly had any rain for months and
the fields are brown and hard.' How fortunate the badgers are here to
have the irrigated fields. If, however, it continues dry, water may be
limited.

As each field of barley here is cut, so Barry Hains and his men are
moving the straw from the edge and ploughing a fire-break all round.

Very few cherries are left now, just pieces of shell. Birds, squirrels,
badgers and foxes have all gathered the cherry harvest, and the
hawfinches have had the kernels. I watched three young foxes squabbling over the last ones on the Wildflower Path. They're handsome
creatures – very leggy and developing fast. At 6.30 a.m., the sun already
well up in a bright blue sky and *hot*.

The sun spotlights the woodland's gloom, and a gnat dances in one
such patch, just above the badger cubs' entrance. A small, sleek head
appears briefly – then is gone. An argument from inside the sett.
Someone late for bed is disturbing another. Much of this place is still
dark, but through the trees the sun has turned the barley of Long Field
to gold. Distant traffic and nearby birdsong are the only sounds.

Saturday 28 July
Have been with Lesley and her cubs as they forage on Barry's
Wheatfield. Now it's ripening, the badgers' diet is changing. Although
more barley is grown here, and they eat a little, wheat is preferred. Went
with them to the up-and-over path at the bank on the top of this field. I
let the family go first and then made to crawl under the wire myself,
whereupon the smallest cub came round and through again with me,
chittering in my face as we did so. Lay on the grassy bank feeling her
snout explore my face. My hair – as always – came in for a lot of
attention, as did my ears. Saw Lesley sitting watching us, placid and
gentle; how trusting and patient she is. Got up carefully to move on
(always fear I may tread on a cub), and happened to look down. Saw my
jeans were a mass of cleavers – that is, the globular fruits of goosegrass
that are covered in hooked spines. Realised for the first time where it is
that the badgers' coats get entangled with the tiny barbed burrs.

Much later when the badgers had gone to earth and it was well light,
saw Josh's vixen come out of the barley on Long Field. Barked to her
once, twice, and she came trotting towards me, brush waving. Knelt to
greet her – haven't met for some time. (I wonder how Tagless's vixen is
faring, now that her mate is dead.) She came with me up Briarmead, and
as we passed the ash tree, six squirrels raced across the lane to the safety
of the wood. I've noticed before that they too glean for the grain once the
combine has finished.

Sunday 29 July

I found the Wheatfield gate wide open. A vehicle has been driven in, flattening the side of the crop and so into the horses' meadow. The fence between Wheatfield and meadow can be moved to allow entrance. This has been done, then the fence replaced. See by the grass that the vehicle was driven over the meadow almost up to the gate into Newby Farm, then turned round and driven back on the same route. Barry's horses haven't been here for the past forty-eight hours. They've been in the home paddock with the other young horse. How fortuitous – wonder if Barry had a suspicion that something was afoot? Left the Wheatfield gate open, so he would see what had happened when he came up the lane later.

4.45 a.m. Met a patrol on Briarmead. Asked about the badger situation; one said he had questioned some men parked here in the afternoon recently. They had cages and dogs with them and said they were after foxes and rabbits. (Whatever they were after, they were doing it illegally as neither the Hainses nor the Council permit such activity on their property – and also, fox pelts are no good now the animals are moulting.) They had checked the vehicle number with their collator – and found they came from the city, and had records. They also told me

296

that Don Francis had some dogs stolen. Found this rather cheering – nothing like having the biter bit!

Monday 30 July
Little 'un, the smallest cub, is limping badly. Met the family as they foraged in the Wheatfield. Her pad was so dusty that I couldn't see what ailed it, especially as she pulled away so. Obviously very painful. Wetted a tissue in my mouth and wiped all over the pad which had swollen up and covered what was embedded there. Laid the cub upside down on the grass by the path and held her there with my knee, to leave both hands free. She cried dreadfully – unlike her mother last year – until I finally drew out a long, straight thorn, as long as the first joint of my thumb. (She must have scrambled through the blackthorn hedge beside the lane; it's quite a thicket in places.) The whole pad was *very* pussy; pressed most of it out. Her sister, upset by the noise, ran off into the wheat, but Lesley just stood quietly by me. When I had finished, I offered her the cub's paw, still holding the youngster down. Her mother set to and washed it very thoroughly, also the pus that had run down the leg – and lastly, my hand! Put the cub on its feet again and scratched behind its stick-up ears. Put my arm round Les – she's her father's daughter all right.

Tuesday 31 July
Sean Cooke, helped by a friend, is putting out the Longworth small mammal traps tonight, then watching for the badgers to emerge. I will meet them on Wednesday morning when they come to check the traps.

Wednesday 1 August
Lapwings feeding on the irrigated fields along Madden Lane. A short distance off, I found badgers – and Tagless's vixen – worming. The ribbons of water running down between the rows of lettuces shine briefly as a vehicle passes on the Motorway.

3.40 a.m. Had just crossed over to the wood side of the road and was checking to see that the cubs didn't follow, when I looked up to see a car with dipped headlights coming along the track that leads from Colts Farm. Still with thoughts on the cubs, I took it mistakenly for a patrol car and came back on to the tarmac to meet it. The driver saw me, there was a blaze of headlights, and the vehicle seemed to leap towards me. Realised my mistake and jumped out of the way just in time. Turned to watch it race off into the darkness; only time to note part of its registration number. Feel sure I've seen this car pass by me on Madden Lane before; a vehicle at this time of night is something of a rarity.

7 a.m. Lovely morning. Much of the barley here is cut; wheat and two spring-sown barleyfields are not quite ripe. Sean Cooke and friend arrived. They heard lots of badger noise last night, but were in the wrong position to view. Walked round to collect the traps. Nothing in any of them – seventy traps in all – what a disappointment. Plenty of small

mammals here, so conclude now is probably the height of their breeding season and, with food aplenty and with young to feed, they would shun anything strange. Sean can't keep the traps out several consecutive nights as people soon connect the markers with the traps, and then they are stolen. He'll try again in September. Speaking to Sean's friend about the nightjars, I found that he had worked with these birds before. Lovely to find someone who knows and likes them as I do. The nightjar's recorded call lures them to the nets for ringing. Sean suggested doing this in the horses' meadow, if the nightjars still frequent it now that the horses have been moved to the paddock. (Their manure attracts insects that, in turn, attract the nightjars.) I'll ask Barry Hains's permission to do this and give him Sean's car number.

After some hesitation, I phoned Pete Williams to tell him about the car. Apologised for having so little to go on, but he seemed grateful that I had bothered. Said he had been driving round the night before until 1 a.m. since so much equipment is being stolen from the fields under cover of darkness. The police are helping; in fact, they stopped him twice last night, once coming down the Motorway bank to do so! Feel rather bad about the thefts as not only do I see patrol cars on Pete's land at night, but other cars also. I merely keep well beyond the headlights, especially if I have the badgers in tow. However, will make an effort to track down any car on the fields and pass on the number. He told me to get him out of bed if there's anything going on.

Monday 6 August
The coldest morning this summer – my breath vaporises before me. Everywhere is damp after the weekend rain. At 5 a.m., even the birds seem reluctant to be the first to sing. Lesley and her cubs, homeward bound, have just squeezed under my gate, crossed the lane and so on to Long Field. Watched the cubs trailing behind their mother, she well up front and progressing at a steady pace between the curving lanes of cut barley stalks, they meandering behind, occasionally stopping to pick up dropped grain, more often to have a game in the straw. A favourite is to run into a pile with snout held low. The cub disappears and the straw heaves convulsively; its sister jumps on the writhing heap with barks of excitement. Sometimes a mouse or vole finds its temporary home disturbed and makes a hasty exit. The twins aren't quick enough to catch them, but it all adds to the game. The youngsters are very wet; their bodies shiny and darker looking. Think their mother is glad to get home and underground. Her cubs, like human children, are lingering before going reluctantly to bed.

All is quiet – the badgers gone. The straw is slowly turned to purest gold as the rising sun touches Long Field. Encouraged by its promised warmth, a lone turtle-dove begins a softly cooing refrain. Below my gate, the rabbits graze, quite oblivious of me up top although my lengthening shadow stretches out to meet them. I like gates!

Thursday 9 August
I picked the year's first blackberries in Briarmead. The only ones ripe as yet are those caught by the sun right on top of the bushes there. Lesley knew exactly what I was doing and came racing up the lane to get her share. She can't remember from last August; she couldn't have smelt a few on top of a bush at that distance; so how did she know? Where her stomach's concerned, Lesley always knows. She's a chip off the old block all right! Her cubs soon realised they were missing out and stood up on hind legs chittering with impatience. There just weren't enough black-berries to go round!

When it was safe to leave the setts this morning, I planted more young trees – willow, gean and sweet chestnut – by Pete's lake. One day, long after I'm gone, perhaps this forgotten corner will be a beautiful place. Have great happiness here, quietly weeding and planting on my own. I don't really notice the Motorway just above. Found a burnished feather – duck? – on the mudflat, like none other that I know. Not a woodland bird, for sure. There are quail in the grass ley by the lake. Sometimes I look up the slope and see them peck-pecking amongst the herbage, or hear their wispy call.

Saturday 11 August
Full moon, cloudy skies; cold, dry dawn. 5.10 a.m. Heard an adult quail and saw a parent and three offspring in the uncut barley along Briarmead. All the barleyfields except this one are cut and many, Long Field included, are baled. It's the busiest time of the farming year.

6.50 a.m. The sun is well up and has broken through the clouds – it has the promise of a lovely day. The bales of straw on Long Field are scattered like so many matchboxes over the golden stubble. Much earlier, the tawny male was using a stack of three for a hunting post. With the dropped grain, there are plenty of gleanings for mice and voles. The tawny fledglings are hunting for themselves now and are no longer dependent on their parents. But this is their most vulnerable time. Gradually this month, they will leave the area in search of one of their own. If they fail to secure a territory, then they starve. Once such a territory is established, however, it is held for life, just as they mate for life. The youngsters get by on beetles and earthworms until their ability to hunt improves and they learn to catch small rodents and moles, like their parents. One was lucky tonight and came upon the still-warm body of a mole that Tagless's vixen had killed and left. (It seems to me that the hunting instinct in a fox is triggered off by *movement* – and sound. A fox does not necessarily eat everything it kills, and shrews, moles and toads are generally left. It's interesting, however, that moles are frequently killed by an adult fox and carried back to be eaten by their cubs.)

At 7.15 a.m., met Tagless's vixen carrying a blackbird. Made the soft contact sound, and she put it down to greet me. Am sorry her mate was shot – have a great regard for my foxes. I followed her as she picked up

299

her prey and went through the underbrush until a short way from the den. Foxes teach their cubs to hunt for themselves by fetching back less and less for them, and by leaving it further and further from the den so that, in searching for the kill, they find small prey for themselves. Beetles are probably the first creatures a very young cub learns to catch.

· Of the three offspring, one young fox is a light sandy colour, in great contrast to the others. It has no black facial markings, or black colouring at all at, for instance, the backs of ears and front of legs; no white tip to tail – another Tagless. At a glance, it appears very un-foxlike.

Tuesday 14 August
Cold, misty night. The badgers are foraging in the firebreak and gleaning on one of the harvested barleyfields just off Briarmead. Sam had a running battle with a gull who was determined to take a high dead rabbit he found amongst the straw; it was probably killed by the combine several days ago. Notice that gulls feeding with the lapwings will take food from them too, even chasing the peewits until they drop it. However, this boar badger wasn't letting the seabirds put anything over him and nearly added gull to his menu. He jumped up and caught one by a leg as it flew off. As its wings flapped round his face, the boar let go and it escaped, though injured.

Left the badgers (I thought!) and walked through the Poplar Row – crossing Clifford's Bank en route. [The old boundary bank between Barry Hains's land and Glebe Farm.] Thought I would pick myself some blackberries as I was very thirsty. However, Les and her cubs caught up with me as I was walking through the orchard. Turned to see them coming up behind me – Lesley wheezy and puffing from her run (badgers aren't built for marathons) – and hit the back of my head *hard* on a low branch laden with near-ripe Conference pears. It rained pears for a moment – I saw stars – and the badgers were delighted! Obviously thought I had knocked the fruit down just for them. A great sound of crunching, munching and slurping – they're noisy animals at times. Of course, they had to have a share of the blackberries too, though these they picked for themselves, wrinkling their snouts back and biting off each sweet, ripe fruit with ease.

7.30 a.m. Weeding at the lakeside with swifts catching insects just above the water. Pulling up clumps of pineapple weed (a very invasive plant here), I found that clouds of insects, probably thriving at ground level in the warm dampness, were coming up with it. First one bird, then another, saw this too. In a moment, I was surrounded by swifts. Diving, banking, turning, twisting around my head. Tiny beaks, yet wide gapes; diminutive legs with long, curved toes; short tails but long, back-curving wings – they're a study in contrasts. Pulled more weed, held it up and more clouds of tiny insects rose in the air. For a long time they took the insects. Have never had such close contact with these birds, even when watching them from the Wheatfield gate.

9.10 a.m. Walking back to Briarmead, saw Alfie taking Long Field's baled straw away. Several bales had to be left as their twine has been deliberately cut.

Sunday 19 August
No early morning mist. Very mild night; clear, starry skies and broken half-moon.

Walked round the edge of Great Chantry Field and amongst the barley stubble I found many sprouting beech mast – tiny trees – which will only be turned under when the field is ploughed. Will plant these also by the lake. I feel I have an affinity with the man who so lovingly planted the Chantry trees two centuries ago. Strange to think that the progeny of *his* beeches may grow there. Is Pete's lake my Chantry, I wonder?

Josh accompanied me round the woods at dawn. At the Main Pond, we met up with his vixen, so I had a two-fox escort! After badger-watch, walked down to the Motorway and planted two more yellow flowering water-lilies in the lake. Had just finished and was standing quietly in the water when the long grass parted and a hen 'red-legs' with her seven chicks came out. The youngsters, cheeping as they came, were busy pecking at the ground when one ahead of the others came to the end of the grass and dropped straight over into the lake! The tiny bird set up a cry as it struggled in the water – I moved – and the adult partridge saw me. In an instant she was running off, calling and trailing a 'broken' wing in an effort to divert my attention to herself. I waded over and gently lifted out the tiny chick, took hold of the end of my jersey and patted it dry, then set it on the ground. (Felt like Gulliver amongst the Lilliputians!) Pretty creature in spite of its wetting; the adult's eye-stripe and back markings were already clear in its down. It ran towards its mother cheep-cheeping loudly and the other chicks (who all this while had remained crouched and still in the grass) ran with him also. Think the hen 'red-legs' was the most confused as, still trailing her 'broken' wing, she led the way with her little brood to the safety of the grass ley above.

I've noticed that this partridge will perch on the wooden posts of the Motorway fence; have never seen the grey partridge here do this. Their calls are quite different, too. 'Red-legs' has a 'chucka-chucka' call, a wheezy call, and another I can't describe in words. The grey partridge (*Perdix perdix*) has a grating 'karr-wick' and an explosive 'krikrikrik' when flushed. Both birds are beautifully marked with bright plumage, yet manage to blend in surprisingly well, when keeping still, on the farmland.

8.30 a.m. Walked back past the sett. Lovely morning, but so silent here. I feel the badgers could be dug out any time of day and no one would know.

When the constable told me on 29 July about the men with dogs and cages here, I had discussed with the patrol *where* we thought badgers

301

might be baited. Talked to a contact in the village today about this and asked – pub cellars apart – where *he* felt this might be carried on. He described the type of people *most likely to be involved at the top*, and to make his point he described a specific incident with people living a few miles away. (He hastened to add that he had no cause to suspect them of anything in connection with the badgers.)

[A property came up for auction in which he and his family were interested, so they went along to bid for it. (I gather it was a large house with land attached, though this wasn't actually stated.) The main bidders were themselves, an unknown man and very 'flash' man bidding through a solicitor. There were many other people there, too, which puzzled the family until the bidding commenced, and they turned out to be friends of Flash. Every time anyone else made a bid, they were quite openly threatened. The auctioneer merely turned a blind eye, and the solicitor remained unmoved. My contact was horrified and stopped bidding, but the other man, undaunted, continued to bid, pushing the price up some thousands. By the time he had reached his maximum and could go no higher, the whole affair had become very ugly with my contact and family regretting they had ever gone. Needless to say, Flash bought with ease and clearly could have gone much higher.

My contact used to be a second-hand car dealer and therefore knows a lot about the hangers-on in the seamier side of that trade, and the money that is made. He says that the buyer, Flash, is such a sort – a typical dealer in second-hand cars and scrap – and although he has never given him and his family any trouble, he wouldn't care to cross him. He added: 'Scrap-yards are ideal places for baiting. Plenty of noise, room and coming and going with no questions asked. These sort of people have the money and will gamble on anything. They are also quite incredibly cruel – even to their own.'

What he said startled me, though not for what was actually said. Certain events clicked into place and for the first time made sense in a more personal matter. The young man accompanying the driver of the car that tried repeatedly to crush me against the side of the Motorway tunnel in June last year. Where I had seen him quite recently – and in whose company.]

Tuesday 28 August
Mild, warm night. Played with Lesley, Sam and the twins on the great Cherry trunk. The adults went off after a while; later, I noticed Sam curled up asleep in the bracken at the field edge. The cubs love running along the trunk to where the tree's three branches lying horizontally form great steps upon which they play chase and King of the Castle. One branch (making the highest step) cracked when the tree fell and now is beginning to rot. This offers great food potential for the badgers as grubs, beetles and insects creep in amongst the splitting heart wood. The breadth of the trunk itself is enormous. Well before the trunk divides to

form the branches, a depression occurs in it which deepens as it continues upwards. I can lie – very comfortably – in this and be completely hidden from view; it's like a smooth, wooden hammock. If the cubs left me long enough, I'd fall asleep! The other family's cubs have just appeared and now all five youngsters are playing chase, up and down, round and round. No, I don't think there's much chance of me falling asleep!

Leaves float down, drifting on the still air. The ground is strewn with them. Autumn has come early this year.

Wednesday 29 August
The night sky is clear with glittering constellations. At 4.10 a.m., a young tawny was 'kewikking' as she went through the wood. She came to the boundary of an adult pair who immediately began caterwauling to push her back. When they make this noise, they sound very much like cats fighting.

The other badger family, complete with their three cubs, have moved out on to the fields and are now denning in what once was the Wheatfield Copse. (This is also part of Clifford's Bank.) It will be a copse again in a few years. The elm brush has sprung up amazingly in the eighteen months since the dead trees were felled. Its thickness well conceals the badgers' spoil heaps. The family still comes into the wood to forage; there is plenty of food and scope here for all nine animals. In the past, this area has contained fourteen badgers with very little fighting or aggression.

First light is now 5.10 a.m. Rabbits grazing between the stubble disappear almost completely. But every few minutes, a pair of ears appears above the dry stalks as their owner pauses to check for danger. To disappear again as the grazing continues. Twenty to thirty rabbits feeding thus are rather comic.

At 6.02 a.m., the sun's orange disc has just cleared the horizon. Colder morning than of late. The swifts have gone. Miss their fast, direct flight and scythe-shaped wings over Briarmead and the Wheatfield. Their stay here seems so short; have never seen them before May and by now, they are gone again.

I contacted Sergeant Warren Hughes of Oakley police station this morning after speaking to the driver of a patrol on Briarmead yesterday at 5.40 a.m. The Sergeant said to phone him when I think there may be another attempt to dig for badgers here, and has also given me his home number.

AUTUMN 1984

Sunday 2 September 1984

It's 6.50 a.m. and a beautiful, sunny but *cold* autumn morning and Alfie is ploughing the far end of Great Chantry Field with gulls wheeling and screaming above the tractor. As he lifts the plough shares to turn at the headland, the sun reflects on the steel blades.

Josh has been much in my company this week. He will suddenly appear about 5.30 a.m. and accompany me as I check for cars. At 7.45 a.m., I came out on the Warby side – still with my foxy escort – intending to go down to the lake. Stood at the wood edge enjoying the morning when a man I've known by sight for many years came round the corner and saw us together. Josh slipped away; the man tried to sound me about him, so I changed the subject. Since we last met, his old dog has died and he was recounting the circumstances, when my fox crept back to my side again though well away from my companion. Warned him on no account to try and touch Josh as he wasn't tame but,

304

rather, a wild fox from the wood that I happened to know. Said goodbye and began to move away. Before I could stop him, the man reached forward and made to stroke the animal's head. Saw Josh duck – then lunge forward as he felt himself trapped between the stranger and the wood edge. The sound of tooth on bone, a cry, and the fox had bitten straight into his hand from the side. Thought the man was going to faint and I offered to go back with him; he lives not far away in Warby. But he shook his head and stumbled down the hillside, still staring at his hand as if unable to believe what had happened. Felt very bad about the whole thing, but couldn't blame the fox.

Went to the lake; all my pond plants including the water-lilies and marsh marigold are doing great. Also, most of the young trees – the willows, in particular, are growing apace.

Tuesday 4 September
2.10 a.m. Gusty wind and rain. First rain of any consequence for some time – very mild. All the stubble except that of Great Chantry has been burnt off. Lapwings and gulls are feeding on it – the burning doesn't seem to deter them one jot.

Was with Tagless's vixen on Pete's land when one of her near-grown cubs approached us (the all-sandy one with no tail tip). Her offspring hunt for themselves now – wonder whether this dog, the only male left of these cubs, will take the dead Tagless's place? Will be interesting to see. Knelt and spoke to Sandy but made no attempt to approach. He slowly walked round me and drank from a puddle, then came up to me. Continued to stroke the vixen's head, at the same time talking to the young dog; then let him smell my hand. Began to stroke gently the side of his face, and behind his ears; think I have a Tagless II here.

Thursday 6 September
Out just after midnight – bitterly cold night. Frost glittering in the moon's rays (the first this autumn); stars etched against a velvet sky; breath vaporising before me. The tawny males are beginning to sound their boundaries more urgently now; the autumn months are a time of territorial challenge and re-statement of boundary rights.

Since the end of June, someone has been shooting very early in the morning here. It is one person and he comes up the footpath from the Main Road, then crosses Briarmead and so into and around these woods. I'm certain it was this individual that shot Tagless (*see* 8 July this year). Well before dawn on that morning, I had heard shots, firstly round Barry's fields and then the woodland. The shooter knows I'm around about the setts and normally keeps clear, and since my first concern is the badgers' safety, I can't chance trying to track him down in case the badger-diggers move in whilst I'm gone.

This morning at 5.25 a.m., I was standing under the shade of the geans on the Wildflower Path listening to the male tawny hooting his boundaries. The owl selects certain trees or 'stations' round the edge of his territory from which to call his challenge to any other male owl, so proclaiming his rights to would-be rivals. At this time of year, he is very consistent in this. The trees are always the same ones – he doesn't dodge about, but goes one to the other consecutively, until he has returned full circle. (It is this predictability, of course, that makes them so vulnerable at dawn and dusk.) I knew, therefore, he was about to fly in front of me to the field maple on the edge of Briarmead. His flight is low, smooth and silent – he seems so large in the poor light; for me, he is one of the pleasures of my morning watch. As the tawny passed me on his expected route, a shot was fired from the direction of the lane and the bird dropped on to the ploughed field. The man saw me and ran back to Briarmead. I followed, determined this time to try and catch up with him – and the badger twins, late home again, chose that moment to cross the lane. The largest cub yelped, nearly ran under his feet and disappeared up the bank and into the wood. Little 'un, in a panic, turned back and ran into me. Picked her up and held her as she tried to burrow her head into the front of my jacket, urinating in her fear. Quite forgot the shooter as I sat on the bank with the young animal on my lap. Had one ear washed and then, inevitably, my hair groomed. What with one thing and another, I finished up rather wet!

Friday 7 September
2.15 a.m. Mild and showery. Met the other badger family (now denning on Clifford's Bank between the fields) worming in the freshly turned earth above the sett. This sow and her three well-grown cubs seem very healthy. None of the youngsters is weakly, though the male cub gets a bit hen-pecked with his mother and sisters putting him in his place! The boar wasn't around, which is usually the way with foraging badgers. The young male approached so I squatted down and stroked behind his ears and rubbed along his back. Badgers have this curious, rubber-like skin; their strong muscles enable the owner to ripple the skin on the back. Rubbing along the spine will generally start a badger off either grooming itself or one's hand. This night was no exception – he promptly began with my hand and graduated to the sleeve of my jacket! It was nice to have the young boar to myself for a bit. His sisters usually swamp him if I am around so I tend to move away rather than cause an upset.

On the grassy path, a sow cub dug down swiftly and turned up and ate a nest of blind and naked rabbits. She had nearly finished them when the other youngsters came up. Whilst she growled threateningly at her sister, then chased her off, the male cub darted in and finished them up.

Left them to check for vehicles and was on Briarmead at 5 a.m. when I heard shooting over what was the Wheatfield. Same man again, I imagined, judging from the direction – the flock of lapwings feeding on the ploughed earth flew up with their plaintive cries sounding all around. Still dark, of course – which is the *stupid* thing about this shooter: at first light, he can see a bird fly but not its colour so he can never be sure of what he is shooting. Stayed at the side of the lane, hoping he would cross at this point; a few minutes went by, a shot close at hand – then a figure dropped down on to Briarmead – as expected, the man I had chased yesterday. Challenged him about the owl, but he was merely abusive. Invited me to try and stop him shooting and, in disgust, I turned my back and started walking away. Had barely gone a few yards when he fired over my head and began laughing. Furious, I ran up to him and, with both hands on his rifle, tried to wrest it from his grasp. Silly thing to do, as I wasn't nearly strong enough. Had no intention of letting go, however, and between us it was fired twice as we struggled in the lane. Oh, for a patrol car – but I don't have that kind of luck! He twisted it out of my reach, then brought the butt down hard across my head – and that was that.

7.30 a.m. All quiet at the Old Cherry Sett. Met Tagless's vixen at the Main Pond area and shared some blackberries with her. In spite of a very dry summer, I have never known them so large and sweet – more like the cultivated varieties. Shortly after, saw Sandy, then the two young vixens, in the field above the sett. Of all the foxcubs born this year, only these three remain. My area now contains six foxes; of those, only two are dogs (Josh and Sandy) so I doubt that any will move out – there is more than enough room here.

Homeward bound, met Barry's car coming along the field track. Told him about my encounters with the shooter; it's his land, so rather frustrating for him as well as me. He said he would tell John Shaw at Glebe Farm to keep an eye on Clifford's Bank for us – it can be seen clearly from the house. At least that will be someone else helping with the badger family there. We both feel this autumn is going to be a nasty one for the badgers here.

Sunday 9 September
4.50 a.m. Raining, with gusty wind. I had just checked for vehicles round the clearing and pond areas, and was walking out of the wood on to the tarmac of Briarmead. A light-coloured van parked to my right, and a lamper's beam coming across-field to my left. Either a badger cub, or just possibly a fox, squealing and crying. Had the choice of remaining hidden and watching developments, though I wouldn't have seen what went into the back of the van as it was facing into the wood, *or* coming into the open to get the van number. Chose the latter and so was kneeling to take the number [omitted] when the man holding the light passed something to a taller man (already holding something else) behind him. He strode up, challenged me, standing between myself and the others and deliberately dazzling me with the light. A boy was with them, holding the lead of a large lurcher-type dog. Whilst the other was putting what they had caught in the back of the van, the lamper barred the way round.

307

I was against the wood edge, the van front and the man, with the entrance to the wood behind me. The crying animal was hidden from me. I was completely taken aback by the child. He was such a tiny lad and stood there just out of the arc of light, apparently indifferent to the crying animal. I love children and was torn between a desire to get to the back of the van and a horror of a fight in front of the child.

The lamper said the van wasn't his, so couldn't care less if I had the number. Declined to say who they were or where they came from. Said they were lamping for foxes and rabbits, but were unlucky and hadn't caught a thing. He only switched the beam off when the others were in the van and he was getting in. For a brief moment before he drove off, I saw he was [full description omitted].

Ran down the lane – still dark and raining – to knock up Mick and Maggie Anderson and phone from their cottage. Couldn't make them hear – no dog barking, though Mick's car was outside. Was going to the phone in Warby, but a short way along the main road I met the car of a CB enthusiast who started off a chain of radio calls, ending up with Warby police. All this took time, however, and it wasn't until 5.45 a.m., almost an hour after the event, that a patrol appeared. Gave the sergeant full particulars and returned to the wood at 6 a.m. Checked and found all six foxes that my area contains – so the cries *couldn't* have been fox. Managed to call up Les, Sam and the twins – all fine; great relief. Will have to leave the Clifford's Bank family until tomorrow; they den in the direction from which the group came.

7.45 a.m. Raining heavily. On the way home, phoned Steve Hammond as felt he should know.

Monday 10th September
Full moon, gusty wind with scudding clouds. The crying animal carried by the lamper yesterday was one of the female cubs from Clifford's Bank. At 5.15 a.m., I spoke to a patrol on Briarmead; also Barry Hains as I started for home at 8 a.m. Told him of yesterday's events and the cub. He said he'd contacted John Shaw about the badgers on the bank, who had promised that he and his tractor-driver, Paddy Mayhew, would try and keep an eye on them, but said there were lampers around, which might complicate things – too true! I told Barry I was concerned for the other cubs; young badgers generally forage near one another and these were no exception. The chances were that the lampers came across them, but their dog could only have tackled one within the beam and kept it occupied until it was netted. Undoubtedly, they saw the others. They, or their friends, will be back.

Earlier, at 7.30 a.m., I had a rather curious encounter with a young man as I was walking away from the Main Pond. Didn't think a lot of it at the time, but feel it could be connected with Sunday's lampers. [Full description of man's stature, clothes, dogs, omitted.] I feel he had been waiting there for me to turn up. Sunday's people saw me come out of the

308

wood here at 4.50 a.m. They have no reason to associate me with anywhere else. Other people, however, know I'm involved with the badgers and can find me at the setts.

Tuesday 11 September
Steve came this afternoon and discussed the taking of the badger cub. He is going to interview the owner of the van, but since I didn't actually *see* the animal in their possession, merely heard it crying, there isn't a great deal that he or the police can do. Feel very stupid and inadequate – I should have insisted they let me see the contents of the van, even if it meant frightening the child or getting hurt. That won't help the young cub now though, or bring her back. Steve also told me that the maximum fine for taking badgers has been raised to £2,000.

Wednesday 12 September
At 3.45 a.m. yesterday, I saw four men plus two lurchers round a small fire on the Ridge. Watched them lamping at 2.20 a.m. this morning near the Poplar Row and on the field directly below Clifford's Bank. (The badger family are on the Madden Lane fields at the moment, where Mick set up the sprays last evening.) Bearing in mind, as Steve says, that it isn't illegal to lamp for rabbits and foxes, I have no right therefore to bother them – except to point out that they are trespassing and neither farmer wants them here. However, when possible in future, I think I will carry Ross's little camera with me. Years ago, I took photos of pelt-hunters shooting badgers, and found to my cost that it caused a very vicious situation – haven't tried it since. Now, in a sense, I haven't a choice. If I'm to stop them being taken, I must *prove* it.

5.15 a.m. Was sitting on a post at the top of Briarmead when a patrol came up the lane. The driver was a young W.P.C. and the constable accompanying her was one of the men to whom I showed the Old Cherry Sett on 25 February. Both had heard about the lamping incident and were interested in the badgers here, asking when the best time would be to patrol Briarmead. I am useless – Sunday's affair has proved that – but *they* could make all the difference in catching such people in future.

Saturday 15 September
Mild, gusty night after a day of rain. All the fields (except two on Glebe Farm) have gone under the plough on the Briarmead side of these woods, so badgers and foxes all foraging here – worms unlimited.

3.50 a.m., Tagless's vixen came to meet me on the Enclosed Path behind the Ridge – spoke softly and stroked her head. Together we followed the field edge and so to Clifford's Bank. There she left me as all *eight* badgers were worming on the field below!

I was with the badgers some while, long enough to time five of them just out of curiosity, to find how many worms each animal could locate and eat in ten minutes. Three adults ate 52, 43 and 49; two cubs ate

309

61 and 63. The sucking of all eight badgers within a relatively small area had to be heard to be believed!

Happened to look up from my absorbing pastime to see a lamper's light very bright like a searchlight, some way down the sloping fields. It would be shining for a while (moving along and covering a considerable distance), then be switched off, only to shine out again some minutes later and getting closer. I trained the monocular on the beam and made out two men and a dog [description of latter omitted]; one man directing the light and the other holding something in his hand. The badgers soon became as aware of it as I; since they were very near the sett, they were not likely to be caught and dazzled in the beam. Different story if they were a way from home. One would look up from worming and stand looking down field – then another and another – until they were all like silent grey statues, snouts raised to scent the air. Then one would move slightly on the wet earth, lower its head to continue foraging – and the others follow suit. The lampers worked round the Poplar Row, then went into the orchard. I was very glad the badgers weren't there as the pears are in process of being picked and packed into crates and any that the pickers drop have to be left as they are bruised. Needless to say, both foxes and badgers generally find their way in that direction during the night!

5.10 a.m. The beam was moving closer so I made sure all four of the Clifford badgers had gone to earth and followed behind Lesley and her family as they crossed the top of Briarmead and went into the wood.

One cub has fallen to lampers already, and even with the vehicle number, it's not enough. I must take Ross's advice and borrow his instamatic camera to track down and photograph these people, their vehicles and their catch. Otherwise it's merely my word against theirs that they wouldn't take a badger if they caught it within the beam. Have an added problem too: yesterday at 5.40 a.m., I saw two lights – torch – at the Old Cherry Sett as I sat on the Wheatfield gate. The badger-diggers are creeping back again.

Sunday 16 September
12.30 a.m. Stood watching two lampers' searchlights, one each side of the Poplar Row: I'm sure these are the same people as last Wednesday; this type of beam and method of working is so distinctive. Wondered if they had left their vehicle somewhere there, although rather too near Glebe Farm, I would have thought. Decided to first find my badgers – have a head count! Then check for their vehicle. Finding the former was easy with all eight animals worming on the wet, ploughed field near by; the vehicle proved to be more difficult. By now the lampers had split up, (working two men and one dog to a beam), though still within contact distance. Found watching the brightness impaired my nightvision, of course. Such beams cover a very wide area. It was hard to keep clear of

both, especially when one switched off; uncertain where it would reappear again, these fields undulate so.

Think Tagless's little vixen must have picked up my scent trail and followed me. A lamper, well to my rear, caught her in his light. The lurcher kept the dazzled animal at bay whilst his companion netted her. She set up a fearful yowling and spitting, very cat-like. I ran up to the man holding her – said he was trespassing and told him to let the fox go. But he refused so I grabbed the net. We were struggling together when I was hit on the head from behind – the lamper had come up behind me. Fell, dragging the net and man holding it with me. Suddenly, the vixen was free and streaking away. Rolled clear as someone began kicking me. No light now – think it might have been dropped. In struggling upright, I accidentally tripped my kicker. With both men sorting themselves out on the ground, I staggered towards the pylon that stands in one of the unploughed fields. Here the straw still lies in great heaps where it was pulled away from the edges before the firebreak was ploughed round, and crawled under a heap of wet straw. Felt dreadful – not very clear what happened after that. Remember standing on Briarmead later, feeling dazed and sick – and seeing the beams again, so they must have continued lamping. Went down the lane and crept under the hedge.

Woke much later in a haze of pain to see the badger twins had found me – Little 'un chittering and trying to scramble into my lap, Sis seated on the ground and chewing the toe of my left boot. They must have found my stillness as odd as I found their energy overwhelming. Somewhere above us in the dogwood tree, the hen robin began singing, and from over the darkened field came the quail's wispy call. Not first light yet, but soon would be – had to make sure the young badgers went to earth.

Walked slowly along the Wildflower Path with Lesley's cubs trailing behind. Had the most curious sensation of seeing everything as if from a great height – things seemed so small and far away. My greatest difficulty was to walk in a straight line – twice found myself on the field. Watched them go below; all quiet at the sett. Felt in my pocket and found the monocular was gone. Was sure I had it under the hedge; hadn't used it there, but had felt its hardness when Little 'un had been chewing my pocket flap. Struggled back along the path and up over the gate. There it lay unharmed, below the hedge; a relief – it's so old I could never replace it. Stood carefully upright again and happened to look towards the eastern skyline now touched with faint colour. A car with dipped lights was creeping along the headland and so on to the Main Road – time 5.45 a.m. Where *had* they left their vehicle? Unsteadily climbed the gate on to Briarmead again. Perched on the top, I automatically looked round the area as I always do from that vantage point. A moving light on the path below the Old Cherry Sett – small, but clear and bobbing as someone carried it. Tried to hurry along, but impossible, so shouted. Heard a man call, another answer, then footsteps running and the light disappeared in the direction of the stiles. The sett was untouched.

Monday 17 September
I have found where the lampers probably parked their car yesterday; on the Top Field just off the path near the beehives. There are fresh tyre-marks – they had left it behind some trees and bramble bushes. After badger-watch, I walked down to Glebe Farm, passing the shed and woodpile where the vixen was cornered, and spoke to John Shaw and Paddy. They know of the lampers' existence, having warned them off the farm on several occasions. Said they were arrogant, abusive and threatening; the last time John had approached them in his van, they had dazzled him. He stayed in his vehicle as he felt sure he would have been assaulted otherwise. He thinks they come from Oakley as he's seen their car [description omitted] drive on to the High Ridge. He also knows they sit round a small fire on the Ridge; that, at full strength, there are four men; and they use searchlight beams. Clearly we have both encountered the same group.

There seems to be a solitary lamper going and coming from the Crosshampton direction, who has a small light and works two dogs. He is quiet, non-abusive, but persistent none the less. I, too, have watched this man, but am not concerned about him: one man on his own can only catch rabbits. There are other groups too, and John Shaw, like Barry Hains, doesn't want them on his land. He has never thought to take vehicle numbers – I find this as incredible as he finds my tussle with them yesterday! He said there were some strange people about, caught my eye and we both started to laugh! Thank God for a sense of humour – he's a likeable man. Explained to him what I had hoped to do and told him

I'd ask Sergeant Warren Hughes if a Special could cover my absence at the Old Cherry Sett next weekend in case of diggers, so I can stay on the fields until they leave. This will depend on how stretched the local police are, of course – the miners' strike is still going strong after six months.

Paddy Mayhew says he sometimes lamps for rabbits with the tractor, and this jogged my memory. Years ago, about ten o'clock one winter's evening, I came across two men and a tractor with a dog. Struck me at the time that it was a rather novel idea.

Speaking to John and Paddy has made me realise why this upsurge of lamping is suddenly upon us. The summer months are pointless. There is little night to lamp by because of the short hours of darkness; also now, of course, there is no standing corn in which the fleeing animals may hide.

Wednesday 19 September
Clear starry sky with bright half-moon; excellent visibility. Have been coming out later these past three mornings as Sunday's blow on the head and kicking have left me feeling pretty rough.

3.45 a.m. Was walking along the Enclosed Path that follows the back of the Ridge when I saw a van [description omitted] moving slowly along the path above Clifford's Bank, going in my direction and some way behind me. That path is a bad one, undermined with holes – hence the vehicle's slow progress. Ran along my path, easily outpacing it; came out at the end and started downfield across the ploughed land. Heard voices and snarling mixed with other sounds as two figures with a light appeared coming *up* the path. They were carrying something between them with difficulty. Stopped to look through the monocular and saw the men carried a net which twisted and turned. A dog didn't help matters by making sudden rushes at it, though it was clearly nervous of the captive animal. By now, the van had reached the group and for a long moment as they held it aloft (partly to lift it into the back of the van and partly to watch the dog, now much braver, jump up and grip on the net), saw the striped mask and heard the challenging 'ung-ung-ung' of a badger swinging there. No frightened animal this, but a savagely angry one – most likely the Clifford boar. Tried to hurry over the chalky clods of earth; wet and slippery from yesterday's rain – hopeless. Knew I'd never reach them as the engine started up and the van began to move. Stood looking through the monocular at the receding number as it swayed down the path and disappeared over the brow. Just not clear enough – the letters moving and dissolving one into another. Haven't seen this group before.

Sat just below the Bank Sett waiting for the badgers there to either re-emerge or come home. 4.20 a.m., and they were out. First the sow carefully scenting the air – scenting then seeing me, she came over – then the two remaining cubs. I waited for the boar. Waited until after 6 a.m., when it was time for me to be at the Old Cherry Sett in the woods,

313

guarding Lesley and her family. Knew the last three members of the Clifford's Bank Sett would, like myself, wait in vain.

Steve came at mid-day in answer to my phone call. Explained to him what I intend doing. He knows he cannot talk me out of it and accepted the situation – that's the good thing about him. I must pass any film I obtain to him to have developed, unless, of course, I photograph a netted, captive badger. This, together with a vehicle number, would be for the police. I want to build up, by observation and photos, a knowledge of the groups lamping here, disregarding those obviously just out for rabbits. The flash range of Ross's little camera is very short which means I'll need to be no more than six feet away to get a man's recognisable likeness. Anything further would be of doubtful value. There is, of course, considerable risk to this, of which I'm only too well aware. I wonder just how many badgers have gone to lampers nationwide. Unlike digging them out, there's no evidence left to show what's happened – it's a terrible thought.

Steve told me he's asked for more patrolling of Briarmead and a two-way radio for me. The first just isn't possible with the chronic shortage of manpower due to the continuing miners' dispute. And the police aren't allowed to equip civilians with their radios – nor could I use their wavelength to contact them. Can understand this.

He would have come to see me yesterday to tell me of the interview with the man from the incident on 9 September, but had someone with him who would have been very curious about me. Steve knows only too well how I hate and fear publicity either for myself or the badgers. Retaliation is rife. Barry Hains's barn being fired was through the linking of our names by the C.P.S. I have always kept a very low profile on people's involvement with me and the badgers here. It just doesn't pay to try and help me, especially when people live in such isolated places. As it happens Steve can't do anything about that lamper – neither can the police. No proof. The man was very contemptuous and cocky.

We both sat there in silence mulling things over, when suddenly Steve said, 'Why don't you write a book about your badgers. Let people *know* what they are really like – you know, the things you tell me. Let them know the frustrations and restrictions involved in trying to protect them. The R.S.P.C.A. work ordinary hours – no shift system like the police. If I spend half the night at a sett, I still have to be at work the next day. Put in your observations of the other animals too.'

He stunned me completely, as I've always had the impression that he didn't approve of my writing these field notes. When Ernest Neal suggested I prepare them for a book, I tried to do so, leaving out the R.S.P.C.A. involvement, but found it was like writing about the badgers leaving out the wood – quite impossible. So I gave it up.

Thursday 20 September
It has been raining heavily – Briarmead is well flooded. Also turned very

314

much colder – autumn is well under way. All this week whilst at the woodland sett, I have been watching – and hearing! – two tawny fledglings contesting the territory of my shot adult male owl (*see* 6 September). The noise begins about 6.15 a.m. and usually continues for half an hour. The adult hen flies to and fro 'kewiking'. Just now, she flew directly at a young male with a sound somewhere between a screech and a hiss. I wonder if *she* will be the one to choose who takes over the territory and who thereby becomes her new mate? Many leaves are falling in the woods – they shine brightly in the wetness underfoot. Light is filtering in again, even to the darkest places. Everywhere are the soft sounds of falling – acorns, chestnuts, beechmast – and a constant patter-patter of moisture dropping from the foliage above.

I phoned Sergeant Warren Hughes this afternoon to see if there is anyone available to watch the Old Cherry Sett at dawn for diggers, whilst I track down the lampers on the open fields. However, nobody is free as more men than usual are seconded to the mining areas. He said rather ruefully that they would be glad when things returned to normal and they could do some proper policing. Can sympathise – must be a rotten job at times.

Saturday 22 September
Arrived on the Ridge at midnight. Very wet everywhere after thirty-six hours of rain. The fields paths are mainly negotiable, but woodland tracts are a morass. Not likely to see lampers tonight, though one just can't tell. No chance of the Old Cherry Sett badgers being dug out, however. Paddy and John Shaw are overseeing the pear-picking and will be around early near Clifford's Bank. Beautiful starry night, fine, sliver of a moon – visibility marvellous.

For the first time ever, I took a flask out with me tonight. Hung it on a small branch and was standing by the damson hedge enjoying hot coffee when Little 'un found me. She reared up on her hind legs, trying to reach the smell and doing her misunderstood whine. I turned my back, pretending I hadn't seen her, so she came round to face me, stood on the bank to be nearer the coffee source, and cried again. It's none too easy ignoring a badger that is determined not to be ignored – it's not impossible, however!

1.20 a.m. Lesley's cubs have had their fill of worms and are now playing Chase the Lapwings – a never-ending source of fun in which the Clifford cubs have joined. Sam is trying to sneak my glove (I've just started wearing them again). We're all feeling relaxed and rather silly! It's strange how this feeling – like unease – can communicate one to another. If I come here one night and sense my badgers and foxes are on edge, I too feel all my senses heightened, alert and tense. Alternatively, I may know someone is around or something afoot or may just be expecting trouble, and very soon after joining one or other animal, it too becomes apprehensive.

315

The lapwing flocks interest me in that they thoroughly go over a harvested field for two to three nights before moving to another. But when the first field is burnt off, they return again to spend a few more nights feeding. So what does the stubble-burning do that re-attracts these birds? Perhaps it clears the ground and so makes more food accessible. Their high crests and white underparts, together with that plaintive call, make them a distinctive feature of this farmland at night. Their method of feeding is like that of the blackbird. They make a short run, then stand motionless listening until a movement reveals the presence of an insect or worm. Then they lean forward and peck it from the earth. They seem very partial to the cranefly larvae – those grey maggots known as leatherjackets. They will eat most insects – also earthworms, slugs and snails. (So do the badgers, of course, and it may be this competition that encourages the cubs to chase them.)

3.50 a.m. Raining hard. No lampers will come now and the badgers are secure, so am starting for home.

Afternoon: Bright and sunny after a morning of heavy rain. In Ashcroft Woods at 1.30 p.m. meaning to do some photography with the OM2N I've been lent; a superior camera to the one I lost, but basically the same. Met Sean Cooke with two friends. He asked me how the badgers were and said he thought they were using a different section of the Old Cherry Sett now. I dishonestly said yes, not because I distrust Sean but because I was interested to hear him say this, and word *does* get around. Actually, Lesley and family are still exactly where they were – only I have disguised their recent digging out (removing the excavated earth and scattering leaves in and about their entrances – then taking the earth trowelful by trowelful, and placing it at unused entrances further along). If this has fooled Sean, I hope it will also fool the diggers – but not if they have terriers with them, of course.

Walked down to the lake – lovely afternoon with this morning's raindrops sparkling in the sun. Have a problem with the thick, green algae that is trying to cover the surface and thereby choking the other plant life. The muddy bed of the lake is like quicksand. Mustn't stand in one place for more than half a minute or my boots get sucked down – it was rather a frightening experience the first time this happened. (I used to be worried about the badgers getting trapped like this, but they soon learnt and went round to the fence part of the Motorway side below the bank to drink.) So I wade in quickly, scoop up a mass of algae, wade back again and pull it in. Go on pulling, hand over hand, for ages as enormous 'curtains' of green trail out. It's heavy with water and leaves a green stain – I feel like a trawler fisherman hauling the catch on board. Extract the freshwater shrimps etc. and put them back in the water. Found three dead rats embedded in it – wonder how they came to be there, though they do swim readily. The sky is a vivid blue with clouds scurrying across. Just a breeze here ruffling the lake surface, but a strong wind in the atmosphere.

Sunday 23 September
Not likely to have lampers as everywhere is still saturated and it's difficult keeping one's balance just walking, but feel uneasy badger-wise so left home 10.50 p.m. Saturday evening. It's a bitterly cold night (unusually low temperatures for September at present), with biting wind. By the orchard, I slipped past the Clifford badger cubs eating fallen pears and walked round the barns of Glebe Farm to imprint the yard on my mind. Paddy at the farmhouse has no telephone, and I wondered how long it would take me from here to reach John Shaw's house in the lane, so I walked there – briskly, to keep warm. It is quite as far as Warby's telephone box, if not further, so will be no use in an emergency. I noticed last Monday that Paddy used an intercom housed in a barn to find where his boss was. It may be connected to John Shaw's bungalow, in which case I might use that. Must see either man and ask.

2.10 a.m. Standing at the Briarmead wood edge with the adult tawny female just by me in the big ash tree there and, close by, the two young male contestants for her and the territory. One fledgling owl is softly calling a quavering 'hoo-oo-oo' – she answers with the soft contact call. He spreads his wings and alights on her branch; touches her face gently with his beak. The other male abruptly hoots. His rival leaves his perch and flies at the hooting bird, talons outstretched. There's a screeching as they collide and the attacker chases his vanquished brother across Briarmead and over the field. The hen begins to preen, turning this way and that, lifting a wing to run her beak carefully along each primary – then scratching her face with a claw. A while later, the young owl returns to her branch – a literal example of billing and cooing!

Monday 24 September
Sitting on the Old Cherry waiting for Lesley to return. Have seen all the other badgers, but not her. 6.15 a.m., and I spied her going to an entrance – called, and she came on to the trunk with me. Am uneasy about the late mornings my badgers are keeping. Only wants a shooter around – badgers are such easy targets. Happily, we've been free of them since 7 September.

6.25 a.m. Heard the tawny pair at the chestnut tree hooting station by Lesley's entrance. Vocally, her young mate has a lot to learn – he's like the newest recruit in the orchestra at present. What's happened to the other young male owl, I don't know, but if he doesn't find a territory of his own very soon, it means death – by starvation – to him. Will try and track him down.

Waited as usual until 7.45 a.m. before leaving. A grey squirrel came down on to the trunk within eighteen inches of where I sat. It knew quite well I was there, but came to drink at a fissure in the bark where water collects. John Shaw caught up with me in his van, and gave me permission to use the telephone in his barn; at night, it should be switched through and have normal dialling tone for outside calls. He told

317

me he had tracked down some lampers recently, at about 11.15 p.m. Couldn't find their vehicle so fired his double-barrelled shotgun in the air as near to their beam as he could get. Said the light went out pretty fast and he hasn't seen them since!

Tuesday 25 September
The twins have been digging out an old, old entrance low down the Cherry slope tonight. They have taken it in turns. Little 'un is underground now – I can hear sounds of digging interspersed with a snort as she clears her nose of earth particles accidentally breathed in. Badgers collect the excavated earth underneath their bodies, then back out kicking and pushing it as they go. At the entrance, normally they kick it out over the spoil heap, but I am busy trowelling it over an old spoil heap at a disused entrance. Whilst her sister pauses for breath and a quick rest, the other goes below to carry on.

It always interests me, this business of rabbit versus badger holes. I have known old, disused badger entrances that, within a year or two, diminish – possibly through the weight of earth all around and lack of use by a large animal. They end up looking just like rabbit holes and a rabbit may then take over. But, years later, a badger (as in the twins' case now) will start digging out and if you're watching you'll see it enlarge with very little effort on the digger's part. You'll notice also, if you're close, the inner walling is often far too wide for any rabbit. If, however, you are unaware of all this, you'll merely come along one day and think a badger has been enlarging that old rabbit burrow.

6.45 a.m. Came round the edge of Long Field this dull, damp morning and there, feeding on the sprouting grain, were twelve Canadas. If I hadn't had Josh accompanying me, I could have gone amongst them but my fox views geese rather differently from me!

Wednesday 26 September
Raining hard by 2.45 a.m. Have been out each night very early hoping to see the searchlight lampers again, or any others that are obviously hunting for more than rabbits – but nothing doing.

Left the badgers happily worming on the ploughed fields in the rain. At the Old Barn ruins, felt I wasn't alone so squatted down and made the soft contact bark. Something moved behind a piece of rotting woodwork, and Tagless's little vixen crept up to me. Put my arms round her wet shoulders, my face into hers. Scarcely seen her since she fled from the lamper's net ten days ago. We went down Briarmead together; the surface a gleaming band of wetness. Met a frog crossing from bank to bank – he never made it, as the vixen snapped him up. Went into my holly tree lean-to shelter near the Old Cherry Sett, out of the rain. Can just curl round in a ball and go to sleep in it – one of three places I have made in this wood that are *completely* weatherproof. Woke suddenly to find my vixen at the entrance. Made room for her wet body as she curled

318

herself up against my chest, inside *my* curled up shape – she's no fool. Think I must be getting more fox-like than human – like her, I instinctively face the entrance and danger. In spite of her thick, wet fur, her body soon warmed mine. (I seem to get easily tired, chilled and cold nowadays, and the pain gets worse.) Don't dislike her foxy smell; in fact, rather enjoy it. Can do without her fleas though!

First light is slow to come – rain very heavy with strong gusts of wind tossing the branches outside and sending flurries of water earthwards. Left the snugness of the shelter to check the Old Cherry slope, just as the young tawny owl flew low towards me en route to his hooting station. He perched in the broken fork of a birch and regarded me solemnly. I began to walk towards the sett but turned where the trail dips, to see him still watching, his head at a 180° angle though his body facing away. On impulse, gave the hen bird's contact call, and held my hand out, fist slightly clenched and thumb projecting. He flew up to me ... round ... made to perch ... then lost courage and returned to the birch.

All undisturbed at the sett. Water racing down the slope with every up-facing crevice of the fallen cherry's trunk a miniature pool. Returned to the vixen and sat next to her, writing up my notes in the dim light of the shelter. Time passed. A head pushed gently between my left arm and body to rest on my thigh. Ceased writing to stroke it – the continuous rain and a wren's sharp, explosive trill outside, the only sounds.

Thursday 27 September
Almost continuous rain since yesterday. After a year of unusually dry weather, water is here with a vengeance. Many places flooded. No one can dig out or lamp for badgers in this – just too much water – which is one consolation. For the first time this year, there has been no need for me to keep vigil. Seems strange. This *should* be a novelty, but I found myself very restless with the pain, so came out just to be here. Owls and badgers quite unbothered – foxes, however, dislike the excessive wet as their thick coats soon become heavily soaked.

I found Tagless's vixen waiting for me in my shelter at 4 a.m.! Saw her eyes' reflective shine as she moved up to make room for me, emitting that soft sound in her throat as she did so. Sat in her warm place with her head resting on my leg and listened to the tawnies parleying from the birch along the way.

5.30 a.m. A noise outside and Lesley's twins have picked up my scent trail and found me here. The vixen, until this moment unnoticed, raises her head from my leg. Her lips draw back in a silent snarl. She likes neither the badgers nor their blocking of the entrance – her only way of retreat. Little 'un, always possessive, fluffs up, stiff-legged, and growls; seems twice her normal size. Save the situation by coming out into the lashing rain. Shoo the young animals in front of me and together go to the Old Cherry Sett, leaving the little vixen to herself.

319

Sunday 30 September

Clear, starry night with gusty wind. Checked for lampers or car headlights on the fields, then walked on to Briarmead and up into the woods – no vehicles parked. Was greeted enthusiastically at the Main Pond by Sam who had been foraging in the wetness there. Took the path down to the Old Cherry Sett to find the twins digging out the extension to their parents' home that they started last Tuesday. Their enthusiasm will be their downfall. This entrance is on the lower slope and, in their efforts to avoid a thick root growing a short distance inside the hole, they have enlarged it drastically. Spent an hour moving the excavated earth trowelful by trowelful. Even so, it's the first thing you notice walking along the lower path as you glance up.

Remembered I was supposed to be looking out for lampers, so returned to the open fields with two *very* muddy badgers. John Shaw's orchard with its pears lying under the trees proved a popular source of easy food and thirst-quenching too! By now, the wind had blown clouds across the sky, though visibility was good. John has a stack of old roll bales at the start of the Poplar Row. One side is sheer, but the loose rolls on the other make it fairly easy to scramble up. Took some pears with me and, on the top, found a space between the bales well out of the wind. Tucked the camera for safety in a crevice and had just made myself at home when I heard a scrambling, then a plaintive whimper. Looked over the edge to see Lesley clambering up the bales with her cubs trying their best to do likewise. Their mother reached me with a final effort and together we looked down at the twins. Then she turned her back on them and disappeared into my retreat, so I slithered down and, going behind them, gave each a helping shove. Received a mud-caked back paw in the face for my pains and stood on the bottom bale wiping dirt from my eyes, watched with interest by two little striped faces now safely on top and peering at me from above!

Just then, I sensed danger and turned – as a man walked round the corner. Stood quite still, staring at him in disbelief. Know him of old as a badger-digger from the woods! In his turn, he saw a figure standing there and said, in a voice sharp with relief, 'Christ, [name omitted], where the hell you been? – thought I'd lost you.' I had quite forgotten that although, with *my* nightvision, I could see his features clearly, he was seeing a shadowy figure made taller by the bale. I recalled the camera up top with the badgers and cursed my own carelessness. At my silence, he repeated the name of the man he was expecting, then realised I wasn't whom he thought, made a sound like a yelp and ran back down the Poplar Row from whence he had come. I climbed back to the badgers and saw that the twins had disappeared in the cavity between the bales. But Les – to my surprise – had flattened herself against the straw on which she had been standing – and part hidden her head under her fore paws! Her white head markings had quite disappeared and she blended into her surroundings wonderfully well. Ernest Neal wrote in *Badgers*, 'Suddenly a dog barked loudly, and although out of sight, it could not have been far away. The cubs reacted by going below ground at once but the sow, which was standing at the time, flattened herself on the ground at the entrance and partly covered her head with her fore paws. The camouflage was perfect.' Have not seen this myself before. In Ernest's observation, these were small cubs. If the twins, therefore, who are nine months old now, had nowhere to hide, they would probably have acted like their mother.

From the top of the bales, I looked all around, but could see no lights or people. Retrieved the camera and climbed down quickly, determined to follow the man. Was halfway along the Row when, above the wind in the trees, I heard a vehicle start up and in the distance saw lights flicking as it passed down the far side of the pear trees. It gathered speed and disappeared from view.

Returned to the badgers feeling I'd missed a golden opportunity – what a fool I am. High above me on the bales, the family had quite recovered from their fright and, having finished off my pears, were grooming the mud from themselves. Suddenly felt a surge of affection for the little pigs. At least they were all right – that was the main thing!

8.30 a.m. Barry Hains's car caught up with me as I was leaving. He told me he had seen lights late yesterday evening on High Ridge as he passed by on the road. Told him what had happened earlier, and he suggested they might have been the men John Shaw fired at on 24 September, checking out the place before lamping – I hadn't thought of that.

Wednesday 3 October
3.10 a.m. Clear skies – very mild with slight wind. Watched a little owl by the haystack near Newby Farm. Its territory doesn't seem to overlap with that of the tawnies here. It pounced on a vole that had ventured from the cover of the pathside grass. Has a bounding flight and its head appears over-large for its body.

All quiet on the lamping front so far this month apart from a man obviously just out for rabbits. At first light – now about 6.40 a.m. – I came along the badger trail of the Old Cherry Sett in time to see the heads of two men moving about by the entrances. They saw me approaching and went off quickly. Had the impression there was a third person ahead of them. Couldn't say whether they carried anything and didn't feel well enough to try following. Stayed around the sett area and, at 7.30 a.m., spoke to Barry Hains on Briarmead. Told him Steve Hammond will be here instead of me next Saturday and Sunday mornings, as I go into hospital on Saturday. Suggested he introduce himself if he sees Steve's van. He told me he had tried tracking down some shooters one morning this week. Couldn't catch up with them, but *did* obtain their car number and has passed it on to the police. Told Barry I hadn't been out much lately, but wish the lampers would turn up now, rather than when I'm out of action – I *do* want to try for photos. Barry clearly doesn't approve, so I asked him if he had any better ideas. He said, 'You can't get on top of these people; they are too many and have the advantage.' Told him impatiently that was a defeatist attitude – what if the police felt that way about enforcing the law? He just looked at me, sighed, and looked away. When I returned to the sett felt sorry I'd been abrupt with him. He's a good man.

Thursday 4 October
6.55 a.m. Vivid dawn sky streaked with mauve, pink, vermilion to the east; the moon's broken disc above the treeline to the west. Hedgerows, trees, fields touched with a strange glow. Birds already busy – their song all around me. Much earlier, I watched the little owl near the farmyard. Now the tawnies are sounding from the woods, interspersed with alarm calls from the smaller birds. Even if I didn't hear or see the tawny owls, I'd know they are near by from these cries. I no longer notice the quail, so think they have left for another year. I'll miss their timorous ways and plaintive call.

Quietly sitting on the Old Cherry's trunk at 7.45 a.m. Distantly thought I heard dogs barking. As the sound approached, I knew it for what it was and went into the open to meet it. Stood on Long Field, facing the wood with the cries coming closer and closer. No mistaking them now as, above the trees, came the largest flock of Canada geese I have ever seen. Two, three broke formation and, losing height, came in to land. Knew them as the geese of previous encounters so approached, stroked their long necks and chin-patches and spoke. I couldn't hear my own voice for the great noise all around; throbbing wingbeats and loudly trumpeting calls. The flock swept low, gained height again clearing the bank between Long Field and Great Chantry; it was lost from sight briefly, then reappeared above the wood. As they passed on their journey once more, my geese rose with them. On powerful wings they left, spreading out across the morning sky in oblique formation – their cries fast fading with them. Stood there on the field – earthbound, infinitessimal – watching the dark line sweep in a great curve over Crosshampton, descending as it did so to the river meadows there.

Friday 5 October
2.50 a.m. Standing on Briarmead looking out across the fields towards Glebe Farm. Lesley and family are on the tarmac here grooming themselves, except Sam who is playing with my glove! A short distance off, the three Clifford badgers are worming in the freshly rolled and sown earth.

Now that the Clifford boar has been taken, the two families often forage close by. There's a half-moon somewhere behind the heavily clouded sky. My favourite kind of night – mild, dark, with good visibility, yet we're safe from human eyes. No humans here fortunately, not even a lamper.

Came out specially though with effort tonight as I may not see Les and the others for some time now. Am loath to leave them, so sit on the lane and let the cubs investigate me. At a glance, they look almost the size of their mother, but they aren't her weight. Lie right back on the tarmac and Little 'un comes and purrs into my upturned face. Her sister carefully examines my hair, then snuffles an ear. The only sounds – apart from those made by the badgers – are lapwings some way off, the tawny male fluting from the woodland behind us and the distant, subdued murmur of motorway traffic. Wish I could stay here for ever and never leave them – they are so vulnerable. How many will be here on my return?

Tuesday 23 October
Back home again, but so far unable to make the journey to and from the woods on foot. Just hope the badgers are all right.

Have spent my enforced rest very profitably, learning about lamping and the different types of equipment used. The searchlight type I have seen used in my area is akin to a Brinkmann Q-Beam Spot Lite 200,000 C.P. Has a considerable range (don't I know!) and can run the length of a field. May be used with a 12-volt, dry cell battery (triple charge) and carried on the lamper's back in a rucksack. The Q-Beam is very light to handle (extremely neat equipment). A dry cell battery is expensive, but is a great advantage over the cheaper, liquid ones which have to be protected in case of leakage. Some gun shops supply them, though model centres also sell them, cheaper, for boats, outboard motors, etc. Rain and wind are the best conditions for lamping. Some new recruits will try in full moonlight, but they soon learn!

Steve came this afternoon. Told me all had been quiet at the sett.

Told him I'd heard Don Francis had had his dogs stolen and, in consequence, has wire-alarmed the fence of Bourne Place against this happening again. (I had best not make him another night visit, then!) I wanted to show Steve the different routes on and off the farmland that are used by the lampers as I will need help quickly when the time comes.

We went in his van along the boundary bank (Clifford's Bank). Barry Hains saw our strange vehicle approaching from a distance and drove to intercept us, just as John Shaw's van appeared up ahead, neatly trapping us between them! Got out laughing and introduced Steve who congratulated the two farmers on their adroitness. Discussed the lamping activities here, also the shooting etc.

We left them and Steve drove the van over High Ridge and down to the gates that open on to Madden Lane. Then back through Glebe Farm and past John Shaw's bungalow. At least Steve knows the routes now and perhaps he'll have an opportunity to pass his knowledge on to the Oakley police.

Friday 26 October

Determined to check on my badgers tonight, so started out at 12.20 a.m. (Tried on Wednesday, but only reached Holmoak Lane and had to turn back – just hadn't the stamina.) Clear skies, cold. Saw three shooting stars.

All seven badgers are fine. What it is to be missed – though their energy and excitement was very exhausting. Didn't stay long. Took me over two hours coming home – twice my normal time. In future, I must avoid being knocked down and kicked by enthusiastic badger-lampers. Takes a bit of getting over!

Saturday 27 October

A clear, cold and very frosty night. No moon, but a star-studded sky. Been watching shooting stars – counted seven. My foxes were in fine voice tonight – especially Josh! But this sort of weather always brings out the vocal in them. I stayed until the sun was well up and did some photography. Each season, the wood has colour. In *spring*, the ground is a mist of blue, yellow and white (bluebells, yellow archangel and wood anemones). *Summer* has the deep green of the mature leaves. *Autumn's* leaves and bracken turn yellow and brown. *Winter* shows the tree trunks' perfection no longer shaded by foliage and sometimes a vivid green if it's a damp season – sometimes white if it snows.

Saturday 3 November

Mild, damp night, clear skies, excellent visibility. Left Briarmead at the Two Oak track with Sam for company and in a *very* playful mood. (I had put my gloves in my inside pocket for safety, but the badger knew full well I had them somewhere.) Turned left at Clifford's Bank, he jumping up every now and again, when suddenly I had the most curious feeling something was about to come round the corner. I think Sam did too as he stopped dead in the middle of the path. Opened the little instamatic camera, activating the flash, just as two men holding a net between them walked round the corner. Recognised one of them, so knew who they were [lampers, once they have found good lamping partners, tend to stay together]. Just took in that a badger was twisting and turning in the net; that one of the lampers had the leash of a lurcher which was doing its best to get at the badger and that the other held a lamp turned off.

I took a photo just as they realised someone was directly in front of them. Next instant, the beam dazzled us and I jumped off the path out of their way. The man I didn't recognise let the net fall as he slipped something off his back. Now I know what he hit me with on 16 September last – the dry cell battery. He swung the pack at my head by its strap and, dodging, I slipped and fell, the camera dropping just out of my reach. Tried to grasp it as I lay on the ground, but a boot got there first. As I rolled clear, thought I heard a crunch. Had the impression it was picked up, but at that moment something came running between us. My mind registered Lesley – *she* was the badger, but netted no more. Now the lampers were making off down Clifford's Bank with, I'm sure, my camera. They would have had a vehicle parked nearer the Main Road and I wanted that number, so I determined to follow on the opposite side of the bank. I was a short distance along when I heard a crying and, looking back, saw Lesley herself trying to catch up with me. Had to turn back of course – no point in both of us chasing after them!

Came back to the bank with her and, sitting down, the trembling badger scrambled on to my lap. Talked to her and stroked her, watching the skyline downfield, hoping to see car lights to give me some idea at least of how far up they had parked. It would probably take them a good twenty minutes to reach the Main Road unless they'd left the car near by – I doubted that, though, since the paths are so wet.

It was as we sat there on Clifford's Bank that I suddenly saw headlights again – this time moving along the Poplar Row. The sow saw it too and froze as the vehicle came to the end of the trees. Which way would it turn – towards us or away? Was it connected with the other lampers? Only as it drove back down the Row did I really look at the *car* and not at the headlights. A patrol car – and by that time too late to stop it. I ran down to Glebe farmyard and phoned for it to return to try and catch the vehicle as it drove off the fields via Clifford's Bank at the Main Road. Too late, however, but they met me at Briarmead and I showed them some of the routes off this farmland.

When Lesley scrambled on to my lap after the lampers had gone, it struck me forcibly what a lovely creature she has become. Even after she cubbed, Les never looked a very attractive specimen. Always had a rather tatty coat, though her long, elegant head made her noticeable. Now she is beautiful with a smooth, sleek grey body and very black legs. Even her tail has a neat, almost clipped appearance. Annoying, of course, that I lost the camera, but not a complete disaster since the lampers were so concerned about the photo that they let slip the net and Lesley got away. Also, I recognised one man from the vixen episode. There's a good chance his companion was the same, so I know both by sight now. Thus the picture is building up, though no vehicle number as yet. That's the next thing, as and when they turn up again.

Sunday 4 November

Tonight the Old Cherry Tree badgers have spent all their time above ground in the vicinity of the sett; very unusual for them in the autumn. Lesley is probably influenced by her fright with Saturday's lampers. But the others too appear unusually nervous though they weren't with her at the time. Wonder if the sett was disturbed in daylight yesterday or is it just a case of the sow communicating her unease? Nevertheless, the family found plenty to occupy their foraging minds. Have photographed some holes the badger cubs made digging out rabbit nestlings (naked, blind and deaf) from their nursery stops. Plenty of small mammals still breeding here, probably due to abundant food supply and mild weather. Sam and Les dug up a nest of a yellow-necked mouse and also that of a wood mouse, and ate the litters. Chestnuts too are plentiful now, and acceptable, though the acorns seem more favoured. Finally, at 4.35 a.m., a mole was unwise enough to throw up earth almost under Sam's snout – and Sam never misses an opportunity!

A patrol stopped at the Briarmead entrance at 5.20 a.m. They said they had twice been on the fields tonight. Thanked them, feeling a bit guilty as, apart from checking for lampers' lights every now and again, I've been woodbound this night with my favourite family.

Earlier I played chase up and down the Old Cherry's trunk with Little 'un and Sis while the adults went underground to sleep off their meal. When I returned from speaking to the constables just before dawn, Les and Sam re-emerged once more and mated long duration (25 minutes). Hope this little family survives.

Wednesday 7 November

12.22 a.m. There's a near full moon behind this thick cloud blanket, so visibility is excellent in spite of the slight rain. Quite warm. Walking up the slope of High Ridge, I saw a fox above me on the top, in silhouette against the swirling sky. Barked softly as I gained the heather near by, and Tagless's vixen came to meet me, the loose pebbles clattering downwards as she sprang. The noise frightened a rabbit crouching in the brambles just below, so that it darted out across the slope. The vixen seemed to change direction even as she leapt and, in one long, continuous movement, landed on the fleeing creature. Spoke to her gently then left her to her meal.

Toadstools have appeared everywhere almost overnight. There are a few of the elegant parasol mushrooms (*Lepiota procera*) in the light, grassy places. By the Enclosed Path, a host of shaggy inkcaps or lawyers' wigs (*Coprinus comatus*) are already shedding drops of ink. Strange to think that this black liquid *was* used once as writing ink.

2.45 a.m. Steady rain and wind. No lampers. All the badgers worming on the fields. Walked down the track towards Newby farmyard hoping to see the little owl and found – not perhaps surprisingly – *two* of them! I'm very interested in these birds. One successfully chased and killed a bank vole simply by running fast after it – you don't see tawnies doing this. The little owls are nesting in the side of Barry Hains's haystack where the bales don't quite meet.

Dawn is so much later now that I cannot stay to guard the sett during the week as I would be late for work. So left the area at 4 a.m. – still raining.

Sunday 11 November
It has been quiet here since Saturday evening with bright light from a waning moon. Viewing life from the top of the old roll bales has become

quite an exercise for Lesley and her cubs – at least, when I'm around. The only requirement is that I fetch a pear cache – and they stay up top for ages. I'm going off pears fast as by now they're either rotting where bruised, or harbouring slugs. Neither condition bothers the badgers, and slugs, of course, are an added bonus. Myself, I prefer to get my protein from other sources!

Hedgehogs are very noisy foragers. One has been working its way up amongst the logs stacked against the poplars – all that is left of the apple orchard now. In the past, I've watched these animals catch and eat centipedes, woodlice, beetles, spiders, snails and slugs – would say it was mainly their acute sense of smell, followed by hearing, that they use to locate their prey. Eyesight seems poor by comparison. Like my foxes, they are attracted by *movement*, but in the hedgehog's case it is *heard* rather than seen/heard. Badgers tend to eat from the vent end – hedgehogs start from the part held down, tearing off pieces and chewing. Like badgers, they thoroughly enjoy earthworms. I would normally use the monocular to see what this particular animal is eating, but three elongated badger heads keep getting in the way as they crane over the top of the bale stack for a better view. These sows are long-headed as it is but, by moonlight, they look most strange, jutting out over the path between bales and logs!

Lesley feels herself slipping, but, unperturbed, slides on her haunches from bale to bale, ending up with a splash in the puddle that covers the path. Shakes herself dog-like and stands on hind legs for a better view of the urchin who by now has disappeared in alarm at all the noise. She can scent him, however, and routs amongst the logs, pushing at them with her long-clawed front paws to send them earthwards with a crash. Now she snuffles at the base of the bales – the hedgehog is there, tightly curled up. Some badgers never learn to unroll hedgehogs but, as a cub, Lesley watched her father Old Joe – so history repeats itself. The same action as his – she squats in front of the animal, bats it slowly over using just her claws, finds the join where head and tail tuck in, then digs her left front claws straight down and into the join, stabbing the hedgehog to the ground. The right paw follows suit and, scraping sideways, makes the hedgehog unroll almost as a carpet unrolls. Pinned at both ends, Les lowers her head, lifts her snout up so her teeth come in contact with the soft belly and bites into the still living body. All the animal is eaten, the skin carefully snuffled over and picked clean, then deftly turned inside out with the spines inside. (Sometimes the skin is left lying flat with spines earthwards. As it shrinks and shrivels the spines are curled inside.) Foxes are said to do this too but I've never known any of my foxes do it.

(Hedgehogs seem to have very wet noses – almost to the point of having a droplet of moisture suspended. The hedgehog family I watch in our garden are easier to observe as they make full use of our lawn. They go right up to an object until they touch it with their wet noses. If it

328

moves and is edible, they will attack and eat; if it's a slug or snail, they will sniff and snuffle at it some while before eating. With the exception of bread soaked in milk, I have found our animals much prefer flesh to vegetable matter. Imagine this is the norm.)

4.55 a.m. Saw Sam on the Briarmead bank and, stroking him, found his left ear swollen and painful. Will bring the hydrogen peroxide solution with me tomorrow night and try to clean it.

8.15 a.m. Walking home, I stood near the stile at the foot of High Ridge watching a magpie come closer and closer to me. It was very aware of me and very inquisitive! A vehicle door banged shut causing the bird to flutter off with its grating cry and a man came over the stile looking round as he did so – but not back, so didn't see me against the fence. How strange life is. I first saw him on 14 April 1983 with a companion, digging out Old Joe's entrance at the Cherry Sett. Have seen him several times since, most recently on 7 October last by the bale stack in the early hours of the morning. He would recognise me, so it's fortunate he didn't notice me standing there. Description [very detailed information omitted]. Waited until he was safely out of sight and took the number of his car [details of make and number omitted] parked on the grass by the roadside.

[Inspector Hogarth discussed this man when we met on 3 December.]

Wednesday 14 November
Phoned Steve as the last two nights have been hectic lamping-wise and I still haven't passed Sunday's vehicle number to him. He came in the afternoon and discussed the situation. Promised to try and convey to Inspector Hogarth the importance of his men knowing the routes off the farmland. To enable Steve to secure a conviction, I must either photograph them with a captive badger or let them be caught in possession of one. However, if they get off this land without the police catching them, I'll never get the badger back.

He met Ross for the first time, which is important – should anything happen to me, my son will need to contact Steve fast. I asked if Steve could take over from me at the Old Cherry Sett next Saturday as I have to work that morning so must leave the area by 7 a.m. Said he would come earlier – as he's done before – both of us stay until 7.30 a.m., and give me a lift back.

Saturday 17 November
It is still pouring with rain after thirty-six hours – everywhere slippery. Sam's ear is much worse and discharging badly. Did manage to clean it last Monday night, but since then he has avoided me. Am determined to catch him as he goes to earth this morning.

5.40 a.m. and there he is. Have thought to coax him with some muscatel raisins, so hold a few outstretched on the palm of my hand. Let him eat, then sit down with him between my knees and facing away from me. He growls and struggles and I fear my legs may be bitten, so smack his snout smartly – that quietens him. Ear *very* pussy and inflamed. Clean with hydrogen peroxide, which bubbles and fizzes – sure sign of infection. Think I'll have to get an antibiotic, though I'm working today so can't go to a vet. Give Sam the last raisins and let him go to earth.

6.40 a.m. Time to meet Steve's van. The little lane is flooded, but not deeply, so we're able to drive to the top of Briarmead. I want to show him and explain the different lights over the fields whilst it's still dull enough to make them out. At night, you can actually see (amongst all the other lights) when a car crosses the little humpback bridge and comes on to these fields – but you need to know where to look. Steve, in his turn, may have the opportunity to explain to some of the constables.

All quiet at the sett; still raining hard. At 7.30 a.m. we leave the area, Steve giving me a lift home. I asked him if he knew anything about the new owner of Crawfords who, I'd heard via the grapevine, was an enthusiastic terrier man and involved in organised dogfighting. (He was also a cat burglar by profession, though that's irrelevant!) Steve looked at me rather thoughtfully and replied that my informant was correct. I remarked that since dog-fighting and badger-baiting often went hand in hand the said gentleman was rather too close to home for comfort; perhaps I'd go and take a walk that way. Steve grinned and said, 'He's got a guard dog, so watch it!' Told him I'd invested in two books on lurchers and lamping – though what goes on over these fields and what is written about are obviously two quite different things! However, I'm learning, both by experience and the written word. (He's given me an antibiotic powder for Sam's ear.)

Sunday 18 November
Went out in thick mist at 3.30 a.m. All quiet. I enjoy the enclosed sensation mist gives to the night.

Surprisingly, Sam came up to me at the Main Pond and made a big fuss, purring and jumping up. Did he recall that last time we met our relationship was strained? I doubt it – much more likely he recalled that he likes raisins! Felt in my pocket and unwrapped them, giving him four. Then put Steve's antibiotic powder and the peroxide on the ground and coaxed him between my knees as I sat there. Was able – aided with muscatels! – to have a good look at his ear, clean it and puff the powder in and all around the infected area. Gave him the remaining raisins – the way to a badger's heart is straight through his stomach – and started to collect together my belongings. Turned in time to see him sneaking off with my glove! He came back when I called, keeping just out of reach; retreated as I approached and followed when I walked on. Obviously, he wanted a game, but I just didn't have the time. Later at 6 a.m., I saw it lying on the ground by the roots of the Old Cherry. Sam had just been digging out a new entrance (doesn't lead anywhere at present) on the

330

hump of the slope with fresh earth thrown up right on to the trunk. Bent to take my glove back, but he was quicker than I, seized it in his jaws and went to earth. What a badger!

Heard the male tawny in the oak by the View Sett (one of his hooting stations), and slipped through the undergrowth to start recording. All last week, he came to my thumb, perching there quite happily, not uttering a sound! All I recorded then was him from a distance – and me making the hen's call and trying to persuade him to answer when he perched almost on top of the recording tape. This morning, however, he perched and hooted in my face twice before flying back to his mate who gave a lovely selection of her varied calls including her 'cat' one. My tape ran out before they finished at 7 a.m.

Walked back to the Old Cherry in case of diggers. Mist fast clearing; the early morning light revealing the autumn browns and yellows of this woodland. Sat on the gnarled trunk and played back my recording with great pleasure; several of a tawny's calls don't sound bird-like at all. Was suddenly brought back to my surroundings by the racket all around – jays, blackbirds, tits, wren, thrushes all sounding their alarm cries at hearing the tawnies in their midst. Don't think they appreciated my tape!

9.15 a.m. On my way home, remembered Steve's remarks about the new owner at Crawfords. Decided to see if any of his vehicles were standing in the open – just in case any turn up in my area. Car visible, but at wrong angle for viewing number. Walked up the footpath to the field above, hoping to see more through the monocular. A man and woman came to the door; a dog came out, too. The man crossed the yard, then back again and they both stood talking. *Knew them.* Saw them in Oakley High Street in the summer, laughing and talking with a car dealer and the young man of the Motorway tunnel incident! By now the dog had picked up my scent trail on the lower track and was barking loudly, so returned to the footpath and walked down as if coming across the field from Weldon. The yard was empty as I walked past, the barking dog following at a safe distance. Not a dog to attack, merely a good guard. Now, how am I going to get vehicle numbers I wonder?

[Five months later, I was to walk past this 'guard' dog sleeping in the sunshine and take all the vehicle numbers I wished and later we became good friends. So much for guard dogs!]

Tuesday 20 November
Just before 4.30 a.m., watched a comet with a fiery tail cross the sky and disappear *outwards* between the stars. Seemed to have a faint whoosh as it went, but that probably was just my imagination. Very exciting and disturbing experience. I've never seen anything quite like that before. Frosty, clear night, no wind. Breath vaporising.

Sam's ear is much improved, though he has been scratching it. Think

331

he and Lesley will produce some more cubs in early February. They mated long duration on three consecutive nights last month. With delayed implantation, early February will probably be right.

Walking home at 6.15 a.m., I heard and watched a little owl on Roger Johnson's land, hunting in the pre-dawn light. Marvellous time of the morning to see things – everything's happening.

Wednesday 21 November
Raining hard with gusty wind. Have been out since midnight expecting to see lampers – this is the ideal weather for them – but nothing.

Sam's ear is much better; its owner in a playful mood. Was nearly knocked over when he jumped up to search for raisins. He has scratched a hole through the back of his ear, mainly, I think, because the forming scab had irritated. The inflamed lump that was behind the ear has quite dispersed and his whole attitude (especially towards me and raisins!) is healthy. Went to puff some powder for the last time round the drying wound, when he turned his head suddenly and got his snout puffed instead! He promptly sneezed, rubbed his nose against my jeans and, pulling out of my grasp, ran round me in circles grunting and barking. Did little runs towards me, crouched down, then ran off and back again, mud flying up in all directions.

2 a.m. Suddenly heard a sound like a fox barking, but not a fox, I'm sure.* Puzzled, I barked back, the 'wow . . . wow' bark – if the sound *was* fox it should answer in kind. Again came the hoarse single bark, nearer this time. Looked round for Sam as he goes for the foxes when he's 'in charge' of me – but my badger had vanished! Felt the hairs rising on the nape of my neck – something very wrong. Climbed quickly up the roll bales and, lying on the top, looked over. Saw a movement the far side of the Poplars. Next moment, a beam shone out, then swept round to cover the area. As it did so, heard a *real* fox bark over the Top Field, 'wow . . . wow . . . wow' , obviously answering me. The light went out as two men passed below me (dog on leash), going towards the sound. Gave them a minute to move off and barked a warning to Josh – knew it was him – then barked again and again. (I remembered him decoying for me all that time ago; now I was doing it for him.) The light shone my way again and, to my surprise, three shots were fired, one going into the base of the bale stack – hadn't realised they were armed. The light turned and moved back over the Top Field. Time went by and occasionally from my vantage point I made out the men and dog distantly quartering the field. Think they eventually went off down Briarmead – vehicle probably parked off the lane.

3 a.m. The rain has ceased. Stars appearing briefly amongst swift clouds. At the corner of Clifford's Bank, a liquid shadow met me. Knelt

*Have found out since that this is known in lamping circles as 'luring' – i.e. what I call 'barking up'.

332

and stroked the sodden fur, his eyes reflecting the starry light. The badgers here I will always try to protect, but my foxes are somehow special. The epitome of grace and beauty, their intelligence and affection rivals that of a dog. Few would agree with me. Perhaps I have gone amongst them too long.

Thursday 22 November
More rain and gale force wind. Holmoak Lane and Briarmead flooded. Lesley and cubs have moved out of these woods and are denning near the other badgers on Clifford's Bank. Lot of disturbance at the Old Cherry Sett – entrances stopped up. Sam is at the View Sett.

The supplier's catalogue of field sports' equipment arrived today. Contents *very* interesting. The 'rabbit' spade (with serrated edge to cut through tree roots) folds down to $9\frac{1}{2}$ inches and can be carried in a small leather case which fits on to a belt, or can be tucked into the pocket of one of the numerous jackets with their 'large proofed interior game pockets' which are illustrated. Which probably accounts for some badger-digging hopefuls in our woods not carrying spades! There are a range of terrier 'finder' sets with transmitting collars and receivers to locate the dog underground, so saving hours of digging and trenching. These are also used to locate the dog-confronted badger for quick digging out. Lamping beams that can be gun-mounted (my lamping friends of last night!), and nets of all descriptions. But perhaps the most interesting pages are those on taxidermy and tanning, with items ranging from embalming fluid and hooks, to the eyes for your stuffed pheasant, fox, BADGER, stoat, squirrel, etc. Wonder how many stuffed badgers are road casualties and how many are helped along? Will send it to Steve.

Sunday 25 November
Dry night – first for some time. Strong wind but very mild. Sam seems unsettled this autumn – probably because it *is* autumn and winter weather will soon be upon us. He has dug out two entrances of the View Sett, two at Old Joe's Chantry Sett and one of the Old Cherry Sett – and now has elected to den at none of them. He is making his home just across the field from Clifford's Bank at the sett inside the wood. Badger hunters nearly excavated this small sett in 1979 in their efforts to find Tossy and his family who had moved out to the adjoining Wheatfield Sett a few nights earlier. Sam has reopened an entrance in the pit and he scrambles in and out via the earth he has dug out and piled up on one side of the great hole.

Have no real need to be in Ashcroft Woods at dawn now, but old habits die hard. 7.10 a.m., returned from listening to the tawny male sounding his boundaries and walked along the winding path to the Old Cherry Sett when I saw two men with shotguns standing by the great fallen trunk and looking around. They ran down the slope when they saw me, one shouting a warning. It was quicker to retrace my steps and catch them on Briarmead – maybe even get a vehicle number – so turned to run back. A man had just come out on to the path behind me – in answer to the shouted warning? Had just time to see he was the voluble digger of 1, 6 and 20 July who had threatened to come back and 'fix' me – and that he held a raised knife. Realised for the first time why his appearance had struck me as odd then and now. The pupils of his eyes are like pin-pricks that give his whole expression a strange look. Very thin face; lots of 'nervous' energy. Definitely unstable, though I wasn't waiting to find out! Ran up the slope with him close behind me. Tried to take him through as much bramble and fallen wood (and a great deal has come down in the recent gales) in an effort to shake him off. Then through the undergrowth beneath the birches where the holes made by the badger cubs digging out rabbit nestlings (*see* 4 November) are hidden now by autumn leaves. Fortunately, he tripped and fell heavily which widened still more the distance between us. Seemed an age before I lost him. Luckily, the Cherry Sett is empty now or I would have been forced to go back.

I don't really think they were after badgers (though wouldn't realise the sett was vacated). The man had merely carried out his threat, using two friends to back him up. Felt ashamed of running; should have stayed my ground, but was very frightened. Bad to yield to intimidation – mustn't do so again.

Monday 26 November
I went to my first ever Badger Group Meeting this evening. Steve had said there was to be a talk given by a police chief from a neighbouring county on how *they* dealt with the badger-digging problem, and I very much wanted to hear him speak. Typically, I arrived much too early in my anxiety not to be late! Just another four people, obviously friends, standing around. Was feeling very awkward and out of place when a man on his own came in, caught my eye, and we started talking. Was relieved to a have a friendly person to talk with; felt so out of my depth. One of those rare occasions (for me) when there's an instant rapport between two strangers – liked him immensely. Neither of us had been before, so we sat talking as we waited for the meeting to begin. In the event, it turned out that the speaker had been sent on picket duty, and a substitute talk was given on How to Watch Badgers. (Could just imagine Ross and Karen's faces at home when they heard!) However, the evening had by no means been wasted, since my friendly stranger turned out to be Inspector Hogarth of Oakley police station.

WINTER 1984–5

Saturday 1 December 1984
Been quiet all week with more rain and gusty winds. Fields probably too
wet for lamping.

Phoned the two farmers as haven't seen them since 23 October. John
Shaw was his usual cheery self. He had heard the patrol go past his
bungalow about three o'clock on 3 November; jumped out of bed to see it
was the police; heard the phone sound a short while after, lifted it and
heard me speak; then the patrol return. He told me to contact him if I
was ever stuck for help, by keeping the receiver on and pushing the
button until he was through – then we could have an intercom
conversation. He said he would always come and help. Thanked him but
said I didn't want him to get hurt, whereupon he roared with laughter,
and remarked that I needn't worry as he always carried a shotgun and
rather enjoyed using it. Think he and I should go into partnership – or
I'd better carry a white flag if I see him coming! This man rather likes

helping, I think, and, unlike Barry, his name has never been linked with mine. John hasn't suffered retaliation – yet. Just hope he never lives to regret helping me. Asked him if he could keep a record of the lamping by noting the *date, time* and *weather conditions.* He was interested when I explained why and promised to do so.

Sunday 2 December
Beautiful mild night with cloudy skies – nightvision excellent – occasional moisture falling. 1.10 a.m. Alfie has ploughed two fields off Briarmead and all seven badgers are busy worming in the wetness. Lesley came up to me after a while as I sat on one of the little posts. Knew what she was going to do and, sure enough, she backed on to and carefully musked my boots. Then turned round, inspected her work, decided it could be bettered, so did it again. Spoke softly to her as she put her fore paws on my knees. Guessed she was about to scramble on to my lap and bent forward to help her as otherwise her long claws dig in and tear. Hadn't realised she was so heavy, lost my balance and both of us ended up on the tarmac. Made the mistake of lying there laughing and found myself surrounded by the whole family, muddy from worming and eager for a game. Think chasing lampers is far less exhausting than being duffed up by Lesley's lot!

3 a.m. Sam has been digging out the fallen leaves from four of the Old Cherry Sett's eleven entrances. Les came to inspect his work and help a little, but by 5.45 a.m. had returned to den on Clifford's Bank. Her mate went to earth at the Cherry Sett. Think she will eventually return to this place when her cubs are due. The disturbance here bothers her, but old habits die hard and she looks upon this woodland sett as home.

I think I have plotted with reasonable accuracy the territories of the three pairs of tawny owls of this wood, taking in, of course, a fair amount of farmland. The territories will harden when and if eggs are laid about March (tawnies have non-laying years). There was so much owl mortality through shooting earlier in the year and the young birds have created new boundaries. I have also mapped the fox boundaries. Badgers not worthwhile as there are so few animals per area and only one adult boar now.

I was sitting on the fallen Cherry trunk writing up my notes before dawn when Tagless's vixen appeared, and trotted up to me. Settling herself at my feet, she turned round dog-like several times before curling up with her chin on my right boot. Bent to stroke her head just as she lifted it and stared up at me, making that slight sound in her throat. (Wonder why people insist animals never look directly into your eyes? They do if they choose to, though they may dislike being looked *at* directly, unless the relationship is good.) She stayed with me until 7.15 a.m. and quite light. We went down the slope together and parted at the path, I to walk the area, she to cross Long Field. Walking towards Briarmead when I thought to look back. There she stood looking back at me – I barked at her and my vixen answered – then we both went our ways.

7.25 a.m. Standing by the many-trunked old crab tree just in the wood when a yellow-neck appeared from the bramble cover and picked up one of the tiny yellow apples. The mouse sat back on its haunches and, holding the fruit stalk downwards, nibbled its way through to the middle of the core, occasionally stopping to listen, whiskers aquiver, before nibbling once more. When it had gone, I picked up the apple and found the indented teeth marks very clear on the now flattened surface – a very neat half left. Tasted the remains myself. Not as sour as I imagined but, like the damsons, best kept until quite ripe.

Monday 3 December
On the strength of our conversation at the meeting last Monday, phoned Inspector Hogarth and arranged to see him. Steve has just been far too busy (*see* 14 November), and I do want the police to know the routes on and off the farmland. Found him just as easy to talk to and really helpful. We discussed:

1) Lamping techniques, and showed him a map of my study area. He took a photocopy on which to write in routes on/off land, also possible parking places.

2) Publicity. I very anti; he mainly anti.

3) Badger-baiting pits that aren't.

4) How to keep lampers' vehicles on the land until police arrived.

5) The suppliers' catalogue and what an eye-opener it has been for me, with its taxidermy and highly sophisticated equipment – their legal/illegal uses.

6) He said there had been digging recently reported at Crawford's. [Went over Tuesday 4 December, but couldn't see anything amiss at the Yewtree Sett.]

7) He asked me if I knew anything about infra-red cameras. No, apart from the fact they are very expensive.

The Inspector is a very busy man who, nevertheless, has given me his time – and has listened. Somehow, I couldn't let his letter – or mine – lie between us. I said that seeing him at the meeting seemed a far cry from the man who wrote to me last year – 'I know very little about badgers. I have no wish to know more than the law requires me to be conversant with.' He looked at me rather thoughtfully and said that he had gone to the meeting hoping (like myself) to hear the police chief talk on the badger-diggers and find out how they dealt with them etc. At the time he wrote to me, he was under a lot of pressure, quite apart from the badger problem. He had received other letters on the subject as well as mine. Difficult to know friend from foe; local rag pressing for quotes and information. He had answered them all in similar vein. Knew nothing about me; not even whether I was a man or woman.

337

I left the folder for him to check – will collect it when he phones.

Thursday 6 December

1 a.m. Cold, clear frosty night with moon near the full. On the Ridge, I watched a cartwheel web being built by a garden spider (Diadem) between the branches of a bramble bush on the slope. First, she spun a four-sided frame with a few supports. Then came the 'spokes' – nearly thirty of them. A small spiral was spun in the middle of the cartwheel to support it whilst she made the permanent spiral beginning at the far edges of the web and working inwards. Once this was accomplished, the inner spiral was taken away. The Diadem spider went carefully over her cartwheel making it sticky by exuding gum from her glands as she went. Her own feet are oil-covered to prevent herself from sticking. Then she clung head downwards in the centre of her web to await a victim. I often stand admiring the cartwheel webs on these bramble bushes – hundreds of them – sparkling with dew or frost as I go home; then they show to perfection. Have been told cartwheel-web spiders make a new web every night.

2 a.m. Was sitting on the chestnut bough seat writing up my notes when the tawnies came on to the Old Cherry trunk close by. Drank from the pool there in the fissured bark (haven't seen them do this before), then parleyed to one another as I recorded – never had it so good. Sadly, I always have a background of motorway traffic – no way of avoiding this.

Friday 14 December

Raining but visibility good. Set out at 10 p.m. Thursday evening to check the area before meeting the Oakley constable at midnight. Inspector Hogarth had suggested a foot patrol (certainly the best way of seeing how the land lies), and found I had the Special Constable who attended both dawn watches at the sett in January. Dave Jones was really interested and very easy to talk to. I showed him the layout including parking places, the different lights, the tracks most frequented by lamping vehicles – and the size of the area covered by the two farms. We spent three hours traversing the land, including High Ridge, during which the rain ceased and a half-moon showed through the clouds. Discussed the difficulties involved and he tried out his radio which had, on the whole, surprisingly good reception. I left him when the area car returned to the top of Briarmead at 3 a.m., feeling the police cover had been very worthwhile. Dave, like myself, had a job to go to later on in the morning.

Meant to spend the rest of the night checking out my badgers who had kept well out of the way throughout our tour, though twice I'd had a brief glimpse of Josh – might have known *he* would be around! However, had no sooner left Briarmead and crossed behind the Old Barn ruins, when Les and twins came cautiously over, then the Clifford sow. Located

338

all seven badgers (or they located me!) within a few minutes and crossed down off the Ridge accompanied by Josh and his vixen who made a great fuss, jumping up with brushes waving. Suppose my escort had made them nervous; now they were relieved? In all the years I have walked these fields by night, I have never had human company before. Must have left both badgers and foxes rather confused.

Wednesday 19 December
7.20 a.m. Dull, grey half-light with steady rain (has been raining for the past three days). Two men at the Old Cherry Sett; one kneeling at an entrance, one standing looking around. They saw me coming through the trees and ran off up the slope. One man whistled several times as he went; a brown terrier running along with them. The second man had been holding something small in his upturned palm, rather as I hold my mini-tape when recording. Put it in his pocket when he moved off. I was too far away to get a photo of them. Didn't follow as have decided doing so is a mistake:

1) I have no radio to contact police in this wood;
2) if I follow to get a vehicle number, I'm liable to be shot at, and
3) if I *do* follow, their friends may move in and dig – that's happened before. All I can do is guard the badgers here on a day-to-day basis simply by being here each morning.

Felt there might be another dog about as the man had whistled, and, sure enough, a little dog suddenly appeared from an entrance near by. Saw it wore a collar and, on impulse, tried to catch it. However, it dodged me, snapping, and ran after the others. Wondered if it was a transmitting collar? If so, the man *could* have been holding the receiver.

Thursday 20 December
Sam and Lesley have been digging out at the Cherry Sett tonight. Found my glove on Sam's spoil heap! In spite of two large holes, shall take it home and wash it. I'm very short of gloves and they don't grow on trees – just on spoil heaps! The twins are still denning with the Clifford family out on the fields. They seem to like the company of the other cubs as they all forage within a short distance of one another. It's a wet, mild night again and raining hard; ponds overflowing.

Met Barry Hains at 8.10 a.m. on Briarmead. He got out of his car to speak, then changed his mind – still pouring down, water running down the lane. He remarked that I didn't seem to mind it – I pointed out one gets used to rain after a while; it's sleet I like least. We discussed yesterday's men at the sett. Barry said at one time he knew people by sight, but now he sees men shooting, ferreting, etc. here that are complete strangers. Conversation moved to lurchers – never has there been such a boom in them. And they are working dogs, hence the surge of coursing, lamping, etc. We both like lurchers as dogs – and discussed the merits of gaze and scent hounds. Wished each other a happy – quiet! – Christmas and went our ways.

I walked out of Ashcroft Woods via the Oak Dell meaning to return the quick way home as talking to Barry had made me late. Suddenly had a certainty I was being followed and, turning, saw a figure in a hooded anorak (still pouring and visibility bad) coming along Madden Lane. No one else about – completely empty landscape, except for the Motorway in the distance. Imagination, or intuitive knowledge? Perhaps I could find out. I turned and walked briskly back – would he merely walk past and avert his head? Instead, he did the stupid thing; turned and walked – almost ran – back the way he had come! I followed without hurrying and saw him go back into the woods via the Oak Dell. I stood for a while, just inside the wood, looking all around and wondering which route to take home.

Walked through the woodland intending to cross from the back of the Ridge, and home over the fields. Had the uncomfortable feeling I was still being followed, although each time I stopped, could only hear the pattering of rain on the dead leaves underfoot. Took the narrow, winding path through the hollies, then ducked under the hanging 'curtain' of an old, old tree and stood against its grey trunk, the thick sweep of evergreen leaves screening me from view. Some minutes passed and then the figure walked by; stopped, looked around. Then, with his back to me, he took a lighter from his pocket and lit a cigarette. Wished he would turn around. Couldn't see his face as the hood protruded beyond it, but his build was informative. After a while, he walked on and I took the other route, crossed the Ridge and came to the stile.

The time was by now 8.45 a.m., still raining, everywhere grey and dull. Noticed a red car as I climbed the stile (know the owner by sight; he walks two dogs each morning). Heard a dog bark close by, and there was a car parked off the road, a whitish terrier inside. This was the lamper's vehicle of 11 November [make and registration number omitted].

Sunday 23 December
Dull, mild morning – raining slightly. At 6.10 a.m., coming from the clearing to the Main Pond, I saw a light (stronger than a torch – security handlamp?) bobbing up through the woods from Briarmead. Stayed well out of the way while the man carrying it carefully checked the area with its four paths, as I had just done. It seemed as though he too was looking for a parked vehicle.

Waited until he returned the way he had come, then hurried through the wood to the Old Cherry Sett where Les and Sam are denning. Came on to the Birch Path between the Hayfield (that was) and the sett slope. Two men were standing on the path looking out towards the lane (lights from a vehicle are visible from that angle – I often stand here myself). Think these men were last Wednesday's two. (If they were, was the man looking for a parked vehicle trying to see if I was around? People who

340

travel in cars find it hard to credit that others walk.) Tried to slip round them unseen in the darkness, but realised too late that one had a couple of terriers on leads which started to bark. His companion dazzled me with a similar security light and told me to 'get out of it'. I tried to get past to the sett, but the one with the dogs brought the butt of his rifle round and sent me sprawling. I wasn't actually hit, more pushed with it. Rolled clear, jumped up and ran down to the entrances. All quiet and untouched there – it would be rather early at 6.30 a.m. to dig out. Stood on the Old Cherry's trunk to make it quite apparent I was there and had no intention of moving. From the trunk is a good view of the whole area and the path below.

Heard nothing more, though at 6.55 a.m., someone passed along the field path and entered the wood. Could have been Mick going to work, although this not his usual route – and am not sure he works Sundays in the winter either. Then nothing until a shooter started at 7.55 a.m. By now the rain had ceased.

9.20 a.m. Phoned the police to let them know of last Wednesday's and today's incidents. Realise they will be too busy with traffic tomorrow morning (Christmas Eve) to patrol Briarmead, but asked if they could do so on Christmas Day and Boxing Day mornings between 6 a.m. and 7 a.m. Know this is an awkward time as duties change over at 6 a.m. He said they would be short-staffed then, but would note it in the book.

Christmas Eve
8 a.m. It has been all quiet here this morning; steady rain. Now a dull, grey light. Les has dug out her entrance – seems settled here now. Her cubs (will soon be able to call them yearlings) play here on the slope, but go to earth on Clifford's Bank. The motorway noise is unusually loud – people already rushing about to shop. Will try recording more tawny owl vocalisation tomorrow; traffic should be minimal on Christmas Day.

Christmas Day
5.55 a.m. Very dark, frosty morning. Standing on Briarmead with my vixen for company. All quiet but for the tawny male in the wood behind us, sounding his boundaries. Have recorded him with very little motorway noise. Every puddle is ice-covered with stars reflected in their glassy surfaces. Sandy is calling my vixen who looks up at me and whines. Kneel to stroke her head, then urge her away. Off she trots across field, looks back a moment, then disappears over the headland.

A few minutes after writing the above, at a little after 6 a.m., I was standing on the bank of Briarmead where the lane is flooded. Around the curve, a vehicle suddenly appeared with headlights dipped and came through the thick ice of the flooded lane with tremendous noise, jagged fragments being thrown up on to the bank. It startled the occupants as much as me, I think. Saw me standing there and reversed at speed back along the lane, turned round neatly at Barry's six-bar gate, and sped off.

341

Saw it was the same Land-rover that I have seen here before (*see* 22 May). Didn't get number; all happened too quickly.

7.25 a.m. and a grey light is stealing into the wood. Birds alarming – the owls are still abroad. Now they have perched in the chestnut above my head. This pair are doing fine and the male regularly comes to my thumb. Hope they have a brood next spring. A crow rises cawing from its roost in the wood, as the sky beyond the Bank Sett slowly turns deep orange. When the rising sun touches the curve of Great Chantry Field, the trees over here will glow. Love this time of day, just before dawn in winter. Bitterly cold; frost lies in the folds of my anorak; breath vaporising. Notice the air above the occupied sett entrances is also steaming – a sure sign to a potential badger-digger!

Some nights ago when the twins were clearing entrances at the Chantry Sett, they pushed out a tiny vase as they did so. Isn't old, probably Victorian, but remembered to collect it to take home this morning; still in the hollow beech trunk where I'd left it. Broke the ice of a puddle at the field edge and washed it. Perfect – no chip or crack anywhere. How did it come to be in the sett?

Walking round to Briarmead at 7.45 a.m., I saw five Canada geese fly overhead calling as they went. See the ice has already re-formed on the flooded lane. Bracken, gean and birch trunks ablaze in the sunlight streaming from the far bank.

Thursday 27 December

A white landscape – deepest frost this winter, −8°C. 1.10 a.m. Thin-edged moon, brilliant stars. No badgers above ground, not even the youngsters. Foxes rutting, very vocal. Seven Canadas round Pete's lake – broke some of the ice for them to drink. Ice has its uses, however: standing at the Bank Sett, I can look over and note the sheet ice still unbroken on flooded Briarmead. So can see without checking that no vehicles have come through to the woodland above.

Blood-red dawn at 7.50 a.m. Sitting on the Old Cherry trunk writing this with three squirrels and a pair of wrens drinking from the tree pool a few feet away. Swear they were waiting for me to break the ice this morning, as I have done the last few days.

Saturday 29 December

A petrified landscape – even the stars seem frozen to the sky. −6°C. Know the badgers on Clifford's Bank are all right, but haven't seen Lesley and Sam since these deep frosts began. Tried whickering, then calling softly at her entrance tonight. Had nearly given up when a long, sleek head came into view, yawning vastly. She came above ground very sleepily; didn't attempt to scratch herself – a badger's favourite occupation on emerging – but came up to and against my anorak as I knelt there. Her body glowed with warmth. Undid the zip and let her nestle against *my* warmth. She snuffled noisily over my jersey, then

curled round, her long muzzle raised, sniffing under my chin. Folded the anorak round her – the long, smooth badger head protruding below my curly one!

7.20 a.m. Poor, early light. Sky a deep red behind me as I sit with my back to a broken branch on the great trunk at the sett. Frost has touched each twist and turn of the gnarled bark. Have just broken the pool water for the squirrels and birds to drink. A wren chink-chinking on a twig jutting out over the slope looks at me pertly with head on one side; decides I'm safe and flies across to drink. Has its back to me – must feel confident.

The foxes are foraging in the woodland now. In spite of deep frosts. many places under the trees are unaffected and merely very wet. Watched Tagless's vixen with Sandy co-ordinating their hunt on the Bank Sett. Caught five birds between them – three pigeons and two crows. Intrigues me when people write that dogfoxes scarcely hunt in the rut as they are too involved with chasing their vixens. They *are* very involved with each other, but they certainly still find food. Who's kidding who, I wonder?

Broke the birds' ice again at 8.30 a.m. as it was solid once more, with a robin peck-pecking. Homeward bound on the Ridge, the air is thick with gossamer seeds drifting from the birches. Think the intense cold has released them as there is no wind. Touch a catkin-like cone and it crumbles into winged bracts that gently cloud about. The light has an eerie dullness, though the sun is risen – has the feel of snow.

Sunday 30 December

After a night of rain, it's a mild, damp morning, and at 8 a.m. is too dark for me to be happy about leaving this place. Much earlier, at 5.40 a.m., was standing in the lane where the wood bank rises high above Briarmead when I heard a man cough from the trees. Could see nothing, but as the ground slopes sharply here, this wasn't surprising. After some minutes was just deciding that I must have imagined it when the cough came again more prolonged – someone spat, then moved into the wood. Couldn't have been a shooter out early as it would be such a long time until first light (7.20 a.m.) and longer still until dawn. Too early to dig out the sett, but not too early to reconnoitre the area. Checked for vehicles, half expecting to see someone doing likewise (as on 23 December), but all quiet. Decided to stand on the Old Cherry's trunk making myself *very* conspicuous. Heard and saw nothing more. Shooting started at 8.28 a.m.

New Year's Day, 1 January 1985

Cold, gusty night with clear skies. The wind is fast drying the sodden land. My pair of tawnies were harmonising well before dawn. The male came to my thumb when I called, his mate flying round my head. Occurred to me she might object to my copying her contact cry. Have never been attacked by an owl – yet! Temperature falling, bitterly cold, $-9°C$. At the Old Cherry Sett, the gale is tossing the treetops; they groan and moan as in pain.

4.10 a.m. Lesley has emerged and comes purring to meet me. Stroke her sleek head and scratch behind her ears. She snuffles the zip of my anorak, and, remembering last Saturday, I undo it and hold the fronts open. She comes inside, snug against my body and I put my arms around her – how she purrs!

7.20 a.m. and first light reveals the frosted landscape. Nothing sounds above the wind-tossed trees. Walk round to keep from becoming too cold, returning to the sett every twenty minutes or so. Enjoy this kind of morning, but pity the squirrels. Their dreys are so vulnerable amongst the crashing, coppiced trunks.

Saturday 5 January

2.15 a.m. Snow has frozen in the hollows and crunches underfoot. No need to stay until dawn – far too frozen for diggers to take the badgers here. Temperature $-11°C$, the coldest so far. Everywhere is very beautiful. Snow is softly falling on frozen snow. Each twig has a tiny ridge of white.

Had thought to find no badgers abroad in such conditions, but hearing noise by the beehives at the corner of Clifford's Bank, I discovered Little 'un (little no more!) and her sister trying to dig out under the beehives. That brings back memories of their parents (17 and 22 December 1983). They were making a great noise amongst the frozen leaves. Crept up and lightly smacked a grey rump protruding from beneath one of the hives. Poor Sis! Hadn't meant to startle her so. She gave a great snort and tried to disappear beneath the hive, but she's grown too sturdy a young badger for that now. When she realised it was me, she ran round grunting and throwing up snow in all directions. Little 'un soon joined her as I pelted them with snowballs; what a noise!

Sunday 6 January
Has been snowing since 3.30 a.m. No wind and not at all cold; a mere −1°C. Earth soft under its snow covering. Fox, rabbit, stoat prints clear on the unblemished surface, though fast disappearing under more snow. Have brought the Olympus out with me, and at 8 a.m. there's enough light to use it. Find it hard not to get the lens wet; tends to get misted up. No one about except a solitary shooter by the Main Pond. No badger prints anywhere; not even in the more sheltered woodland places or round the hives.

8.45 a.m. In the distance see Ralph's car going up Briarmead – the first and only vehicle to do so. Photographed old-man's-beard snow-covered and trailing from Barry's six-bar gate, as his friend's car carefully returned down the winding lane, skidding on the treacherous surface. Sounded his horn and waved, shaking his head at me and laughing. Think he needs looking after more than me!

Tuesday 8 January
Great orange moon, seeming too heavy in a glittering sky. Snow hard-frozen underfoot. Temperature −16°C! But the cold is bearable, as there's no wind. The vixens are in oestrus now, and for a mere two to three nights of this three-week period they are receptive to their mates. Such is the way of the fox.

I left my gear (including the thermometer) on the snow near Briarmead, for I'd need to travel light in order to follow Josh and his vixen. They were running in front of Glebe Farm, obsessed, in a world of their own. A strangely still, silent world. Just the crunch, crunch of pads on snow, the quick breath, and the sudden startled cry of a lark rising clumsily as they passed. By the first pylon, Josh stopped and scent-marked its base. His mate, now some distance off, turned and screamed. Four feet squarely planted, body forward, rigid, brush curled up and over. Scream upon scream, not human, yet not animal. Can understand the old belief in witches and banshees – this was one in the flesh.

[It's interesting that for the brief period a vixen is fertile, her mate will appear to smell the side of her head and ears a great deal – almost heading her off to do so. Josh was doing this now. His mate's ears had flattened back and her head was lowered submissively. To my knowledge, they have no gland there, so don't know the reason for this.]

Then they were off again, crossing Top Field to Prosser's Wood. On to the bottom of High Ridge and up the track to the snow-laden bracken

345

behind. Then out again full circle to Glebe Farm and the small barn between the trees of the Poplar Row. There, a short while later, the pair were locked in coitus for approx. twenty minutes. From now until the birth of their cubs in early March, they will be inseparable. They will run together, play together, mutually groom, often hunting together. One will never be far from the other.

Thursday 10 January
Steve came this afternoon, and told me that the lamper and his companion of 9 September last had been discovered last Friday afternoon on land belonging to the Electricity Board. They had a caged fox in their van, apparently taken from beneath an out-house which had a broken drain outside giving the fox entry. The police had called in the R.S.P.C.A. as a) a dog had been left below ground, and b) they wondered if it could also be a badger sett. However, it definitely wasn't badger, but the sort of place where a fox would go to earth. A constable, a W.P.C. and Steve were on site when the young man returned with seven friends, all armed with picks etc. to break up the cement and release the dog. He is called Roger Smith and, as before, was very cocky and full of himself. (Can scarcely blame him really; as the law stands at present, he's laughing.) Drives a van [description and number omitted]. Steve said I should call the police if it's seen in my area, since Roger and his friend Graham Jones will be up to no good. Steve recalled the incident in Ashcroft Woods on 9 September but Roger denied ever being in the vicinity, let alone netting a badger. The latter I can understand (who's going to admit taking a badger?), but denying he had been on Briarmead was a bit silly in the circumstances. To think I let him get away with the young Clifford sow, to my everlasting regret – how useless I am. I'm sure the young man that turned up early the following morning (10 September) was connected.

Steve told me that whenever he gets called out anywhere in the area, or is passing, he drives up Briarmead and has a look round if at all possible. Says there's usually someone walking their dog, so doesn't feel there would be trouble there during the day. (However, the constable one weekday afternoon last summer came across a van containing cages owned by men with police records, so one just can't tell.)

Saturday 12 January
4.10 a.m. Mild morning just below freezing. Snow still lying, clear skies, no wind. The badgers have been out foraging in the snow-free places. Plenty of food still to be found, like beechmast, chestnuts, *many* acorns, crab apples. The yearlings, Little 'un and Sis, are now denning by their parents at the Old Cherry Sett. They cleared some entrances for themselves. The dark brown earth shows with startling clarity on the whiteness. Had to leave the area earlier than I like as I work this morning. Before going, I brushed lightly over the badger prints indented

on the snow. It's obvious exactly where they are denning without that.

Left work at 1.20 p.m. and walked home via Briarmead and Ashcroft Woods. Sun shining in a blue sky; the young corn on Long Field showing green through the snow. Men's boot marks all round the sett entrances – at three of them, someone had knelt. Realised I had either overlooked some prints, or one of the badgers had been out after I left. The twins slide down part of the slope but few people would know it was badger – looks very like children – only I've watched the yearlings doing it. Checked where Josh and vixen are denning at the Felled Logs Sett – no human prints round that, though plenty of fox. Walked down the hillside to the lake, its frozen surface shimmering under the dying sun.

At 3.15 p.m. the sun touches the horizon – long shadows creep across the landscape – the day is nearly done.

Tuesday 14 January
From the fifth of this month, snow showers have fallen, slowly accumulating. The deep frost makes it rigid underfoot. The wind whistles through the glistening bones of the trees. No badgers above ground since Saturday. Tonight, Sandy mated with Tagless's vixen. I found one of his sisters dead in the bracken behind the Ridge. Brushed the snow off her body – beautiful coat. She had curled up for warmth there and died – malnutrition and cold. The other young vixen is healthy, but not yet in oestrus. Foxes are mature at nine months, but a vixen under a year comes into season slightly later.

Wednesday 16 January
Steve came this afternoon and told me there was another meeting of the C.P.S. Planned for 22 January – was I interested? A police chief was to talk on the baiting problem. Will go, but am none too happy about the outcome.

Steve was called out to Bramley Woods recently. A constable on patrol saw a man and a dog walking round the outskirts of the wood in the snow. Checked his vehicle number to find he came from Barksham. Rather a long ride to walk one's dog? Steve and the constable followed his footprints. They think the stranger was probably checking for occupied setts or dens, but can't be sure of course. Alan has heard of several reports recently of lorries in fields being used for baiting. The driver keeps look-out and, at the first sign of trouble, puts up the tailboard and drives off with the badger. The onlookers, their dogs and vehicles are left but, without the badger, nothing can be proven. Actually, that's a pretty good way of getting over the problem of pits. Imagine this has been going on a good while. Discussed baiting pits (real ones, that is), and some possibles he and his colleagues have checked out.

Friday 18 January
Wind has drifted the snow on to Briarmead; the smooth curves assume

347

strange shapes where the lane slopes most steeply. Met my little vixen and her new mate close by. (Have always known her as Tagless's vixen, but she's Sandy's now.) Their snow prints are interesting: where it is deep, they have to jump to make any progress; quite different from their prints in shallow snow. I had a good look at the dogfox – can't help wondering what a pelt-hunter would think of him. With no black *or* white markings, he's curiously un-foxlike. Imagine where he should be white (belly etc.) he's a creamy colour, but haven't seen him yet in full daylight so can't be one hundred per cent sure. He's certainly *not* white, however. Might be worth tracking them down during a quiet daytime to find out. [2 February. Beige to coffee colour.]

Phoned Barry Hains, and passed on the lampers' van number that Steve had given me. I happened to say that I was glad snow drifts had blocked Briarmead and he said he had made sure the tractors hadn't used the lane – they would have reopened it by so doing – but had sent them round the longer (field) way instead. He asked me how things were badger-wise and I mentioned the boot and kneeling marks last Saturday. I feel that when it thaws, the diggers will move in. After all, first bitter frost, then snow, to say nothing of me around, must be frustrating for them, at the very least. He promised to keep an eye on things during the day, when it does thaw. Think that's called co-operation!

Sunday 20 January
Noticeably warmer though the snow still lies thick on the fields, paths and lane. The woodland badgers have been out foraging and playing tonight – sliding down the sett slope has been a great favourite. They seem to have two methods of doing this; either sitting back on their haunches, or putting head between front legs and rolling down like a ball.

3.10 a.m. and standing at the top of the slide, now smooth and icy from their play, when Lesley and one of her daughters began quarrelling over something just behind me. They sometimes do this over a tasty titbit each feels is rightly hers, though all the fuss is soon over and forgotten. This time, however, one cannoned into my legs. I put out a foot to steady myself, unfortunately on to the ice, and next moment was travelling down the slide in (painful) style. The force of my fall landed me on the level ground below and, looking backwards, I saw three heads above the ridge, regarding me with interest. Then the yearlings came sliding down too, one giving me a powerful push in the back and the other narrowly missing me. Les came down on her haunches – making a far neater and more composed job of it than her daughters – almost with dignity, one might say. She came to a halt close by, reached over and whickered softly. The twins scampered up the slope again with great enthusiasm; only Sam went off on his own towards the field above.

Stroked the mother's long head and neck; then found myself with an armful of badger as she came on to my lap. She *is* pregnant.

Remembered last January, almost at the same spot, when I held her and discovered she was in cub. It isn't noticeable until I feel her. Am delighted. That night, I was waiting to show the men through the wood (15 January 1984). Now she already has two well-grown daughters and so much has happened in that time!

Will soon be first light. The whole area is covered with paw prints and slide marks. They have scratched away the snow under the trees to forage – plenty of sprouting bulbs, bluebells especially, acorns, crab apples, etc. The earth below its white blanket is not particularly hard.

9.15 a.m. I walked straight across the lake and back again after photographing it – snow over solid ice. As I left the lakeside, Pete Williams's jeep caught up with me. Said he had been meaning to contact me as his boss was thinking of clearing the dump end of the copse and levelling it in an effort to reduce the rabbit population there. Pete's three children had told him there were badgers living at the other end and he wanted to make sure they wouldn't be disturbed. I said Les and the twins had dug out there in the autumn, but weren't denning there now. Would check and let him know.

Left him to check the copse. As I approached, a covey of partridge (common/grey) rose from its cover and, keeping close together, flew low across the field. To my surprise and pleasure, found the sett *is* badger-occupied (more than one animal by the snowprints), and they've been out recently. Pete has sharp-eyed lads, but then children are often most

349

observant. Will see if I can get them involved and interested in keeping an eye on it. The future lies with today's children – they are tomorrow's people.

Monday 21 January
Has been raining all day; snow fast disappearing; strong wind. Met Pete's wife Jean and three children this evening (Alex, 11; James, 8; Rebecca, 5), all interested in watching over the badger sett. Explained what to do and watch for – I think their parents are as interested as they. Will check on it myself from time to time, but it's a considerable way from Clifford's Bank (two farms plus a wood distant) and from the Old Cherry Sett.

Left Colts Farm just after 9 p.m. Still pouring, with a strong wind. As I came out of the darkness of Warby Road on to the lit Madden Lane, saw two men approaching. The first held the leash of a grey lurcher, the man behind had two terriers and carried a light (switched off). They stopped when they saw me; must have been surprised to see anyone walking along there (lonely, dark and weather so bad); even more so, a woman. They stood watching me walk along until the curve of the road hid us one from another. I waited a moment, then went back. Sure enough, they were going through the farm. Couldn't follow on to the fields as I had no boots and was already wet through in that short time. Wondered where they had left their vehicle. Came home and changed, then went out again to search the whole area. By now quite a time had elapsed, of course. No sign of anyone at all.

Tuesday 22 January
No point in returning home, so stayed out until morning. Steady rain. Snow has gone except where it drifted and packed hard on the fields and on Briarmead.

Went to find the new badgers at Colts Farm bank. Stood looking down over the sloping field at the bank. I was wrong when I thought quarrying etc. during the last century had caused the odd shapings in this land. Whatever *has* caused them is far older, and because the area was difficult to farm with machinery, it was left. In time, colonising birch, bramble and bracken has covered it, so that today it is a field stretching up to Ashcroft Woods with a deep coppice in the middle of the area. The small sett here is not old – probably less than fifty years.

The badgers here are two (yearling?) sisters. Was able to come very close and watched them for more than two hours. Glad the children discovered these animals rather than I. Have told the boys and their sister that they are *their* badgers. Feel they will take a pride in watching over and recording the sett, especially as their parents are so enthusiastic, too. I am very lucky in my farmers, as are the badgers.

Evening: Went with Steve to the C.P.S. Badger Group Meeting to hear the police chief talk on the badger-digging problem (should have heard

350

him on 28 November last). An interesting talk. Met Sergeant Warren Hughes for the first time (whom I originally phoned on 25 August). He was representing Inspector Hogarth, who was unable to attend.

I had asked Barry Hains to come, but he couldn't make it. At the time I was disappointed, but from the remarks made by the C.P.S. about farmers tonight, I'm relieved. Recalled a similar meeting over the future of Ashcroft Woods with Pete Williams present in the audience. Didn't know him very well then, but admired his quiet way of answering his questioners. He must have felt the atmosphere against him – as I did – but was courteous, calm and controlled. Glad Barry didn't come. Steve spoke up very well for our local farmers, but it was like speaking to closed minds. What a pity we can't all work together; a Badger Group is surely about badgers, not bigotry. Feel very disheartened. Don't think I'll attend another meeting.

Friday 25 January
Still raining slightly. Dull first light at 7.10 a.m. and the tawnies are calling in the Scots pines at the Felled Logs Sett. Here, by the fallen Cherry, however, all is silent but for the drip-drip, of moisture falling from the coppiced trunks. Lesley is *very* near her time and taking great care of herself – good badgers are scarce! One sign that her cubs are due is her snappiness towards Sam. He will soon be banished for a while from the sett. She will let her yearlings in but then they are young sows.

Tuesday 29 January
Clear skies, crescent moon, frost – no wind. Sandy mated with the young vixen tonight. It will be interesting to see if the older vixen will tolerate a rival, or whether her ten-month-old rival will stay a loner.

2.10 a.m. A stoat has just killed a young rabbit feeding out in a field of young corn. Interesting how they stalk one relentlessly through a colony of grazing animals who just continue to feed – rats act similarly in ignoring the pursued and the pursuer in their midst. The prey soon became panic-stricken and stopped running. Crouched down squealing, body pressed against the bare earth. The kill was made as usual with a bite at the back of the neck. (A larger rabbit would have been gripped at nape.) Blood oozed from the wound and the stoat licked this away before commencing eating. Tawny owl perched in a blackthorn on Clifford's Bank watched each movement with great interest – its head turning almost the complete circle though the body quite stationary.

3.15 a.m. and Lesley came into my anorak again; has become a habit. Sam was growled at when he approached us. Partly possession of me, but mostly because parturition near at hand. Felt rather sorry for him – remembered last year.

Thursday 31 January
Came home early from work today and went straight out again to

Ashcroft Woods while the light was still good. Rarely have a chance during the winter months to look at things in daylight. Was walking slowly and quietly along the top path that eventually leads down to the Old Cherry Sett when first a lurcher and then two border collies appeared in front of me – having forestalled their owners. Made a fuss of the lurcher and was standing, head bent talking to her as two men came on the scene. Said without glancing their way what a lovely dog she was. Silence. And I looked up into the thin face of a young man with dark hair. Have never seen such malevolence on a human face. Looked from him to his companion – a big, stocky man in his mid-forties and well dressed in a flashy way. The latter eyed me narrowly and said something out of the corner of his mouth to his friend. I walked round them, all the time watching the younger as I knew where I had seen him before and felt he might rush me, produce a knife, anything. That sort of situation. His face no longer contorted, he gathered saliva in his mouth and spat full at me – which I avoided.

Moved quickly away along the path to the top of the sett, then walked down the slope and sat on the chestnut bough, stunned by the memory of a previous encounter with the younger man. Then he had sat next to the driver of the van who had tried repeatedly to run me down in the Motorway tunnel (8 June 1983). If they had succeeded, of one thing I'm sure, my body would not have been found in the tunnel. More likely dumped in the fast lane of the Motorway just above while it was still dark. Couldn't say if the older man was the driver, but suspect not. (*See also* 18 November 1984.)

Sometime I'll mention this to Steve. That van incident wasn't my first encounter with the young man. Have seen him about these woods before, sometimes in the company of some badger-diggers. Even so, feel he knows me a lot better than I know him.

Sunday 3 February
Very mild night, excellent visibility, slight rain about dawn. After badger-watch, took a seeding head of reedmace down to the lakeside and broadcast it there. I see the Motorway bank just above the lake (but nowhere else) has been prepared for planting – dug-out holes infilled with dark earth extending upwards in neat rows. Could make a good screen. Wonder what trees or shrubs are to be put there? The Motorway verges in other local places have been planted with foresight using indigenous species.

At the copse bank, I see the badgers have been digging out very recently – the sandy earth spilling down the slope. The birches seem full of redpolls, tits and siskins – the air is alive with their twitterings as they search these trees for food. Glad this sett is on private land where the people here are interested; the woodland is so vulnerable. Hope Les and Sam's little family prosper; they could be dug out so easily in the day. Paddy Mayhew and family and John Shaw himself keep an eye on

Clifford's Bank. It's the concern and help of people like these that makes all the difference.

Tuesday 5 February

Deep frost, full moon. I haven't seen Lesley since Sunday – think she now has her cubs. Sam crossed Briarmead in my company and together we walked along the Two Oak track – he foraging at the path side, I watching the lapwings and gazing all around. At 4 a.m., heard a terrier barking, then another joining in. It was coming from the next field, beyond Clifford's Bank. Left Sam standing uneasily on the track, quivering snout uplifted to catch any scent, his striped head clear in the moonlight.

I saw across-field near the bank another badger, surrounded by three dogs (two terriers and one lurcher), caught in a beam held by a man with his back to me, and another man running up to them. The latter saw me; everything so clear under the moon. The dogs were slipped on leashes and though they pulled backwards briefly, the men holding them reached the far bank and ran along the bottom of it. The Clifford sow, heavy with cub, gained the bank further along and in a moment had vanished below ground. By the time I too had gained the bank, the lampers had disappeared from view. The men seemed to be wearing balaclava-type head gear, but I was too far away to see details. This is my first confirmed incidence of terriers being used in lamping. They're not really lamping dogs – haven't the speed and are noisy. Useful to hold a larger animal though, be it fox or badger.

All night, I had been carrying the expensive Olympus over my shoulder (no flash attached) for use about dawn, so I left my thick coat with the OM2N hidden under it in the elm brush there, and unhampered but for Ross's instamatic, turned the corner of Clifford's Bank towards the Ridge. I was gaining on the men when the one with the lurcher turned and brought his arm up. I know that gesture of old and threw myself flat as the gun went off. Stayed where I was for a moment, getting my breath, then stood up and watched them run on to the Ridge.

On the Ridge, I looked all around wondering if this was where their vehicle was parked and what had happened to them now. A man whistled once, then again, over by the scree slope, almost as if calling a dog up. Came to the sudden conclusion that others were here besides the two lampers; were they connected or just a coincidence? I wasted valuable time searching for a car, then realised the lampers had moved back on to the fields.

Decided I was getting nowhere on my own, so ran back the way I had come (collecting anorak and camera en route), then along the Poplar Row to the farmyard telephone. The police number was ringing but no answer – obviously busy at counter – so rang John Shaw (by now 4.40 a.m.), who said he'd take the van to search the lane entrances and those of the farm. Next, got through to the station to ask if a patrol could check the perimeter of the area, apart from that which John was covering. Left the Olympus by the telephone for safety and returned to search the fields. Thought I saw a smallish light briefly by one of the pylons (though metal, like glass, can reflect brightly under the moon), but nothing there when I reached it. Shortly after, John's van – without lights – picked me up and drove towards Briarmead where the headlights of a patrol car shone out at the wood entrance. No one had seen anything. As we stood on the lane looking out over the fields, the headlights of the other patrol appeared as it came across the bridge.

I stayed a moment explaining the set-up, then John went off home, promising to pick up the Olympus for me. I left the constables – one of whom was Len Watts who came with me to look at the Old Cherry Sett (25 February 1984) – I to search round the pear orchard, they to check the wood edge. No luck. The three of us met up behind High Ridge and walked back together to Briarmead and their car. I apologised for wasting their time. Len said they would rather be called out like this than not be and hear later that a badger had been taken. Warmed to them – can't be much fun tramping across farmland at night. They asked me how John Shaw happened to be up; I laughed and told them how I'd got him out of bed! Discussed the Old Barn as we neared its ruins, Len saying he had played there as a boy. Sometime I must ask him what he remembers of the Barn. He describes himself as a 'townee' but, from that, he hasn't always been. They gave me a lift home, by now 5.40 a.m., and was told to be careful or they would be finding my body under a bush!

Phoned John Shaw later, who said that last Wednesday, 30 January, there were lampers on his land; at about 9.15 p.m., some friends visiting Paddy's family at the cottage saw lamping lights on the field as they came. Paddy rang his boss, but John was out. Understandably, as he had company, Paddy didn't investigate. He learnt later that when his friends left about midnight, they noticed the lampers were still around.

Wednesday 6 February

Lesley has had her cubs. Sat on the ground in the moonlight with my back against the Old Cherry's fallen trunk as she scrambled on to my lap purring like a great cat, the smell of sweet, warm milk clinging to her chunky body. We sat facing one another with her long snout nearly touching my cheek. Take back all I have ever said of foxes being the most attractive animals. Lesley is a beautiful creature – young, healthy and fulfilled. Just then Little 'un came close. Les growled, so I held her snout in both hands and shaking it gently, growled back. Then spoke softly to the yearling sow who came up again, musked my gloves as they lay on the ground, and whickered quietly to her mother. Les accepted her daughter by grooming her neck. Sat a long time there, an arm round each sow, the long tree shadows snaking darkly over the ground, the moon seemingly caught in the bare branches above.

Thursday 7 February
Very mild, overcast night. Too warm for my anorak, so left it hanging from a tree on Clifford's Bank. Played with my vixen, whilst her mate Sandy hunted along the path edge. She had caught and eaten a wood mouse, biting off the tail before swallowing. [My first observation of this was 21 February 1982.] I picked up the tail, then hid it in my cupped hands; now opening, now closing them. Twice she tried to take it before I covered it again. Then she brought her paw up and attempted to scratch it away. This failing, my vixen jumped up, a paw on each of my shoulders, her brush waving. I made the soft contact sound and, opening my hands, let her take it. She gently picked it off my palm and held it a moment dangling from her mouth. Then, coming to lie down next to me, she let it drop in front of us. Stroked her head, then her thick shoulder fur. She, smelling the fresh blood from my scratched hand, licked it away. If ever rabies comes to England, I'll be one of the first to get it.

Saturday 9 February
2.15 a.m. After twenty-four hours of rain and wind, it has turned to snow. Earlier, *all* badgers were foraging on the fields (including the Clifford sow who, like Lesley, is lactating). Both sows are finding food very close to their cubs, that is, at the nearest field edge. Plenty of worms, the supply seems inexhaustible – I sometimes wonder what Darwin would have thought of my badgers!

But now, at 5 a.m., a frozen world. Each twig on the lower branches has a ridge of white, though high above, the strong wind is punishing the rasping treetops. No badgers or foxes are abroad now, though a tawny calls briefly from the Chantry. And still it snows, drifting across the open land in the bitter wind. The day has come early, aided by the snow and, at 7 a.m., it's quite light. Could go home as no badger could be dug out in this but a) am glowing with warmth and enjoying myself! and b) wish to collect the Olympus left in John Shaw's care from last Tuesday and don't want to call on them too early.

Walked about to keep warm and, going along the Wildflower Path towards Briarmead, happened to look back. A small grey figure was following – jumping up and down in its efforts to reach me through the snow! It was Lesley. Amazed she was about so late.

Went to meet her and was made a great fuss of by the playful creature, who thrust a warm, *wet* snout into my anorak where I'd left the zip undone. Backtrailed our snow prints to discover she could only have emerged recently and clearly had followed my footprints – or badger-like, their scent – her paw prints superimposed in places over mine. Already their impression was blurring as they infilled with continuously fresh snowflakes.

When she went to earth once more I walked down the lane, now hidden like all else, under its blanket of white. My boot knocked something hard and, reaching down, I found a large, frozen rabbit below

355

the snow; probably run over yesterday evening in the rain. Pleased with my find, I returned to the sett. Les would have meat and plenty of it for a while! It was heavy and kept slipping from my fingers, so I hugged it in my arms for easier carrying. Found, to my surprise, that the snow covering my anorak front was frozen hard in the wind, and noticed for the first time the icicles hanging from the edge of my hood and from the hair that shows around my face. Hadn't been conscious of the cold to any degree – wondered what the temperature was. At Lesley's entrance, I let the carcass drop into her hole, and was startled to watch the speed with which the rabbit shot downwards, disappearing in style round the tunnel's curve!

Walking is difficult along the exposed farm track to Glebe Farm, fighting the wind all the way. It's a comforting thought, however, that homeward bound it will be to my back! Gulls are sweeping the airways above, blown where the wind wills on their screeching quest for food – the only sign of life anywhere. Paddy's cottage, like the clustered barns, seems fast sinking into snow, and knowledge not sight tells me those strange shapes nearby are machinery. John's farmyard has the raw hardship of a Bruegel landscape.

8.40 a.m. At the bungalow I get John out of bed! Seem to be making a habit of that, though he laughs and doesn't appear to mind. With the Olympus over my shoulder I retrace my steps, the route stretching endlessly straight ahead. 'It's a long lane that has no turning' and this is a lane in point! The wind lashes to a fury, screaming its rage in the wires. The blizzard intensifies as stinging snowflakes make a rawness of my face. To my mind comes a picture of Lesley, snug underground with her newborn cubs – and her rabbit. Think she's the more intelligent of us two!

[By Sunday 10 February, the snow had ceased, the wind sending drifts to block railways, lanes and larger roads. No more snow fell that week, but the cold was intense at night, and even by day it was minus degrees centigrade owing to the bitter wind. Fortunately for the badgers, no one could lamp or dig out under those conditions. I had influenza, then bronchitis from Monday 11 February, so didn't return to the area for some days.]

Monday 18 February
I've made it! First time out since 9 February. Sunny morning, though the raw air makes me cough. 1.30 p.m. Sett untouched – felt a great surge of relief. Snow on the higher slope all melted, but lower down the snow still lies and the great tree is still covered. Birds busy in the sunshine – a lone shooter somewhere. Briarmead was blocked with drifts halfway up but, unfortunately, not until well past the Old Cherry Sett.

Came here via Colts Farm, having left some things for the Williams' children. I saw that half the bank has been cleared, leaving the mature birches. The sett there quite all right; Pete's men have been very careful.

356

Sat on the chestnut-bough seat looking carefully around at the different entrances. The sun shining down one hole revealed the digging claw marks clear on the inner wall. Strange how quite intelligent people insist that badgers live as deep as twenty to thirty feet below ground in an ancient sett like this. Tunnels will run that *length* but a badger is rarely as much as six feet *below* the ground level. Commonsense should tell anyone that twenty to thirty feet down just isn't possible – or necessary.

Watched a nuthatch hammering at a hazelnut he had wedged in the bark of a cherry tree. Stayed until my coughing got the better of me – enjoying the knowledge that no harm has come to the badgers since I was last here. The way back seemed miles, but worth it for the peace of mind.

Wednesday 20 February
Snow gradually disappearing though the drifts have compacted and likely to remain so until it rains. First light is now about 6.15 a.m. Everywhere the birds are busy. All quiet at the Old Cherry Sett; the earth is not frozen there. The twins were out earlier, but not Les or Sam.

7.45 a.m. Walked down to photograph the sheet of ice covering the lake. Watched a skylark on throbbing wings, singing high above these fields. A tractor was working in the far distance, with many gulls and lapwings feeding on the ploughed land. Was called in by Pete as I passed his house, and sat in the kitchen drinking tea and talking to the children

and their parents. Whilst there, Roy the tractor driver phoned in to say he'd seen someone on the fields checking the sett. Pete was able to reassure him, explaining it had been me, too far away for him to make out. Shows his men are alert.

Steve came this afternoon. I never realised, till I knew him, how few inspectors the R.S.P.C.A. have. Talking to me today, he made an estimate of the area he covers. Approximately 1½ million human inhabitants with their pets, livestock – and, of course, the wild animals and birds. All complaints of cruelty in that area to be investigated by one man. (No wonder I had to wait a while for help when I first phoned the Society. I was, after all, a non-urgent case compared with, for instance, a road casualty, or an animal in immediate pain.) His area isn't exceptionally large but if, like Steve, you are conscientious, then your workload is heavy indeed. Preparing court cases takes an enormous part of his time. That he has never lost a case is a credit to him and an indication of his meticulous preparation. A lot of this spills over into his off-duty time, since one man can only do so much in the hours allotted to him.

We discussed the increase in wild bird traffic; also of organised dog-fighting. Not only the Staffordshire bull terrier, but that dreaded fighting machine the American pit bull terrier is betted on; the R.S.P.C.A. believe that large sums of money change hands. As with badger-baiting, however, those who inform may experience swift and terminal retribution, so information is very hard to come by.

Saturday 23 February
Came over at 10 p.m. to check the fields for lampers, since I felt uneasy about the situation now that the weather is milder. All quiet and peaceful. Snow drifts linger here and there on the fields and Briarmead still partially blocked. Josh and his vixen are denning on Clifford's Bank, further along from the badgers. They have also dug out in Prosser's Wood and on the Ridge – alternative places if the vixen is disturbed when in whelp. The solitary vixen is denning in the wood edge near the Old Barn ruins; she has probably dug out at least one other but I haven't got round to locating them – as I'm still not one hundred per cent in health. Sandy and vixen are denning at the Felled Logs Sett and have also dug out two entrances at the far end of the Old Cherry Sett – nowhere near the badgers.

By 3.30 a.m., a dense fog covered the land, blotting out all lights and the motorway sounds. A strange, cold, shrouded night; visibility poor but exciting none the less. Suddenly smelt the fresh musky odour of fox and barked softly. Walked down to the lake with Sandy's vixen close behind me. Somewhere along the route we picked up her mate. It was bitterly cold around the sheet of ice-covered water, spirals of writhing vapour rising from the freezing surface.

358

Wednesday 27 February
Went out in fog at 2.10 a.m. It was not as dense or as freezing as last Saturday. The drifts covering Briarmead have nearly gone and vehicles can go to the top of the lane once more. Seems strange that in spite of several spring-like days and above normal temperatures snow can still be found here and there on these fields. Some entrances dug out at *all* occupied setts – the badgers are making the most of the mild, damp weather. Lesley is using the nursery entrance for her cubs again. She has also dug out the entrance opposite the Old Cherry itself. The bright, sandy earth has dropped into and partly filled the place where her mother and brother were dug out in October 1983.

Before I left home tonight, I picked up and petted Karen's cat. Lesley was very interested in the cat smell on the front of my anorak, snuffling over it, then carefully investigating inside when I undid the zip. Played with her on the Old Cherry trunk, now slippery and wet with the mist. Sam tried to join in but was warned off by his mate. She's very possessive over me at present – probably to do with her having the cubs. When she had gone to earth, I made a fuss of Sam. The only fault I find with this boar (apart from a love of my gloves!) is his habit of butting me when he gets very excited. Badger cubs do this when playing – that is, one charging at another with lowered head which strikes the other's body between fore legs and hind. Adults do this in play and also as an aggressive action. In Sam's case, it catches me on the front of the legs and bumps appear on the bone. He's the only badger ever to do this to me and, obviously, it's meant in play. However, it's extremely painful and my left leg has two permanent bumps now from last spring. Cubs love to bowl one another over in this fashion – perhaps Sam has still to grow up!

Saturday 2 March
Lovely mild, damp night. Snow on Briarmead has gone at last. Came round to the Old Cherry Sett at first light, 5.50 a.m., to be confronted by two men carrying rifles – and wearing balaclava-type masks! [A supplier's catalogue arrived today, 9 March: under 'Headgear' they stock SAS-style balaclavas, exactly as described later.] They looked bizarre in the dimness; my efforts at photography are having odd repercussions! This may have been what the lampers wore on 5 February, but they were at a distance, so can't be sure. Challenged them. They said, in effect, they were sick of me being around and I was getting too nosey. (This remark has since given me food for thought as the two people about whom I've been making enquiries may have heard of my interest.)

I jumped on the Old Cherry's trunk to be on a level or higher than them – felt less vulnerable like that. However, an unfortunate move in this case as one came after me on to the trunk the other following on the ground. Ran out over the slope where the trunk divides, the man behind me swearing and slipping on the wet, gnarled bark. Had to jump down where the limb is rotten and was faced by his companion who punched me. Grabbed at his mask (a knitted helmet with round holes for the eyes and a triangle cut out for the bridge of the nose and the mouth). Couldn't drag it off and by now was being hit over the head by the one behind me on the trunk. Felt my feet slip in the wetness. Afraid of being kicked on the ground, I let myself roll down the slope under the great tree. Went with some force, ending up directly under the trunk with all the twigginess of the branches around me. Registered that I must be about where Sam disappears to here. He has dug out an entrance but the great weight above has crumbled it into a small cave and I was wedged in this, but safe. The men were furious that I had escaped them and fired down the slope. Couldn't possibly see where they were aiming, though several bullets ricocheted unpleasantly close.

There was a long pause and hopefully I thought them gone. Then the timber just above me shifted, debris covering my face, mouth and eyes. They were on the trunk, jumping up and down, probably where it was rotten. For the first time that morning I was frightened – had a horrible vision of being crushed beneath the enormous weight just above.

Took me some while to realise they really had gone. Found it easier to go *down* the slope to get out. By now, it was just 6.15 a.m. and getting light. Took my anorak off and shook it – felt like something off a refuse tip. Heard Canadas calling and, leaving my coat, ran down on to Long Field just as three of these geese rose off Great Chantry, sounding as they went. They've probably been feeding on the autumn-sown barley there during the night.

Decided action was needed and ran to check each possible parking place round the wood, though probably the two men had already left. No dawn as such, the sky heavy and leaden – light poor. Went through the wood and passed the Main Pond, turned right on to Briarmead and started down the lane. Saw something through the trees off the path that hadn't been there before, well camouflaged – green against the grassy bank. The van was [make and condition omitted; also registration number]. It takes a good vehicle (Land-rovers apart) to come into this wood at the moment via the lane, as the spring has overflowed since the snow and has flooded it. Whether this was *the* vehicle I rather doubted, as by now it was 6.40 a.m. I hadn't seen or heard anyone else but that's not conclusive.

Spent a long time at the Old Cherry Sett, writing up what I remembered while it was still fresh in my mind. Watched the squirrels' mating chases, and a great spotted woodpecker drumming; the birds all about seemed to be singing for the joy of it. Difficult to believe what had happened here such a short time ago. Left at 8 a.m., having had no further trouble and seen no other people. Checked for the vehicle, but it had gone.

Evening: Phoned Steve, asking him to check the van. If it's an unknown, then I'd say it had no connection with this morning's affair.

[22 March: Steve reckoned this was, in fact, the vehicle they used. The owner is employed by a man I have been enquiring about and is known to the police.]

Sunday 3 March
8.30 a.m. Ralph's car caught up with me on Briarmead as I was leaving. Discussed the digging/lamping situation. Am never sure what his police connection is and he always smiles and drives off if I start probing! Today he said, 'Recently, we caught people digging for badgers in Barksham Woods and chased them but they got away.' He also said he has tried catching lampers on these fields at night, but it's very difficult even with a car as the area is so large and variable – don't I know, regardless of car! Told him of yesterday's two men at the sett; also of the vehicle that just might have a bearing. Have come to rather like Barry's mystery friend.

Monday–Wednesday 4–6 March
These nights have been frosty with clear skies and moon near the full. Spent much of the time recording fox vocalisation; these conditions perfect. One day would like to do a serious study of this aspect of *Vulpes vulpes*, but would need more sensitive equipment.

Thursday 7 March
Full moon. Night started clear and frosty, but by 2 a.m. light rain occasionally falling from a cloudy sky; visibility excellent. Badgers in great form. Clifford sow greeted and musked me. Has never done this before, so feel it's something of a landmark.
At 4.50 a.m. as I was walking down Briarmead heard a shot from just inside the wood. No possible doubt about it – a single shot coming from somewhere near the field edge above the Old Cherry Sett. Warning or signal? Ran down to the sett, but nothing more. (Sam came home after 6 a.m. and wanted a game – trust him!)

Friday 8 March
Clear skies, moon just past the full – deep frost. 3.30 a.m. Tawnies vocalising – they have chosen their nest site.
Josh doesn't tolerate Sandy as he did Tagless (his dead son). The two dogs had a snapping contest tonight. Sandy's vixen kept me company, leaving the males to quarrel. No physical contact apart from jumping up, paws on each other's shoulders and yowling – just a war of nerves that, I imagine, Josh won. Would like to have taped the tawnies parleying, but not with my vixen escort. Foxes and owls just don't mix!
5.15 a.m. Walking down Briarmead, having checked the Main Pond areas etc. for vehicles, saw movement on the bank so called out to let them (?) know they'd been seen. Went on walking down to where the bank stands high above the lane. Someone fired several times over my head from the bank – only just above me and obviously meant to

361

intimidate. Have been through all this before in the past – was not impressed.

Stayed at the setts till 6.30 a.m. Ran home (good exercise!) through Colts Farm – and found I had a tractor pacing me along Madden Lane. Driver waved and laughed. All right for him, he's already at work!

Sunday 10 March
Mild, damp night; waning moon in a mackerel sky. Lesley's yearlings (Little 'un and Sis) are on the move. They dug out tonight at Old Joe's favourite sett in the Chantry. See that the dead tree at the View Sett which obscured two den entrances there has been moved very recently – by whom, and why?

It is going to be difficult watching over this family now they are so widely spaced apart – inevitable, of course. Birdsong everywhere. Wood spurge's green flowers and hazel catkins both heavy with pollen – spring is here once more. Simultaneously watched a lesser spotted woodpecker drumming as a 'yaffle' sounded from the Chantry and my tawny pair call and answer near by. What more could one wish for!

8.30 a.m. At Holmoak Lane, en route for home. Met a man I know well by sight who told me a fox was snared up on the bank there. At night, going to Ashcroft Woods, I sometimes see badgers cross the tarmac at this point to follow the up-and-over path on the bank and so under the wire. Sure enough, a fox was caught by its hindquarters in a *badger* snare. It was meant to pass over the larger animal's snout and tighten where the slender neck meets the body, but in the smaller creature it had passed straight on to the pelvis. Fortunately, it was not made from cutting wire, but insulating cord. The man returned with a pair of pincers, so whilst he set to on the wire, I kept the little vixen occupied – stroked her head and made the soft contact call. The man was, at first, anxious that the animal shouldn't bite him but I, to my own surprise, found calming this stranger fox quite easy. Gently, with one hand still stroking, I ran the other under her belly and took the strain of the cord, gradually easing her body backwards. Although she would be bruised from her earlier efforts to escape, she wasn't cut. This wire cord was meant to hold and secure, not damage the animal. How beautiful these creatures are – always very interested in foxes unknown to me. My companion remarked that he had seen this type of snare before, fixed at this part of the fence. (Didn't say to him that it wasn't intended for foxes at all, as I never think it wise to betray my badger interest.)

At last she was free and I felt the tension on my hand relax – the man and I grinned at one another. As I gently took my hands away, the one from under her belly felt wet, and glancing down I saw milk on my palm! This was a lactating vixen with cubs to feed. Her sharp little face looked at us briefly, then off she raced – nothing much wrong with her! Halfway across the field, she turned and stared back at us, gave herself a quick shake, then casually trotted away. We scrambled back down the bank

362

together laughing. It's a marvellous feeling, releasing an animal unharmed – and the way that vixen moved, she would soon be back feeding
her cubs.

We collected the pieces of cut-through wire, as Steve will want them.
My companion said he'd check the rest of the fence, though he'd never
found snares except in this spot.

[Saturday 6 April: Discussed this stranger vixen allowing me to
handle her. The man and I feel it was probably reared in captivity.]

Tuesday 12 March
Frosty with clear, starry skies. Met Sandy carrying back a rabbit for his
vixen – she has her cubs now. Believe Josh's mate had her cubs during
the night of 1/2 March, and Sandy's vixen 10/11 March. The young vixen
that also mated with Sandy should cub-about 26 March (but *see* 22
March).

Came home early from the woods as I wanted to check the horses' field
near Roger Johnson's land for snares. None there. The horses, very
interested, came up to see what I was doing. Was standing quietly in the
midst of them watching a little owl hunting when a large boar badger
appeared from under the wire fence and ambled past me. Think the
horses' scent possibly covered mine – no wind, everywhere quite still.
One horse put his head down towards the badger as if mildly curious; the
boar snuffling under some manure was too preoccupied to notice! It had
come up the bank from Holmoak Lane and under the wire at the point
where Sunday's snare had been set.

[Later, at the end of March, I was given permission to check for badger setts in the grounds of a large house in the neighbourhood. The owner was indisposed (had told me previously that he would take me round), but had left a message saying there *was* a sett, though it hadn't been badger-occupied since they moved in two years ago. Must admit this suited me best, as I prefer to wander around unaccompanied. One area of the grounds well overgrown with rhododendrons houses a sett in its bank. A fox has a den in one part, but three entrances are badger and in regular use. Searched and found beneath the bushes four fresh dung pits. Standing at the edge of the property, I could see a clear path across the field from the horses' pasture where the snare was set. This then was where the boar badger was returning on that morning.]

Saturday 17 March

Yesterday's snow lies frozen on each twig; everywhere a tracery of white. On Thursday night, Little 'un dug out two entrances of the Bank Sett, though she's not denning there. Am regularly checking the horses' field by Holmoak Lane as I come to the woods, but to date have found no more snares. Find I have to tear myself away from the horses though — they seem to enjoy a nightly visitor!

First light at 5.20 a.m., the snow making it even lighter. Everywhere a perfect whiteness — bracken, cherry blossom buds, all snow-covered. In these woods the Clifford yearlings (boar and sow) have joined Lesley's yearlings, and earlier all four animals were digging out in the sheltered Chantry. Old Joe's favourite sett is coming into its own again; also the View Sett, another of his homes. The four young animals play and mutually groom together. The hollow makes a natural depression in which to roll and rub their backs. Smaller, basin-like hollows are often to be found near setts, made by the continual rubbing and rolling (also mutual grooming) of their badger occupants.

The elder leaves are well advanced although snow-covered now. Watched a pheasant feeding on the path below the Old Cherry Sett at 6 a.m.; a gaudy splash of colour against white.

Thursday 21 March

Deep frost, clear skies, no moon — visibility excellent. The tawny hen is incubating her clutch now, so her mate is hunting for them both. Recorded their vocalisation for two hours — her calls to him for food; the soft noises he made on returning with first a vole, then a sparrow. The bond between tawnies is for life and very strong.

Came out on to Briarmead about 1 a.m. to get warm again after sitting for so long, and saw a lamper's beam on the field. No idea where the badgers were but, with the paths hardened by the deep frost, had a suspicion where I might find a vehicle. Sure enough, it was parked just above the sett on Clifford's Bank [number omitted], Roger Smith and Graham Jones in action once more (*see* 9 September 1984 and 10

January this year). No way of immobilising the vehicle – no keys left in ignition and doors locked. Had the choice of going to the farmyard and phoning the police from there and chancing that the lampers might net a badger and get away in the interval, or staying to make sure that they didn't but not getting help. Chose the latter – Hobson's choice really. Watched them, keeping well out of range of their spotlight beam. They caught only a few rabbits and left about 2.20 a.m. Didn't switch on their headlights until nearly out of sight.

Lesley's cubs haven't appeared above ground yet, but we've had nights of either deep frost or snow.

Friday 22 March
Another mild, showery night. 12.15 a.m., met four young badgers rooting on Briarmead bank below the damson trees: Little 'un, Sis, plus the two Clifford yearlings. Though not yet sexually mature, the three young sows (like human teenagers) seem rather to enjoy leading on the young boar, then dropping him flat. One moment he has all their attention – then, thoroughly aroused and excited, he is growled at and rebuffed. They literally turn their backs on him at times as, ignored, he ambles after their swaying figures. No need to feel sorry for him though; in another few months he'll come into his own! Don't quite know what they were after on the bank where eight large snuffle holes have been left in the moist earth and a heap of soft soil has spilled on to the tarmac. (Vole nestlings? Watched Josh do likewise at this point on 26 March.)

Went on my way across the field intending to watch the little owls. Never made it, however, as the Four Musketeers reappeared and decided to accompany me. At Glebe Farm, I tried to dodge them by slipping round the back of the barn, but it ended up as a game of chase – with me as the quarry! Oh well, I ought to be flattered, I suppose. All too soon, the sows will be adults occupied with the serious business of rearing cubs of their own.

In the farmyard, water, water everywhere. Probably a tap left partly on. Hastily moved aside as the badgers had a splashing contest – excitement mounting, their soaked bodies shining. Round and round, in and out of the machine parts stacked against a barn wall. The boar scrambled on to a big wooden block, then jumped down, nearly flattening Sis. Over and over they rolled, mud flying in all directions – the noise deafening! How Paddy's dog in the cottage over the way didn't hear them, I don't know. Imagine that if anyone *did* come to investigate the din, though, the yearlings would disappear and I, red-faced, would be left to explain to an irate Paddy. So, cowardly, but discreet, I crept away and left the hoodlums to it.

Found plenty to interest me on the field bank. Two stoats bounding back and forth, their bodies sinuous as they chased through the vegetation growing there. Disappeared briefly, then saw them again further off along the path. Then they disappeared for good as my Four

365

Musketeers came into view. Imagine they had trailed me; seemed very pleased with themselves! They immediately scented the stoats. I find it fascinating to see at close quarters what information a first-rate nose can tell its owner. They might have been watching with me as their snouts followed each twist and turn the mustelids had made.

3.40 a.m. Heard a noise and looked up to see a van with no lights on creeping over the bridge. For a moment, I imagined it to be people from one of the cottages, late home from an evening out – but no lights! Looked more closely and saw the number [omitted]; the digger/lamper and companion from 11 November last. Watched its slow progress towards the farm. Fortunately for us, they hadn't used their lights or we would have been seen, being so close to the track side. The badgers were barely interested, and who could blame them? It had come quietly and passed on; after all, people *do* live at the end of this road.

Decided it best to get these young animals back to the wood and safety, then try and find where the Clifford sow living on this bank might be – not far from her young cubs and too near the lampers for comfort, I felt. Worry made me impatient with the yearlings. The male wanted a game with me and, knowing that if I could get *him* safely clear of the area, the three sows would come too, I sternly slapped his snout! Painful yes, but it had the desired effect and fifteen minutes later left them worming in the wet edge of the Bank Sett and Long Field.

Found the van empty where the Top Field meets the Ridge. The van doors were locked – two cages in the back. Again, I had no way of immobilising the vehicle. Was puzzled to see two beams and four men with dogs working close together. They must be linked, but where was the other vehicle? Couldn't chance leaving the area to phone – by now the men were lamping the Top Field and that behind the Ridge. Time passed as I searched for the Clifford sow, then came across her by chance and enticed her (quite easily, as it happened) back to the sett – just as I heard a shot. Puzzled. All the badgers were accounted for and the dogs kill the rabbits – so a fox? By now the beams had gone; the sky lightening, 4.50 a.m., and it would soon be first light. Ran across the Ridge and started down the scree slope in time to see *two* vans in the distance slip out on to Madden Lane and disappear.

Walked back across the Ridge. Think the shot could have been for the lone vixen very soon to whelp and denning further along Clifford's Bank from the badger sow – will find out soon enough. If so, there will be only two pairs of adult foxes now in the whole of my study area, though they have cubs. [Later: Checked that the lone vixen *is* missing. Also, that her den is empty – fortuitously, she hadn't cubbed, though if she had, it's doubtful if she would have been above ground at all.]

Crossing the fields, a skylark rose on pulsing wings, singing high up in the still-dark sky. They seem the first to sing from these fields. As I passed the posts of Briarmead at the Crosshampton side of Ashcroft Woods, heard – then saw – a woodcock roding. See one of the badgers has used a snuffle hole on the bank here as a dung pit. Hastily pushed earth into it with my boot. It's obvious enough that these animals are around, without that!

At 7.20 a.m. it's a dull, mild, misty morning. At the Dump hollow with Josh in time to see a cock pheasant slowly traversing the field outside, peck-pecking as he went. The fox crouched down, belly to ground, 'elbows' above shoulder blades, and moved stealthily after it. A short distance from his quarry he made a dash and caught the bird (not by its tail, as I had expected, but side on) before it could rise properly.

Just then, the sun breaking through the mist bathed both in golden light. The memory of the moment lingered long after I returned home.

Steve Hammond came today complete with one of Roger Smith's nets. Seems the police had caught the pair trespassing after foxes for the umpteenth time and had taken their equipment, saying that if they wanted it back, they could call at the station within three weeks and sign for it. The police can only touch them for taking a badger and the young men know they can't be charged. Even though Smith is cocky, the constables guessed he wouldn't voluntarily present himself at the station – and they were right. The loss of his property would hurt his pocket and inconvenience him, though clearly from my experience yesterday, it didn't for long!

Steve told me (on 2 March) the van does belong to [name omitted]; he is very well known to the police, who were surprised his vehicle was seen parked so near home as he tends to operate further afield. Was able to tell Steve that he works for a man I've been enquiring about [information omitted] and it was obvious that he had been sent with another man to find me. The odd thing about all this is that I had come to a dead-end in my search for information; Steve's news has spurred me on to try again.

Saturday 23 March
Mild, showery night. 1.30 a.m. saw a lamper working off Holmoak Lane as I went by.

Saw Lesley's cubs for the first time! *Three* very unsteady little characters moving about in the play-pen of their entrance. They are seven weeks old now (born approx. two days earlier than those of the Clifford sow), and have the typically fluffy fur and rounded face of the very young. They kept close contact with each other by touch and smell – had the impression that focusing was still poor. Nose to earth (scarcely long enough to be called a snout at present), they moved timorously within the confines of the trench the badger-baiters dug seventeen months ago, feeling and smelling the dead leaves and crumbly clods of sandy soil Lesley cleared out when making their nursery.

Their mother came to me, purring, as I knelt on the slope above, watching her young. At the sound, they set up a shrill warbling, stretching up soft, myopic faces in our direction. Still with her paws on my knee, she looked down at her cubs, then up at me. Suddenly felt very

367

humble. How privileged I am to be trusted so. For the next half hour, I sat amongst the leaves and brambles there, watching as she lay on her side in the trench feeding her cubs. They snuffled as they suckled. One let go of a teat momentarily, then whimpered as it sought to regain it. Traffic in the far distance, muffled fluting of the male tawny on the field below. Arms hugging legs, chin resting on my knees, I watched the second litter of the young badger so many people have helped me to protect – farmers, their men, Steve and the constables. Surely I must be the luckiest person in the world.

INDEX

369

373